HARDCORE PROGRAMMING FOR MECHANICAL ENGINEERS

T0093613

HARDCORE PROGRAMMING FOR MECHANICAL ENGINEERS

Build Engineering Applications from Scratch

by Ángel Sola Orbaiceta

no starch press

San Francisco

HARDCORE PROGRAMMING FOR MECHANICAL ENGINEERS. Copyright © 2021 by Ángel Sola Orbaiceta

Printed in the United States of America

25 24 23 22 21   1 2 3 4 5 6 7 8 9

ISBN-13: 978-1-7185-0078-5 (print)
ISBN-13: 978-1-7185-0079-2 (ebook)

Publisher: Bill Pollock
Production Manager: Rachel Monaghan
Production Editor: Katrina Taylor
Developmental Editor: Alex Freed
Cover Illustrator: Gina Redman
Interior Design: Octopod Studios
Technical Reviewer: Peter Kazarinoff
Copyeditor: Kim Wimpsett
Proofreader: Lisa Devoto Farrell

For information on book distributors or translations, please contact No Starch Press, Inc. directly:
No Starch Press, Inc.
245 8th Street, San Francisco, CA 94103
phone: 415.863.9900; fax: 415.863.9950; info@nostarch.com; www.nostarch.com

Library of Congress Control Number: 2021930213

To my wife Jen, the person I most admire.

About the Author

Ángel Sola majored in industrial engineering with a focus in mechanics from the Public University of Navarra. He's a self-taught programmer, who has been working in the software industry since 2013. He currently works at Glovo (*https://glovoapp.com/*), a thriving start-up in the heart of Barcelona. In his spare time, he develops his own applications (like InkStructure, which solves 2D structure problems), brews beer, and cooks food from around the world.

About the Technical Reviewer

Peter D. Kazarinoff, PhD, is a faculty member in Engineering and Engineering Technology at Portland Community College. Peter earned a PhD in materials science and engineering from the University of Washington and a BA from Cornell University. He teaches courses in engineering programming, mechanical engineering, and material science. Peter lives in Portland, Oregon with his wife and two inquisitive daughters. He is the author of the book *Problem Solving with Python* and blogs at *pythonforundergradengineers.com*.

BRIEF CONTENTS

CONTENTS IN DETAIL

PART I
BASICS

1
A SHORT PYTHON PRIMER   **3**

2
TWO PYTHON PARADIGMS   23

3
THE COMMAND LINE   49

PART II
2D GEOMETRY

4
POINTS AND VECTORS

5
LINES AND SEGMENTS

PART III
GRAPHICS AND SIMULATIONS

8
DRAWING VECTOR IMAGES

9
BUILDING A CIRCLE FROM THREE POINTS

10
GRAPHICAL USER INTERFACES AND THE CANVAS

11
ANIMATIONS, SIMULATIONS, AND THE TIME LOOP

12
ANIMATING AFFINE TRANSFORMATIONS

PART IV
SYSTEMS OF EQUATIONS

13
MATRICES AND VECTORS   337

14
LINEAR EQUATIONS   359

PART V
TRUSS STRUCTURES

15
STRUCTURAL MODELS

387

16
STRUCTURE RESOLUTION

427

19
ASSEMBLING OUR APPLICATION 529

BIBLIOGRAPHY 547

INDEX 549

ACKNOWLEDGMENTS

The person I want to thank most is my wife Jen. Without her emotional support, this book would have been impossible to finish.

Second, I want to thank my parents, Angel and Raquel. They taught me the importance of hard work and paying attention to the details. Those lessons are some of the most valuable we can learn from our parents. I couldn't have had better mentors.

Big thanks to Bill Pollock, who believed in this project and gave me the opportunity to make it happen. I'm also very thankful to Alex Freed, the editor for the book. Without her edits, the book's quality wouldn't be half of what it is. Her editorial skills have made a huge difference. I'm very thankful to Katrina Taylor as well, who made a great job reviewing unifying the language of the book and moving it to production. I want to also say thanks to the team at No Starch Press who were involved in producing this book; working with them has been a very pleasurable experience. And I can't forget about Gina Redman, who I want to thank for the book's cover illustration.

Lastly, I want to thank Peter Kazarinoff for his invaluable technical feedback. A lot of his advice was crucial to shaping the code and explanations in the book.

INTRODUCTION

Knowing how to write code empowers you to solve complex problems. By harnessing the capabilities of modern CPUs, which can accomplish billions of operations per second, we can quickly and correctly work out the solutions to difficult problems.

This is a book about solving engineering problems with Python. We'll learn how to code geometric primitives that will serve as the basis of more complex operations, how to read and write from files, how to create vector images and animated sequences to present the results, and how to solve large systems of linear equations. Finally, we'll put all this knowledge together to build an application that solves truss structure problems.

Who This Book Is For

This book is targeted at engineering students, graduated engineers, or just about any person with a technical background who wants to learn how to write applications to solve engineering problems.

A background in math and mechanics is a must. We'll be using concepts from linear algebra, 2D geometry, and physics. We'll also use some mechanics of materials and numerical methods, which are subjects common to many engineering degrees. We won't go too far into these topics to allow a larger number of readers to find the material of the book useful. The techniques learned in this book can later be used to solve problems that involve more complex concepts.

To follow along, you'll need to have some coding skills and basic Python knowledge. This is not an introductory book to programming; there are lots of other good books covering that. I can recommend *Python Crash Course* by Eric Matthes (No Starch Press, 2019) if you're looking for such a book. There's also a lot of great material online, from which I'd pick *https://real python.com* as my favorite. The official Python website is also full of good tutorials and documents: *https://www.python.org/about/gettingstarted/*.

We're going to write a lot of code, so I strongly recommend you have a computer with you as you read and that you enter and test all the code in this book.

What You'll Learn

In this book, we'll explore techniques to write robust applications that correctly, and quickly, solve engineering problems. To ensure correctness, we'll be testing our code using automated tests. Every application you build should be properly tested using automated testing, as we'll discuss throughout the book.

Engineering applications usually require some amount of data to be fed in, so we'll also learn how to read the input of our programs from a file, parsing it using regular expressions.

Engineering applications typically need to solve a large system of equations, so we'll cover how to write numerical methods that can do these complex computations. We'll focus on linear systems, but the same techniques can easily be applied to write numerical algorithms for nonlinear equations.

Lastly, engineering applications need to produce a result. We'll learn how to write text to files that we can later inspect. We'll cover how to produce beautiful vector diagrams and animated sequences to present the results of our programs. As they say, a diagram is worth a thousand words: looking at a well-drawn diagram that describes the result with the most relevant solution values makes programs much more valuable.

To illustrate all these concepts, we'll conclude the book by building an application that solves two-dimensional truss structures. This application will have everything you need to build engineering applications. The knowledge acquired building this application can easily be translated to writing other kinds of engineering applications.

About This Book

In this section, we'll explain three things: the meaning behind the title of this book, the choice of Python, and the table of contents.

What Is the "Hardcore" About?

The word *Hardcore* in the title of this book refers to the fact that we'll write all the code ourselves, relying only on the Python standard libraries (libraries that ship with Python); we won't use any third-party library to solve equations or draw vector images.

You may be wondering why. If there's code already written by someone that does all this for us, why not simply use it? Aren't we re-inventing the wheel?

This is a book about learning, and to learn you need to do things yourself. You'll never understand the wheel unless you re-invent it. Once your software skills are solid and you've written thousands of lines of code and worked on a lot of projects, you'll be in a good position to decide which external libraries fit your needs and how to leverage them. But if you use those libraries from the beginning, you'll get used to using them and take the solutions for granted. It's important to always ask yourself, how does this library's code work to solve my problem?

Like anything else, coding takes practice. If you want to become good at coding, you need to write a lot of code; there are no shortcuts. If you're getting paid to write software or want to take an idea to market as fast as possible, then use existing libraries. But if you're learning and want to become proficient in the art of writing code, don't use libraries. Write the code yourself.

Why Python?

Python is one of the most beloved programming languages. According to Stack Overflow's 2020 developer survey (*https://insights.stackoverflow.com/survey/2020*), Python is today's third most loved language, with 66.7 percent of its users willing to continue using it in the future, just behind TypeScript and Rust (see Figure 1).

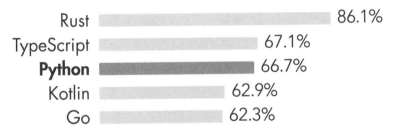

Rust 86.1%
TypeScript 67.1%
Python 66.7%
Kotlin 62.9%
Go 62.3%

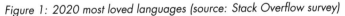

Figure 1: 2020 most loved languages (source: Stack Overflow survey)

This same survey puts Python first when it comes to "desired" languages: 30 percent of the surveyed developers who are not currently using Python expressed interest in learning it (see Figure 2).

Python		30.0%
JavaScript		18.5%
Go		17.9%
TypeScript		17.0%
Rust		14.6%

Figure 2: 2020 most wanted languages (source: Stack Overflow survey)

These results are not surprising; Python is an extremely versatile and productive language. Writing code in Python is a delight, and its Standard Library is well equipped: for just about anything you want to do, Python has something ready to help.

We'll use Python in this book not only because of its popularity but also because it's easy to use and versatile. One nice thing about Python is that, if you are reading this book but have no prior knowledge of the language, it won't take you long to get started. It's a relatively easy language to learn and the internet is filled with tutorials and courses to help you.

What Python is typically not seen as is a fast language, and indeed, Python's execution times are not one of its strengths. Figure 3 below shows a comparison of the execution times in seconds of the same three programs written both in Python and in Go (a very fast language developed by Google). In every case, Python takes much longer than Go to execute.

reverse-complement

source	secs	mem	gz	busy	cpu load
Python 3	16.41	1,772,696	434	17.57	1% 78% 28% 0%
Go	3.73	826,488	611	4.10	88% 6% 2% 14%

k-nucleotide

source	secs	mem	gz	busy	cpu load
Python 3	72.58	183,484	1967	276.33	95% 95% 94% 97%
Go	12.67	150,584	1722	47.44	95% 90% 93% 96%

fasta

source	secs	mem	gz	busy	cpu load
Python 3	63.63	841,056	1947	127.80	58% 61% 44% 37%
Go	2.11	4,228	1358	5.66	69% 65% 64% 70%

Figure 3: Python benchmark (source: https://benchmarksgame-team .pages.debian.net/benchmarksgame/fastest/python3-go.html)

So, don't we care about speed? We do, but for the purposes of this book, we care more about development time and the development experience. Python has lots of constructs that make coding delightful; for example, things like filtering or mapping a collection can be done out of the box using Python's list comprehensions, whereas in Go, you need to do those operations using good old for loops. For almost every program we'll write, execution time will never be a concern, as we'll get more than acceptable results. The skills you learn in this book will transfer to other, faster languages if you encounter speed issues in your applications.

But before we start learning anything, let's have a quick overview of the topics you'll find in this book.

Contents at a Glance

We'll cover a lot of ground in this book. Each chapter builds on top of the previous ones, so you'll want to make sure to read the book in order and work on the code each chapter presents.

The book includes the following chapters:

Part I: Basics

Chapter 1: A Short Python Primer   Introduces some intermediate Python topics that we'll use throughout the book. We'll cover how to split our code into modules and packages, how to use Python's collections, and how to run Python scripts and import modules.

Chapter 2: Two Python Paradigms   Covers functional and object-oriented programming paradigms and explores techniques to write code in those styles.

Chapter 3: The Command Line   Instructs you on how to use the command line to run programs and other simple tasks such as creating files.

Part II: 2D Geometry

Chapter 4: Points and Vectors   Covers the most basic, but crucial, geometric primitives: points and vectors. The rest of the book relies on the implementation of these two primitives, so we'll also learn about automated testing to make sure our implementations are bug-free.

Chapter 5: Lines and Segments   Adds the line and segment geometric primitives to our geometry toolbox. We'll take a look at how to check whether two segments or two lines intersect and how to calculate the intersection points.

Chapter 6: Polygons   Adds rectangles, circles, and generic polygons to our geometry toolbox.

Chapter 7: Affine Transformations   Covers affine transformations, an interesting algebraic construct we'll use to produce beautiful images and animations.

Part III: Graphics and Simulations

Chapter 8: Drawing Vector Images   Introduces the Scalable Vector Graphics (SVG) image format. We'll write our own library to produce these images using our geometric primitives.

Chapter 9: Building a Circle from Three Points   Takes all the knowledge from the previous chapters to build our first application, one that finds the circle that goes through three given points and draws the result to a vector image.

Chapter 10: Graphical User Interfaces and the Canvas   Covers the basics of the Tkinter package, which is used to build user interfaces in Python. We'll spend most of the time learning how to use the Canvas widget, which is used to draw images to the screen.

Chapter 11: Animations, Simulations, and the Time Loop   Guides you through the process of creating an animation by drawing inside Tkinter's Canvas. We'll explore the concept of the time loop used by engineering simulations and video game engines to render scenes to the screen.

Chapter 12: Animating Affine Transformations   Creates an application that animates the effect of applying an affine transformation to some geometric primitives.

Part IV: Systems of Equations

Chapter 13: Matrices and Vectors   Introduces the vector and matrix constructs and covers how to code these primitives, which will be extremely useful when we're working with systems of equations.

Chapter 14: Linear Equations   Shows how numerical methods can be implemented to solve large systems of linear equations. We'll implement the Cholesky factorization method together; this algorithm will solve the systems of equations that will appear in the next and last part of the book.

Part V: Truss Structures

Chapter 15: Structural Models   Reviews the basic mechanics of materials concepts we'll use in this part of the book. We'll also write the classes to represent a truss structure. Using this truss structure model we'll build a complete structural analysis application.

Chapter 16: Structure Resolution   Using the model built in the previous chapter, we'll cover all the computations required to find the structure's displacements, deformations, and stresses.

Chapter 17: Reading Input from a File   Covers the implementation of file reading and parsing so that our truss analysis application can rely on data that's stored as plaintext.

Chapter 18: Producing an SVG Image and Text File   Discusses the generation of SVG image diagrams based on the structure solution. Here we'll use our own SVG package to draw the diagrams, which will contain all the relevant details such as the geometry of the deformed structure and the stress label next to each bar.

Chapter 19: Assembling Our Application   Explains how to put together the pieces built in the previous chapters to build the complete truss resolution application.

Setting Up Your Environment

In this book, we'll use Python 3 and provide instructions to work with Py-Charm, a development environment program that'll let us work effectively. The code has been tested using Python versions 3.6 through 3.9, but it'll most likely continue to work equally well with future versions of the language. Let's download the code that accompanies the book, install the latest Python 3 interpreter, and set up PyCharm.

Downloading the Book's Code

All the code for this book is available on GitHub at *https://github.com/angel solaorbaiceta/Mechanics*. Again, while I strongly recommend that you write all the code yourself, it's a good idea to have it with you for reference.

If you are familiar with Git and GitHub, you may want to clone the repository. Also, I suggest fetching and pulling from the repository from time to time, as I may add new features or fix bugs in the project.

If you are not familiar with the Git version control system or GitHub, your best option is to download a copy of the code. You can do this by clicking the **Clone** button and choosing the **Download ZIP** option (see Figure 4).

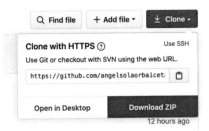

Figure 4: Downloading the code from GitHub

Unzip the project and place it inside the directory of your choice. As you'll see, I documented every package and subpackage in the project using *README files* (*README.md*). These files are usually found in software projects; they explain and document the features of a project and also include instructions on how to compile or run the code. A README file is the first thing you want to read when you open a software project, as they describe how to configure the project and get the code running.

NOTE *README files are written using the Markdown format. If you want to know more about this format, you can read about it here:* https://www.markdownguide.org/.

The *Mechanics* project on GitHub contains more code than we cover in this book. We didn't want to make this book too long, so we couldn't cover everything included in the project.

For example, in Chapter 14, "Linear Equations," we talk about numerical methods to solve systems of linear equations and explain the Cholesky factorization in detail. There are some other numerical methods in the project, such as the conjugate gradient, which we don't have time to cover in the book; the code is there for you to analyze and use. There are also many automated tests that we skip in the book for brevity reasons; use those tests as a reference when you write your own.

It's time to install Python.

Installing Python

You can download Python for macOS, Linux, and Windows from *https://www.python.org/downloads/*. For Windows and macOS you'll need to download the installer and run it.

Linux typically comes with Python preinstalled. You can check which version is installed on your computer using the following command in the shell:

```
$ python3 -V
Python 3.8.2
```

To install a version of Python on a Linux computer, you use the *os* package manager. For Ubuntu users using the *apt* package manager, this would be

```
$ sudo apt install python3.8
```

For Fedora users, using the *dnf* package manager, this would be

```
$ sudo dnf install python38
```

If you are using a different Linux distribution, a quick Google search should get you the instructions to install Python using your package manager.

It's important that you download a version of Python 3, such as 3.9, which is the current version at the time of writing. Any version above 3.6 (included) will work.

NOTE *Python versions 2 and 3 are not compatible; code written targeting Python 3 will very likely not work with Python's version 2 interpreter. The language evolved in a non-backwards-compatible way, and some features in version 3 are not available in version 2.*

Installing and Configuring PyCharm

As we develop our code, we'll want to use an *integrated development environment* (or IDE for short), a program equipped with features that help us write code more effectively. An IDE typically offers autocompletion features to let you know what options you have available as you type, as well as build, debug, and test tools. Taking some time to learn the main features of your IDE of choice is worth the effort: it'll make you much more productive during the development phase.

For this book we'll be using PyCharm, a powerful IDE created by Jet-Brains, a company that makes not only some of the best IDEs on the market but also its own programming language: Kotlin. If you already have some Python experience and prefer to use another IDE, such as Visual Studio Code, you're welcome to do so, but you'll need to figure out some things on your own using your IDE's documentation. If you don't have a lot of previous experience with any IDE, I recommend you stick to using PyCharm so you can follow along with the book.

To download PyCharm, head to *https://www.jetbrains.com/pycharm/* and click the **Download** button (see Figure 5).

Figure 5: Downloading PyCharm IDE

PyCharm is available for Linux, macOS, and Windows. It has two different versions: Professional and Community. You can download the Community version for free. Follow the installer steps to install PyCharm on your machine.

Opening the Mechanics Project

Let's use PyCharm to set up the *Mechanics* project you downloaded earlier so you can play with it and have its code for reference.

Open PyCharm and click the **Open** option on the welcome screen. Locate the *Mechanics* project folder you downloaded or cloned from GitHub and select it. PyCharm should open the project and configure a Python interpreter for it, using the version of Python installed in your computer.

Every project inside PyCharm requires that a Python interpreter be set. Since you could have several different versions of Python installed on your machine and because you may have chosen custom install locations, you need to tell PyCharm which of those versions of Python you want to use to interpret your project's code and where to find Python's interpreter in your system. For Windows and Linux users, go the menu and choose **File ▶ Settings**. For macOS users, choose **PyCharm ▶ Preferences**. In the Settings/Preferences window, click the **Project: Mechanics** section in the left column to expand it and choose **Python Interpreter** (see Figure 6).

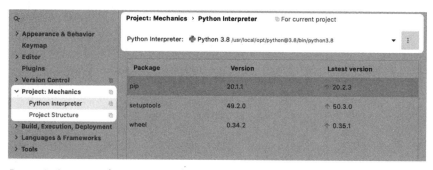

Figure 6: Setting up the project's Python interpreter

On the right side of the window, click the down arrow beside the Python Interpreter field, and from the drop-down, choose the version of the Python binary you installed on your computer. If you followed the previous instructions, Python should have been installed to a default directory where PyCharm can find it, so the interpreter should appear in the list. If you've installed Python somewhere else, you'll need to tell PyCharm the directory where you did so.

NOTE *If you have any trouble setting the project's interpreter, check PyCharm's official documentation:* https://www.jetbrains.com/help/pycharm/configuring-python-interpreter.html. *This link contains a detailed explanation of the process.*

Now that you've opened the *Mechanics* project, it should already be set up. Open the *README.md* file inside PyCharm by double-clicking it. By default, when you open a Markdown file in PyCharm, it'll show you a split view: to your left is the Markdown raw file and to your right is the rendered version of the file. See Figure 7.

This *README.md* file explains the basic structure of the project. Feel free to navigate through the links in the preview; give yourself some time to read through the README files inside each of the packages. This will give you a good sense of the amount of work we'll do together throughout the book.

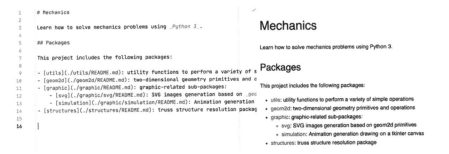

```
1    # Mechanics
2
3    Learn how to solve mechanics problems using _Python 3_.
4
5    ## Packages
6
7    This project includes the following packages:
8
9    - [utils](./utils/README.md): utility functions to perform a variety of s
10   - [geom2d](./geom2d/README.md): two-dimensional geometry primitives and o
11   - [graphic](./graphic/README.md): graphic-related sub-packages:
12       - [svg](./graphic/svg/README.md): SVG images generation based on _geo
13       - [simulation](./graphic/simulation/README.md): Animation generation
14   - [structures](./structures/README.md): truss structure resolution packag
15
16   |
```

Mechanics

Learn how to solve mechanics problems using Python 3.

Packages

This project includes the following packages:

- utils: utility functions to perform a variety of simple operations
- geom2d: two-dimensional geometry primitives and operations
- graphic: graphic-related sub-packages:
  - svg: SVG images generation based on geom2d primitives
  - simulation: Animation generation drawing on a tkinter canvas
- structures: truss structure resolution package

Figure 7: README.md *file with PyCharm's split view*

Creating Your Own Mechanics Project

Now that you have the *Mechanics* project you downloaded set up for reference, let's create a new empty project where you can write your code. Close the project if you have it open (select **File ▸ Close Project**). You should see the welcome page, as in Figure 8.

PyCharm
Version 2020.1.2

Create New Project

Open

Get from Version Control

Figure 8: *PyCharm welcome screen*

From the welcome page choose **Create New Project**. You'll be asked to name your project: use *Mechanics*. Then, for the interpreter, instead of the default, which is New environment using, select the **Existing interpreter** option (see Figure 9). Locate the version of Python you downloaded earlier in the introduction and click **CREATE**.

Figure 9: PyCharm, creating a new project

You should have a new empty project created and ready for you to write code. Let's take a quick look at PyCharm's main features.

PyCharm Introduction

This section is by no means a thorough guide to using PyCharm. To get a more complete overview of the IDE, you should read the documentation at *https://www.jetbrains.com/help/pycharm*. The official documentation is complete and up-to-date with the latest features.

PyCharm is a powerful IDE, and its Community (free) version even comes packed with lots of functionality; it makes working with Python a delightful experience. Its user interface (UI) can be divided into four main sections (see Figure 10).

Navigation bar On the top of the window is the navigation bar. To its left is the breadcrumb navigation of the currently open file. To its right are buttons to run and debug the program, as well as the drop-down list that shows the current run configuration (we'll cover run configurations later in the book).

Project Tool window This is the directory structure of your project, including all its packages and files.

Editor This is where you'll write your code.

Terminal PyCharm comes with two terminals: your system's terminal and Python's terminal. We'll use both of them throughout the book. We'll cover these in Chapter 3.

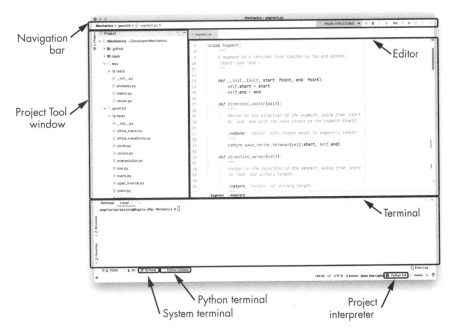

Navigation bar

Editor

Project Tool window

Terminal

Python terminal

System terminal

Project interpreter

Figure 10: PyCharm UI

PyCharm also includes the project's Python interpreter in the lower-right corner of the UI. You can change the interpreter's version from here, choosing from a list of versions installed on your system.

Creating Packages and Files

We can create new Python packages (we'll cover packages in Chapter 1) in your project using the Project Tool window. To create a new package, go to the Project Tool window and right-click the folder or package where you want to create the new package; from the menu that appears, select **New ▶ Python Package**. Similarly, select **New ▶ Python File** to create Python files. You can see these options in Figure 11.

You can also create regular directories with New ▶ Directory and all types of files using New ▶ File, which will let you choose the file's extension yourself. The difference between a regular directory and a Python package is that the latter includes a file named *__init__.py* that instructs Python's interpreter to understand the directory as a package with Python code. You'll learn more about this in Chapter 1.

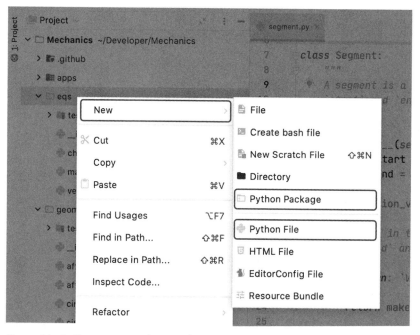

Figure 11: PyCharm new package or file

Creating Run Configurations

A *run configuration* is just a way of telling PyCharm how we want our project (or a part of it) to run. We can save this configuration to use as many times as we need. With a run configuration in place, we can execute our application by simply pressing a button, as opposed to having to write a command in the shell, which potentially entails copy-pasting parameters, inputting file-names, and the like.

Among other things, a run configuration can include information about the entry point for our application, what files to redirect to the standard input, what environment variables have to be set, and what parameters to pass to the program. Run configurations are a convenience that will save us time when developing; they also allow us to easily debug Python code, as we'll see in the next section. You can find the official documentation for run configurations here: *https://www.jetbrains.com/help/pycharm/run-debug-configuration .html*.

Let's create a run configuration ourselves to get some hands-on experience. To do this, let's first create a new empty project.

Creating a Test Project

To create a new project from the menu, choose **File ▶ New Project**. In the Create Project dialog, enter *RunConfig* for the project's name, select the **Existing interpreter** option, and then click **CREATE**.

In this new empty project, add a Python file by right-clicking the *Run-Config* empty directory in the Project Tool window and then selecting **New ▶ Python File**. Name it *fibonacci*. Open the file and enter this code:

```
def fibonacci(n):
    if n < 3:
        return 1

    return fibonacci(n - 1) + fibonacci(n - 2)


fib_30 = fibonacci(30)
print(f'the 30th Fibonacci number is {fib_30}')
```

We've written a function to compute the *n*th Fibonacci number using a recursive algorithm, which we then use to compute and print the 30th number. Let's create a new run configuration to execute this script.

Creating a New Run Configuration

To create a new run configuration, from the menu select **Run ▶ Edit Configurations**; the dialog in Figure 12 should appear.

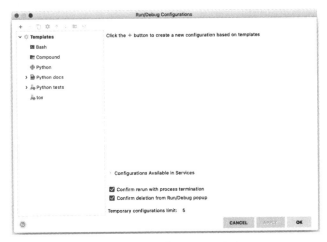

Figure 12: The Run/Debug Configurations dialog

As you can see, there are a few templates we can use to create a new run configuration. Each template defines parameters to help us readily create the right kind of configuration. We're only going to use the Python template in this book. This template defines a run configuration to run and debug Python files.

In the dialog, click the **+** button in the top-left corner and select **Python** from the list of available templates (see Figure 13).

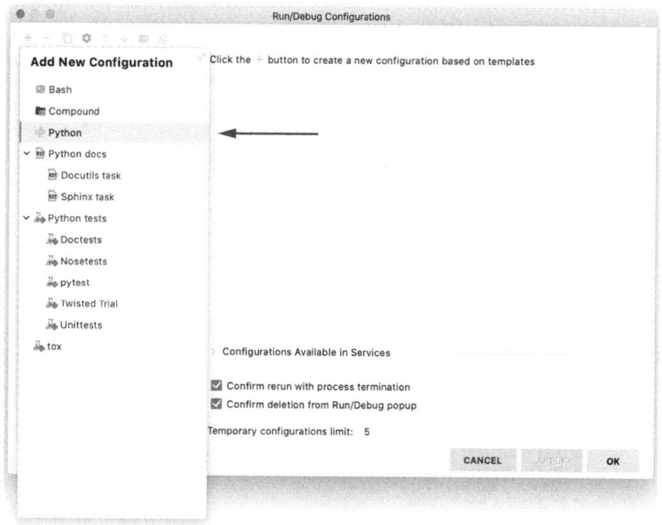

Figure 13: Creating a new Python run configuration

Once you've chosen the configuration template, the right side of the dialog displays the parameters we'll need to provide for this configuration to run our code. We only need to fill two of these parameters: the configuration's name and the script path.

Locate the Name field at the top of the dialog and enter **fibonacci**. Then locate the Script path field under the Configuration section, and click the folder icon to its right. Upon clicking this icon, a file dialog should open inside the project's root folder, exactly where we've added our *fibonacci.py* file. Choose this file as the script path. Your new configuration dialog should look similar to Figure 14. Click **OK**.

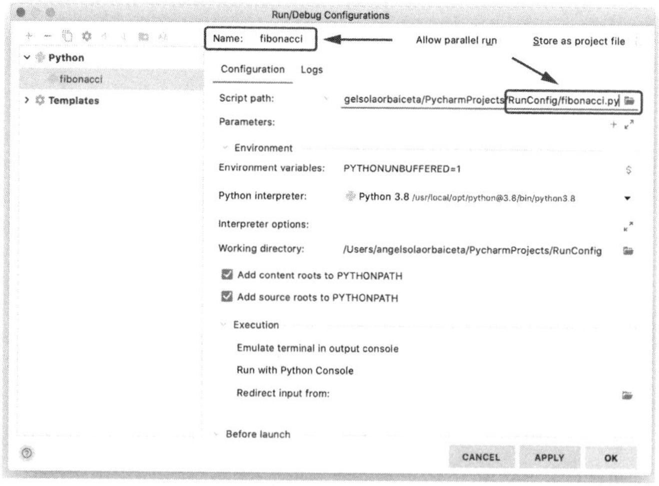

Figure 14: The run configuration parameters

You've successfully created a run configuration. Let's use it.

Using the Run Configuration

In the navigation bar, toward the right, locate the run configuration selector. Figure 15 shows this selector.

Figure 15: The run configuration selector

In the drop-down list, select the run configuration you just created and click the green play button to execute it. You should see the following message in the shell of the IDE:

```
the 30th Fibonacci number is 832040

Process finished with exit code 0
```

You can also launch a run configuration from the menu by selecting **Run ▸ Run 'fibonacci'**.

We've successfully used a run configuration to launch our *fibonacci.py* script. Let's now use it to learn about debugging Python code.

Debugging Python Code

When our programs are misbehaving and we don't know why, we can debug them. To debug a program, we can execute it line by line, one step at a time, and inspect the values of the variables.

Let's modify our fibonacci function a little bit before we debug the script. Imagine that the users of this function are complaining about it being too slow for large numbers. For example, they state they have to wait several minutes for the function to compute the 50th Fibonacci number:

```
# this will fry your CPU... be prepared to wait
>>> fibonacci(50)
```

After careful analysis, we realize that our current implementation of the fibonacci function could be improved if we cached the already computed Fibonacci numbers to avoid repeating the calculations over and over again. To speed up the execution, we decide to save the numbers we've already figured out in a dictionary. Modify your code like so:

```
cache = {}


def fibonacci(n):
    if n < 3:
        return 1

    if n in cache:
        return cache[n]
```

```
    cache[n] = fibonacci(n - 1) + fibonacci(n - 2)
    return cache[n]
```

```
fib_30 = fibonacci(30)
print(f'the 30th Fibonacci number is {fib_30}')
```

Before we start our debugging exercise, try to run the script again to make sure it still yields the expected result. You can go further and try to compute the 50th number: this time it will compute it in a matter of milliseconds. The following:

```
--snip--

fib_50 = fibonacci(50)
print(f'the 50th Fibonacci number is {fib_50}')
```

yields this result:

```
the 50th Fibonacci number is 12586269025

Process finished with exit code 0
```

Let's now stop the execution exactly at the line where we call the function:

```
fib_50 = fibonacci(50)
```

To do this, we need to set a *breakpoint* where we want the Python interpreter to stop the execution. You can set a breakpoint in two ways: either click in the editor, slightly to the right of the line number where you want to stop (where the dot appears in Figure 16), or click your cursor anywhere in the line, and then from the menu select **Run ▶ Toggle Breakpoints ▶ Line Breakpoint**.

If you've added the breakpoint successfully, you should see a dot like the one in Figure 16.

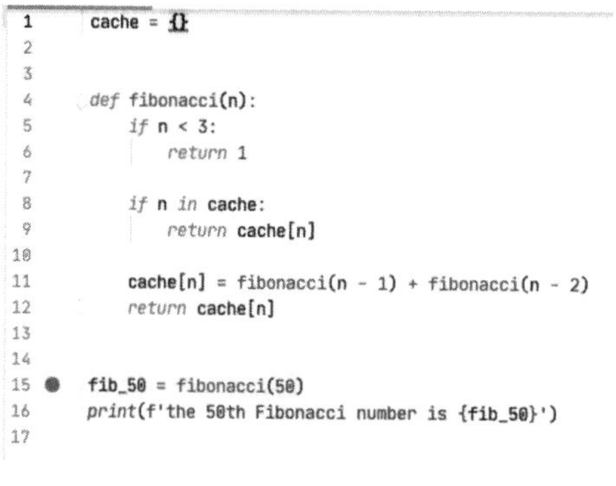

```
 1      cache = {}
 2
 3
 4      def fibonacci(n):
 5          if n < 3:
 6              return 1
 7
 8          if n in cache:
 9              return cache[n]
10
11          cache[n] = fibonacci(n - 1) + fibonacci(n - 2)
12          return cache[n]
13
14
15  ●   fib_50 = fibonacci(50)
16      print(f'the 50th Fibonacci number is {fib_50}')
17
```

Figure 16: Setting a breakpoint in the code

To launch the Fibonacci run configuration in debug mode, instead of clicking the green play button, you want to click the red bug button (see Figure 15) or select **Run ▶ Debug 'fibonacci'** from the menu.

PyCharm launches our script and checks for breakpoints; as soon as it finds one, it stops execution before executing that line. Your IDE should've halted execution in the line where we set the breakpoint and displayed the debugger controls in the lower part, as in Figure 17.

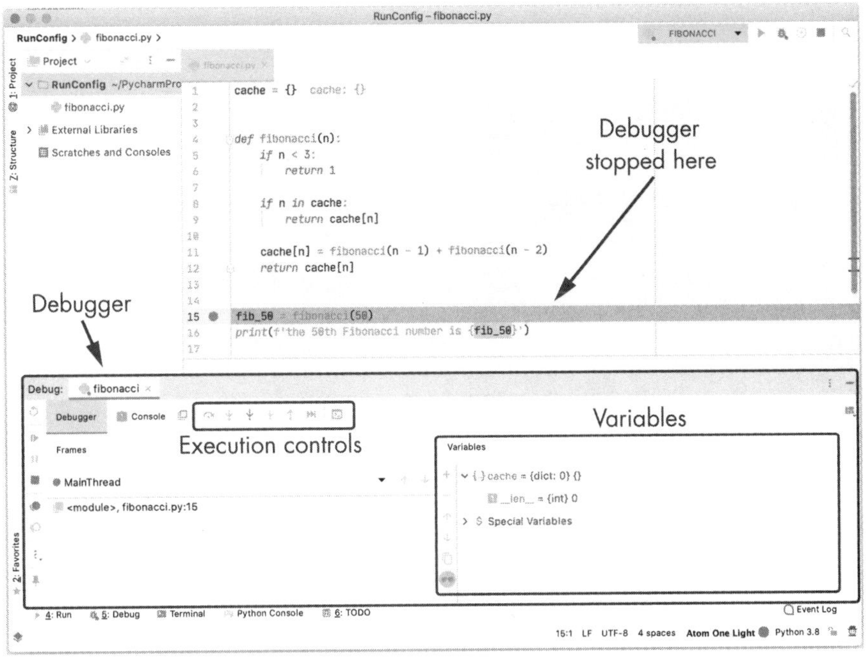

Figure 17: PyCharm's debugger

The debugger has a bar near the top to control the execution of the program (see Figure 18). There are a few icons, but we're mainly interested in the first two: Step over and Step into. With the Step over option, we can execute the current line and jump to the next one. The Step into option goes inside the function body of the current line. We'll look at these two in a minute.

The right side of the debugger has a Variables pane where we can inspect the current state of our program: the values of all the existing variables. For instance, we can see the cache variable in Figure 17, which is an empty dictionary at the moment.

Figure 18: Debugger execution controls

Let's now click the Step into icon in the execution control's section of the debugger. The execution enters the fibonacci function body and stops in its first instruction (Figure 19).

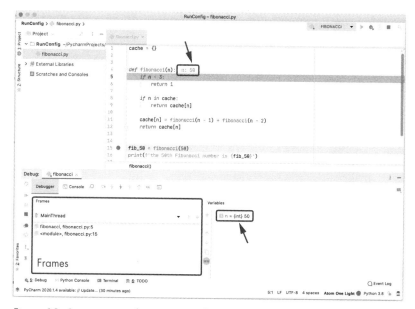

Figure 19: Stepping into the fibonacci function

The debugger's Variables pane now shows the n variable with its current value, 50. This value also appears beside the fibonacci function definition, as you can see in Figure 19 (both places are indicated with arrows).

The left side of the debugger displays the Frames pane. This pane contains the stack frames of our program. Each time a function is executed, a new frame is pushed to the stack with the function's local variables and some more information. You can go back and forth in time by clicking a frame to inspect the state of the program before that function got called. For instance, you can click the <module>, fibonacci.py:15 stack frame to go back in time before the fibonacci function got called. To go back to the current execution point, simply click the topmost stack frame, fibonacci, fibonacci.py:5 in this case.

Try to continue debugging the program using the Step over and Step into controls. Make sure you watch the cache and n variables as they change their values. Once you're done experimenting, to stop the debugging session, you can either execute all the instructions in the program until it finishes or click the Stop button in the debugger. You can do this from the menu by selecting **Run ▶ Stop 'fibonacci'** or by clicking the red square icon on the left side of the debugger.

Let's try one last debugging exercise. Run the program again in debug mode; when the execution stops at the breakpoint, click the Step over icon. Inspect the cache variable in the Variables pane. As you can see, the cache is now filled with all the Fibonacci numbers from 3 up to 50. You can expand the dictionary to check all of the values inside, as in Figure 20.

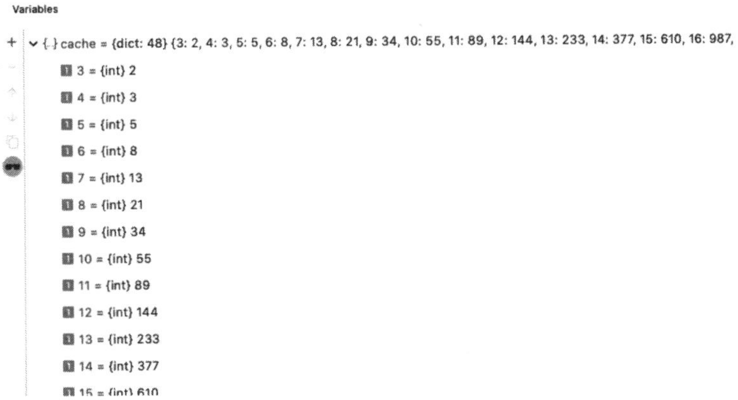

Variables

+ ⌄ { } cache = {dict: 48} {3: 2, 4: 3, 5: 5, 6: 8, 7: 13, 8: 21, 9: 34, 10: 55, 11: 89, 12: 144, 13: 233, 14: 377, 15: 610, 16: 987,

    🔢 3 = {int} 2

    🔢 4 = {int} 3

    🔢 5 = {int} 5

    🔢 6 = {int} 8

    🔢 7 = {int} 13

    🔢 8 = {int} 21

    🔢 9 = {int} 34

    🔢 10 = {int} 55

    🔢 11 = {int} 89

    🔢 12 = {int} 144

    🔢 13 = {int} 233

    🔢 14 = {int} 377

    🔢 15 = {int} 610

Figure 20: Debugger variables

You can also interact with the current status of the program using the debugger's console (Figure 21). In the debugger view, click the **Console** tab next to the Debugger tab. In this console, you can interact with the state of the current program and do things like check whether a given Fibonacci number is cached:

```
>>> 12 in cache
True
```

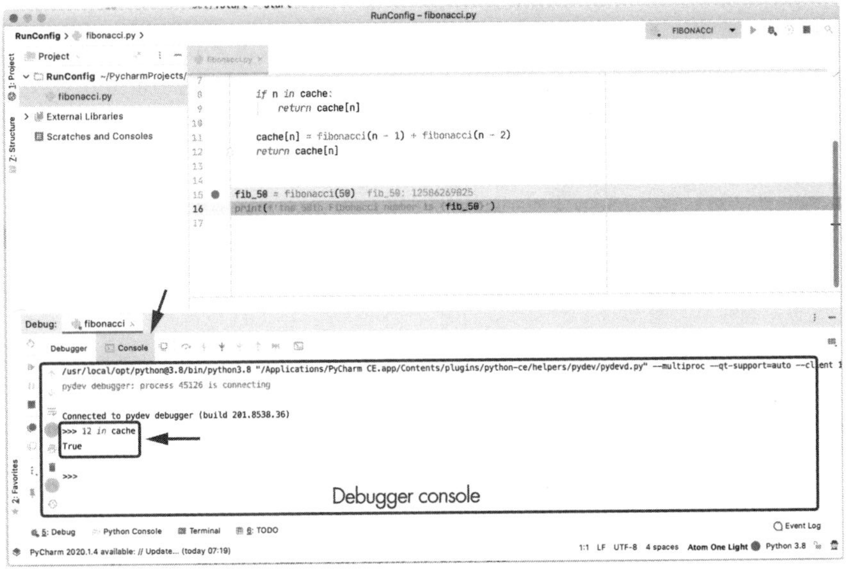

Figure 21: Debugger console

Summary

In this introductory chapter, we've taken a look at the contents of the book and the prerequisites you'll need to follow along and make the best of it. We also installed Python and configured our environment to work effectively throughout the book.

The last section was a sneak peek into PyCharm and its powerful debugging tools, but as you can imagine, we've barely scratched the surface. To learn more about PyCharm debugging, take a quick look at the official documentation at *https://www.jetbrains.com/help/pycharm/debugging-code.html*.

Now, let's start learning about Python.

PART I

BASICS

1

A SHORT PYTHON PRIMER

In this first chapter, we'll take a look at some of the Python features we'll use throughout the book. This is not meant to be an introduction to Python; I'm assuming you have a basic understanding of the language. If you don't, there are plenty of good books and online tutorials that'll get you started.

We'll first explore how Python code can be split into packages and how to import these packages into our programs. We'll learn how to document Python code and how to consult this documentation using Python. Then, we'll review tuples, lists, sets, and dictionaries, which are the most popular Python collections.

Python Packages and Modules

Software projects of a reasonable size usually consist of lots of source files, also called *modules*. A coherent bundle of Python modules is referred to as a *package*. Let's start our discussion on Python by taking a look at these two concepts: modules and packages.

Modules

A Python *module* is a file that contains Python code that's meant to be imported by other Python modules or scripts. A *script*, on the other hand, is a Python file that's meant to be run.

Python modules allow us to share code between files, which spares us from having to write the same code over and over again.

Every Python file has access to a global variable named __name__. This variable can have two possible values:

- The name of the module, that is, the name of the file without the *.py* extension
- The string '__main__'

Python determines the value of __name__ based on whether the file is imported by some other module or run as a script. When the module is imported inside another module or script, __name__ is set to the name of the module. If we run the module as a script, for example,

```
$ python3 my_module.py
```

then the value of __name__ is set to '__main__'. This may seem a bit abstract at the moment, but we'll explain why we care about the __name__ global variable later in the chapter. As we'll see, knowing if a given module is being imported or run as a script is an important piece of information we'll want to consider.

As we write more and more Python modules for our project, it makes sense to separate them into groups according to functionality. These groups of modules are called *packages*.

Packages

A *package* is a directory containing Python modules and a special file whose name is required to be *__init__.py*. Python's interpreter will understand any folder containing an *__init__.py* file as a package.

For instance, a folder structure like:

```
geom2d
  |- __init__.py
  |- point.py
  |- vector.py
```

is a Python package called *geom2d* containing two files, or modules: *point.py* and *vector.py*.

The *__init__.py* file is executed whenever something is imported from the package. This means that the *__init__.py* file can contain Python code, usually initialization code. Most of the time, however, this *__init__.py* file remains empty.

Running Files

When Python imports a file, it reads its contents. If this file contains only functions and data, Python loads these definitions, but no code is actually executed. However, if there are top-level instructions or function calls, Python will execute them as part of the import process—something we usually don't want.

Earlier, we saw how when a file is run (as opposed to imported), Python sets the __name__ global variable to be the string '__main__'. We can use this fact to execute the main logic only when the file is being run, and not when the file is imported:

```
if __name__ == '__main__':
    # only executes if file is run, not imported
```

We'll refer to this pattern as the "if name is main" pattern, and we'll use it in the applications we'll write in this book.

Remember that when a file is imported, Python sets the __name__ variable to the name of that module.

Importing Code

Let's say you had some Python code you wanted to use in multiple files. One way to do that would be to copy and paste the code every time you wanted to use it. Not only would this be tedious and boring, but imagine what would happen if you changed your mind about how that code works: you'd need to open every single file where you pasted the code and modify it in the same way. As you can imagine, this is not a productive way of writing software.

Fortunately, Python provides a powerful system to share code: importing modules. When *module_b* imports *module_a*, *module_b* gains access to the code written in *module_a*. This lets us write algorithms in a single place and then share that code across files. Let's look at an example using two modules we'll write in the next part of the book.

Say we have two modules: *point.py* and *vector.py*. Both modules are inside the package we saw earlier:

```
geom2d
|- __init__.py
|- point.py
|- vector.py
```

The first module, named *point.py*, defines the geometric primitive Point, and the second one, *vector.py*, defines the Vector, another geometric primitive. Figure 1-1 illustrates these two modules. Each module is divided into two sections: a section in gray, for the code in the module that has been imported from somewhere else, and a section in white, for the code defined by the module itself.

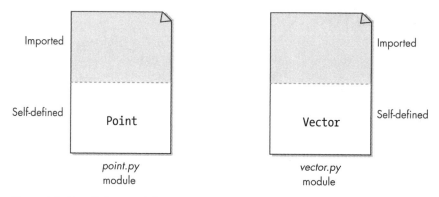

Figure 1-1: Two Python modules

Now, say we need our *point.py* module to implement some functionality that uses a Vector (like, for example, displacing a point by a given vector). We can gain access to the Vector code in *vector.py* using Python's import command. Figure 1-2 illustrates this process, which brings the Vector code to the "imported" section of the *point.py* module, making it available inside the entire module.

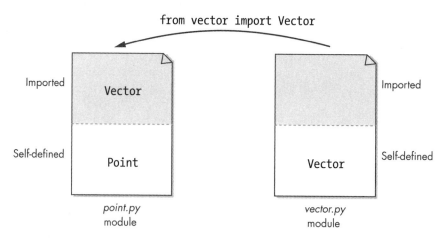

Figure 1-2: Importing the Vector class from the vector.py

In Figure 1-2, we use the following Python command:

```
from vector import Vector
```

This command brings just the Vector class from *vector.py*. We're not importing anything else defined in *vector.py*.

As you'll see in the next section, there are a few ways to import from modules.

Different Import Forms

To understand the different ways we can import modules and names inside a module, let's use two packages from our *Mechanics* project.

```
Mechanics
  |- geom2d
  |    |- __init__.py
  |    |- point.py
  |    |- vector.py
  |
  |- eqs
  |    |- __init__.py
  |    |- matrix.py
  |    |- vector.py
```

For this example, we'll use the *geom2d* and *eqs* packages, using two files, or modules, inside of each. Each of these modules defines a single class that has the same name as the module, only capitalized. For example, the module in *point.py* defines the Point class, *vector.py* defines the Vector class, and *matrix.py* defines the Matrix class. Figure 1-3 illustrates this package structure.

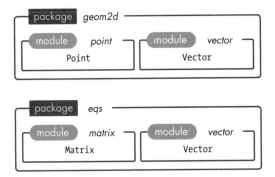

Figure 1-3: Two packages from our Mechanics project and some of their modules

With this directory set up in our minds, let's analyze several scenarios.

Importing from a Module in the Same Package

If we are in module *point.py* from the package *geom2d* and we want to import the entire *vector.py* module, we can use the following:

```
import vector
```

Now we can use the *vector.py* module's contents like so:

```
v = vector.Vector(1, 2)
```

It's important to note that since we imported the entire module and not any of its individual entities, we have to refer to the module-defined entities using the module name. If we want to refer to the module using a different name, we can alias it:

```
import vector as vec
```

Then we can use it like so:

```
v = vec.Vector(1, 2)
```

We can also import specific names from a module instead of importing the entire module. As you saw earlier, the syntax for this is as follows:

```
from vector import Vector
```

With this import, we can instead do the following:

```
v = Vector(1, 2)
```

In this case, we can also alias the imported name:

```
from vector import Vector as Vec
```

When we *alias* an imported name, we simply rename it to something else. In this case, we can now write it as follows:

```
v = Vec(1, 2)
```

Importing from a Module in a Different Package

If we wanted to import the *point.py* module from inside the *matrix.py* module, which is in a different package, we could do the following:

```
import geom.point
```

or equivalently

```
from geom import point
```

This lets us use the entire *point.py* module inside *matrix.py*:

```
p = point.Point(1, 2)
```

Once again, we can choose to alias the imported module:

```
import geom.point as pt
```

or equivalently

```
from geom import point as pt
```

Either way, we can use pt as follows:

```
p = pt.Point(1, 2)
```

We can also import names from the module, instead of bringing the entire module, like so:

```
from geom.point import Point

p = Point(1, 2)
```

As before, we can use an alias:

```
from geom.point import Point as Pt

p = Pt(1, 2)
```

Relative Imports

Finally, we have relative imports. A *relative import* is one that refers to a module using a route whose start point is the file's current location.

We use one dot (.) to refer to modules or packages inside the same package and two dots (..) to refer to the parent directory.

Following our previous example, we could import the *point.py* module from within *matrix.py* using a relative import:

```
from ..geom.point import Point

p = Point(1, 2)
```

In this case, the route ..geom.point means this: from the current directory move to our parent's directory and look for the *point.py* module.

Documenting the Code with Docstrings

When we write code that other developers will use, it's good practice to document it. This documentation should include information about how to use our code, what assumptions the code makes, and what each function does.

Python uses *docstrings* to document code. These docstrings are defined between triple quotes (""") and appear as the first statement of the function, class, or module they document.

You may have noticed how the code for the *Mechanics* project you downloaded earlier uses these docstrings. For example, if you open the *matrix.py* file, the methods of the Matrix class are documented this way:

```
def set_data(self, data: [float]):
    """
    Sets the given list of 'float' numbers as the values of
    the matrix.

    The matrix is filled with the passed in numbers from left
    to right and from top to bottom.
    The length of the passed in list has to be equal to the
```

```
number of values in the matrix: rows x columns.

If the size of the list doesn't match the matrix number
of elements, an error is raised.

:param data: [float] with the values
:return: this Matrix
"""
if len(data) != self.__cols_count * self.__rows_count:
    raise ValueError('Cannot set data: size mismatch')

for row in range(self.__rows_count):
    offset = self.__cols_count * row
    for col in range(self.__cols_count):
        self.__data[row][col] = data[offset + col]

return self
```

If you ever find yourself using this code and can't figure something out, Python has the help global function; if you give help a module, function, class, or method, it returns that code's docstring. For example, we could get the documentation for this set_data method inside a Python interpreter console as follows:

```
>>> from eqs.matrix import Matrix
>>> help(Matrix.set_data)
```

```
Help on function set_data in module eqs.matrix:
set_data(self, data: [<class 'float'>])
    Sets the given list of 'float' numbers as the values of
    the matrix.

    The matrix is filled with the passed in numbers from left
    to right and from top to bottom.
    The length of the passed in list has to be equal to the
    number of values in the matrix: rows x columns.

    If the size of the list doesn't match the matrix number
    of elements, an error is raised.

    :param data: [float] with the values
    :return: this Matrix
```

There are automated tools, like Sphinx (*https://www.sphinx-doc.org/*), that generate documentation reports in HTML, PDF, or plaintext using the docstrings in a project. You can distribute this documentation along with your code so that other developers have a good place to start learning about the code you write.

We won't be writing the docstrings in this book as they take up considerable space. But they should all be in the code you downloaded, and you can look at them there.

Collections in Python

Our programs often work with collections of items, sometimes very large ones. We want to store these items in a way that is convenient for our purposes. Sometimes we'll be interested in knowing whether a collection includes a particular item, and other times we'll need to know the order of our items; we may also want a fast way of finding a given item, maybe one that fulfills a particular condition.

As you can see, there are many ways to interact with a collection of items. As it turns out, choosing the right way to store data is crucial for our programs to perform well. There are different collection flavors, each good for certain cases; knowing which type of collection to use in each particular situation is an important skill every software developer should master.

Python offers us four main collections: the set, the tuple, the list, and the dictionary. Let's explain how each of these collections stores elements and how to use them.

Sets

The *set* is an unordered collection of unique elements. Sets are most useful when we need to quickly determine whether an element exists in a collection.

To create a set in Python, we can use the set function:

```
>>> s1 = set([1, 2, 3])
```

We can also use the literal syntax:

```
>>> s1 = {1, 2, 3}
```

Notice that when using the literal syntax, we define the set using curly brackets ({}).

We can get the number of elements contained inside a set using the global len function:

```
>>> len(s1)
3
```

Checking whether an element exists in the set is a fast operation and can be done using the in operator:

```
>>> 2 in s1
True

>>> 5 in s1
False
```

We can add new elements to the set using the add method:

```
>>> s1.add(4)
# the set is now {1, 2, 3, 4}
```

If we try to add an element that's already present, nothing happens because a set doesn't allow repeated elements:

```
>>> s1.add(3)
# the set is still {1, 2, 3, 4}
```

We can remove an element from a set using the remove method:

```
>>> s1.add(3)
>>> s1.remove(1)
# the set is now {2, 3, 4}
```

We can operate with sets using the familiar mathematical operations for sets. For example, we can compute the difference between two sets, which is the set containing the elements of the first set that aren't in the second set:

```
>>> s1 = set([1, 2, 3])
>>> s2 = set([3, 4])
>>> s1.difference(s2)
{1, 2}
```

We can also compute the union of two sets, which is the set containing all the elements that appear in both sets:

```
>>> s1 = set([1, 2, 3])
>>> s2 = set([3, 4])
>>> s1.union(s2)
{1, 2, 3, 4}
```

We can iterate through sets, but the order of the iteration is not guaranteed:

```
>>> for element in s1:
...     print(element)
...
3
1
2
```

Tuples

Tuples are immutable and ordered sequences of elements. *Immutable* means that, once created, the tuple cannot be changed in any way. Elements in a tuple are referred to with the index they occupy, starting with zero. Counting in Python always starts from zero.

Tuples are a good option when we're passing a collection of ordered data around our code but don't want the collection to be mutated in any way. For example, in code like:

```
>>> names = ('Anne', 'Emma')
>>> some_function(names)
```

you can be sure the names tuple won't be changed by some_function in any way. By contrast, if you decided to use a set like:

```
>>> names = set('Anne', 'Emma')
>>> some_function(names)
```

nothing would prevent some_function from adding or removing elements from the passed-in names, so you'd need to check the function's code to understand whether the code alters the elements.

NOTE *In any case, as we'll see later, functions shouldn't mutate their parameters, so the functions we'll write in this book will never modify their input parameters in any way. You might, nevertheless, use functions written by other developers who didn't follow the same rule, so you want to check whether those functions have these kinds of side effects.*

Tuples are defined between parentheses, and the elements inside a tuple are comma-separated. Here's a tuple, defined using literal syntax, containing my name and age:

```
>>> me = ('Angel', 31)
```

If we want to create a tuple with only one element, we need to write a comma after it:

```
>>> name = ('Angel',)
```

It can also be created using the tuple function, passing it a list of items:

```
>>> me = tuple(['Angel', 31])
```

We can get the number of items in a tuple using the len global function:

```
>>> len(count)
2
```

We can also count how many times a given value appears inside a tuple using the tuple's count method:

```
>>> me.count('Angel')
1

>>> me.count(50)
0
```

```
>>> ('hey', 'hey', 'hey').count('hey')
3
```

We can get the index of the first occurrence of a given item using the index method:

```
>>> family = ('Angel', 'Alvaro', 'Mery', 'Paul', 'Isabel', 'Alvaro')
>>> family.index('Alvaro')
1
```

In this example, we're looking for the index of the string `'Alvaro'`, which appears twice: at indices 1 and 5. The index method yields the first occurrence's index, which is 1 in this case.

The in operator can be used to check whether an element exists inside a tuple:

```
>>> 'Isabel' in family
True
```

```
>>> 'Elena' in family
False
```

Tuples can be multiplied by numbers, a peculiar operation that yields a new tuple with the original elements repeated as many times as the multiplier number:

```
>>> ('ruby', 'ruby') * 4
('ruby', 'ruby', 'ruby', 'ruby', 'ruby', 'ruby', 'ruby', 'ruby')
```

```
>>> ('we', 'found', 'love', 'in', 'a', 'hopeless', 'place') * 16
('we', 'found', 'love', 'in', 'a', 'hopeless', 'place', 'we', 'found', ...
```

We can iterate through tuple values using for loops:

```
>>> for city in ('San Francisco', 'Barcelona', 'Pamplona'):
...     print(f'{city} is a beautiful city')
...
San Francisco is a beautiful city
Barcelona is a beautiful city
Pamplona is a beautiful city
```

Using Python's built-in enumerate function, we can iterate through the items in the tuple with their indices:

```
>>> cities = ('Pamplona', 'San Francisco', 'Barcelona')
>>> for index, city in enumerate(cities):
...     print(f'{city} is #{index + 1} in my favorite cities list')
...
Pamplona is #1 in my favorite cities list
```

```
San Francisco is #2 in my favorite cities list
Barcelona is #3 in my favorite cities list
```

Lists

The *list* is an ordered collection of nonunique elements referenced by their index. Lists are well suited for cases where we need to keep elements in order and where we know the index at which they appear.

Lists and tuples are similar, with the tuple's immutability being the only difference; items in a list move around, and items can be added and removed. If you are sure the items in a large collection won't be modified, use a tuple instead of a list; tuple manipulations are faster than their list equivalents. Python can do some optimizations if it knows the items in the collection won't change.

To create a list in Python, we can use the list function:

```
>>> l1 = list(['a', 'b', 'c'])
```

Or we can use the literal syntax:

```
>>> l1 = ['a', 'b', 'c']
```

Note the usage of the square brackets ([ ]).

We can check the number of items in a list using the len function:

```
>>> len(l1)
3
```

List elements can be accessed by index (the index of the first element is zero):

```
>>> l1[1]
'b'
```

We can also replace an existing element in the list:

```
>>> l1[1] = 'm'
# the list is now ['a', 'm', 'c']
```

Be careful not to use an index that doesn't exist in the list; it'll raise an IndexError:

```
>>> l1[35] = 'x'
Traceback (most recent call last):
  File "<input>", line 1, in <module>
IndexError: list assignment index out of range
```

Items can be appended to the end of the list using the append method:

```
>>> l1.append('d')
# the list is now ['a', 'm', 'c', 'd']
```

Lists can be iterated, and the order of iteration is guaranteed:

```
>>> for element in l1:
...     print(element)
...
a
m
c
d
```

Often enough, we're interested not only in the element itself but also in its index in the list. In those cases, we can use the enumerate function, which yields a tuple of the index and element:

```
>>> for index, element in enumerate(l1):
...     print(f'{index} -> {element}')
...
0 -> a
1 -> m
2 -> c
3 -> d
```

A new list can be created by taking contiguous elements from another list. This process is called *slicing*. Slicing is a big topic that requires a section of its own.

Slicing Lists

Slicing a list looks a bit like indexing into the list using square brackets, except we use two indices separated by a colon: [*<start>* : *<end>*]. Here's an example:

```
>>> a = [1, 2, 3, 4]
>>> b = a[1:3]
# list b is [2, 3]
```

In the previous example, we have a list a with values [1, 2, 3, 4]. We create a new list, b, by slicing the original list and taking the items starting at index 1 (inclusive) and ending at index 3 (noninclusive).

NOTE *Don't forget that slices in Python always include the element in the start index and exclude the element in the end index.*

Figure 1-4 illustrates this process.

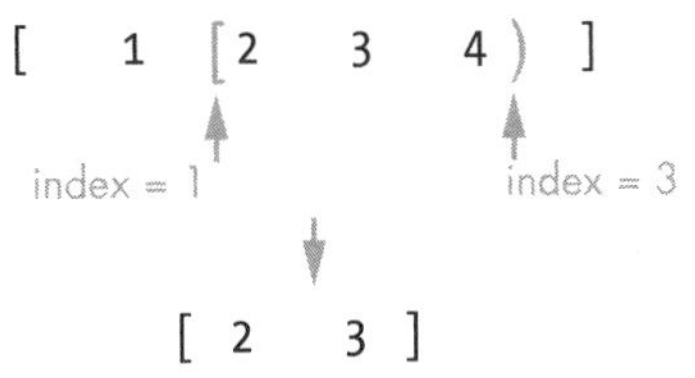

Figure 1-4: Slicing a list

Both the start and end indices in the slice operator are optional because they have a default value. By default, the start index is assigned the first index in the list, which is always zero. The end index is assigned the last index in the list plus one, which is equal to len(the_list).

```
>>> a = [1, 2, 3, 4]

# these two are equivalent:
>>> b_1 = a[0:4]
>>> b_2 = a[:]
```

In this example, both b_1 and b_2 lists are a copy of the original a list. By copy we really mean they're different lists; you can safely modify b_1 or b_2, and list a remains unchanged. You can test this by doing the following:

```
>>> a = [1, 2, 3, 4]
>>> b = a[:]
>>> b[0] = 55

>>> print('list a:', a)
list a: [1, 2, 3, 4]

>>> print('list b:', b)
list b: [55, 2, 3, 4]
```

Negative indices are another trick you can use. A negative index is an index that is counted starting from the end of the list and moving toward the beginning of the list. Negative indices can be used in slicing operations the same way as positive indices, with a small exception: negative indices start at −1, not at −0. We could, for instance, slice a list to get its two last values as follows:

```
>>> a = [1, 2, 3, 4]
>>> b = a[-2:]
# list b is [3, 4]
```

Here we're creating a new list starting at the second position from the end all the way to the last element of the list. Figure 1-5 illustrates this.

Slicing lists is a versatile operation in Python.

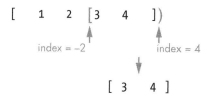

$$[\quad 1 \quad 2 \quad [3 \quad 4 \quad])$$

index = -2   index = 4

$$[\quad 3 \quad 4 \quad]$$

Figure 1-5: Slicing a list using negative indices

Dictionaries

A *dictionary* is a collection of key-value pairs. Values in a dictionary are mapped to their key; we retrieve elements from a dictionary using their key. Finding a value in a dictionary is fast.

Dictionaries are useful when we want to store elements referenced by some key. For example, if we wanted to store information about our siblings and wanted to be able to retrieve it by the name of the sibling, we could use a dictionary. We'll take a look at this in the following code.

To create a dictionary in Python, you can either use the dict function,

```
>>> colors = dict([('stoke', 'red'), ('fill', 'orange')])
```

or use the literal syntax,

```
>>> colors = {'stoke': 'red', 'fill': 'orange'}
```

The dict function expects a list of tuples. These tuples should contain two values: the first one is used as the key, and the second is used as the value. The literal version for creating dictionaries is much less verbose, and in both cases the resulting dictionary is the same.

As with a list, we access values in a dictionary using square brackets. However, this time we use the key of the value between the brackets, as opposed to the index:

```
>>> colors['stroke']
red
```

You can use anything that's immutable as the key in a dictionary. Remember that tuples are immutable, whereas lists are not. Numbers, strings, and booleans are also immutable and thus can be used as dictionary keys.

Let's create a dictionary where the keys are tuples:

```
>>> ages = {('Angel', 'Sola'): 31, ('Jen', 'Gil'): 30}
```

In this example, we map the age to a key composed of a name and a surname in a tuple. If we want to know Jen's age, we can ask for the value in a dictionary by using its key:

```
>>> age = ages[('Jen', 'Gil')]
>>> print(f'she is {age} years old')
she is 30 years old
```

What happens when we look for a key that's not in the dictionary?

```
>>> age = ages[('Steve', 'Perry')]
Traceback (most recent call last):
  File "<input>", line 1, in <module>
KeyError: ('Steve', 'Perry')
```

We get an error. We can check whether a key is in a dictionary before getting its value using the in operator:

```
>>> ('Steve', 'Perry') in ages
False
```

We can also get a set-like view of all the keys in the dictionary:

```
>>> ages.keys()
dict_keys([('Angel', 'Sola'), ('Jen', 'Gil')])
```

We can do the same for the values:

```
>>> ages.values()
dict_values([31, 30])
```

We can use the in operator to check for the existence of a value in both the keys and values stored in Python dictionaries:

```
>>> ('Jen', 'Gil') in ages.keys()
True

>>> 45 in ages.values()
False
```

Dictionaries can be iterated in a few ways. Let's imagine we have the following ages dictionary:

```
>>> ages = {'Angel': 31, 'Jen': 30}
```

We can use for loops to iterate through the dictionary keys:

```
>>> for name in ages.keys():
...     print(f'we have the age for {name}')
...
we have the age for Angel
we have the age for Jen
```

We can do the same for the values:

```
>>> for age in ages.values():
...     print(f'someone is {age} years old')
...
someone is 31 years old
someone is 30 years old
```

And we can do the same for the key-value tuples:

```
>>> for name, age in ages.items():
...     print(f'{name} is {age} years old')
...
Angel is 31 years old
Jen is 30 years old
```

That's about all we need to know about Python's collections for now. Let's continue our Python tour by looking at destructuring collections.

Destructuring

Destructuring or *unpacking* is a technique that allows us to assign values inside a collection to variables. Let's look at some examples.

Imagine we have a tuple containing information about a person, including her name and favorite beverage:

```
>>> anne_info = ('Anne', 'grape juice')
```

Say we want to have those two pieces of information in separate variables. We could separate them out like so:

```
>>> name = anne_info[0]
>>> beverage = anne_info[1]
```

This is perfectly fine, but we can do it in a more elegant way using destructuring syntax. To destructure the two strings inside the tuple into two variables, we have to use another tuple with the variable names on the left side of the assignment:

```
>>> (name, beverage) = anne_info

>>> name
'Anne'

>>> beverage
>>> 'grape juice'
```

We can also destructure lists. For example, if we had a list containing similar information about another person, like

```
>>> emma_info = ['Emma', 'hot chocolate']
```

we could destructure the name and favorite beverage using a list on the left side of the assignment:

```
>>> [name, beverage] = emma_info

>>> name
'Emma'

>>> beverage
'hot chocolate'
```

The left-side tuple or list has to match the size of the one on the right side, but there might be cases where we're not interested in all of the unpacked values. In such cases, you can use an underscore in those positions where you want to ignore the corresponding value. For example,

```
[a, _, c] = [1, 2, 3]
```

assigns the value 1 to variable a and assigns 3 to variable c, but it discards the value 2.

This is another technique that helps us write more concise code.

Summary

This chapter has been a tour of some intermediate and advanced Python techniques we'll use throughout the book. We took a look at how Python programs are made of modules bundled into packages and how to import these modules from other parts of our code.

We also explained the "if name is main" pattern, which is used to avoid executing portions of the code when the file is imported.

Then, we briefly touched on the four basic Python collections: tuples, lists, sets, and dictionaries. We also looked at how to destructure, or unpack, these collections.

Now let's shift gears and talk about a few programming paradigms.

2

TWO PYTHON PARADIGMS

 Now that we've explored some topics in the Python programming language, let's learn about the two main paradigms we can use to write code. In this second chapter on Python, we'll discuss the functional and object-oriented programming paradigms and the benefits each brings. We'll wrap up with a brief look at type hints. Let's get started.

Functional Programming

Functional programming is a programming paradigm, which means that it's a style of writing code we can decide to adhere to. For us to say "we're writing functional-style code" we have to follow some simple rules that define what functional programming is about.

The central elements of the functional programming paradigm are pure functions and the immutability of data. We'll break these concepts down in the next sections.

Not all programming languages have good support for writing functional-style code. For example, languages like C have no good support for it. On the other hand, there are languages, like Haskell, that are purely functional, meaning you can only write functional-style code. By design, Python isn't a functional language, but it does have support for the functional programming style.

Let's learn about pure functions.

Pure Functions

Let's quickly review the syntax for a Python function:

```
def function_name(parameters):
    <function body>
```

The definition of a function starts with the def keyword followed by the name of the function and the input parameters inside parentheses. A colon (:) marks the end of the function header. The code in the body of the function is indented one level.

A function, in the functional programming paradigm, is similar to the mathematical concept of a function: a mapping of some input to some output. We say a function is *pure* if

- It consistently returns the same outputs for the same set of inputs.

- It doesn't have side effects.

A *side effect* happens when something outside the body of the function is mutated by the function. A side effect also occurs when the function's inputs are modified by the function, because a pure function never modifies its inputs. For example, the following function is pure:

```
def make_vector_between(p, q):
    u = q['x'] - p['x']
    v = q['y'] - p['y']

    return {'u': u, 'v': v}
```

Given the same input points p and q, the output is always the same vector, and nothing outside the function's body is modified. In contrast, the following code is an impure version of make_vector:

```
last_point = {'x': 10, 'y': 20}

def make_vector(q):
    u = q['x'] - last_point['x']
    v = q['y'] - last_point['y']
    new_vector = {'u': u, 'v': v}
    last_point = q

    return new_vector
```

The previous snippet uses the shared state of `last_point`, which is mutated every time `make_vector` is called. This mutation is a side effect of the function. The returned vector depends on the `last_point` shared state, so the function doesn't return the same vector consistently for the same input point.

Immutability

As you saw in the previous example, one key aspect of functional programming is *immutability*. Something is immutable if it doesn't change with time. If we decide to write code in the functional programming style, we make the firm decision of avoiding data mutations and modeling our programs using pure functions.

Let's take a look at an example. Imagine we had defined a point and a vector in the plane using dictionaries:

```python
point = {'x': 5, 'y': 2}
vector = {'u': 10, 'v': 20}
```

If we wanted to compute the point resulting from displacing the existing point by the vector, we could do it in a functional way by creating a new point using a function. Here's an example:

```python
def displaced_point(point, vector):
    x = point['x'] + vector['u']
    y = point['y'] + vector['v']

    return {'x': x, 'y': y}
```

This function is pure: given the same `point` and `vector` inputs, the resulting displaced point is consistently the same, and there is nothing that escapes the function's body that is mutated in any sense, not even the function parameters.

If we run this function, passing in the `point` and `vector` defined earlier, we get the following:

```python
>>> displaced_point(point, vector)
{'x': 15, 'y': 22}

# let's check the state of point (shouldn't have been mutated)
>>> point
{'x': 5, 'y': 2}
```

Conversely, a nonfunctional way of solving this case could involve mutating the original point using a function like the following:

```python
def displace_point_in_place(point, vector):
    point['x'] += vector['u']
    point['y'] += vector['v']
```

This function mutates the point it receives as an argument, which violates one of the key rules of the functional style.

Note the use of in_place in the function name. This is a commonly used naming convention that implies that the changes will happen by mutating the original object. We'll adhere to this naming convention throughout the book.

Now let's see how we'd go about using this `displace_point_in_place` function:

```
>>> displace_point_in_place(point, vector)
# nothing gets returned from the function, so let's check the point

>>> point
{'x': 15, 'y': 22}
# the original point has been mutated!
```

As you can see, the function isn't returning anything, which is a sign that the function isn't pure, because to do some kind of useful operation it must have mutated something somewhere. In this case, that "something" is our point, whose coordinates have been updated.

An important benefit of the functional style is that by respecting the immutability of data structures, we avoid unintended side effects. When you mutate an object, you may not be aware of all the places in your code where that object is referenced. If there are other parts in the code relying on that object's state, there may be side effects you are not aware of. So, after the object was mutated, your program may behave differently than expected. These kinds of errors are extremely hard to hunt down and can require hours of debugging.

If we minimize the number of mutations in our project, we make it more reliable and less error prone.

Let's now take a look at a special kind of function that has a central role in functional programming: the lambda function.

Lambdas

Back in the 1930s, a mathematician named Alonzo Church invented lambda calculus, a theory about functions and how they are applied to their arguments. Lambda calculus is the core of functional programming.

In Python, a *lambda function*, or *lambda*, is an anonymous, typically short function defined on a single line. We'll find lambdas to be useful when passing functions as parameters to other functions, for instance.

We define a lambda function in Python using the `lambda` keyword followed by the arguments (separated by commas), a colon, and the function's expression body:

```
lambda <arg1>, <arg2>, ...: <expression body>
```

The expression's result is the returned value.

A lambda function to sum two numbers can be written as follows:

```
>>> sum = lambda x, y: x + y
>>> sum(1, 2)
3
```

This is equivalent to the regular Python function:

```
>>> def sum(x, y):
...     return x + y
...
>>> sum(1, 2)
3
```

Lambdas are going to appear in the next sections; we'll see there how they're used in several contexts. The place we'll be using lambdas the most is as arguments to the filter, map, and reduce functions, as we'll discuss in "Filter, Map, and Reduce" on page 29.

Higher-Order Functions

A *higher-order* function is a function that either receives a function (or functions) as input parameters or returns a function as its result.

Let's take a look at examples for both cases.

Functions As Function Arguments

Imagine we want to write a function that can run a function a given number of times. We could implement this as follows:

```
>>> def repeat_fn(fn, times):
...     for _ in range(times):
...         fn()
...

>>> def say_hi():
...     print('Hi there!')
...

>>> repeat_fn(say_hi, 5)
Hi there!
Hi there!
Hi there!
Hi there!
Hi there!
```

As you can see, the repeat_fn function's first parameter is another function, which is executed as many times as the second argument times dictates. Then, we define another function to simply print the string "Hi there!" to the screen: say_hi. The result of calling the `repeat_fn` function and passing it say_hi is those five greetings.

We could rewrite the previous example using an anonymous lambda function:

```
>>> def repeat_fn(fn, times):
...     for _ in range(times):
...         fn()
...
>>> repeat_fn(lambda: print("Hello!"), 5)
Hello!
Hello!
Hello!
Hello!
Hello!
```

This spares us from having to define a named function to print the message.

Functions As Function Return Values

Let's take a look at a function that returns another function. Imagine we want to define validation functions that validate if a given string contains a sequence of characters. We can write a function named `make_contains_validator` that takes a sequence and returns a function to validate strings that contain that sequence:

```
>>> def make_contains_validator(sequence):
...     return lambda string: sequence in string
```

We can use this function to generate validation functions, like the following one,

```
>>> validate_contains_at = make_contains_validator('@')
```

which can be used to check whether the passed-in strings contain the @ character:

```
>>> validate_contains_at('foo@bar.com')
True
>>> validate_contains_at('not this one')
False
```

Higher-order functions are a useful resource we'll use throughout the book.

Functions Inside Other Functions

Another convenient technique we'll use throughout this book is defining a function inside another function. There are two good reasons we may want to do this: for one, it gives the inner function access to everything inside the outer function, without needing to pass that information as parameters; and also, the inner function may define some logic that we don't want to expose to the outside world.

A function can be defined inside another function using the regular syntax. Let's take a look at an example:

```
def outer_fn(a, b):
    c = a + b

    def inner_fn():
        # we have access to a, b and c here
        print(a, b, c)

    inner_fn()
```

Here, the inner_fn function is defined inside the outer_fn function, and thus, it can't be accessed from outside this host function, only from within its body. The inner_fn function has access to everything defined inside outer_fn, including the function parameters.

Defining subfunctions inside of functions is useful when a function's logic grows complex and it can be broken down into smaller tasks. Of course, we could also split the function into smaller functions all defined at the same level. In this case, to signal that those subfunctions are not meant to be imported and consumed from outside the module, we'll follow Python's standard and name those functions starting with two underscores:

```
def public_fn():
    # this function can be imported

def __private_fn():
    # this function should only be accessed from inside the module
```

Note that Python has no access modifiers (public, private, . . .); thus, all the code written at the top level of a module, that is, a Python file, can be imported and used.

Remember that the two underscores are just a convention that we have to respect. Nothing really prevents us from importing and using that code. If we import a function that starts with two underscores, we have to understand that the function was not written by its authors to be used from the outside, and we may get unexpected results if we call that function. By defining our subfunctions within the functions that call them, we prevent this behavior.

Filter, Map, and Reduce

In functional programming, we never mutate a collection's items, but instead always create a new collection to reflect the changes of an operation over that collection. There are three operations that form the cornerstone of functional programming and can accomplish every modification to a collection we can ever think of: `filter`, `map`, and `reduce`.

Filter

The *filter* operation takes a collection and creates a new collection where some items may have been left out. The items are filtered according to a *predicate function*, which is a function that accepts one argument and returns either `True` or `False` depending on whether that argument passes a given test.

Figure 2-1 illustrates the filter operation.

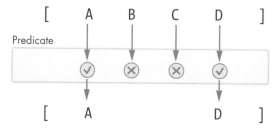

Figure 2-1: Filtering a collection

Figure 2-1 shows a source collection made of four elements: A, B, C, and D. Below the collection is a box representing the predicate function, which determines which elements to keep and which to discard. Each element in the collection is passed to the predicate, and only those that pass the test are included in the resulting collection.

There are two ways we can filter collections in Python: using the `filter` global function and, if the collection is a list, using list comprehensions. We'll focus on the `filter` function here; we'll cover list comprehensions in the next section. Python's `filter` function receives a function (the predicate) and collection as parameters:

```
filter(<predicate_fn>, <collection>)
```

Let's write a predicate lambda function to test whether a number is even:

```
lambda n: n % 2 == 0
```

Now let's use our lambda function to filter a list of numbers and obtain a new collection with only even numbers:

```
>>> numbers = [1, 2, 3, 4, 5, 6, 7, 8]
>>> evens = filter(lambda n: n % 2 == 0, numbers)
>>> list(evens)
[2, 4, 6, 8]
```

One thing to note is that the `filter` function doesn't return a list, but rather an iterator. Iterators allow for iteration over a collection of items, one at a time. If you want to know more about Python iterators and how they work under the hood, please refer to the documentation at *https://docs.python.org*

/3/library/stdtypes.html#typeiter and *https://docs.python.org/3/glossary.html# term-iterator.*

We can consume all the iterator values and put them into a list using the list function we saw earlier. We can also consume the iterator using a for loop:

```
>>> for number in evens:
...     print(number)
...
2
4
6
8
```

Map

The *map* operation creates a new collection by taking each item in the source collection and running it through a function, storing the results in a new collection. The new collection is the same size as the source collection.

Figure 2-2 illustrates the map operation.

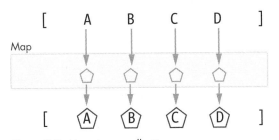

Figure 2-2: Mapping a collection

We run our source collection made of items A, B, C, and D through a mapping function, illustrated within a rectangle in Figure 2-2; the result of the mapping is stored in a new collection.

We can map a collection either using the global map function or, if we have a list, using list comprehensions. We'll discuss list comprehensions in a moment; for now, let's study how to map collections using the map function.

The map global function receives two parameters: a mapping function and a source collection:

```
map(<mapping_fn>, <collection>)
```

This is how we would map a list of names to their length:

```
>>> names = ['Angel', 'Alvaro', 'Mery', 'Paul', 'Isabel']
>>> lengths = map(lambda name: len(name), names)
>>> list(lengths)
[5, 6, 4, 4, 6]
```

As with the `filter` function, `map` returns an iterator that can be consumed into a list using the `list` function. In the previous example, the resulting list contains the number of letters in each of the names in the `names` list: five letters in *Angel*, six letters in *Alvaro*, and so on. We've mapped each name into a number representing its length.

Reduce

The *reduce* operation is the most complex, but at the same time, it's the most versatile of the three. It creates a new collection that can have fewer items than, more items than, or the same number of items as the original. To construct this new collection, it first applies a reducer function to the first and second elements. It then applies the reducer function to the third element *and* the result of the first application. It then applies the reducer function to the fourth element and the result of the second application. In this way, the results accumulate. A figure will help here. Take a look at Figure 2-3.

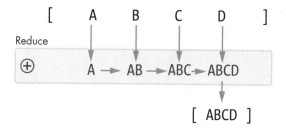

Figure 2-3: Reducing a collection

The reduction function in this example concatenates every element in the collection (A, B, C, and D) into a single element: ABCD.

The reducer function takes two parameters: the accumulated result and an item in the collection:

```
reducer_fn(<accumulated_result>, <item>)
```

The function is expected to return the accumulated result after the new item has been processed.

There's no global `reduce` function provided by Python, but there is a package named *functools* with some useful operations for working with higher-order functions, including a `reduce` function. This function doesn't return an iterator, but rather it returns the resulting collection or item directly. The function's signature looks like this:

```
reduce(<reducer_fn>, <collection>)
```

Let's work with an example:

```
>>> from functools import reduce

>>> letters = ['A', 'B', 'C', 'D']
```

```
>>> reduce(lambda result, letter: result + letter, letters)
'ABCD'
```

In this example, the reduce function returned a single item: `'ABCD'`, the result of concatenating each letter in the collection. To start the reduction process, the reduce function takes the first two letters, *A* and *B*, and concatenates them into *AB*. For this first step, Python uses the initial item of the collection (*A*) as the accumulated result and applies the reducer to it and the second item. Then, it moves to the third letter, *C*, and concatenates it with the current accumulated result *AB*, thus producing the new result: *ABC*. The last step does the same with the *D* letter to produce the result *ABCD*.

What happens when the accumulated result and the items of the collection have different types? In that case, we can't take the first item as the accumulated result, and thus the reduce function expects us to provide a third argument to use as the starting accumulated result:

```
reduce(<reducer_fn>, <collection>, <start_result>)
```

For example, imagine that we have the collection of names from earlier and we want to reduce it to obtain the total sum of the lengths of those names. In this case, the accumulated result is numeric, whereas the items in the collection are strings; we can't use the first item as the accumulated length. If we forget to provide reduce with the start result, Python is nice enough to remind us by raising an error:

```
>>> reduce(lambda total_length, name: total_length + len(name), names)
Traceback (most recent call last):
  File "<input>", line 1, in <module>
  File "<input>", line 1, in <lambda>
TypeError: can only concatenate str (not "int") to str
```

For this case, we should pass `0` as the initial accumulated length:

```
>>> reduce(lambda total_length, name: total_length + len(name), names, 0)
25
```

One interesting note here is that if the accumulated result and the items of the collection have different types, you can always concatenate a map with a reduce to obtain the same result. For example, in the previous exercise we could have also done the following:

```
>>> from functools import reduce

>>> names = ['Angel', 'Alvaro', 'Mery', 'Paul', 'Isabel']
>>> lengths = map(lambda name: len(name), names)
>>> reduce(lambda total_length, length: total_length + length, lengths)
25
```

In this code we first map the names list into a list of the name lengths: lengths. Then, we reduce the lengths list to sum all the values, with no starting value necessary.

When reducing items using a common operation—like a sum of two numbers or a concatenation of two strings—we don't need to write a lambda function ourselves; we can simply pass the reduce function an existing Python function. For example, when reducing numbers, there's a useful module provided by Python named *operator.py*. This module defines functions to operate with numbers, among others. Using this module, we can simplify our previous example to the following:

```
>>> from functools import reduce
>>> import operator

>>> names = ['Angel', 'Alvaro', 'Mery', 'Paul', 'Isabel']
>>> lengths = map(lambda name: len(name), names)
>>> reduce(operator.add, lengths)
25
```

This code is shorter and more readable, so we'll prefer this form throughout the book.

The operator.add function is defined by Python as follows:

```
def add(a, b):
    "Same as a + b."
    return a + b
```

As you can see, this function is equivalent to the lambda function we defined to sum two numbers. We'll see more examples of functions defined by Python that can be used with reduce throughout the book.

So far, all of our examples have reduced collections to a single value, but the reduce operation can do much more. In fact, both the filter and map operations are specializations of the reduce operation. We can filter and map a collection using only a reduce operation. But this isn't something we'll stop to analyze here; try to figure it out on your own if you feel motivated.

Let's see an example where we want to create a new collection based on the names list, where every item is the concatenation of all the previous names with the current name separated by the hyphen character (-). The result we're looking for should be something like this:

```
['Angel', 'Angel-Alvaro', 'Angel-Alvaro-Mery', ...]
```

We can do this using the following code:

```
>>> from functools import reduce

>>> names = ['Angel', 'Alvaro', 'Mery', 'Paul', 'Isabel']
>>> def compute_next_name(names, name):
...     if len(names) < 1:
...         return name
```

```
...     return names[-1] + '-' + name
...
>>> reduce(
...     lambda result, name: result + [compute_next_name(result, name)],
...     names,
...     [])
['Angel', 'Angel-Alvaro', 'Angel-Alvaro-Mery', 'Angel-Alvaro-Mery-Paul', ...]
```

Here, we use `compute_next_name` to determine the next item in the sequence. The lambda used inside `reduce` concatenates the accumulated result, which is the list of stitched-together names, with a new list consisting of the new item. The initial solution, an empty list, needs to be provided, since once again the type of each item in the list (string) is different from the result (list of strings).

As you can see, the reduce operation is very versatile.

List Comprehensions

As mentioned earlier, we can filter and map lists in Python using list comprehensions. This form is typically preferred over the `filter` and `map` functions when dealing with lists, as its syntax is more concise and readable.

A list comprehension to map items has the following structure:

```
[<expression> for <item> in <list>]
```

There are two parts to it:

- `for <item> in <list>` is the `for` loop that iterates over the items in `<list>`.

- `<expression>` is a mapping expression to map `<item>` into something else.

Let's repeat the exercise we did earlier where we mapped a list of names to a list of the lengths of each name, this time using a list comprehension:

```
>>> names = ['Angel', 'Alvaro', 'Mery', 'Paul', 'Isabel']
>>> [len(name) for name in names]
[5, 6, 4, 4, 6]
```

I hope you see why Python programmers favor list comprehensions over the `map` function; the example almost reads like plain English: "length of name for (each) name in names." In the example, `for name in names` iterates over the names in the original list and then uses the length of each name (`len(name)`) as the result.

To filter a list using a list comprehension we can add an `if` clause at the end of the comprehension:

```
[<expression> for <item> in <list> if <condition>]
```

If we wanted to, for example, filter a list of names, this time keeping only those that start with *A*, we could write the following list comprehension:

```
>>> [name for name in names if name.startswith('A')]
['Angel', 'Alvaro']
```

Note two things from this example: the mapping expression is the `name` itself (an identity mapping, which is the same as no mapping), and the filter uses the string `startswith` method. This method returns `True` only if the string has the given argument as a prefix.

We can filter and map in the same list comprehension. For example, let's say we want to take our list of names and filter out those that have more than five letters and then construct a new list whose elements are a tuple of the original name and its length. We could do this easily:

```
>>> [(name, len(name)) for name in names if len(name) < 6]
[('Angel', 5), ('Mery', 4), ('Paul', 4)]
```

For comparison's sake, let's see what this would look like if we decided to use the `filter` and `map` functions:

```
>>> names_with_length = map(lambda name: (name, len(name)), names)
>>> result = filter(lambda name_length: name_length[1] < 6, names_with_length)
>>> list(result)
[('Angel', 5), ('Mery', 4), ('Paul', 4)]
```

As you can see, the result is the same, but the list comprehension version is simpler and more readable. What's easier to read is easier to maintain, so list comprehensions are going to be our preferred way of filtering and mapping lists.

Let's now turn our attention to the second paradigm we'll be exploring in this chapter: object-oriented programming.

Object-Oriented Programming

In the previous section, we talked about functional programming and some functional patterns. Now we'll learn about another paradigm: the *object-oriented paradigm*. As the function is to functional programming, the object is to object-oriented programming. So, first things first: What's an object?

There are several ways we could describe what an object is. I'm going to deviate from the standard academic definition of an object in object-oriented programming theory and try a rather unconventional explanation.

From a practical standpoint, we can think of objects as experts on a given subject. We can ask them questions, and they will give us information; or we can request that they do things for us, and they will do them. Our questions or requests may require complex operations, but these experts hide the complexity from us so that we don't need to worry about the details—we just care about getting the job done.

For example, think of a dentist. When you go to the dentist, you don't need to know anything about dentistry yourself. You rely on the dentist's expertise to get your cavities fixed. You can also ask the dentist questions about your teeth, and the dentist will respond using a language that you can understand, hiding the real complexity of the subject. In this example, the dentist would be an object you'd rely on for odontology-related tasks or queries.

To request things from an object, we call one of the object's *methods*. Methods are functions that belong to a given object and have access to the object's internals. The object itself has some memory that contains data that is typically hidden to the outside world, although the object may decide to expose some of this data in the form of *properties*.

NOTE   *A method is a function that belongs to a class: it's part of the class definition. It needs to be called (executed) on the instance of the class where it's defined. By contrast, a function doesn't belong to any class; it works on its own.*

In Python's parlance, any function or variable in an object is called an *attribute*. Both properties and methods are attributes. We'll be using these equivalent terms throughout this chapter and the rest of the book.

Let's now get practical and see how we can define and work with objects in Python.

Classes

A *class* defines how objects are constructed and what characteristics and knowledge they have. Some people like to compare classes to blueprints; they are general descriptions of what information the object holds and what it can do. Objects and classes are related but distinct; if the class is the blueprint, the object is the finished building.

We define a new class in Python using the reserved class keyword. By convention, class names start with an uppercase letter and use an uppercase letter at the start of every new word (this case is commonly known as *Pascal case*). Let's create a class that models a coffee machine:

```
class CoffeeMachine:
    def __init__(self):
        self.__coffees_brewed = 0
```

In this listing we define a new class representing a coffee machine. We can use this class to generate new coffee machine objects, in a process referred to as *instantiation*. When we instantiate a class, we create a new object of that class. A class is instantiated by calling its name as if it were a function that's returning the instantiated object:

```
>>> machine = CoffeeMachine()
```

Now we have the `machine` object whose functionality is defined by the Coffee Machine class (which is still empty, but we'll complete it in the following sections). When a class is instantiated, its __init__ function is called. Inside this __init__ function, we can perform one-time initialization tasks. For example, here we add a count of the number of brewed coffees and set it to zero:

```
def __init__(self):
    self.__coffees_brewed = 0
```

Notice the two underscores at the beginning of __coffees_brewed. If you remember from our discussion on access levels earlier, in Python, by default, everything is visible to the outside. The double underscore naming pattern is used to signify that something is private and no one is expected to access it directly.

```
# Don't do this!
>>> machine.__coffees_brewed
0
```

In this case, we don't want the outside world to access __coffees_brewed; they could change the coffees brewed count at will!

```
# Don't do this!
>>> machine.__coffees_brewed = 5469
>>> machine.__coffees_brewed
5469
```

So if we can't access __coffees_brewed, how do we know how many coffees our machine has brewed? The answer is properties. Properties are a class's read-only attributes. Before we can discuss properties, however, we have some syntax to cover.

self

If you look at the previous example, you'll see that we make frequent use of a variable named `self`. We could use any other name for this variable, but `self` is used by convention. As you saw earlier, we pass it to the definition of every function inside the class, including the initializer. Thanks to this first parameter, `self`, we gain access to whatever is defined in the class. In the __init__ function, for example, we append the __coffees_brewed variable to `self`; from that point on, this variable exists in the object.

The variable `self` needs to appear as the first parameter in the definition of every function inside the class, but it doesn't need to be passed as the first argument when we call those functions on instances of the class. For example, to instantiate the CoffeeMachine class, we wrote the following:

```
>>> machine = CoffeeMachine()
```

The initializer was called without parameters (no `self` here). If you think about it, how could we possibly pass the initializer as `self` in this case if we haven't yet initialized the object? As it turns out, Python takes care of that for us: we'll never need to pass self to the initializer or any of the object's methods or properties.

The self reference is how different attributes of a class have access to the other definitions in the class. For example, in the brew_coffee method we'll write later, we use self to access the __coffees_brewed count:

```
def brew_coffee(self):
    # we need 'self' here to access the class' __coffees_brewed count
    self.__coffees_brewed += 1
```

With an understanding of self, we can move on to properties.

Class Properties

An object's *property* is a read-only attribute that returns some data. A property of an object is accessed using *dot notation*: *object.property*. Following our coffee machine example, we could add a coffees_brewed property (the number of coffees brewed by the machine), like so:

```
class CoffeeMachine:
    def __init__(self):
        self.__coffees_brewed = 0

    @property
    def coffees_brewed(self):
        return self.__coffees_brewed
```

Then we could access it:

```
>>> machine = CoffeeMachine()
>>> machine.coffees_brewed
0
```

Properties are defined as functions using the @property decorator:

```
@property
def coffees_brewed(self):
    return self.__coffees_brewed
```

Properties shouldn't accept any parameter (except for the customary self), and they should return something. A property that doesn't return anything or expects parameters is conceptually wrong: properties should just be read-only data we request the object to give us.

We mentioned that @property is an example of a decorator. Python decorators allow us to modify a function's behavior. The @property modifies the function of a class so that it can be consumed as if it were an attribute of the class. We won't use any other decorators in this book, so we won't cover them here, but I encourage you to read up on them if you're interested.

Properties get us information about an object. For instance, if we wanted to know whether a given instance of a CoffeeMachine has brewed at least one coffee, we could include a property like the following:

```
class CoffeeMachine:
    def __init__(self):
        self.__coffees_brewed

    @property
    def has_brewed(self):
        return self.__coffees_brewed > 0

    --snip--
```

We can now ask instances of the CoffeeMachine class whether they've brewed at all:

```
>>> machine.has_brewed
False
```

This machine hasn't prepared any coffee yet, so how can we ask a CoffeeMachine instance to brew a coffee for us? We use methods.

Class Methods

Properties allow us to know something about an object: they answer our queries. To request an object to perform some task for us, we use methods. A *method* is nothing more than a function that belongs to a class and has access to the attributes defined in that class. In our CoffeeMachine class example, let's write a method to request it to brew some coffee:

```
class CoffeeMachine:
    def __init__(self):
        self.__coffees_brewed = 0

    @property
    def coffees_brewed(self):
        return self.__coffees_brewed

    @property
    def has_brewed(self):
        return self.__coffees_brewed > 0

    def brew_coffee(self):
        self.__coffees_brewed += 1
```

Methods get self as their first parameter, which gives them access to everything defined inside the class. As we discussed earlier, when calling a method on an object, we never pass self ourselves; Python does it for us.

Note that properties are like methods decorated with @property. *Both properties and methods expect* self *as their first argument. When calling a method, we use parentheses and optionally pass it arguments, but properties are accessed without parentheses.*

We can call the brew_coffee method on an instance of the class:

```
>>> machine = CoffeeMachine()
>>> machine.brew_coffee()
```

Now that we've brewed our first coffee, we can ask the instance this:

```
>>> machine.coffees_brewed
1
>>> machine.has_brewed
True
```

As you see, methods have to be called on a particular instance of a class (an object). This object will be the one responding to the request. So, whereas functions are called without a particular receiver, like

```
a_function()
```

methods have to be called on an object, like

```
machine.brew_coffee()
```

Objects can only respond to the methods defined in the class that created them. If a method (or any attribute for that matter) is called on an object but this method wasn't defined in the class, an AttributeError is raised. Let's try this. Let's order our coffee machine to brew tea even though we never gave it the instructions on how to do so:

```
>>> machine.brew_tea()
Traceback (most recent call last):
  File "<input>", line 1, in <module>
AttributeError: 'CoffeeMachine' object has no attribute 'brew_tea'
```

Okay, our object complained: we never told it we expected it to know how to prepare tea. Here's the key to its complaint:

```
'CoffeeMachine' object has no attribute 'brew_tea'
```

Lesson learned: don't ever request an object to do something it wasn't taught; it'll just freak out and make your program fail.

Methods can accept any number of parameters, which in our class have to be defined after the first mandatory argument: self. For example, let's add a method to our CoffeeMachine class that allows us to fill it with a given amount of water.

```
class CoffeeMachine:

    def __init__(self):
        self.__coffees_brewed = 0
        self.__liters_of_water = 0

    def fill_water_tank(self, liters):
        self.__liters_of_water += liters
```

We can fill the coffee machine instance by calling our new method:

```
>>> machine = CoffeeMachine()
>>> machine.fill_water_tank(5)
```

One last thing to know about methods before we move on is how powerful their dynamic dispatch nature is. When a method is called on an object, Python will check whether the object responds to that method or not, but, and here's the key, Python doesn't care about the object's class as long as this class has the requested method defined.

We can use this feature to define different objects that respond to the same method (by same method we mean same name and arguments) and use them interchangeably. For instance, we could define a new, more modern coffee-producer entity:

```
class CoffeeHipster:
    def __init__(self, skill_level):
        self.__skill_level = skill_level

    def brew_coffee(self):
        # depending on the __skill_level, this method
        # may take a long time to complete.
        # But apparently the result will be worth it?
        --snip--
```

Now we can write a function that expects a coffee producer (any object whose class defines a brew_cofee() method) and does something with it:

```
def keep_programmer_awake(programmer, coffee_producer):
    while programmer.wants_to_sleep:
        # give the coder some wakey juice
        coffee_producer.brew_coffee()
        --snip--
```

This function works with both an instance of CoffeeMachine and CoffeeHipster:

```
>>> machine = CoffeeMachine()
>>> hipster = CoffeeHipster()
>>> programmer = SleepyProgrammer('Angel')
```

```
# works!
>>> keep_programmer_awake(programmer, machine)

# also works!
>>> keep_programmer_awake(programmer, hipster)
```

For this technique to work, we need to make sure that the methods have the same signature, that is, they're called the same and expect exactly the same parameters with the same names.

Magic Methods

There are some special methods our classes may define that are known as *magic methods* or *dunder methods* (short for *double underscore*). These methods aren't typically called by us directly, but Python uses them under the hood, as we'll see in the following examples.

We've already used one such method: __init__, which we used as the initializer when instantiating objects. This __init__ method defines the code that's executed when a new instance of a class is created.

One prominent use case for magic methods (which we'll use a lot throughout the book) is overloading operators. Let's see this through an example. Imagine we implement a class to represent complex numbers:

```
class ComplexNum:
    def __init__(self, re, im):
        self.__re = re
        self.__im = im

    @property
    def real(self):
        return self.__re

    @property
    def imaginary(self):
        return self.__im
```

How would we go about implementing the addition operation on ComplexNum instances? A first option could be including a method called plus:

```
class ComplexNum:

    --snip--

    def plus(self, addend):
        return ComplexNum(
            self.__re + addend.__re,
            self.__im + addend.__im
        )
```

which we could use like so:

```
>>> c1 = ComplexNum(2, 3)
>>> c2 = ComplexNum(5, 7)

>>> c1.plus(c2)
# the result is: 7 + 10i
```

This is okay, but it would be nicer if we could instead use the + operator like we do with any other number:

```
>>> c1 + c2
```

Python includes a magic method, __add__; if we implement that method, then we can use the + operator as shown earlier, and Python will call this __add__ method under the hood. So if we rename our plus method __add__, we can automatically add ComplexNums using the + operator:

```
class ComplexNum:

    --snip--

    def __add__(self, addend):
        return ComplexNum(
            self.__re + addend.__re,
            self.__im + addend.__im
        )
```

There are more magic methods we can implement in our classes to perform subtraction, division, comparisons, and more. You can take a brief look at Table 4-1 on page 70 for a reference of the operations we can implement with magic methods. For example, subtracting two of our complex numbers using the - operator would be as simple as implementing the __sub__ method:

```
class ComplexNum:

    --snip--

    def __sub__(self, subtrahend):
        return ComplexNum(
            self.__re - subtrahend.__re,
            self.__im - subtrahend.__im
        )
```

Now we can use the - operator:

```
>>> c1 - c2
# yields: -3 - 4i
```

What about comparing two instances for equality using the == operator? Simply implement the __eq__ magic method:

```
class ComplexNum:

    --snip--

    def __eq__(self, other):
        return (self.__re == other.__re) and (self.__im == other.__im)
```

Now we can easily compare complex numbers:

```
>>> c1 == c2
False
```

We'll be using some magic methods throughout the book; they really improve the readability of the code.

Let's now change topics and learn about type hints.

Type Hints

Python *type hints* are a small help we can use when writing code to make sure we don't mistype the name of a method or property of a class.

For example, let's use the implementation of a complex number from the previous section:

```
class ComplexNum:

    def __init__(self, re, im):
        self.__re = re
        self.__im = im

    @property
    def real(self):
        return self.__re

    @property
    def imaginary(self):
        return self.__im
```

Now say that we write a function that takes an instance of ComplexNum as an argument, and we want to extract the imaginary part of the number, but we're a bit sleepy and mistakenly write the following:

```
def defrangulate(complex):
    --snip--
    im = complex.imaginry
```

Did you spot the typo? Well, since we know nothing about the complex argument, there's no visual clue our IDE can give us. As far as the IDE knows, imaginry is a perfectly valid attribute name, and it won't be until we run the program and pass a complex number that we get an error.

Python is a dynamically typed language: it uses type information at runtime. For example, it checks whether a given type of object responds to a method at runtime, and if it doesn't, an error is raised:

```
AttributeError: 'ComplexNum' object has no attribute 'imaginry'
```

A bit unfortunate, isn't it? In this case, we know that this function only expects instances of the ComplexNum class, so it would be nice if our IDE warned us about that property being mistyped. And in fact, we can do this using type hints.

In a function or method definition, a type hint goes after the argument name, separated by a colon:

```
def defrangulate(complex: ComplexNum):
    --snip--
    im = complex.imaginry
    -------------^-------
    'ComplexNum' object has no attribute 'imaginry'
```

As you can see, the IDE has signaled to us that ComplexNum has no attribute named imaginry.

In addition to the types we define using classes, we can use Python's built-in types as type hints. For instance, the complex-number initializer expecting two floating-point numbers could be written like so:

```
class ComplexNum:
    def __init__(self, re: float, im: float):
        self.__re = re
        self.__im = im
```

And now our IDE would warn us if we tried to instantiate the class with the wrong parameter types:

```
i = ComplexNumber('one', 'two')
------------------^------------
Expected type 'float', got 'str' instead.
```

We can use float for floating-point numbers, int for integers, and str for strings.

These type hints help us during development but have no effect at runtime. We'll be using type hints in many places throughout the book: it takes no time to add them, and we get a bit of extra safety.

Summary

We discussed two programming paradigms in this chapter: functional programming and object-oriented programming. Of course, both of these are huge topics, and whole books could be, and have been, written about them. We only scratched the surface.

We also talked about magic methods and type hints, two techniques we'll use extensively throughout the book.

In the next chapter, we'll discuss the command line. After that, we'll start writing code.

3

THE COMMAND LINE

Command line interfaces let us give direct instructions to our computer. From the command line, we can run programs, search files, create and delete directories, connect to the internet, and do much more. With two exceptions, the applications that we'll create in this book are all designed to be executed from the command line. In this chapter, we'll briefly cover the basics of command line interfaces. Feel free to skip this chapter if you already know how to use them.

Unix and Windows

Every operating system comes with a different flavor of a command line interface, but they all have a similar purpose: issuing commands directly to the operating system. Linux and macOS are both based on Unix, so they share a common syntax and use similar *command line processors*, which are programs that interpret your commands, issued in the form of plaintext, and translate them into a language the machine can execute. Several Unix command line processors exist; bash, bourne, and zsh are a few examples.

The command line application in these systems is often called a *shell*, *terminal*, or *prompt*. Apple had macOS come bundled with a bash shell, but recently, it replaced bash with zsh, which is, arguably, more modern and feature rich. We won't be worrying too much about the differences of these shell flavors; for our purposes, we can think of them as interchangeable.

Windows has its own command line system, and it uses a different syntax than macOS or Linux. Fortunately enough, since most developers are more familiar with Unix-like shells, Windows decided to allow its users to install a Linux subsystem. In the next section, we'll look at how to install this Windows Subsystem for Linux (WSL) support in case you're following this book with a Windows machine.

Finding Your Shell

If you are a Linux or macOS user, you don't need to install any additional software: your system comes with a shell. You can find it inside your applications directory.

If you're a Windows user, your system also has a command line, but we won't be using that one; we'll install the WSL instead. This system will give you access to a shell you can use to follow along with this book. Let's look at how to get it installed on your machine. If you aren't a Windows user, feel free to skip this section.

Installing the Windows Subsystem for Linux

The *Windows Subsystem for Linux*, WSL for short, is an installation of a Linux operating system inside your Windows operating system. The WSL will let you access Linux's main tools, including the shell.

Since installation instructions tend to evolve with time, please refer to the official documentation if you find any issue with the following steps. You can find the official documentation at *https://docs.microsoft.com/windows/wsl*, where you'll also find detailed information and a step-by-step installation guide.

As of the time of this writing, to install a Linux subsystem you first need to enable the WSL optional feature in your machine. To do this, open the PowerShell application as Administrator and then execute the following command:

```
PS C:\> dism.exe /online /enable-feature
    /featurename:Microsoft-Windows-Subsystem-Linux
    /all /norestart
```

Note that you should write this command on a single line; I had to break the line because it didn't fit in the print version of the book. It may take a few seconds to finish. Once the command has run, restart your machine.

When your machine is fully restarted, you can proceed to install any Linux distribution (also known as *distro*) of your choice. If you have no favorite Linux distro, I suggest you install Ubuntu; it's reliable and developer-friendly.

To install a Linux subsystem, open the Microsoft Store and search for *Ubuntu* (or your distro of choice). For this book, I'll be using Ubuntu's 20 LTS version. Run the installer for the Linux subsystem; once the installation process finishes, open it.

When you open your Linux subsystem for the first time, it'll need to perform some installations, which may take a few minutes. As you will see, this installation includes the Linux operating system and a shell to communicate with it, but not the graphical interface. The shell will prompt you to create a new username and password. Don't hesitate to read the documentation if you find yourself stuck at any point during the installation and configuration of the system.

Taking a First Look at the Shell

When you open your shell, it shows something like the following:

```
angel@MacBook ~ %
```

You may see some different characters toward the end, but the first part is the logged-in user and the name of the machine separated by an at sign:

```
<user>@<machine> ~ %
```

For the remainder of the book, we'll use the dollar sign ($) to signify the shell, and we won't show the user and machine names:

```
$
```

Now that you know how to open a shell, let's look at some useful commands.

Files and Directories

Let's try our first command: pwd (short for *print working directory*). Type **pwd** in the shell and press ENTER or RETURN. This command shows the path of the current directory, that is, the directory the shell is currently in:

```
$ pwd
/Users/angel
```

In this case, the shell is telling us the current working directory is *angel*, which is inside the *Users* directory.

Using the whoami command, we can also ask the shell to tell us the currently logged-in user:

```
$ whoami
angel
```

We can then list the contents inside the current directory using the `ls` command:

```
$ ls
Desktop          Downloads        Music            PycharmProjects
Applications     Developer        Library          Pictures
Documents        Git              Movies           Public
```

Moving Around

We can change directories using `cd` followed by the name of the directory we want to go to:

```
$ cd Documents
$ pwd
/Users/angel/Documents
```

To go back one directory, to the parent directory, we use two dots:

```
$ cd ..
$ pwd
/Users/angel
```

In these two examples of the `cd` command, we've changed directories using relative paths. A *relative path* is a path that starts from the current location. For example, if we want to change directories using a relative path, we simply provide the route like so:

```
$ cd Documents/Video
$ pwd
/Users/angel/Documents/Video
```

We can use one dot (.) to signify the current directory. So, the following is an alternative way of switching to the *Documents/Video* directory:

```
$ cd ./Documents/Video
$ pwd
/Users/angel/Documents/Video
```

We may also change directories using an *absolute path*, which is a path relative to the root directory. The root directory's name is simply a slash character (/). Let's try to change directories to the root directory using an absolute path:

```
$ cd /
$ pwd
/
```

Now let's move back to our home directory. The home directory also has a special shortcut name, a tilde (~):

```
$ cd ~
$ pwd
/Users/angel
```

Creating Files and Directories

We can create new directories using the `mkdir` command followed by the name of the directory we want to create:

```
$ mkdir tmp/mechanics
```

Here we've just created a new directory named *tmp* inside the working directory, which has another new directory inside it named *mechanics*. We could have done the same thing in two steps, first creating the *tmp* directory,

```
$ mkdir tmp
```

and then changing directories to *tmp* (`cd tmp`) and creating the *mechanics* directory,

```
$ mkdir mechanics
```

The result is the same in both cases.

Let's `cd` into that new directory:

```
$ cd tmp/mechanics
```

To create a new file, we can use the `touch` command followed by the filename:

```
$ touch file.txt
$ ls
file.txt
```

We can write some text to the file using input redirection, which we'll explain a bit more in the next section:

```
$ echo write me to the file > file.txt
```

This command is a bit more complex than the ones we've seen so far, and it has two parts. The first part, on the left side of the > symbol, uses the `echo` command to output `write me to the file`. We can run this command separately to see what it does:

```
$ echo write me to the file
write me to the file
```

As we can see, the echo command simply prints what we pass it. With the
> symbol, we can redirect the output target from the standard output (the
shell) to a file so that the message is written to the file instead of the shell.

To prove that we did this, let's read the contents of the file using the **cat**
command:

```
$ cat file.txt
write me to the file
```

The cat command prints the contents of the file. The command is short for
concatenate and it concatenates the contents of the file passed to it. In fact,
we can pass cat to the same file twice to see the concatenated result:

```
$ cat file.txt file.txt
write me to the file
write me to the file
```

Let's now delete the file and directories we just created.

Deleting Files and Directories

To remove a file, we use the **rm** command:

```
$ rm file.txt
```

The file is now gone forever: there's no trash bin or any other safety mechanism when working with the command line. We need to be extra careful
when deleting files or directories.

Let's go back two directories to get out of the *tmp/mechanics* folder:

```
$ cd ../..
$ pwd
/Users/angel
```

If a directory is empty, we can remove it using the -d command line option. A *command line option* is an argument that we can pass to the command
to modify its behavior. Command line options appear in two forms: as a single dash followed by one or more lowercase letters, as in -f, or as a double
dash followed by a single or compound word, as in --file or --file-name.

Removing an empty directory is done like so:

```
$ rm -d tmp
rm: tmp: Directory not empty
```

As you can see, the shell returned an error message because our *tmp* directory is not empty (it has a subdirectory). If we want to remove a directory
and all its subdirectories, we can use the -r option instead:

```
$ rm -r tmp
```

If the directory or any subdirectory had files inside, the previous command would fail. This command is useful when we want to remove directories that contain no files, because if a file is encountered, the command won't remove anything as a safety measure. To remove directories with files inside, we can use the -rf option:

```
$ rm -rf tmp
```

You want to be *extremely careful* with the rm -rf command. You can do some nasty, unrecoverable harm with this one.

Commands Summary

Table 3-1 summarizes the commands we've explored in this section.

Table 3-1: Shell Commands for Files and Directories

Command	Description
whoami	Displays the effective user ID
pwd	Returns the working directory name
ls	Lists the directory's contents
cd	Changes the directory
mkdir	Creates a new directory
echo	Writes arguments to the standard output
cat	Concatenates and prints files
rm	Removes a file
rm -d	Removes an empty directory
rm -r	Removes a directory with other directories inside
rm -rf	Removes directories and files (recursively)

Using Windows Subsystem for Linux

Now that we know the basic commands we need to move around the directories of a machine, let's take a look at some specifics when working with the Windows Subsystem for Linux.

Finding Your C: Drive

Every time you open your Linux subsystem, the shell's working directory will be set to the Linux subsystem's home directory. You can reveal this current directory using the pwd command:

```
$ pwd
/home/angel
```

The WSL has its own directory structure disconnected from your computer's. But, since you'll be writing the code for this book on your Windows machine, you'll need a way of accessing your C: drive. WSL offers a simple way of accessing the C: drive.

Your local drives are mounted inside a directory in your Linux subsystem called /mnt. Let's **cd** into /mnt and then list its contents:

```
$ cd /mnt
$ ls
c    d
```

It's important to use the absolute path (starting with /) to navigate to /mnt. The ls command listed my two drives: C: and D:. To open one of them, simply change directories:

```
$ cd c
```

Now your WSL's working directory is your C: drive. You can find your *Users* home directory or whatever folder you'll be using to write your code:

```
$ cd Users/angel
```

Ensuring Python's Installation (Ubuntu)

Ubuntu comes already packed with Python version 3 installed. You can check the installed version from the shell:

```
$ python3 --version
Python 3.8.2
```

You can update Python to its latest version using Ubuntu's apt command line tool. First you'll need to update the apt package lists so that they are up-to-date with the latest versions of the available software. You need to run this command as *superuser*. You can do this by prefixing the command you want to run with sudo, short for *superuser do*. You'll need to provide your password for any command you run as superuser:

```
$ sudo apt update
[sudo] password for angel: <write your password here>
```

When you write your password, you won't see anything written in the shell. As you type, the prompt will remain blank, mainly for security reasons. Once the package lists are up-to-date, you can upgrade Python's version:

```
$ sudo apt upgrade python3
```

Now you can be sure you have the latest stable release for Python's version 3 available for Ubuntu. You are now ready to learn how to run Python scripts.

Running Python Scripts

Running a Python file using the command line is a straightforward process:

```
$ python3 <filename.py>
```

It's important that we use Python's version 3 interpreter because we'll use some features available only in this version. As Python versions 2 and 3 can both be installed on the same machine, the version 3 interpreter is named with a 3 at the end.

Let's create a Python file and execute it. In your shell, use the following command to create a new Python file:

```
$ touch script.py
```

This will create a new file, *script.py*, in the shell's working directory. Open the file in PyCharm, or your editor of choice, and enter a **print** statement:

```
print('hello, World!')
```

Make sure to save the file. Let's check that our *script.py* file was correctly written:

```
$ cat script.py
print('hello, World!')
```

Finally, let's execute our Python script from the command line:

```
$ python3 script.py
hello, World!
```

As expected, our program gives us a `hello, World!` greeting.

Passing Arguments to the Script

Command line programs can accept arguments. Let's try this and accept an argument in our Python script to personalize the greeting. Open the *script.py* file and modify it so that it now contains the following:

```
import sys

name = sys.argv[1] if len(sys.argv) > 1 else 'unknown'
print(f'Hello, {name}')
```

Python's sys.argv is a list of the arguments passed in to the executing script. This first item of the list is always the name of the executing program, in this case, *script.py*. For this reason, we first need to check whether the list of arguments contains more than one item to know whether the name was passed to the program as an argument. If we detect that the user passed an argument, we use it as the name of the person we want to greet, but if no argument is passed, we default the name to `unknown`.

We can now run our program without arguments to get an impersonal greeting:

```
$ python3 script.py
Hello, unknown!
```

We can also pass the script a name to get a more personalized greeting:

```
$ python3 script.py Jenny
Hello, Jenny!
```

Standard Input and Output

Programs executed in the shell can read and write data. When a program, like our *script.py* from earlier, prints something, it appears as output in the shell. Our earlier program outputted a string like `Hello, Jenny!` that was then displayed in the shell. The shell's screen is generally referred to as the *standard output*.

Redirecting the Output to a File

Earlier, we wrote the result of an `echo` command to a file by redirecting the output with the > character.

Try this in your shell:

```
$ python3 script.py Jenny > greeting.txt
$ cat greeting.txt
Hello, Jenny!
```

This time, the result of the *script.py* program wasn't printed to the shell's screen, but instead it was written to a new file, *greeting.txt*.

Using the > character, we can redirect the output of a program to a new file. If the target file already exists, it gets overwritten. We can also use the >> characters to append something to an existing file instead of creating a new one:

```
$ python3 script.py Angel >> greeting.txt
$ cat greeting.txt
Hello, Jenny!
Hello, Angel!
```

This is a useful technique, and we'll use it throughout the book to write the result of our programs to an external file.

Redirecting the Input from a File

Much like we can redirect the shell's standard output, we can redirect the shell's input. Let's create a new script. Instead of reading a name from the program's argument, it prompts the user to write their name. First, create a new empty file:

```
$ touch script2.py
```

Open the file and enter the following code:

```
print("What's your name?")
name = input()
print('Hello there, {name}')
```

If we run our new script now, it'll prompt us to write our name:

```
$ python3 script2.py
What's your name?
Angel
Hello there, Angel
```

This program reads the name from the *standard input*, that is, the shell. We had to write the name in the shell and press RETURN for our program to read it. We can redirect the input from a file to our program, this time using the ‹ character. In this case, the program reads the contents of the file instead of reading from the shell.

Let's write a name inside a new file:

```
$ echo Mary > name.txt
```

Now, let's redirect the input to be read from this file to our program:

```
$ python3 script2.py < name.txt
What's your name?
Hello there, Mary
```

This time, instead of having to write anything ourselves when the program prompts for a name, the shell read in the contents of the *name.txt* file.

The applications we'll write in this book will use input redirecting to read the contents of an input file into our Python programs.

Using PyCharm's Python Console

As we saw in the introduction of the book, PyCharm comes with two consoles: a Python console and your system's shell. The former is especially interesting as it allows us to run Python code directly as well as inspect all the loaded symbols. You can open your PyCharm's Python console by clicking the Python Console button in the lower bar or by selecting View ▶ Tool Windows ▶ Python Console in the menu.

The Python console, as you can see in Figure 3-1, is divided into two panes: the left pane is the console where you write Python code, and the right pane includes a list of all the variables you've defined. Let's do a practical exercise to learn how this works.

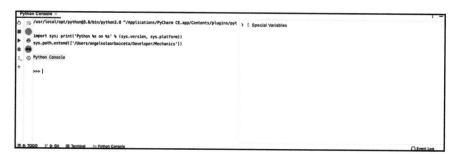

Figure 3-1: PyCharm Python console

In the Python prompt, enter the following:

```
>>> names = ['Angel', 'Alvaro', 'Mary', 'Paul', 'Isabel']
```

Now the right pane includes a list of symbols that you can explore (see Figure 3-2). You can expand the names symbol to inspect the items inside the list.

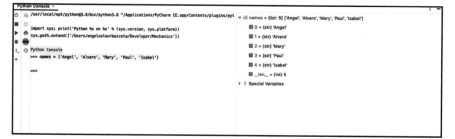

Figure 3-2: Declaring a list of names

Let's now write a function to filter a list of strings, keeping only those that are shorter than a given length. Write the following in the console (note the three dots marking the indentation when writing code in the console):

```
>>> def filter_list_shorter_than(lst, length):
...     return [item for item in lst if len(item) < length]
...

>>> filter_list_shorter_than(names, 5)
['Mary', 'Paul']
```

If you want to keep a reference of the filtered list, you can save the result to a variable:

```
>>> result = filter_list_shorter_than(names, 5)
```

Now you can use the Python console's right pane to explore the result list.

You can also import Python modules from the console. You can import modules from your own project or from the standard library. For instance, if you have the *Mechanics* project you downloaded earlier open in PyCharm, you can import the Point class.

```
>>> from geom2d import Point
>>> p = Point(10, 15)
```

Importing a module from the standard library is equally simple. For instance, to import the JSONDecoder class from the json module, use the following:

```
>>> from json import JSONDecoder
```

From time to time we may want to reload the console so that all the imported modules and defined variables are cleared. This is a good idea, because the modules you import and the variables you define might interact with the new code you write. We can reload the Python's console by clicking the reload button located at the top left of the console (see Figure 3-3).

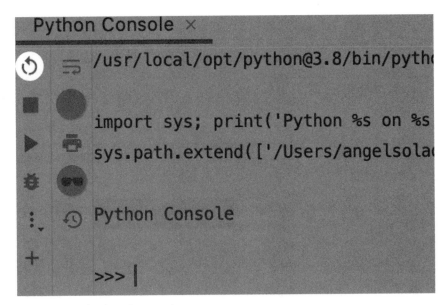

Figure 3-3: Reloading the console

Take your time exploring PyCharm's Python console, as you'll find it useful throughout the book; we'll often test our code by running quick experiments in it.

Summary

In this short chapter, we covered the basics of using the bash/zsh command line. From this shell we can issue commands to the computer, and we'll execute our Python scripts from here. We also explored the standard input and output redirection, a technique we'll use extensively throughout the book.

Without further ado, let's start creating our *Mechanics* project. Let the fun begin!

PART II

2D GEOMETRY

4

POINTS AND VECTORS

 Points and vectors are the basis of geometry. In this book, we'll use them as our *primitives*, the building blocks for the rest of our geometry library. For our geometry library to be usable, it's crucial that we implement points and vectors using bug-free code. A bug in our code will not only cause errors in the library's functions but also could propagate to all the other libraries we build on top of it, giving us all sorts of false calculations.

In this chapter, we have two main tasks. First, we need to implement classes to represent both points and vectors. Then, we need to make sure our code is bug-free by unit testing, a process we'll repeat throughout this book. Before we can do either, though, we need to implement a few useful methods.

Comparing Numbers

When it comes to representing real numbers, computers don't have infinite precision. Most computers use floating-point numbers to store these values, which cannot represent every rational number, let alone irrational numbers.

Thus, when comparing floating-point numbers, you have to specify a *tolerance*: a number ϵ as small as you need such that

$$|a - b| < \epsilon$$

where a and b are the two numbers you want to compare.

A tolerance's order of magnitude needs to be consistent with the problem's magnitudes and your desired precision. For example, it wouldn't make much sense to use a tolerance of $1E^{-20}$ mm when working with a planet's orbital lengths, which are on the order of millions of kilometers. Similarly, it would be pointless to use a tolerance of $1E^{-2}$ cm when working with atomic distances.

Before we start writing our primitives, we'll need a way of knowing whether two floating-point numbers can be considered equal or not given a tolerance ϵ. But we can't rely on the computer to compare floating-point numbers, as a different digit in the hundredth decimal is logically considered to be a completely different number. So, we'll start this chapter by writing a function that compares two numbers using a given tolerance. For our geometrical calculations, we'll use a default tolerance of $1E^{-10}$, which is an acceptable level of precision for most of the calculations we'll do throughout the book.

Open your project in the IDE, right-click the project's root folder, and select **New ▶ Python Package**. Name it *geom2d* and click **OK**. This will be the package for all of our geometry code.

Because the package name establishes that everything inside is in 2D, we won't repeat this piece of information when giving names to our files and classes. Inside the package, we'll use names like point *or* segment *instead of* point2d *or* segment2d. *If we wanted to create a three-dimensional geometry package,* geom3d, *we'd still use* point *and* segment, *only with different, three-dimensional implementations.*

Create a new file by right-clicking the *geom2d* package folder and selecting **New ▶ Python File**. Name it *nums*, leave the Kind drop-down as is, and click **OK**.

With the file created, let's implement our first comparison function. Listing 4-1 has the code for our function.

```
import math


def are_close_enough(a, b, tolerance=1e-10):
    return math.fabs(a - b) < tolerance
```

Listing 4-1: Comparing numbers

First, we import the *math* module, part of Python's standard library that contains useful mathematical functions. Our function takes two numbers, a and b, and an optional tolerance parameter that will default to $1E^{-10}$ if no other value is provided. Last, we use the math library's fabs function to check whether the absolute value of the difference between a and b is smaller than the tolerance, and we return the appropriate boolean.

In practice, we'll find there are two particular values we're comparing against: zero and one. To save us from repeatedly writing something like

```
are_close_enough(num, 1.0, 1e-5)
```

or

```
are_close_enough(num, 0.0, 1e-5)
```

let's implement them as functions. After the previous function, add the code in Listing 4-2.

```
--snip--

def is_close_to_zero(a, tolerance=1e-10):
    return are_close_enough(a, 0.0, tolerance)


def is_close_to_one(a, tolerance=1e-10):
    return are_close_enough(a, 1.0, tolerance)
```

Listing 4-2: Comparing number to zero or one

Functions like the ones in Listing 4-2 aren't strictly necessary, but they are convenient, and they make the code more readable.

The Point Class

A point, according to Euclid's first volume of the *Elements*, is "that of which there is no part." In other words, a point is an entity with no width, length, or depth. It is just a position in space, something you can't see with your naked eye. Points are the basis of all Euclidean geometry, and everything else in his writings is based on this simple concept. Accordingly, our geometry library will also be based on this powerful primitive.

A point consists of two numbers, *x* and *y*. These are its coordinates, sometimes also called *projections*. Figure 4-1 depicts a point *P* and its coordinates in the Euclidean plane.

Figure 4-1: A point P
in the plane

Let's implement a class representing a two-dimensional point. As before, we'll create a new file by right-clicking the *geom2d* package folder and selecting **New ► Python File**. Name it *point* and click **OK**. Inside the file, enter the code in Listing 4-3.

```
class Point:
    def __init__(self, x, y):
        self.x = x
        self.y = y
```

Listing 4-3: Our Point class

The coordinates are passed to the initializer method (__init__) and stored as attributes of the class.

With our initializer written, let's implement some functionality.

Calculating Distance Between Points

To compute the distance $d(P, Q)$ between the two points P and Q, we use Equation 4.1.

$$d(P, Q) = \sqrt{(Q_x - P_x)^2 + (Q_y - P_y)^2} \qquad (4.1)$$

Here, P_x and P_y are P's coordinates, and Q_x and Q_y are Q's coordinates. We can see this graphically in Figure 4-2.

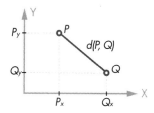

Figure 4-2: Distance between the points P and Q

We can implement our distance calculation in two ways. We could call the method on a point p to compute the distance to another point q, as in p.distance_to(q). We could also implement the same calculation as a function where both points are given as arguments: distance_between(p, q). The former is the object-oriented style; the latter is functional. Because we're doing object-oriented programming here, we'll go with the former.

Listing 4-4 has the code to implement Equation 4.1 in our class.

```
import math


class Point:
    --snip--

    def distance_to(self, other):
        delta_x = other.x - self.x
```

```
        delta_y = other.y - self.y
        return math.sqrt(delta_x ** 2 + delta_y ** 2)
```

Listing 4-4: Calculating the distance between two points

First, we need to import the *math* module, which loads a bunch of useful mathematical operations into our class. We define the `distance_to` method with `self` and `other` as arguments: `self` is the current point, and `other` is the point we want to calculate the distance to. We then calculate the distance (or *delta*) between the two coordinates and use the power (**) operator to square both deltas and return the square root of their sum.

Now let's test this out. Open the Python console from the IDE and try the following:

```
>>> from geom2d.point import Point
>>> p = Point(1, 3)
>>> q = Point(2, 4)
>>> p.distance_to(q)
1.4142135623730951
```

Exciting! We've taken the first major step in building our geometry library—Euclid would be proud. You can try that same operation with your calculator and see whether our implementation yields the correct result. Later in the chapter, we'll automate a test that checks that the distance method yields the right result.

While we have the console open and p and q loaded, try the following:

```
>>> p
<geom2d.point.Point object at 0x10f8a2588>

>>> p.__dict__
{'x': 1, 'y': 3}
```

Evaluating point p yields a string telling us p is an object of the `Point` class at memory position `0x10f8a2588`. Note that the memory address you obtain will likely be different than mine. Without knowing everything in the computer's memory (and reading hexadecimal), this description isn't much help. You can also inspect the `__dict__` attribute of any class to get a dictionary of all the attributes it holds. That gives you more interesting information about the instance. Later in the chapter, we'll be implementing a special method that will help print a cleaner description of the object, something like (2, 5).

Let's now focus our attention on overloading the + and − operators for the `Point` class.

Addition and Subtraction Operators

The next basic operations we'll need are addition and subtraction, operations that we'll also implement for vectors. We'll use these basic methods quite often, both on their own and to build more complex methods. We could implement them as normal methods, calling them with something like `p.plus(q)` and `p.minus(q)`, but we can do better. Python allows us to overload + and − operators (as we learned in "Magic Methods" on page 43) so that we can write `p + q` and `p - q` and have Python know to add and subtract the points correctly. Overloading operators makes code like this much easier to read and understand.

Overloading an operator in Python involves implementing a method using a specific name that corresponds to the operator. Then, when Python finds the operator, it will replace it with the method you've defined and call it. For the + operator, the name is __add__, and for −, it is __sub__. Table 4-1 contains common operators we can overload in our classes.

Table 4-1: Python's Overloadable Operators

Operator	Method Name	Description
+	__add__(self, other)	Addition
-	__sub__(self, other)	Subtraction
*	__mul__(self, other)	Multiplication
/	__truediv__(self, other)	Division
%	__mod__(self, other)	Modulo
==	__eq__(self, other)	Equality
!=	__ne__(self, other)	Inequality
<	__lt__(self, other)	Less than
<=	__le__(self, other)	Less than or equal to
>	__gt__(self, other)	Greater than
>=	__ge__(self, other)	Greater than or equal to

Let's implement the addition and subtraction operations as methods. Inside the `Point` class and after the `distance_to` method, add the code in Listing 4-5.

```python
class Point:
    --snip--

    def __add__(self, other):
        return Point(
            self.x + other.x,
            self.y + other.y
        )

    def __sub__(self, other):
        return Point(
            self.x - other.x,
            self.y - other.y
        )
```

Listing 4-5: Adding and subtracting points

The method __add__ creates and returns a new `Point` where its projections are the sum of the two parameters' projections. This operation doesn't make a lot of sense algebraically speaking, but we may find it useful later.

The method __sub__ does the same where the resulting projections are the subtraction of the input points' projections. Subtracting two points $P - Q$ yields a vector going from Q to P, but we haven't created a class for vectors yet. We will refactor this code in the next section so that it returns a vector instance.

Let's implement our next major primitive: the vector.

The Vector Class

Similar to points, *vectors* in the Euclidean plane are composed of two numbers, called the coordinates, that encode a magnitude and a direction. The vector $\langle 3, 5 \rangle$, for instance, can be understood as the displacement achieved by moving 3 units in the positive direction of the horizontal axis and 5 units in the positive direction of the vertical axis. Figure 4-3 depicts a vector $\vec{p}$ in the Euclidean plane.

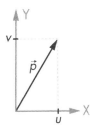

Figure 4-3: A vector $\vec{p}$
in the plane

Many physical quantities are vectorial: they require both a magnitude and a direction to be completely defined. For example, velocities, accelerations, and forces are all vector quantities. Since vectors are so common, let's create a class to represent them.

Right-click the *geom2d* package folder and select **New ▶ Python File**. Name it *vector* and click **OK**. Then enter the code in Listing 4-6.

```
class Vector:
    def __init__(self, u, v):
        self.u = u
        self.v = v
```

Listing 4-6: Vector class

The implementation of Vector is similar to that of the Point class. The coordinates are named u and v instead of x and y. This is just a convention to avoid mixing points and vectors unwittingly.

Before we move on, let's refactor the Point class's __sub__ method so that it returns a Vector. Recall that subtracting two points $P - Q$ yields a vector going from Q to P. Modify your *point.py* file so that it now matches the code in Listing 4-7.

```
import math

from geom2d.vector import Vector


class Point:
    --snip--

    def __sub__(self, other):
        return Vector(
            self.x - other.x,
            self.y - other.y
        )
```

Listing 4-7: Refactoring Point __sub__ method

We'll take a closer look at this operation in "Vector Factories" on page 89, where we'll use this operation to create vectors.

Let's now implement some useful methods for the Vector class.

Addition and Subtraction Operators

Like with points, adding vectors and subtracting them are common operations. For example, we can get the sum of two forces (which are vector quantities) by summing the vectors representing them.

After the __init__ method, enter the code in Listing 4-8.

```
class Vector:
    --snip--

    def __add__(self, other):
        return Vector(
            self.u + other.u,
            self.v + other.v
        )

    def __sub__(self, other):
        return Vector(
            self.u - other.u,
            self.v - other.v
        )
```

Listing 4-8: Vector addition and subtraction

In both the __add__ and __sub__ methods, we create a new instance of Vector to hold the addition or subtraction of projections.

Figure 4-4 depicts the addition and subtraction operations of two vectors, $\vec{p}$ and $\vec{q}$. Notice how subtracting $\vec{p} - \vec{q}$ can be interpreted as the sum of $\vec{p}$ and $-\vec{q}$.

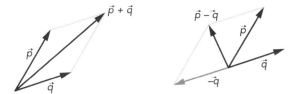

Figure 4-4: A sum of two vectors: $\vec{p} + \vec{q}$ and a subtraction of two vectors: $\vec{p} - \vec{q}$

Now you might be wondering if we'll do the same thing for the other operators. Addition and subtraction translate easily to the world of points and vectors, but for something like the __mul__ operator (used to overload the multiplication operation), it's not as simple. It's unclear whether multiplication would be the dot product, the cross product, or a vector scaling operation. Instead of using a single operator, we'll simply implement these operations as methods with descriptive names: scaled_by, dot, and cross.

We'll begin with scaling.

Scaling Vectors

To *scale* a vector $\vec{u}$, you multiply it by a magnitude k called a *scalar*, which will stretch or shrink the vector. Mathematically, the scalar multiplication looks like Equation 4.2:

$$k \cdot \vec{u} = k \cdot \left\{ \begin{array}{c} u_x \\ u_y \end{array} \right\} = \left\{ \begin{array}{c} k \cdot u_x \\ k \cdot u_y \end{array} \right\} \tag{4.2}$$

Let's create a scaling method in the Vector class. Enter the code in Listing 4-9 under the __sub__ method.

```
class Vector:
    --snip--

    def scaled_by(self, factor):
        return Vector(factor * self.u, factor * self.v)
```

Listing 4-9: Scaling a vector

In the previous code, we simply return a new Vector whose u and v attributes are multiplied by factor, the passed-in scalar.

Displacing Points

Using the scaled method, we can implement another operation: displacing a point P by a given vector $\vec{u}$ k times. Mathematically, that looks like Equation 4.3.

$$\left(\begin{array}{c} P_x \\ P_y \end{array} \right) + k \cdot \left\{ \begin{array}{c} u_x \\ u_y \end{array} \right\} = \left(\begin{array}{c} P_x + k \cdot u_x \\ P_y + k \cdot u_y \end{array} \right) \tag{4.3}$$

Graphically it looks like Figure 4-5.

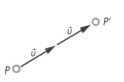

Figure 4-5: Displacing a point P
by a vector $\vec{u}$ a given number
of times k (2 in this case)

Let's implement it programmatically inside our Point class, as the displacement subject is the point (Listing 4-10).

```
class Point:
    --snip--

    def displaced(self, vector: Vector, times=1):
        scaled_vec = vector.scaled_by(times)
        return Point(
            self.x + scaled_vec.u,
            self.y + scaled_vec.v
        )
```

Listing 4-10: Displacing a point P by a vector $\vec{u}$ a given number of times k

The method gets passed two arguments: a vector vector and a scalar times. The vector is scaled according to times to produce the net displacement. For instance, a vector $\langle 3, 5 \rangle$ scaled with times = 2 would result in a displacement of $\langle 6, 10 \rangle$. Note the parameter times gets a default value of 1, as often the passed vector already has the desired length. The returned point results from adding the coordinates of the source point and the displacement vector's coordinates.

Let's try to move a point in the Python shell. Restart the console so the previously imported Point and Vector classes don't get in the way, and enter the following:

```
>>> from geom2d.point import Point
>>> from geom2d.vector import Vector

>>> p = Point(2, 3)
>>> v = Vector(10, 20)
>>> p_prime = p.displaced(v, 2)
>>> p_prime.__dict__
{'x': 22, 'y': 43}
```

You can use a calculator to confirm that the math works as expected.

Vector Norms

A *norm* of a vector is its length. A *unitary norm* is a norm whose length is exactly one unit. Vectors with a unitary norm are useful for defining directions; hence, we'll frequently want to know whether a vector has a unitary norm (whether it's *normal*). We'll also frequently want to *normalize* a vector: keep its direction but scale it to have a length of 1. The norm of a two-dimensional vector is given by Equation 4.4.

$$\|\vec{u}\| = \sqrt{u_x^2 + u_y^2} \tag{4.4}$$

Let's implement a property that returns the norm of Vector, and let's implement another property that checks whether the vector is normal. Both are included in Listing 4-11.

```
import math

from geom2d import nums


class Vector:
    --snip--

    @property
    def norm(self):
        return math.sqrt(self.u ** 2 + self.v ** 2)

    @property
    def is_normal(self):
        return nums.is_close_to_one(self.norm)
```

Listing 4-11: Norm of a vector

The value obtained from the norm property follows exactly the definition from Equation 4.4. To know whether a vector has a norm of 1, we use our numeric comparison is_close_to_one and pass in the vector's norm.

We'll implement two other important operations: a method that normalizes a vector $\vec{u}$, yielding a vector $\hat{u}$ with the same direction but unitary length, and a method that scales a vector to have a given length. A normalized version of a vector, which we'll call a *unit vector* or *versor*, can be obtained using Equation 4.5.

$$\hat{u} = \frac{\vec{u}}{\|\vec{u}\|} = \frac{1}{\sqrt{u_x^2 + u_y^2}} \cdot \left\{ \begin{array}{c} u_x \\ u_y \end{array} \right\} = \left\{ \begin{array}{c} \frac{u_x}{\sqrt{u_x^2+u_y^2}} \\ \frac{u_y}{\sqrt{u_x^2+u_y^2}} \end{array} \right\} \tag{4.5}$$

A vector computed this way will have a length of 1. Multiplying that vector by a scalar k results in a vector $\vec{u}_k$, which has the same direction as the original but with a new length that's exactly the value of the scalar, as shown in Equation 4.6.

$$\vec{u}_k = k\frac{\vec{u}}{\|\vec{u}\|} = \frac{k}{\sqrt{u_x^2 + u_y^2}} \cdot \left\{ \begin{array}{c} u_x \\ u_y \end{array} \right\} = \left\{ \begin{array}{c} \frac{k \cdot u_x}{\sqrt{u_x^2+u_y^2}} \\ \frac{k \cdot u_y}{\sqrt{u_x^2+u_y^2}} \end{array} \right\} \tag{4.6}$$

In Listing 4-12, we'll turn those equations into code.

```
class Vector:
    --snip--

    def normalized(self):
        return self.scaled_by(1.0 / self.norm)

    def with_length(self, length):
        return self.normalized().scaled_by(length)
```

Listing 4-12: Vectors with unit or chosen length

To normalize a vector, we scale it by the inverse of its norm (which is equivalent to dividing the vector's length by its norm). When we want a vector scaled to a given length, we simply normalize the vector and then scale it by the desired length.

Immutable Design

You may have realized by now that we never mutate the attributes of any of our objects but rather create and return a new Point or Vector instance. To normalize a vector, for instance, we could have used the code in Listing 4-13.

```
def normalize(self):
    norm = self.norm
    self.x = self.x / norm
    self.y = self.y / norm
```

Listing 4-13: Normalization of a vector in place

Calling that method would result in a *normalization in place*, that is, a mutation of the current object's attributes. Normalizing in place is faster and requires less memory but is also much more error-prone. It's easier than it seems for your program to mistakenly mutate an object that is being used by other parts of the program not expecting the change. Finding these kinds of bugs is really tricky and requires extensive debugging. Furthermore, programs using immutable data are much easier to understand and reason about, as you don't need to keep track of how objects change their state with respect to time.

Take a look at the following code. It implements the normalize method in a similar way to the previous one, but it contains a subtle error. In this case, the normalization would yield a wrong result. Can you spot why?

```
def normalize(self):
    self.x = self.x / self.norm
    self.y = self.y / self.norm
```

This is a tricky one. By mutating the `self.x` attribute in the first line, the second call to get the `self.norm` property will use the updated value for `self.x`. The first and second calls to `self.norm` yield different results, which is why we had to store the value of `self.norm` in a variable.

When the amount of data the object has is small, you're better off avoiding mutations altogether. Your program will behave correctly if executed concurrently, and your code will be simpler to understand. Reducing mutability to a minimum will make your code more robust; as you'll see throughout the book, we'll adhere to this principle as much as we can.

Naming Convention

Notice the naming convention for methods. Methods mutating the state of the object upon calling are named as follows:

`normalize`   Normalizes the vector in place

`scale_by`   Scales the vector in place

Methods creating a new object as their result are named as follows:

`normalized`   Returns a new normalized vector

`scaled_by`   Returns a new scaled vector

Next, we'll implement the dot and cross products in our Vector class. These simple products will open the door to some useful operations such as computing the angle between two vectors or testing for perpendicularity.

Dot Product

The *dot product* between two vectors $\vec{u}$ and $\vec{v}$ yields a scalar value, a measure of how different the directions of the two vectors are. In two dimensions, with θ being the angle between the vectors, this product is given by Equation 4.7.

$$\vec{u} \cdot \vec{v} = \|\vec{u}\| \cdot \|\vec{v}\| \cdot \cos\theta = u_x \cdot v_x + u_y \cdot v_y \qquad (4.7)$$

To understand the different values the dot product can have depending on the relative directions of the two operand vectors, let's take a look at Figure 4-6. This figure depicts a reference vector $\vec{v}$ and three other vectors: $\vec{a}$, $\vec{b}$, and $\vec{c}$. A line perpendicular to $\vec{v}$ divides the space in two half-planes. Vector $\vec{b}$ lies on that line, so the angle θ between $\vec{v}$ and $\vec{b}$ is 90°, and since $\cos(90°) = 0$, then $\vec{v} \cdot \vec{b} = 0$. Perpendicular vectors yield a dot product of zero. Vector $\vec{a}$ happens to be on the same half-plane as $\vec{v}$; therefore, $\vec{v} \cdot \vec{a} > 0$. Lastly, $\vec{c}$ is on the opposite half-plane of $\vec{v}$; hence, $\vec{v} \cdot \vec{c} < 0$.

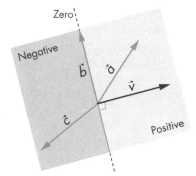

Figure 4-6: Vector directions with respect to $\vec{v}$ yield different dot products.

Implementing the dot product is straightforward from Equation 4.7. Inside the Vector class, enter the code in Listing 4-14.

```
class Vector:
    --snip--

    def dot(self, other):
        return (self.u * other.u) + (self.v * other.v)
```

Listing 4-14: Dot product

Before we move on to the cross product, let's stop for a minute and analyze one of its applications: obtaining the projection of a vector in a given direction.

Projecting Vectors

When one of the vectors involved in a dot product is a unit vector, this operation's result is the length of the projection of one vector over the other vector. To see why, let's use Equation 4.7. Given a vector $\vec{u}$ and a unit vector $\hat{v}$, the dot product is:

$$\vec{u} \cdot \hat{v} = \|\vec{u}\| \cdot \|\hat{v}\| \cdot \cos\theta = \|\vec{u}\| \cdot 1 \cdot \cos\theta = \|\vec{u}\| \cdot \cos\theta$$

where $\|\vec{u}\| \cdot \cos\theta$ is exactly the projection of $\vec{u}$ over the direction of $\hat{v}$. This will be handy for computing projections over a direction, which we could use to obtain the axial component of a force on a truss member, for example, as illustrated in Figure 4-7. In this case, we'd simply have to do $\vec{F}_a = \vec{F} \cdot \hat{u}$ to compute the axial component $\vec{F}_a$.

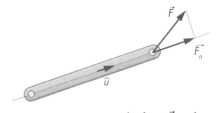

Figure 4-7: Projection of a force $\vec{F}$ in the axial direction $\hat{u}$ of a truss member

Let's implement this operation as a new method. Enter the code from Listing 4-15 into your class.

```
class Vector:
    --snip--

    def projection_over(self, direction):
        return self.dot(direction.normalized())
```

Listing 4-15: Projection of a vector over another vector

Note that the `direction` argument may not be a unit vector. To make sure our formula works, we normalize it.

Cross Product

The *cross product* of two three-dimensional vectors yields a new vector that is perpendicular to the plane containing the other two. The order of operands matters and defines the direction of the resulting vector. You can figure out the direction of the cross product using the right-hand rule. Notice that this product is therefore noncommutative: $\vec{u} \times \vec{v} = -\vec{v} \times \vec{u}$. Figure 4-8 illustrates this phenomenon.

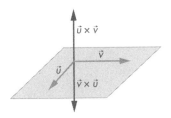

Figure 4-8: Cross products are noncommutative.

In 3D space, the cross product can be computed using Equation 4.8.

$$\vec{u} \times \vec{v} = \left\{ \begin{array}{c} u_y \cdot v_z - u_z \cdot v_y \\ u_z \cdot v_x - u_x \cdot v_z \\ u_x \cdot v_y - u_y \cdot v_x \end{array} \right\} \tag{4.8}$$

When working in two dimensions, every vector is contained in the same plane; thus, every cross product yields a vector perpendicular to that plane. That is easy to observe from the previous expression by simply noting that $u_z = v_z = 0$:

$$\vec{u} \times \vec{v} = \left\{ \begin{array}{c} u_y \cdot 0 - 0 \cdot v_y \\ 0 \cdot v_x - u_x \cdot 0 \\ u_x \cdot v_y - u_y \cdot v_x \end{array} \right\} = \left\{ \begin{array}{c} 0 \\ 0 \\ u_x \cdot v_y - u_y \cdot v_x \end{array} \right\}$$

In two-dimensional applications, the cross product is therefore considered to yield a scalar value, which is the z-coordinate of the previous expression's resulting vector. You can think of this coordinate as being the length of the resulting vector. Since the x- and y-coordinates are zero, this magnitude given by the z-coordinate is all we need to keep. Given θ as the angle between vectors $\vec{u}$ and $\vec{v}$, the cross product operation in two dimensions can be obtained by applying Equation 4.9.

$$\vec{u} \times \vec{v} = \|\vec{u}\| \cdot \|\vec{v}\| \cdot \sin \theta = u_x \cdot v_y - u_y \cdot v_x \qquad (4.9)$$

Let's implement the cross product. Enter the code in Listing 4-16.

```
class Vector:
    --snip--


    def cross(self, other):
        return (self.u * other.v) - (self.v * other.u)
```

Listing 4-16: Cross product

One important application of the cross product in two dimensions is determining the rotational direction of angles. From Figure 4-8 you can see that $\vec{u} \times \vec{v} > 0$, since going from $\vec{u}$ to $\vec{v}$ describes a positive (counterclockwise) angle. Conversely, going from $\vec{v}$ to $\vec{u}$ describes a negative angle resulting in a negative cross product $\vec{u} \times \vec{v} < 0$. Lastly, note that parallel vectors have a cross product of zero, which is easy to see because $\sin 0 = 0$. Let's take a closer look at this fact and write methods in our class that determine whether two vectors are parallel or perpendicular.

Parallel and Perpendicular Vectors

Using the dot and cross products, it's easy to test whether two vectors are parallel or perpendicular to each other. Listing 4-17 contains the code for these operations.

```
class Vector:
    --snip--


    def is_parallel_to(self, other):
        return nums.is_close_to_zero(
            self.cross(other)
        )
```

```
def is_perpendicular_to(self, other):
    return nums.is_close_to_zero(
        self.dot(other)
    )
```

Listing 4-17: Checking whether vectors are parallel or perpendicular

Checking whether two vectors are parallel to each other is as simple as checking that their cross product is zero. Likewise, checking whether two vectors are perpendicular is as simple as checking whether the dot product is zero. Notice that we use the function is_close_to_zero to account for floating-point number comparison difficulties in the calculations.

Angles Between Vectors

Computing the angle between two vectors can be done with the help of the dot product expression:

$$\vec{u} \cdot \vec{v} = \|\vec{u}\| \cdot \|\vec{v}\| \cdot \cos\theta$$

Dividing the dot product term on one side by the norm product on the other and taking the inverse of the cosine of that expression, we get Equation 4.10:

$$\theta = \text{acos}\left(\frac{\vec{u} \cdot \vec{v}}{\|\vec{u}\| \cdot \|\vec{v}\|)}\right) \tag{4.10}$$

This expression computes only the magnitude of the angle; if we want to know the direction, we'll need to make use of the cross product. The sign of the angle can be obtained using

$$\text{sgn}(\vec{u} \times \vec{v})$$

where sgn, the sign function, is defined as follows:

$$\text{sgn}(x) = \begin{cases} -1 & \text{if } x < 0 \\ +1 & \text{if } x \geq 0 \end{cases}$$

To understand why we only get the magnitude of the angle using Equation 4.10, we need to remember an important property of the cosine function. Recall from basic geometry that a unit vector's angle cosine is exactly the value of its horizontal projection. As you can see by inspecting the unit circle from Figure 4-9, two vectors with opposite angles (angles where the sum equals zero) get assigned the same cosine value. In other words, $\cos\alpha = \cos(-\alpha)$, which means that once an angle goes through the cosine function, its sign is forever lost. That makes it impossible to determine what the angle's sign is from a computed value of the dot product.

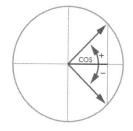

Figure 4-9: Cosines of
opposite angles are equal.

For many of our applications, we'll be needing both the magnitude and sign of angles; with the help of the cross product, we can bring this information back. Let's create two new methods, one that yields the absolute value of the angle (for those cases where the magnitude is enough) and another one that includes the sign. Enter the code in Listing 4-18 in your Vector class.

```
class Vector:
    --snip--

    def angle_value_to(self, other):
        dot_product = self.dot(other)
        norm_product = self.norm * other.norm
        return math.acos(dot_product / norm_product)

    def angle_to(self, other):
        value = self.angle_value_to(other)
        cross_product = self.cross(other)
        return math.copysign(value, cross_product)
```

Listing 4-18: Calculating the angle between two vectors

The first method, angle_value_to, computes the angle between self and other using Equation 4.10. We first obtain the dot product value and divide it by the product of norms. The angle is then the arc cosine of the result. The second method, angle_to, returns the value of the angle with the sign from the cross product. The math.copysign(x, y) function in Python returns the magnitude of x with the sign of y.

Let's try these two methods in the console. Reload it and write the following:

```
>>> from geom2d.vector import Vector
>>> u = Vector(1, 0)
>>> v = Vector(1, 1)

>>> v.angle_value_to(u)
0.7853981633974484 # result in radians

>>> v.angle_to(u)
-0.7853981633974484 # result in radians
```

Just for reference, the angle value of 0.78539... is $\pi/4$ rad (45°).

Now let's suppose we have a vector and want to create a new one by rotating the original by a certain angle.

Rotating Vectors

Imagine that in the case of the bar subject to an external force, as we saw in Figure 4-7, we're also interested in knowing the projection of force $\vec{F}$ in the direction perpendicular to the bar. This is the force's shear component. To find the projection of the force, we first need to figure out a vector perpendicular to the direction of the bar $\hat{u}$, which is obtained by rotating this vector $\pi/2$ radians, as illustrated in Figure 4-10.

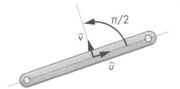

Figure 4-10: Rotating the bar's direction
vector $\pi/2$ radians

A rotation preserves the length of the original vector because a rotation is a transformation that respects lengths. Assuming α is the angle that we want the vector rotated by, we can use Equation 4.11:

$$\vec{u}\big|_{\alpha} = \begin{pmatrix} \cos\alpha & -\sin\alpha \\ \sin\alpha & \cos\alpha \end{pmatrix} \cdot \left\{ \begin{array}{c} u_x \\ u_y \end{array} \right\} = \left\{ \begin{array}{c} u_x \cdot \cos\alpha - u_y \cdot \sin\alpha \\ u_x \cdot \sin\alpha + u_y \cdot \cos\alpha \end{array} \right\} \qquad (4.11)$$

which in Python becomes the code in Listing 4-19.

```python
class Vector:
    --snip--

    def rotated_radians(self, radians):
        cos = math.cos(radians)
        sin = math.sin(radians)
        return Vector(
            self.u * cos - self.v * sin,
            self.u * sin + self.v * cos
        )
```

Listing 4-19: Rotating a vector

The rotated_radians function returns a new vector, the result of rotating the original one by the given number of radians. Following our immutability guidelines, we never mutate the source vector; instead, we return a new one with the rotation applied.

There's one angle, $\pi/2$ rad (90°), which is quite useful for rotating a vector. Using $\pi/2$ rad, we get a new vector perpendicular to the original one.

To avoid writing `v.rotated_radians(math.pi / 2)` over and over again, we can define a new method in our Vector class. Knowing that $\cos(\pi/2) = 0$ and $\sin(\pi/2) = 1$, the angle in Equation 4.11 simplifies to the following:

$$\vec{u}\,|_{(\pi/2)} = \left\{ \begin{array}{c} u_x \cdot 0 - u_y \cdot 1 \\ u_x \cdot 1 + u_y \cdot 0 \end{array} \right\} = \left\{ \begin{array}{c} -u_y \\ u_x \end{array} \right\}$$

Let's call the method perpendicular. In Python, it looks like Listing 4-20.

```
class Vector:
    --snip--

    def perpendicular(self):
        return Vector(-self.v, self.u)
```

Listing 4-20: Obtaining a perpendicular vector

There's another angle we'll often use for rotations: π rad (180°). Rotating a vector π rad results in a vector that is colinear but in the opposite direction. This time, $\cos(\pi) = -1$ and $\sin(\pi) = 0$. The angle in Equation 4.11 now looks like this:

$$\vec{u}\,|_{(\pi)} = \left\{ \begin{array}{c} u_x \cdot (-1) - u_y \cdot 0 \\ u_x \cdot 0 + u_y \cdot (-1) \end{array} \right\} = \left\{ \begin{array}{c} -u_x \\ -u_y \end{array} \right\}$$

Let's call the method opposite. In Python, it looks like Listing 4-21.

```
class Vector:
    --snip--

    def opposite(self):
        return Vector(-self.u, -self.v)
```

Listing 4-21: Obtaining the opposite vector

These two methods, perpendicular and opposite, don't really add anything we didn't have before; we could just use rotated_radians. Nevertheless, they're convenient, and we'll be using them often.

Sine and Cosine

To project a vector quantity in the x- and y-axes, we use the sine or cosine values of the vector's angle, as depicted in Figure 4-11.

We'll use these to compute the stiffness matrices in global coordinates of truss structure bars in Part V of the book. The stiffness matrix of a bar is computed relative to a reference frame whose x-axis is in the direction of the bar's directrix, but we'll need to project this matrix in the direction of the global x- and y-axes to build the structure's global system of equations.

If the Vector class didn't provide these two properties, clients of this class could get its angle value and then compute the sine or cosine of it. Even though this is perfectly acceptable, it requires a few operations to first compute the angle and then one extra sine or cosine operation. But as you

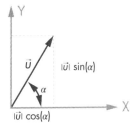

Figure 4-11: Vector projections

know, we can compute the sine and cosine values much more efficiently by their mathematical definition.

Say we have vector $\vec{a}$ with norm $\|\vec{a}\|$, whose projections are labeled u and v. The sine and cosine can be computed as follows:

$$\sin\theta = \frac{v}{\|\vec{a}\|} \quad \cos\theta = \frac{u}{\|\vec{a}\|}$$

Let's implement these as attributes of the Vector class. Enter the code in Listing 4-22.

```
class Vector:
    --snip--

    @property
    def sine(self):
        return self.v / self.norm

    @property
    def cosine(self):
        return self.u / self.norm
```

Listing 4-22: Vector's direction sine and cosine

The implementation is straightforward given the previous expressions. Let's complete our Point and Vector classes by adding the last touches.

Completing Our Classes

Our Point and Vector classes are looking good, but they're missing some small details. If we compare two instances of any of them, Python may not be able to determine whether they are equivalent; we'll fix that shortly. Also, if you remember, Python prints object instances to the console giving their class name accompanied with a memory address, which is not that helpful for us; we'll also fix this here.

Checking Equality

Try entering the following in the shell (don't forget to reload it).

```
>>> from geom2d.point import Point
>>> p = Point(1, 0)
>>> p == p
```
❶ True

```
>>> q = Point(1, 0)
>>> p == q
```
❷ False

I bet ❶ didn't surprise you: a Point is equal to itself. What about ❷? Did you raise your eyebrows? We are comparing two points with the same coordinates, but Python states they are different. Shouldn't $(1, 0)$ be equal to $(1, 0)$? It should, but first we have to teach Python how to compare two given instances of our class. By default Python considers two instances of a class to be equal if they're effectively the same instance, that is, if they live in the same memory region. To be more explicit, write this to the console:

```
>>> p
<geom2d.point.Point object at 0x10baa3f60>
```

```
>>> q
<geom2d.point.Point object at 0x10c63b438>
```

Python sees instance p as the one on the memory address 0x10baa3f60 and instance q on 0x10c63b438. Don't forget that the memory addresses of your instances will differ from these. We must instruct Python to compare our Point instances by checking whether the projections are close enough to be considered the same. If you recall from Table 4-1, by implementing a method called __eq__(self, other), you are effectively overloading the == operator. Let's do this for both the Point and Vector classes.

Listing 4-23 contains the code for the Point class (don't forget to import nums).

```
import math

from geom2d import nums


class Point:
    --snip--

    def __eq__(self, other):
        if self is other:
            return True

        if not isinstance(other, Point):
            return False
```

```
        return nums.are_close_enough(self.x, other.x) and \
            nums.are_close_enough(self.y, other.y)
```

Listing 4-23: Point equality implementation

Listing 4-24 contains the code for the Vector class.

```
import math

from geom2d import nums


class Vector:
    --snip--

    def __eq__(self, other):
        if self is other:
            return True

        if not isinstance(other, Vector):
            return False

        return nums.are_close_enough(self.u, other.u) and \
            nums.are_close_enough(self.v, other.v)
```

Listing 4-24: Implementing vector equality

As you can see, in both cases the idea is the same: comparing coordinates against another given instance. Prior to that, we do two important checks, though. The first one is to check for the case where we are comparing the same instance against itself, in which case we don't require any further comparison, so we directly return True. The second check is for the case where other is not an instance of the class. Since Python allows us to compare any two objects, we may be comparing an instance of Vector against a string, for example. If we detect this case where we try to compare instances from different classes, we return False, and we're done. You'll see this comparison pattern throughout the book, as all of our classes implementing __eq__ will use this same approach.

To make sure we got it right, let's repeat the experiment. Don't forget to reload the console to import the last version of the code, and enter the following code:

```
>>> from geom2d.point import Point
>>> p = Point(1, 0)
>>> p == p
True

>>> q = Point(1, 0)
>>> p == q
True
```

There you go! Now our `Point` and `Vector` classes comparison actually works as it is supposed to work.

String Representation

As you've seen in the console when evaluating an instance of a class, the output is not super helpful:

```
>>> from geom2d.vector import Vector
>>> v = Vector(2, 3)
>>> v
<geom2d.vector.Vector object at 0x10c63b438>
```

If we try to convert the instance to its string representation using the str function, we get the same result:

```
>>> str(p)
'<geom2d.vector.Vector object at 0x10c63b438>'
```

When printing the string representation of `Vector` instances to the console, we'd find something like the following much more useful:

```
>>> str(p)
'(2, 5) with norm 5.385164807134504'
```

That message has the information of the coordinate values and the value of the norm. Function str() in Python converts an instance of a class to its string representation. This function first checks whether the passed argument implements method __str__. If it does, the function calls it and returns the result. If it doesn't, the function simply returns the default string representation, which in our case is that unhelpful memory position mess.

Let's implement __str__ in our classes. Enter Listing 4-25 inside the Point class.

```
class Point:
    --snip--

    def __str__(self):
        return f'({self.x}, {self.y})'
```

Listing 4-25: Overriding string representation for `Point`

Then enter Listing 4-26 inside the `Vector` class.

```
class Vector:
    --snip--

    def __str__(self):
        return f'({self.u}, {self.v}) with norm {self.norm}'
```

Listing 4-26: Overriding string representation for `Vector`

We include instance attributes in the string using *f-strings* (f''). The attributes are inserted between curly brackets, and Python calls their __str__ methods to get their string representation and concatenate the result. For example, you can think of the f-string,

```
f'({self.x}, {self.y})'
```

as being translated by Python to something like this:

```
"(" + str(self.x) + ", " + str(self.y) + ")"
```

Now when using str() on instances of our classes, a much nicer description will be printed. Let's reload the Python shell and give it a second try:

```
>>> from geom2d.vector import Vector
>>> v = Vector(2, 3)
>>> str(v)
'(2, 3) with norm 3.605551275463989'
```

Much better, isn't it?

Vector Factories

A *factory function* is just a function that builds an object. Factory functions are a good option for initializing objects that require some calculation. An initializer should ideally only set its class attributes and avoid any computation; for that we will use factories.

A factory function is also helpful to improve the readability of the code. For instance, if you wanted to create a Vector from a point *P* to another point *Q*, the code

```
make_vector_between(p, q)
```

reads much better than this code:

```
Vector(q.x - p.x, q.y - p.y)
```

Not only that, but the latter is likely to be written many times, which should tell you there is an algorithm that needs to be abstracted into its own concept. In this particular case, the algorithm is the formula to create a vector between two ordered points (see Equation 4.12).

NOTE   *A missing abstraction is a common problem. It happens when an algorithm representing a concrete concept is not properly encapsulated into its own function or class with a descriptive name. Its main hazards are that it takes longer for our brains to understand code when abstractions are not well encapsulated and that the same algorithm is copied and pasted in many places, making it difficult to maintain.*

Create a new file inside *geom2d*, call it *vectors*, and enter the code from Listing 4-27.

```
from geom2d.point import Point
from geom2d.vector import Vector


def make_vector_between(p: Point, q: Point):
    return q - p


def make_versor(u: float, v: float):
    return Vector(u, v).normalized()


def make_versor_between(p: Point, q: Point):
    return make_vector_between(p, q).normalized()
```

Listing 4-27: Vector factory functions

This file defines several functions, all of which have the purpose of creating vectors. The first function we define, make_vector_between, creates a vector going from a point p to another point q. We've harnessed our Point class's __sub__ implementation to create the vector between the points. That is one handy way of creating vectors, expressed mathematically as shown in Equation 4.12.

$$\vec{u}_{P \to Q} = \left\{ \begin{array}{c} Q_x - P_x \\ Q_y - P_y \end{array} \right\} \tag{4.12}$$

Next, we have a function called make_versor, which creates versors, or vectors of unit length. *Versors* are frequently used to express direction or orientation, so we'll want a convenient way of creating them. Note that versors are written with a hat over them, as in $\hat{u}$, signifying their length is unitary.

Lastly, we have make_versor_between to create a versor between two points, which reuses the make_vector_between function to return the normalized result of it. The resulting versor could also be computed with Equation 4.13.

$$\hat{u}_{P \to Q} = \frac{1}{\sqrt{(Q_x - P_x)^2 + (Q_y - P_y)^2}} \cdot \left\{ \begin{array}{c} Q_x - P_x \\ Q_y - P_y \end{array} \right\} \tag{4.13}$$

Unit Testing

So far we've implemented a couple of methods on classes Point and Vector, and we've tested some of them in the console by hand, but now we face some big questions: How can we convince someone else that our code always works as expected? How can we be sure what we've written works all the time? How can we make sure we don't break anything when we modify existing code or add new code?

Often enough, you'll need to go back to some piece of code you wrote a long time ago to fix a bug. The problem comes when you want to change that code but don't know whether making that change will break what's already working. In fact, you may not be aware of what all the code is supposed to be doing, so you end up changing something you shouldn't have and break something else. This phenomenon happens so regularly it has its own name: *regression*.

Testing code by hand in the console is tiresome and boring, ensuring that you probably won't test everything you need to test. Besides that, it's not a repeatable process: you'll forget about which tests you executed for each method, or if someone else needs to run them, they'll have to figure out what to test and how. But still, we really need to make sure our changes won't break anything. Code is entirely useless if it doesn't do what it's supposed to.

What would make our lives much easier is an automated test we could execute, which takes a few milliseconds to run and spits out output that clearly states whether anything went wrong, where, and why. This is the basic idea behind *unit testing*, a crucial activity for any serious developer. Your code cannot be considered finished until it's accompanied with good unit tests that prove its quality. I consider this part of development so vital I want to cover it early in the book and make extensive use of it. Writing automated, unitary tests for our code is a simple process, and there's really no excuse for not doing it.

Creating unit tests for your code is simple: create a new file, and inside it add a new class with methods that test small portions of the test subject. Each test case has an *assertion* function that ensures a specific result is obtained given a set of inputs. The test is considered to pass when the assertion succeeds and to fail otherwise. When the test class is executed (as we'll see next), the methods are executed, and their assertions are checked.

Don't worry if this still doesn't make sense; we're going to use unit testing so much in this book you'll get to fully understand it.

Testing Distances

The first method we wrote for Point was distance_to, so let's start our unit test adventure there. In the *geom2d* package, create a new file named *point _test.py*. Your project's structure should look like the following:

```
Mechanics
  |- geom2d
  |    |- __init__.py
  |    |- nums.py
  |    |- point.py
  |    |- point_test.py
  |    |- vector.py
  |    |- vectors.py
```

In *point_test.py*, enter the code from Listing 4-28.

```python
import unittest

from geom2d.point import Point


❶ class TestPoint(unittest.TestCase):

    ❷ def test_distance_to(self):
        p = Point(1, 2)
        q = Point(4, 6)
        expected = 5
        actual = p.distance_to(q)

        ❸ self.assertAlmostEqual(expected, actual)
```

Listing 4-28: Distance between points test

We start by importing the *unittest* module, shipped with Python. This module provides us with most of the infrastructure we need to write and execute unit tests. After importing our `Point` class, we define the class `TestPoint`, which inherits `unittest.TestCase` ❶. The `TestCase` class defines a good collection of assertion methods that we gain access to inside our class when we inherit it.

Next we have the `test_distance_to` method ❷. It's important that the method name starts with the word *test_*, because this is how the class discovers which of its methods are tests to be executed. You can define other methods in the class, but as long as their names don't start with *test*, they won't be executed as tests. Inside the test we create two points that we know are 5 units apart from each other and assert that their distance `p.distance_to(q)` is close to that value.

NOTE *The* unittest *module's choice of words may be confusing. The name* UnitTest *is used for the class even though the tests themselves are actually the methods inside the class. Our class extending* UnitTest *is just a way of grouping related test cases.*

The assertion method `assertAlmostEqual` ❸ (defined in the class we inherited from: `unittest.TestCase`) checks for floating-point number equality with a given tolerance, which is expressed as the number of decimal positions to compare. The default number of decimal positions to check is 7, and in this test, we'll stick to the default (as we didn't provide any other value). Remember that when dealing with floating-point number comparisons, a tolerance must be used or, in this case, a given number of decimal positions (see the "Comparing Numbers" on page 4).

There are several ways to run tests. Let's explore how to do it from both PyCharm and the console.

Running the Test from PyCharm

If you take a look at your test file in PyCharm, you'll see a little green play button to the left of the class and method definitions. The class button executes all the tests inside of it (so far we have only one), whereas the button next to the method will run only that one test. Click the class one; from the menu, select **Run 'Unittest for point**.' The Run pane appears in the lower part of the IDE, and the result of executing your tests is displayed. If you did everything right, you should see the following:

```
--snip--

Ran 1 test in 0.001s

OK

Process finished with exit code 0
```

Let's now learn how to run the same test from the console.

Running the Test from the Console

IDEs other than PyCharm may have their own way to run tests. But regardless of the IDE you use, you can always run tests from the console. Open the console or shell and make sure you're in the *Mechanics* project directory. Then run the following command:

```
$ python3 -m unittest geom2d/point_test.py
```

You should see the following result:

```
Ran 1 tests in 0.000s

OK
```

We'll run most of the tests throughout the book from the IDE, but feel free to run them from the console if you prefer.

Assertion Errors

Let's see what would've happened if the assertion detected a wrong result. Inside *point_test.py*, change the expected value for the distance:

```
expected = 567
```

This assertion is expecting points $(1, 2)$ and $(4, 6)$ to be 567 units apart, which is totally wrong. Now execute the test again by clicking the green play button beside the class. This is the result you should see:

```
Ran 1 test in 0.006s

FAILED (failures=1)
```

```
Failure
Traceback (most recent call last):
  --snip--
  File ".../geom2d/tests/point_test.py", line 14, in test_distance_to
    self.assertAlmostEqual(expected, actual)
  --snip--

AssertionError: 567 != 5.0 within 7 places (562.0 difference)
```

The message with the most valuable information is the last one. It's telling us that there was an assertion error; that is, the assertion failed when it found 5.0 where 567 was expected. It used 7 decimal places in the comparison and still found a difference of 562.

Before this assertion error is the *traceback*, the execution path Python took until it got the error. As the message states, calls closer to the failure appear last in the list. As you can see, the test execution failed in file *point _test.py* (no surprise) on line 14 (yours may be different), in a test named test_distance_to. This information will prove invaluable when you modify existing code and run the tests only to find out whether a test fails, as it can tell you what exactly broke. These test failure messages will give you precise information.

Don't forget to put our unit test back to how we initially wrote it and make sure it still runs successfully.

Testing Vector Plus and Minus Operations

To ensure + and − operations work properly for vectors (doing the same for the Point class is left as an exercise for you), let's use the following test cases:

$$\left\{ \begin{array}{c} 1 \\ 2 \end{array} \right\} + \left\{ \begin{array}{c} 4 \\ 6 \end{array} \right\} = \left\{ \begin{array}{c} 5 \\ 8 \end{array} \right\}$$

and

$$\left\{ \begin{array}{c} 1 \\ 2 \end{array} \right\} - \left\{ \begin{array}{c} 4 \\ 6 \end{array} \right\} = \left\{ \begin{array}{c} -3 \\ -4 \end{array} \right\}$$

Create a new file inside package *geom2d* for testing the Vector class. Name it *vector_test* and enter the code from Listing 4-29.

```
import unittest

from geom2d.vector import Vector


class TestVector(unittest.TestCase):
    u = Vector(1, 2)
    v = Vector(4, 6)

    def test_plus(self):
```

```
        expected = Vector(5, 8)
        actual = self.u + self.v
        self.assertEqual(expected, actual)

    def test_minus(self):
        expected = Vector(-3, -4)
        actual = self.u - self.v
        self.assertEqual(expected, actual)
```

Listing 4-29: Tests for plus and minus operations

Run all tests using the green play button to the left of the class definition. If you got everything right, your two new tests should succeed. Yay! Our operations were properly implemented. The nice thing is, if there had been a bug in the implementation, these tests would have pointed out where and why.

It's worth noting that this time we're using assertion method `assertEqual`, which under the hood compares both arguments using the `==` operator. If we hadn't overloaded this operator in the `Vector` class, the tests would fail even if the results were right. Try this: comment out the `__eq__(self, other)` method definition (by appending a # character at the beginning of the line) in the `Vector` class and rerun the tests.

You'll find how the last two tests fail with a message like the following:

```
<geom2d.vector.Vector object at 0x10fd8d198> !=
<geom2d.vector.Vector object at 0x10fd8d240>

Expected :<geom2d.vector.Vector object at 0x10fd8d240>
Actual   :<geom2d.vector.Vector object at 0x10fd8d198>
```

Familiar? That's Python assuming two objects from the class can be equal only if they are the same actual object living in the same memory position. Our `__eq__` operator overload explains to Python the rules to determine when two objects should be considered the same. Don't forget to uncomment the method.

Testing Vector Product Operations

Let's add two new test cases for dot and cross products using the same two vectors defined in the test class:

$$\begin{Bmatrix} 1 \\ 2 \end{Bmatrix} \cdot \begin{Bmatrix} 4 \\ 6 \end{Bmatrix} = 4 + 12 = 16$$

and

$$\begin{Bmatrix} 1 \\ 2 \end{Bmatrix} \times \begin{Bmatrix} 4 \\ 6 \end{Bmatrix} = 6 - 8 = -2$$

In code, this looks like Listing 4-30.

```
import unittest

from geom2d.vector import Vector


class TestVector(unittest.TestCase):

    --snip--

    def test_dot_product(self):
        expected = 16
        actual = self.u.dot(self.v)
        self.assertAlmostEqual(expected, actual)

    def test_cross_product(self):
        expected = -2
        actual = self.u.cross(self.v)
        self.assertAlmostEqual(expected, actual)
```

Listing 4-30: Tests vector dot and cross products

Run all test cases to make sure the new ones also succeed. Note that, as we're comparing numbers again, we use assertion method assertAlmostEqual.

Testing Vector Parallelism and Perpendicularity

Next we'll test the is_parallel_to and is_perpendicular_to methods. Since we're checking a Boolean expression, we want to have two tests, one checking that the two vectors are parallel (a positive test) and one checking whether they're not (a negative test). For the positive case, we'll rely on the fact that a vector is always parallel to itself. Enter the Listing 4-31 code inside TestVector.

```
import unittest

from geom2d.vector import Vector

class TestVector(unittest.TestCase):

    --snip--

    def test_are_parallel(self):
        self.assertTrue(self.u.is_parallel_to(self.u))

    def test_are_not_parallel(self):
        self.assertFalse(self.u.is_parallel_to(self.v))
```

Listing 4-31: Testing vector parallelism

There are two new assertion methods in this listing that are interesting ones: assertTrue, which checks whether a given expression evaluates to True; and assertFalse, which checks whether a given expression evaluates to False.

We'll follow the same pattern for checking perpendicularity. After the last two tests, enter the two in Listing 4-32.

```
import unittest

from geom2d.vector import Vector


class TestVector(unittest.TestCase):

    --snip--

    def test_are_perpendicular(self):
        perp = Vector(-2, 1)
        self.assertTrue(self.u.is_perpendicular_to(perp))

    def test_are_not_perpendicular(self):
        self.assertFalse(self.u.is_perpendicular_to(self.v))
```

Listing 4-32: Testing vector perpendicularity

Run all tests inside the TestVector class to make sure they succeed. Congratulations! You've implemented your first unit tests. These tests will ensure the methods in our geometry classes work as expected. Additionally, if you find a better implementation for one of the methods we covered with tests, to make sure it still works as expected, just run its tests. Tests also serve to document the expected behavior of your code. If at some point you need a reminder about what the code you wrote is supposed to do in a particular case, unit tests should help.

Writing good tests is not a simple endeavor. One gets good at it by writing many, but there are some guidelines we can follow that will help us. Let's take a look at three simple rules that will make our tests much more resilient.

Three Golden Rules for Unit Testing

We've covered tests for a small fraction of the methods from the Point and Vector classes. Now that you have the required knowledge, try testing all the methods that we wrote in both the Point and Vector classes. I'll leave this for you as an exercise, but you can take a look at the code provided with the book if you need help: it includes a lot of unit tests. Look for all the methods we didn't test and write the tests you think are needed to make sure they work properly. I encourage you to try, but if you still feel like unit testing is foreign to you, don't worry, we'll be writing unit tests in other chapters of this book.

As mentioned, I believe writing unit tests is an integral part of coding, and handling software not covered by unit tests should be considered a poor practice. Moreover, writing code for the open-source community requires good unit tests. You've got to give the community a reason to believe what you did actually works. Proving this with automated tests that anybody can easily run and see for themselves is always a good approach, as it's unlikely anybody is going to take the time to think about how to test your code and then open the console and manually try it all.

You'll get better at writing reliable unit tests as you practice. For now, I'd like to give you some basic rules to follow. Don't expect to fully grasp their meanings now, but come back to this section from time to time as you move through the book.

Rule 1: One Reason to Fail

Unit tests should have one and only one reason to fail. This sounds simple, but in many cases the *test subject* (what you are testing) is complex and made up of several components working together.

If tests fail for only one reason, it's straightforward to find the bug in the code. Imagine the opposite: a test that could fail for, say, five different reasons. When that test fails, you'll find yourself spending too much time reading error messages and debugging code, trying to understand what made it fail this particular time.

Some developers and test professionals (testing is a profession on its own, which I spent several years doing) state that each test should have one and only one assertion. Being pragmatic, sometimes having more than one assertion is not that harmful, but if it's one, that's much better.

Let's analyze a particular case. Take the test we wrote for checking whether two vectors are perpendicular. If instead of

```python
def test_are_perpendicular(self):
    perp = Vector(-2, 1)
    self.assertTrue(self.u.is_perpendicular_to(perp))
```

we had written

```python
def test_are_perpendicular(self):
    perp = u.perpendicular()
    self.assertTrue(self.u.is_perpendicular_to(perp))
```

then the test could fail because of an error in the is_perpendicular_to method or because of an error in the implementation of perpendicular, which we use to compute a perpendicular vector to $\vec{u}$. See the difference?

Rule 2: Controlled Environment

We use the word *fixture* to refer to the environment where a test runs. The environment includes all pieces of data surrounding our test and the state of the test subject itself, all of which may alter the results of the test. This rule states that you should have total control of the fixture where your test runs.

Inputs and expected outputs of the test should always be known beforehand. Everything happening inside your tests should be *deterministic*; that is, there should be no randomness or dependence on anything out of your control: dates or times, operating systems, machine environment variables not set by the test, and so on.

If your tests seem to fail at random, they are useless, and you should get rid of them. People get used to random failing tests fast and start ignoring them. The problem comes when they also ignore tests that are failing because of a bug in the code.

Rule 3: Test Independence

Tests should never depend on other tests. Each test should run on its own and never depend on a fixture set by other tests.

There are at least three reasons for this. First, you'll want to run or debug tests independently. Second, many test frameworks do not guarantee the execution order of tests. Finally, it's much simpler to read and understand tests that don't depend on other surrounding tests.

Let's illustrate this with the TestSwitch class in Listing 4-33.

```
class TestSwitch(unittest.TestCase):

    switch = Switch()

    def test_switch_on(self):
     self.switch.on()
     self.assertTrue(self.switch.is_on())

    def test_switch_off(self):
     # Last test should have switched on
     self.switch.toggle()
     self.assertTrue(self.switch.is_off())
```

Listing 4-33: Test depending on another test

See how test_switch_off depends on test_switch_on? By using a method called toggle, we could get the wrong result if the tests run in a different order and the switch has a state of *off* when this test runs.

Never rely on test execution order; that results in trouble. Tests should always run independently: they should work the same way no matter the order of execution.

Summary

In this chapter, we created two important classes: Point and Vector. The rest of our *geom2d* library will be built upon these simple but powerful abstractions. We taught Python how to determine whether two given instances of Point or Vector are logically equal by implementing the special method __eq__, and provided a better textual representation with __str__. We covered some of the methods in these classes with unit tests, and I encouraged you to extend the coverage on your own. The best way to learn to write good unit tests is by practicing. In the next chapter, we'll add two new geometrical abstractions to *geom2d*: lines and segments. These provide a new dimension that can be used to construct more complex shapes.

5

LINES AND SEGMENTS

A point and a direction describe an infinite, straight line, with no start or end. Two distinct points bound a segment, which has a finite length but contains infinite points. In this chapter, we'll focus on these two primitives, line segments and lines. We'll implement both with the help of the points and vectors we implemented in the previous chapter.

We'll also spend some time understanding and implementing two algorithms: one that computes the closest point to a segment, and another that computes segment intersections. These algorithms use some vital concepts from geometry that will serve as the foundation for more complex problems. We'll take our time implementing these operations to make sure we understand them, so get your Python IDE ready and grab a pen and paper—it'll be helpful to sketch some diagrams the old-school way.

Segment Class

Between any two points in the plane exists a unique *segment*, a straight line with finite length containing infinite points. Figure 5-1 depicts a segment between two points: *S* and *E*.

Figure 5-1: Segment defined
between the points S and E

Let's start by creating a class named Segment with two attributes: a start
point *S* and an end point *E*. This is how our project's structure looks so far:

```
Mechanics
  |- geom2d
  |     |- __init__.py
  |     |- nums.py
  |     |- point.py
  |     |- point_test.py
  |     |- vector.py
  |     |- vector_test.py
  |     |- vectors.py
```

Right-click the *geom2d* package, select **New ▶ Python File**, name it
segment, and click **OK**. PyCharm adds the *.py* extension for you, but if you're
using another IDE, you may need to add it yourself. In the file, enter the
class as it's written in Listing 5-1.

```
from geom2d.point import Point


class Segment:
    def __init__(self, start: Point, end: Point):
        self.start = start
        self.end = end
```

Listing 5-1: Segment initialization

We start by importing the Point class from the *geom2d.point* module.
Then, we define the Segment class with an initializer that accepts two points:
start and end. These are stored in corresponding attributes.

Note that we are typing the parameters; more specifically, we're saying they must be of type Point. These are the *type hints* we saw in Chapter 2,
mostly for the IDE to give us some context help. If the IDE knows both start
and end are objects from Point, it'll detect if we're trying to use any attribute
the class doesn't implement. But it's important to realize this won't prevent
us from passing the wrong argument type at runtime. In fact, if you try the
following in the console:

```
>>> from geom2d.segment import Segment
>>> s = Segment("foo", "bar")
```

```
>>> s.start
'foo'
```

you should see that Python allowed us to pass strings instead of `Points` without complaining, as type hints are ignored by Python's interpreter at runtime.

The Segment's Direction

An important property of a segment is its *direction*, defined as a vector going from its start point S to its end point E. If we call it $\vec{d}$, we can compute it using Equation 5.1.

$$\vec{d} = E - S = \left\{ \begin{array}{c} E_x - S_x \\ E_y - S_y \end{array} \right\} \tag{5.1}$$

The normalization of the direction vector yields the direction versor, also commonly used in many operations with segments. The *direction vector* is a vector with the same length as the segment and parallel to it, with a direction going from its start point toward the end point. The *direction versor* is the normalized version of the direction vector, that is, a vector with the same direction but with unitary length.

The direction versor $\hat{d}$, given the segment with a length of l, is then as shown in Equation 5.2.

$$\hat{d} = \frac{\vec{d}}{\|\vec{d}\|} = \left\{ \begin{array}{c} \frac{E_x - S_x}{l} \\ \frac{E_y - S_y}{l} \end{array} \right\} \tag{5.2}$$

NOTE   *Most of the time when we say segment's direction, we'll mean direction versor $\hat{d}$, but we'll also sometimes use that phrase to refer to the direction vector $\vec{d}$. If that's the case, we'll explicitly note it. So, if nothing is said, assume by direction we mean the direction versor.*

Let's implement both as properties of the class. Enter the code in Listing 5-2 in your *segment.py* file.

```
from geom2d.point import Point
from geom2d.vectors import make_vector_between, make_versor_between


class Segment:
    --snip--

    @property
    def direction_vector(self):
        return make_vector_between(self.start, self.end)

    @property
    def direction_versor(self):
```

```
        return make_versor_between(self.start, self.end)
```

Listing 5-2: Calculating a segment's direction vector and versor

Since we're using the `make_vector_between` and `make_versor_between` factory functions we defined in *vectors.py*, these two attributes are straightforward to implement. We simply make a vector or versor between our start and end points.

Now, as important as the direction of the segment is, it's just as important that we know the direction perpendicular to it. We might use this perpendicular direction, for instance, to compute the velocity direction of a particle colliding against a straight line, which may represent a wall or the ground, such as the case in Figure 5-2.

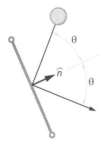

Figure 5-2: Computing the collision angle using the normal direction

Rotating the direction versor $\hat{d}$ $\pi/4$ radians (90°) yields the segment's *normal versor*. Computing this versor is quite simple using Vector's perpendicular attribute. Enter the new property in Listing 5-3 in the Segment class.

```
class Segment:
    --snip--

    @property
    def normal_versor(self):
        return self.direction_versor.perpendicular()
```

Listing 5-3: Computing a vector perpendicular to the segment's direction

This new property we have added works by chaining two attributes: `direction_versor` and `perpendicular`. We first call self's `direction_versor` to obtain the segment's direction versor. The result is an instance of Vector, upon which we call the `perpendicular` method, which returns a versor perpendicular to the segment's direction.

We could have stored the direction versor in a new variable and then called the `perpendicular` method on that variable:

```
def normal_versor(self):
    d = self.direction_versor
    return d.perpendicular()
```

In this case, the d variable doesn't add readability to the code, and since we use it only once, we can chain both methods and return the result. You'll see this pattern used often in our code.

You can see a visual representation of the concepts we just implemented in Figure 5-3. The segment on the left shows the direction vector $\vec{d}$, with its origin at S (the start point) and tip at E (the end point). The segment on the right shows the normalized version $\hat{d}$ of the direction vector and its perpendicular counterpart $\hat{n}$, the direction and normal versors, respectively.

Figure 5-3: Segment direction vector (left) and direction and normal versors (right)

We'll skip writing unit tests in this section, but that doesn't mean you shouldn't do them. From here on out, I won't write tests for every method we do, just some chosen ones, so we can keep focus and get through the content. But it's a great exercise for you to write unit tests for these untested methods. You can refer to the tests in the *Mechanics* project accompanying the book.

The Segment's Length

Another important property of a segment is its *length*, or the distance between its end points.

Calculating Length

There are at least two ways we can compute the length of the segment: we can either compute the distance between points S and E or compute the length of the direction vector $\vec{d}$.

We'll use the first one, which is shown in Listing 5-4, but if you prefer, you can implement the second one. The result should be the same.

```
class Segment:
    --snip--

    @property
    def length(self):
        return self.start.distance_to(self.end)
```

Listing 5-4: Calculating the length of a segment

Note again that using our previously implemented methods makes this calculation a breeze. Your *segment.py* file should look like Listing 5-5 at this point.

```
from geom2d.point import Point
from geom2d.vectors import make_vector_between, make_versor_between


class Segment:
    def __init__(self, start: Point, end: Point):
        self.start = start
        self.end = end

    @property
    def direction_vector(self):
        return make_vector_between(self.start, self.end)

    @property
    def direction_versor(self):
        return make_versor_between(self.start, self.end)

    @property
    def normal_versor(self):
        return self.direction_versor.perpendicular()

    @property
    def length(self):
        return self.start.distance_to(self.end)
```

Listing 5-5: Segment class

Let's test the method we just wrote.

Unit Testing Length

To make sure we made no mistakes implementing the length property, let's write a unit test. Start by creating a new test file. Right-click the *geom2d* package, select **New ▶ Python File**, name it *segment_test.py*, and click **OK**. Then enter the code in Listing 5-6.

```
import math
import unittest

from geom2d.point import Point
from geom2d.segment import Segment


class TestSegment(unittest.TestCase):

    start = Point(400, 0)
    end = Point(0, 400)
    segment = Segment(start, end)
```

```
def test_length(self):
    expected = 400 * math.sqrt(2)
    actual = self.segment.length
    self.assertAlmostEqual(expected, actual)
```

Listing 5-6: Testing a segment's length property

We import the *unittest* and *math* modules and the `Segment` and `Point` classes. Then, we define two points: start at $(400, 0)$ and end at $(0, 400)$. Using these points, we create segment, which is our test subject. Following Rule 1 for good unit tests, a test should fail for one and only one reason, our expected result is expressed directly as $400\sqrt{2}$, which comes from $\sqrt{(400 - 0)^2 + (0 - 400)^2}$ $= \sqrt{2 \cdot 400^2}$. The temptation here would be to write the following:

```
expected = self.start.distance_to(self.end)
```

However, that would violate Rule 1, as the test could fail for more than one reason. Moreover, in this case, both the expected and actual values would be computed using the same method: `distance_to`. This breaks the test's independence from the code it's supposed to test.

Run the test by clicking the green play button to the left of the `TestSegment` class definition and selecting **Run 'Unittests for segment'**. You can run it from the console like so:

```
$ python3 -m unittest geom2d/segment_test.py
```

It may seem silly to test the `distance` property because the only thing it does is call the `distance_to` method, which has already been tested. Even with such simple implementations we could have made mistakes such as, for example, trying to compute the distance using the same point twice:

```
self.start.distance_to(self.start)
```

As you probably know from your own experience, we developers make mistakes like this more often than not.

The t Parameter and Middle Points

We said earlier that there are an infinite number of points between the endpoints E and S of a segment. How do we go about obtaining them? It's common to use a parameter with values going from 0 to 1 (inclusive) to obtain every point along the segment. We'll call this parameter t and define it as done in Equation 5.3.

$$\{t \in \mathbb{R} \mid 0.0 \leq t \leq 1.0\} \tag{5.3}$$

All points between the segment's start and end points can be obtained by varying the value of t. For $t = 0$, we get exactly the segment's start point S. Similarly, for $t = 1$, we get the end point E. To compute any middle point P given a value of t, we can use Equation 5.4.

$$P = \begin{pmatrix} S_x \\ S_y \end{pmatrix} + t \left\{ \begin{array}{c} E_x - S_x \\ E_y - S_y \end{array} \right\} \qquad (5.4)$$

By realizing that the vector in the previous expression is exactly the direction vector as defined in Equation 5.1, we can simplify the expression as in Equation 5.5.

$$P = S + t \cdot \vec{d} \qquad (5.5)$$

We can easily implement Equation 5.5 using Point's displaced method. Enter the method point_at in Listing 5-7 into your Segment class file (*segment.py*).

```
class Segment:
    --snip--

    def point_at(self, t: float):
        return self.start.displaced(self.direction_vector, t)
```

Listing 5-7: Obtaining a point from a segment using parameter t

By displacing the start point by the direction vector t times (with $0.0 \leq t \leq 1.0$), we obtain any point on the segment. Let's implement a property that directly yields the middle point of the segment, that is, the point for $t = 0.5$ (see Figure 5-4).

Figure 5-4: A segment's
middle point

This is a special point we'll be computing often, so we want a convenient way of obtaining it. Enter the code in Listing 5-8).

```
class Segment:
    --snip--

    @property
    def middle(self):
        return self.point_at(0.5)
```

Listing 5-8: Segment's middle point

Validating t Values

You may have realized that in point_at, we don't check that the passed-in t value is inside the expected range given by Equation 5.3. We can pass it a wrong value for t, and it works without complaining, yielding points that are out of the segment. For instance, if we passed it a value of $t = 1.5$, we'd obtain the point depicted in Figure 5-5.

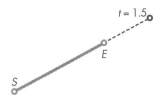

Figure 5-5: Point out of the
segment for t = 1.5

Without validating the *t* value, this method silently fails by returning a point that the user may be tricked into thinking lies between the segment end points. By *silently fail*, we mean that the result is conceptually wrong, but the method happily computes it for us without any kind of warning or complaint that there may be some kind of error.

Robust software *fails fast*, meaning that as soon as an erroneous condition is detected, the program panics and quits, if possible with a message giving comprehensive information about the error.

This may sound scary, but it helps a lot. Imagine we allow users to pass a wrong value of *t* to our point_at(t) method. Now say that the user without noticing passes in a *t* like 739928393839. . . You can imagine the point obtained from this value is quite far from the segment that is supposed to contain it. Such a value wouldn't crash our program, and it would continue to execute. We may not notice that we've gotten such a value until some calculation several minutes later, when everything fails. Debugging all of what happened before we found the error could take hours (or maybe days, depending on the complexity of the code and how far the error spread). It'd be much simpler if we could detect the wrong value right away. Perhaps we could tell the user something like this:

```
Oops! We were expecting the value of 't' to be in the  range [0, 1],
but you gave us a value of '739928393839'.
```

This message is crystal clear. It's telling the user the program had to quit because of an error. This error could have gotten worse had the program continued to execute. The nice thing is the user gets the chance to analyze where the wrong value came from and take action to prevent it from happening again.

NOTE *Here we're using the word user to reference anyone using our code, not the end user of the applications we write. This includes yourself, as you'll be the user of your own code quite often.*

Since there's going to be a bunch of functionality defined for the *t* parameter, we'd better create a module for it. At this point, your project's structure should look like this:

```
Mechanics
    |- geom2d
    |    |- __init__.py
    |    |- nums.py
```

```
|   |- point.py
|   |- point_test.py
|   |- segment.py
|   |- segment_test.py
|   |- vector.py
|   |- vector_test.py
|   |- vectors.py
```

Create a new file inside the *geom2d* package named *tparam.py*. Inside it, enter the code from Listing 5-9.

```python
MIN = 0.0
MIDDLE = 0.5
MAX = 1.0


def make(value: float):
    if value < MIN:
        return MIN

    if value > MAX:
        return MAX

    return value


def ensure_valid(t):
    if not is_valid(t):
        raise TParamError(t)


def is_valid(t):
    return False if t < MIN or t > MAX else True


class TParamError(Exception):
    def __init__(self, t):
        self.t = t

    def __str__(self):
        return f'Expected t to be in [0, 1] but was {self.t}'
```

Listing 5-9: Validating parameter t values

We start by defining three useful constants. There's MIN, the minimum value t can take. There's MIDDLE, the value of (MIN + MAX) / 2. Finally, there's MAX, the maximum value t can take.

These values are going to be used a lot, so instead of writing *magic numbers* (numbers that appear hard-coded without explanation about their nature) everywhere, we've given them a name to understand what they refer to.

Once we've defined the values, we define the function make to create a parameter with a valid value. Then comes the function ensure_valid, which checks that *t* is not less or greater than the range limits using another method: is_valid. If *t* has a value outside the valid range, an exception is raised. TParam Error is an implementation of Python's Exception. This is a user-defined exception we provide with a nice formatted message. In the initializer for TParam Error, we pass the offending *t* value, and in the special method __str__, we return the actual message. Recall that a class may define the __str__ method to provide a textual (string) representation of the instance when it's called.

To see how it prints the message, try the following in the console:

```
>>> from geom2d import tparam
>>> tparam.ensure_valid(10.5)
Traceback (most recent call last):
  --snip--
geom2d.tparam.TParamError: Expected t to be in [0, 1] but was 10.5
```

The error message is nice and clear:

```
Expected t to be in [0, 1] but was 10.5
```

Let's use this validation in the point_at method from the Segment class. First, import the module in your *segment.py* file:

```
from geom2d import tparam
```

Go back to *segment.py* and refactor point_at(t) to include the validation, as in Listing 5-10.

```
def point_at(self, t: float):
    tparam.ensure_valid(t)
    return self.start.displaced(self.direction_vector, t)
```

Listing 5-10: Validating values of t in segment's point_at method

Then refactor the middle property to remove the 0.5 magic number as shown in Listing 5-11.

```
@property
def middle(self):
    return self.point_at(tparam.MIDDLE)
```

Listing 5-11: Removing the magic number from our middle point computation

If you followed along, your *segment.py* file should look like Listing 5-12.

```
from geom2d import tparam
from geom2d.point import Point
from geom2d.vectors import make_vector_between, make_versor_between
```

```
class Segment:
    def __init__(self, start: Point, end: Point):
        self.start = start
        self.end = end

    @property
    def direction_vector(self):
        return make_vector_between(self.start, self.end)

    @property
    def direction_versor(self):
        return make_versor_between(self.start, self.end)

    @property
    def normal_versor(self):
        return self.direction_versor.perpendicular()

    @property
    def length(self):
        return self.start.distance_to(self.end)

    def point_at(self, t: float):
        tparam.ensure_valid(t)
        return self.start.displaced(self.direction_vector, t)

    @property
    def middle(self):
        return self.point_at(tparam.MIDDLE)
```

Listing 5-12: The Segment class

With our Segment class complete, let's write some tests.

Unit Testing Segment Points

Since we'll use point_at as part of more complex computations, we really
want to make sure it works, so let's start with a test to assert that if it passes
a wrong value of *t*, an exception is actually raised. This gives us the opportunity to learn a new assertion method: assertRaises.

In the file *segment_test.py*, start by importing the *tparam* module:

```
from geom2d import tparam
```

Then write the test in Listing 5-13.

```
class TestSegment(unittest.TestCase):

    start = Point(400, 0)
    end = Point(0, 400)
```

```
    segment = Segment(start, end)

--snip--

def test_point_at_wrong_t(self):
    self.assertRaises(
      ❶ tparam.TParamError,
      ❷ self.segment.point_at,
      ❸ 56.7
    )
```

Listing 5-13: Testing wrong values of t

This assertion is a bit more complex than the ones we've seen so far. We are passing it three arguments. First is the expected exception to be raised (TParamError) ❶. Second, we pass the method that is expected to raise the exception ❷. Last, we pass the arguments to be passed into the previous method (point_at in this case) as comma-separated arguments ❸.

The assertion can be read as follows:

```
assert that method 'point_at' from instance 'self.segment'
raises an exception of type 'tparam.TParamError'
when called with arguments '56.7'
```

If point_at accepted more than one argument, you would include them as arguments of assertRaises. Now, let's include the two test cases from Listing 5-14.

```
class TestSegment(unittest.TestCase):

    start = Point(400, 0)
    end = Point(0, 400)
    segment = Segment(start, end)

    --snip--

    def test_point_at(self):
        t = tparam.make(0.25)
        expected = Point(300, 100)
        actual = self.segment.point_at(t)
        self.assertEqual(expected, actual)

    def test_middle_point(self):
        expected = Point(200, 200)
        actual = self.segment.middle
        self.assertEqual(expected, actual)
```

Listing 5-14: Testing the point_at method

In the first test case, we ensure that a middle point for a valid t value, 0.25 in this case, yields the expected point. Using Equation 5.4, this point can be computed as follows:

$$P = \underbrace{\begin{pmatrix} 400 \\ 0 \end{pmatrix}}_{S} + \underbrace{0.25}_{t} \cdot \underbrace{\left\{ \begin{array}{c} 0 - 400 \\ 400 - 0 \end{array} \right\}}_{E-S} = \begin{pmatrix} 400 \\ 0 \end{pmatrix} + \left\{ \begin{array}{c} -100 \\ 100 \end{array} \right\} = \begin{pmatrix} 300 \\ 100 \end{pmatrix}$$

The second test is for the `middle` attribute, which computes the point at $t = 0.5$. Take a pen and some paper and make sure point $(200, 200)$ is right in our test. Then run all the tests in the *segment_test.py* file to make sure all of them pass. You can do this from the console as follows:

```
$ python3 -m unittest geom2d/segment_test.py
```

Closest Point

Now suppose we want to know what the segment's point is that is closest to an outside point. If the outside point is not aligned with the segment, that is, a line perpendicular to the segment going through the point doesn't intersect with the segment, then the closest point has to be one of the two end points: S or E. If, on the other hand, the point is aligned with the segment, the intersection between the perpendicular line and the segment itself yields the closest point. Figure 5-6 illustrates this.

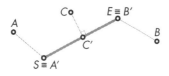

Figure 5-6: A segment's closest points

In the figure, point $S \equiv A'$ is the closest point to A, point $E \equiv B'$ is the closest point to B, and C' is the closest point to C. Let's see how we can implement this procedure.

The Algorithm

With the help of the method `projection_over` from Chapter 4, we can find the closest point easily. We'll use P as the external point, l as the length of the segment, and the various points, segments, and vectors in Figure 5-7.

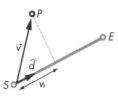

Figure 5-7: Auxiliary vectors for the algorithm that computes a segment's closest point

The algorithm is as follows:

1. Compute a vector $\vec{v}$ going from segment's S to external point P.

2. Compute the projection of $\vec{v}$ over the segment's direction versor, $\hat{d}$.

3. Depending on the value of the projection, call it v_s. The closest point P' can be calculated using Equation 5.6.

$$P' = \begin{cases} S & \text{if } v_s < 0 \\ E & \text{if } v_s > l \\ S + v_s \cdot \hat{d} & \text{if } 0 \leq v_s \leq l \end{cases} \qquad (5.6)$$

If the value of the projection v_s is negative, the projection lies outside the segment on S's side; hence, the closest point is S. For numbers greater than l, the projection over the segment's direction is longer than the segment itself. Thus, the result is the end point E. For any value of v_s in the closed range $[0, l]$, we obtain the point by displacing S in the direction of $\hat{d} \, v_s$ times. Figure 5-7 depicts this last case where the external point P is aligned with the segment.

The code for this operation is in Listing 5-15.

```
class Segment:
    --snip--

    def closest_point_to(self, p: Point):
        v = make_vector_between(self.start, p)
        d = self.direction_versor
        vs = v.projection_over(d)

        if vs < 0:
            return self.start

        if vs > self.length:
            return self.end

        return self.start.displaced(d, vs)
```

Listing 5-15: Closest point to a segment

We start by computing vector $\vec{v}$. We then get v_s: the projection of $\vec{v}$ over the segment's direction versor $\hat{d}$. If v_s is smaller than zero, we return the start point. If greater than the length of the segment, we return the end point; otherwise, we compute the displacement of the start point that yields the resulting point on the segment.

Unit Testing Closest Points

Let's test the three different cases defined earlier, namely, $v_s < 0$, $v_s > l$, and $0 < v_s < l$. Listing 5-16 shows the code for the tests.

```
class TestSegment(unittest.TestCase):

    start = Point(400, 0)
    end = Point(0, 400)
    segment = Segment(start, end)

    --snip--

    def test_closest_point_is_start(self):
        p = Point(500, 20)
        expected = self.start
        actual = self.segment.closest_point_to(p)
        self.assertEqual(expected, actual)

    def test_closest_point_is_end(self):
        p = Point(20, 500)
        expected = self.end
        actual = self.segment.closest_point_to(p)
        self.assertEqual(expected, actual)

    def test_closest_point_is_middle(self):
        p = Point(250, 250)
        expected = Point(200, 200)
        actual = self.segment.closest_point_to(p)
        self.assertEqual(expected, actual)
```

Listing 5-16: Testing a segment's closest point

To better understand the tests, it may be a good exercise to draw the segment and each of the external points by hand to see whether you can figure out why the expected results have the values they have. Your drawing should look similar to Figure 5-8. Furthermore, trying to solve the three cases by hand will presumably give you some insight into the algorithm.

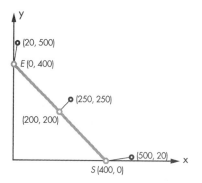

Figure 5-8: The segment's closest points and their test cases

Don't forget to run all tests and make sure they all succeed. You can do this from the console as follows:

```
$ python3 -m unittest geom2d/segment_test.py
```

Distance to a Point

Now that we know the closest point in the segment to an external point, we can easily compute the distance between it and the segment. Enter the method in Listing 5-17.

```
class Segment:
    --snip--

    def distance_to(self, p: Point):
        return p.distance_to(
            self.closest_point_to(p)
        )
```

Listing 5-17: Computing the distance from a point to the segment

As you can see in the code, the distance between the segment and any given external point is the distance between the point and that in the segment that is closest to it. Simple, isn't it?

Segment Intersections

Now we get to the fun stuff. How do we test whether two segments intersect? If they do intersect, how do we compute the intersection point? Consider the cases from Figure 5-9.

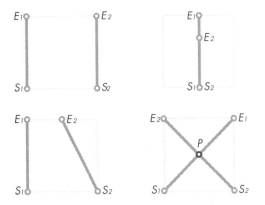

Figure 5-9: Possible segment intersection cases

The two cases from the left column have no intersection, but there is a difference between them. In the first case, the direction vectors of the segments are parallel ($\vec{d}_1 \times \vec{d}_2 = 0$). Thus, it's easy to know there will be no intersection. In the other case, if instead of segments we had infinite lines, there would be an intersection point. It might be far from where the segments are, but there'd be one nonetheless. As we'll see in the following equations, we'll have to compute the intersection point as if we were working with lines and then ensure the point lies inside both segments.

In the upper-right case, the two segments overlap; hence, there is more than one intersection point—an infinite number, to be precise. For our analysis we'll define two possible cases: segments either have an intersection point or don't intersect at all (we won't be considering the upper-right case). We'll forget about the overlapping case since we won't be needing it for our applications, and we want simplified code.

Overlapping Segments

If we were to include the case where the segments overlap, the return object for the intersection function could be either a Point or a Segment. A function that returns different object types is hard to work with. Once we have the result, we'd need to check what type of object we got and act accordingly. This could look as follows:

```
result = seg_a.intersection_with(seg_b)

if type(result) is Point:
    # intersection is a point
elif type(result) is Segment:
    # intersection is a segment
else:
    # no intersection
```

But this code is messy. There are better ways of handling this logic, but we won't get into it, as for us there will be either an intersection point or no intersection at all. That will make our code simpler and easier to work with.

Let's take a look at the algorithm.

The Algorithm

Let's find the intersection point of a case like the one in the lower right of Figure 5-9. Say we have two segments:

- Segment 1 with start point S_1 and end point E_1
- Segment 2 with start point S_2 and end point E_2

We can compute every point in segment 1, let's call it P_1, using the following expression,

$$P_1(t_1) = S_1 + t_1 \cdot \vec{d}_1$$

where t_1 is the parameter that goes from 0 to 1 and $\vec{d}_1$ is the direction vector (not versor) for the segment. Similarly, here is segment 2:

$$P_2(t_2) = S_2 + t_2 \cdot \vec{d}_2$$

To find the intersection point, we have to look for a pair of values t_1 and t_2 such that $P_1(t_1) = P_2(t_2)$:

$$S_1 + t_1 \cdot \vec{d}_1 = S_2 + t_2 \cdot \vec{d}_2$$

If both segments intersect, plugging those t parameter values in their respective segment expressions should result in the same point, the intersection point P. Let's rewrite the expression in its vector form:

$$\begin{pmatrix} S_{1x} \\ S_{1y} \end{pmatrix} + t_1 \cdot \left\{ \begin{matrix} d_{1x} \\ d_{1y} \end{matrix} \right\} = \begin{pmatrix} S_{2x} \\ S_{2y} \end{pmatrix} + t_2 \cdot \left\{ \begin{matrix} d_{2x} \\ d_{2y} \end{matrix} \right\}$$

We can use this form to obtain a scalar system of two equations and two unknowns, t_1 and t_2:

$$\begin{cases} S_{1x} + t_1 \cdot d_{1x} = S_{2x} + t_2 \cdot d_{2x} \\ S_{1y} + t_1 \cdot d_{1y} = S_{2y} + t_2 \cdot d_{2y} \end{cases}$$

I'll spare you the details and give you the result, though it may be a good exercise to solve the system yourself for t_1 and t_2. The final expressions for the t parameters are as shown in Equations 5.7 and 5.8.

$$t_1 = \frac{\Delta S_x \cdot d_{2y} - \Delta S_y \cdot d_{2x}}{\vec{d}_1 \times \vec{d}_2} \tag{5.7}$$

$$t_2 = \frac{\Delta S_x \cdot d_{1y} - \Delta S_y \cdot d_{1x}}{\vec{d}_1 \times \vec{d}_2} \tag{5.8}$$

Here, $\Delta S_x = S_{2x} - S_{1x}$, $\Delta S_y = S_{2y} - S_{1y}$, and $\vec{d}_1 \times \vec{d}_2 \neq 0$. Note that these formulas would yield ∞ if the segments were parallel ($\vec{d}_1 \times \vec{d}_2 = 0$). We can't attempt a division by zero; that would raise an exception in our Python code, so we'll need to detect this case before we try to compute the values of t_1 and t_2.

With these two values computed for the case where segments were not parallel, we have two possible outcomes:

- Values t_1 and t_2 are both inside range [0, 1]. The intersection point belongs to both segments.

- One or both of t_1 and t_2 are outside range [0, 1]. The intersection point is outside of at least one of the segments.

Now we're ready to implement the logic in an algorithm. In your *segment.py* file, implement the intersection_with method as shown in Listing 5-18.

```
class Segment:
    --snip--

    def intersection_with(self, other):
        d1, d2 = self.direction_vector, other.direction_vector
```

```
if d1.is_parallel_to(d2):
    return None

cross_prod = d1.cross(d2)
delta = other.start - self.start
t1 = (delta.u * d2.v - delta.v * d2.u) / cross_prod
t2 = (delta.u * d1.v - delta.v * d1.u) / cross_prod

if tparam.is_valid(t1) and tparam.is_valid(t2):
    return self.point_at(t1)
else:
    return None
```

Listing 5-18: Intersection between two segments

We start by storing both segments' direction vectors in the variables d1 and d2 using Python's multiple assignment. With the multiple assignment, several values can be assigned to variables at once. Then we check whether the directions are parallel, in which case we return None. If we find the segments aren't parallel, we compute $\vec{d}_1 \times \vec{d}_2$ and ΔS and store them in the variables cross_prod and delta. With the help of these values, we then compute t_1 and t_2. If these values are inside their valid range, we then return the resulting intersection point by calling point_at on the current Segment object (self). Make sure you understand that we could have computed P using t_2 and called point_at on other. The result would've been the same.

NOTE   *Similarly to other languages such as Java or C# with null, one should use None judiciously. Use it for cases where having an empty-like value is a perfectly valid outcome. For instance, in our intersection_with method, None represents the case where there exists no intersection point.*

Unit Testing Segment Intersections

As we advance with the book material and our code becomes more complex, testing these code fragments will become more involved. The method we just wrote for computing intersection between segments has a couple of branches or paths the execution can take. With the objective of being as exhaustive as possible with our unit tests, let's compile every case we want covered (see Table 5-1).

Table 5-1: Segment Intersection Algorithm Outcomes

Segment Directions	t_1	t_2	Intersection Result
$\vec{d}_1 \parallel \vec{d}_2$	—	—	None
$\vec{d}_1 \nparallel \vec{d}_2$	Out of range	Out of range	None
$\vec{d}_1 \nparallel \vec{d}_2$	In range	Out of range	None
$\vec{d}_1 \nparallel \vec{d}_2$	Out of range	In range	None
$\vec{d}_1 \nparallel \vec{d}_2$	In range	In range	$P = S_1 + t_1 \cdot \vec{d}_1$

We'll be writing unit tests for the first and last cases from Table 5-1; I'll leave the other three as an exercise for you. In file *segment_test.py*, include the tests in Listing 5-19 in the TestSegmentclass.

```
class TestSegment(unittest.TestCase):

    start = Point(400, 0)
    end = Point(0, 400)
    segment = Segment(start, end)

    --snip--

    def test_parallel_segments_no_intersection(self):
        other = Segment(Point(200, 0), Point(0, 200))
        actual = self.segment.intersection_with(other)
        self.assertIsNone(actual)

    def test_segments_intersection(self):
        other = Segment(Point(0, 0), Point(400, 400))
        expected = Point(200, 200)
        actual = self.segment.intersection_with(other)
        self.assertEqual(expected, actual)
```

Listing 5-19: Testing segment intersections

So, in the first test, we construct a parallel segment and assert that the intersection between the two is None with the assertion assertIsNone, which checks that the passed-in value is None. In the second, we construct a segment perpendicular to the first one that intersects it at $(200, 200)$ and assert we get that point as the result. You can run all the tests in the file from the IDE by clicking the green play button or from the console as follows:

```
$ python3 -m unittest geom2d/segment_test.py
```

Can you come up with the segments needed for the other three cases?

Equality and String Representation

Just as we did with the Point and Vector classes, we want to overload the == operator so that Python understands two segments with equal start and end points as logically equal, and we want to implement a __str__ method so we can get a nice string representation of the segment. Enter the code in Listing 5-20 in the *segment.py* file.

```
class Segment:
    --snip--

    def __eq__(self, other):
        if self is other:
            return True
```

```
            if not isinstance(other, Segment):
                return False

            return self.start == other.start \
                and self.end == other.end

    def __str__(self):
        return f'segment from {self.start} to {self.end}'
```

Listing 5-20: Equality of segments and string representation

We'll add one last property once we've developed the Line class. If you
followed along, your Segment class should look similar to Listing 5-21.

```
from geom2d import tparam
from geom2d.point import Point
from geom2d.vectors import make_vector_between, make_versor_between


class Segment:
    def __init__(self, start: Point, end: Point):
        self.start = start
        self.end = end

    @property
    def direction_vector(self):
        return make_vector_between(self.start, self.end)

    @property
    def direction_versor(self):
        return make_versor_between(self.start, self.end)

    @property
    def normal_versor(self):
        return self.direction_versor.perpendicular()

    @property
    def length(self):
        return self.start.distance_to(self.end)

    def point_at(self, t: float):
        tparam.ensure_valid(t)
        return self.start.displaced(self.direction_vector, t)

    @property
    def middle(self):
        return self.point_at(tparam.MIDDLE)
```

```python
    def closest_point_to(self, p: Point):
        v = make_vector_between(self.start, p)
        d = self.direction_versor
        vs = v.projection_over(d)

        if vs < 0:
            return self.start

        if vs > self.length:
            return self.end

        return self.start.displaced(d, vs)

    def distance_to(self, p: Point):
        return p.distance_to(
            self.closest_point_to(p)
        )

    def intersection_with(self, other):
        d1, d2 = self.direction_vector, other.direction_vector

        if d1.is_parallel_to(d2):
            return None

        cross_prod = d1.cross(d2)
        delta = other.start - self.start
        t1 = (delta.u * d2.v - delta.v * d2.u) / cross_prod
        t2 = (delta.u * d1.v - delta.v * d1.u) / cross_prod

        if tparam.is_valid(t1) and tparam.is_valid(t2):
            return self.point_at(t1)
        else:
            return None

    def __eq__(self, other):
        if self is other:
            return True

        if not isinstance(other, Segment):
            return False

        return self.start == other.start \
                and self.end == other.end

    def __str__(self):
        return f'segment from {self.start} to {self.end}'
```

Listing 5-21: The Segment class

Line Class

An infinite line can be described by a base point B and a direction vector $\vec{d}$, like that in Figure 5-10.

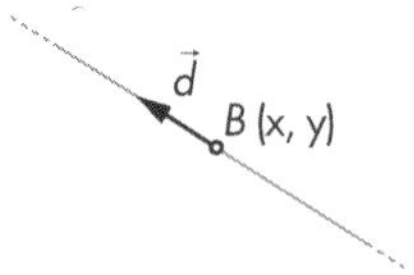

Figure 5-10: A line with a
base point B and direction
vector $\vec{d}$

Lines are useful helper primitives; with them we can build more complex geometries and operations. One common usage of lines, for example, is finding where two nonparallel directions intersect. You'll see in the next chapter how operations such as constructing a circle out of three points are effortless using line intersections.

Let's create a new Line class with these two properties: a base point and a direction. In the *geom2d* package, add a new file named *line.py* and enter the code in Listing 5-22.

```
from geom2d.point import Point
from geom2d.vector import Vector


class Line:
    def __init__(self, base: Point, direction: Vector):
        self.base = base
        self.direction = direction
```

Listing 5-22: Line initialization

The initializer sets our properties base and direction based on the values passed into their corresponding arguments. Like before, we've typed the base and direction arguments so our IDE can warn us of any potential errors.

Let's now provide two methods that check whether a line is parallel or perpendicular to another line (Listing 5-23).

```
class Line:
    --snip--

    def is_parallel_to(self, other):
        return self.direction.is_parallel_to(other.direction)

    def is_perpendicular_to(self, other):
        return self.direction.is_perpendicular_to(other.direction)
```

Listing 5-23: Checking whether lines are parallel or perpendicular

We didn't implement these methods for Segment, because our concern was with the segment's infinite points and how they're located in the plane; here, on the other hand, we're working with directions. Working with directions requires knowledge of their relative positioning; Are they parallel? Are they perpendicular?

With lines, the question is usually about how they are positioned with respect to other lines; with segments, the question is usually about how they are positioned themselves.

To check whether two lines are parallel, we could simply access their direction properties and use their methods like so:

```
d1 = line_one.direction
d2 = line_two.direction
d1.is_parallel_to(d2)
```

This is definitely possible, but it's not considered good practice. There is a guideline commonly known as the *principle of least knowledge* or *law of Demeter*, which states that "you should only talk to your immediate friends." In this case, as we are working with lines, lines are our immediate friends. The Line properties base point and direction vector are not our immediate friends; thus, we shouldn't ask them for stuff. If we need something from them, we have to ask our immediate friend, the Line holding such properties, to do it for us.

So, here's how we should check whether two lines are parallel or perpendicular:

```
line_one.is_parallel_to(line_two)
```

Let's also include two more methods to create new lines that are perpendicular or parallel to an existing line and that go through a point. In your file, enter the code in Listing 5-24.

```
from geom2d.point import Point
from geom2d.vector import Vector


class Line:
    --snip--

    def perpendicular_through(self, point: Point):
        return Line(point, self.direction.perpendicular())

    def parallel_through(self, point: Point):
        return Line(point, self.direction)
```

Listing 5-24: Creating perpendicular and parallel lines

The method perpendicular_through receives point as an argument and returns a new line, which uses that base point and direction vector perpendicular to the original line. Similarly, `parallel_through` constructs a new line with the given base point but using the same direction vector as the original line.

Line Intersections

A general algorithm to compute the intersection between two segments was explained in depth earlier in the chapter. The algorithm was based on the start point and direction vector of segments but can be extended to work with lines by using the base point of the line instead of the start point of the segment. The nice thing is that in the case of lines, parameters t_1 and t_2 are not bounded to range $[0, 1]$; they can go from $-\infty$ to ∞.

If we rewrite Equations 5.7 and 5.8 for lines, we get Equations 5.9 and 5.10.

$$t_1 = \frac{\Delta B_x \cdot d_{2y} - \Delta B_y \cdot d_{2x}}{\vec{d_1} \times \vec{d_2}} \tag{5.9}$$

$$t_2 = \frac{\Delta B_x \cdot d_{1y} - \Delta B_y \cdot d_{1x}}{\vec{d_1} \times \vec{d_2}} \tag{5.10}$$

In this case, $\Delta B_x = B_{2x} - B_{1x}$, and $\Delta B_y = B_{2y} - B_{1y}$. For these formulas to yield the correct values, recall that $\vec{d_1} \times \vec{d_2} \neq 0$. Since the t values are not bounded anymore, there's no need to compute both t_1 and t_2 and check whether they fall into the range $[0, 1]$. Computing one of them will suffice in getting the resulting intersection point. Let's choose Equation 5.9 to compute t_1. With t_1, we can determine the actual intersection point as follows:

$$P = B_1 + t_1 \cdot \vec{d_1}$$

Implement method `intersection_with` in your `Line` class as in Listing 5-25.

```
from geom2d.point import Point
from geom2d.vector import Vector
from geom2d.vectors import make_vector_between


class Line:
    --snip--

    def intersection_with(self, other):
        if self.is_parallel_to(other):
            return None

        d1, d2 = self.direction, other.direction
        cross_prod = d1.cross(d2)
        delta = make_vector_between(self.base, other.base)
        t1 = (delta.u * d2.v - delta.v * d2.u) / cross_prod

        return self.base.displaced(d1, t1)
```

Listing 5-25: Calculating the intersection between two lines

The code looks similar to the algorithm in Segment, but it's a bit simpler. To check for parallelism, we use the self method instead of using the directions. As we implemented is_parallel_to on the Line class, it makes sense to use it (and it helps the code read even better!).

Unit Testing Line Intersections

Let's make sure our tweaked algorithm works. Create a new file *line_test.py* and enter the test for the Line class in Listing 5-26.

```python
import unittest

from geom2d.line import Line
from geom2d.point import Point
from geom2d.vector import Vector


class TestLine(unittest.TestCase):

    def test_parallel_lines_no_intersection(self):
        l1 = Line(Point(0, 0), Vector(1, 1))
        l2 = Line(Point(10, 10), Vector(1, 1))
        self.assertIsNone(l1.intersection_with(l2))

    def test_lines_intersection(self):
        l1 = Line(Point(50, 0), Vector(0, 1))
        l2 = Line(Point(0, 30), Vector(1, 0))
        actual = l1.intersection_with(l2)
        expected = Point(50, 30)
        self.assertEqual(expected, actual)
```

Listing 5-26: Testing line intersections

In the first test, test_parallel_lines_no_intersection, we create two parallel lines with different base points but the same direction vectors. We then assert intersection_with returns None. The second test, test_lines_intersection, creates two lines, the first of which is vertical at $x = 50$ and the second horizontal at $y = 30$; hence, the intersection point is $(50, 30)$.

Run the tests by clicking the green play button beside the class definition. You should see this in the console:

```
Ran 2 tests in 0.001s

OK

Process finished with exit code 0
```

You can also run the tests from the console:

```
$ python3 -m unittest geom2d/line_test.py
```

Listing 5-27 contains all the code we wrote for the Line class.

```python
from geom2d.point import Point
from geom2d.vector import Vector
from geom2d.vectors import make_vector_between


class Line:
    def __init__(self, base: Point, direction: Vector):
        self.base = base
        self.direction = direction

    def is_parallel_to(self, other):
        return self.direction.is_parallel_to(other.direction)

    def is_perpendicular_to(self, other):
        return self.direction.is_perpendicular_to(other.direction)

    def perpendicular_through(self, point: Point):
        return Line(point, self.direction.perpendicular())

    def parallel_through(self, point: Point):
        return Line(point, self.direction)

    def intersection_with(self, other):
        if self.is_parallel_to(other):
            return None

        d1, d2 = self.direction, other.direction
        cross_prod = d1.cross(d2)
        delta = make_vector_between(self.base, other.base)
        t1 = (delta.u * d2.v - delta.v * d2.u) / cross_prod

        return self.base.displaced(d1, t1)
```

Listing 5-27: The Line class

Segment's Bisector

Now that we have both segments and lines, we can implement a new attribute in Segment: its *bisector*. This attribute is the line going through the segment's middle point *M* that's perpendicular to it. Figure 5-11 illustrates this concept.

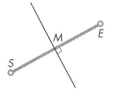

Figure 5-11: A segment's bisector

Computing a bisector line for a segment is simple since we already have access to the segment's middle point and normal versor (don't forget to import the Line class), as shown in Listing 5-28.

```
from geom2d import tparam
from geom2d.line import Line
from geom2d.point import Point
from geom2d.vectors import make_vector_between, make_versor_between


class Segment:
    --snip--

    @property
    def bisector(self):
        return Line(self.middle, self.normal_versor)
```

Listing 5-28: Segment's bisector

In the next chapter, we'll be using the bisectors of segments to create a circle passing through three points—a common way of obtaining circles in CAD software. In Part III of the book, we'll create a program that computes a circle passing through three points and draws a beautiful image with captions indicating its center and radius.

Summary

In this chapter, we used the Point and Vector classes to create two new primitives: Segment and Line. Both have a defined direction, and both represent a set of infinite aligned points, but segments are bounded between two points, whereas lines have no ends.

We also implemented a way of obtaining the infinite points in Segment using a parameter *t* that is defined in the range [0, 1]. There was no need to do the same for Line, as we're not usually interested in what points make it up.

We then created two algorithms: we included a method in the Segment class that looks for its closest point to an external point. Although we didn't implement it in Line, we could have done so. We used this method to compute the distance from a point to a segment. We also implemented an algorithm to compute intersections between two segments and two lines. These intersections result in a point or the value None returned. Lastly, we used the Line class to represent the bisector of a segment.

These linear primitives are going to prove invaluable for building more complex ones called polygons, the topic of our next chapter.

6

POLYGONS

Our next primitive, polygons, builds on points and segments. Polygons can be used to describe colliding geometries, portions of the screen that need redrawing, body boundaries, and much more. It turns out these primitives are extremely useful when it comes to processing images, as you can use them to figure out whether different parts of the image overlap. In dynamics simulations, they help determine when two bodies collide. In user interfaces for graphic-intensive applications, you can use simple polygons to easily figure out whether the user's mouse is over an entity that may be selected.

In this chapter, we'll be implementing three primitives: generic polygons, described by their vertices; circles, defined by a center point and a radius; and rectangles, defined by an origin point, a width, and a height. Because it may be more convenient in some applications to work only with generic polygons, both the circle and the rectangle will implement a method to convert themselves into a generic polygon. We'll also write a few other algorithms, including one that determines whether a polygon overlaps with another of its class and one that tests whether a polygon contains a given point.

Polygon Class

A *polygon* is a two-dimensional figure defined by a sequence of a minimum of three ordered and noncoincident vertices connected to form a closed *polygonal chain*. Each connection is a segment going from one vertex to the next one, where the last vertex is connected back to the first. Given vertices $[V_1, V_2, \ldots, V_n]$, each of the segments defined as $[(V_1 \rightarrow V_2), (V_2 \rightarrow V_3), \ldots, (V_n \rightarrow V_1)]$ is called a *side* (see Figure 6-1).

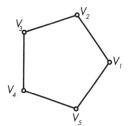

Figure 6-1: A polygon defined by its vertices

At this point, your *geom2d* package should look like this:

```
Mechanics
|- geom2d
|    |- __init__.py
|    |- line.py
|    |- line_test.py
|    |- nums.py
|    |- point.py
|    |- point_test.py
|    |- segment.py
|    |- segment_test.py
|    |- vector.py
|    |- vector_test.py
|    |- vectors.py
```

Let's create a class to represent polygons defined by their vertices as a sequence of points (instances of class Point). Create a new file inside the package *geom2d*, name it *polygon.py*, and enter the code from Listing 6-1.

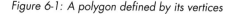

```
from geom2d.point import Point


class Polygon:
    def __init__(self, vertices: [Point]):
        if len(vertices) < 3:
            raise ValueError('Need 3 or more vertices')
```

```
self.vertices = vertices
```

Listing 6-1: Polygon initialization

First we import `Point` from `geom2d.point`. Then we define class `Polygon` with an initializer that accepts a sequence of points ordered according to the polygonal chain; connected vertices should be adjacent in the sequence. If the list contains fewer than three points, we raise an exception of type `ValueError`. Remember the fail fast strategy? We want to fail as soon as we detect something that doesn't make sense and may cause trouble, such as a polygon with fewer than three vertices.

NOTE   *According to Python's documentation, a `ValueError` should be raised when "an operation or function receives an argument that has the right type but an inappropriate value, and the situation is not described by a more precise exception."*

Sides

A *side* is a segment going from one vertex to the next in a polygon's sequence of vertices. The sides of a polygon together make up its *perimeter*. To close the polygonal chain, the last vertex needs to connect with the first. Generating the sides of a polygon thus requires pairing up a sequence of vertices. This sounds like a generic operation we could use for any sequence of objects, not just vertices, so we want to implement it in its own module.

For the sections that follow, you'll need a good understanding of Python's list comprehensions. You can refer to "List Comprehensions" on page 35 for a refresher.

Pairing Vertices

Given a list of items (of whatever type),

```
[A, B, C]
```

the pairing algorithm should create a new list where each item is a tuple of the original item at that position paired up with the next, including a pair of the last element with the first, as follows:

```
[(A, B), (B, C), (C, A)]
```

Let's write this code in a new package inside our Python project. Create a new package at the same level as *geom2d* and name it *utils*. In this package we'll keep small pieces of generic logic that are potentially reusable by the rest of our project modules. Your project's folder structure should look like the following:

```
Mechanics
|- geom2d
|   |- __init__.py
|   |- line.py
```

```
|   |   ...
|- utils
|   |- __init__.py
```

Many software projects end up having a *utils* package or module where all kinds of unrelated algorithms are bundled together. Although convenient, this practice is ultimately doomed and hinders the project's maintainability. A *utils* package is for pieces of code that aren't big enough to be promoted to their own package but are still reused by many other parts inside the project. When related code inside *utils* starts to grow, you're better off moving it to its own dedicated package. For example, if our pairing logic started to specialize, covering lots of different cases and types of collections, we would move it to a new package called *pairs*. That's not the case here, so we'll keep it simple.

In the package create a new file named *pairs.py* and include the function in Listing 6-2.

```
def make_round_pairs(sequence):
    length = len(sequence)
    return [
    ❶ (sequence[i], sequence[(i + 1) % length])
    ❷ for i in range(length)
    ]
```

Listing 6-2: Pairing up list elements

The function uses a *list comprehension* to create a new list from a range of values, starting from 0 and going all the way to length ❷. For each value it creates a tuple with two items ❶: the element at index i from the original list and the next one at i + 1. When we reach index i = length, i + 1 would be out of bounds in sequence, so we want to wrap around and go back to index 0 so that the last and first elements are also paired up. We do this with the modulo operator (%), which returns the remainder when you divide one number by another. The neat thing is that n % m returns n for every $n < m$, and it returns 0 for $n = m$.

To better understand modulo, try this in the shell:

```
>>> [n % 4 for n in range(5)]
[0, 1, 2, 3, 0]
```

See how for $n = 4$ the result is 0, but for all other values the result is n itself? Try to increase the range parameter:

```
>>> [n % 4 for n in range(7)]
[0, 1, 2, 3, 0, 1, 2]
```

Numbers in a modulo 4 operation never go beyond 3. Once that number is reached, the next one wraps around to 0 again.

If you want to know more about this "wrapping around" phenomenon resulting from the modulo operator, search for modular arithmetic. *It's widely used in modern cryptography and has some really interesting properties.*

We're now ready to implement the method that will generate the sides for our Polygon class.

Generating Sides

Once vertices are properly paired, writing the code to generate the sides is simple: we just need to create a Segment instance per pair of vertices. To compute them, first add the following imports in your file *polygon.py*:

```
from geom2d.segment import Segment
from utils.pairs import make_round_pairs
```

Then, enter the method in Listing 6-3.

```
from geom2d.point import Point
from geom2d.segment import Segment
from utils.pairs import make_round_pairs


class Polygon:
    --snip--

    def sides(self):
        vertex_pairs = make_round_pairs(self.vertices)
        return [
            Segment(pair[0], pair[1])
            for pair in vertex_pairs
        ]
```

Listing 6-3: Computing polygon sides

Using the make_round_pairs function, we pair vertices up such that each tuple in vertex_pairs contains the start and end points of a segment. Then, using a list comprehension, each of these tuples is mapped into a segment.

Testing Sides

Let's create a unit test for the sides attribute. Create a new file named *polygon_test.py* inside the package *geom2d* and enter the code for class TestPolygon (Listing 6-4).

```
import unittest

from geom2d.point import Point
from geom2d.polygon import Polygon
from geom2d.segment import Segment
```

```
class TestPolygon(unittest.TestCase):
    vertices = [
        Point(0, 0),
        Point(30, 0),
        Point(0, 30),
    ]
    polygon = Polygon(vertices)

    def test_sides(self):
        expected = [
            Segment(self.vertices[0], self.vertices[1]),
            Segment(self.vertices[1], self.vertices[2]),
            Segment(self.vertices[2], self.vertices[0])
        ]
        actual = self.polygon.sides()
        self.assertEqual(expected, actual)
```

Listing 6-4: Testing sides of a polygon

Inside the test class we create a list of vertices—$(0, 0)$, $(30, 0)$, and $(0, 30)$—that make a triangle. We use these points as vertices for the creation of the test subject: polygon. Figure 6-2 illustrates the polygon. To ensure the sides are properly computed, we construct the list of expected sides using the original vertices properly paired up.

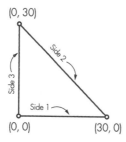

Figure 6-2: The polygon used in the test

Since we overloaded the == operator in the Segment class (by implementing the special method __eq__), the equality comparison will work as intended. If we hadn't done so, the equality assertion would consider segments different even if bounded by the same end points, and thus the test would fail.

Run the test using the following command to make sure it succeeds.

```
$ python3 -m unittest geom2d/polygon_test.py
```

If everything went well, you should get this output:

```
Ran 1 tests in 0.000s
```

```
OK
```

Centroid

A noteworthy point in a polygon is its *centroid*, the arithmetic mean of the position of all vertices. Assuming n is the number of vertices, the *centroid* can be expressed using Equation 6.1.

$$G = \frac{1}{n}\left(\begin{array}{c} \sum\limits_{i=1}^{n} x_i \\ \sum\limits_{i=1}^{n} y_i \end{array} \right) \tag{6.1}$$

Here, x_i and y_i are the coordinates of vertex i.

Implementing the Centroid

Let's implement the centroid property. To do so, we first need to import the following at the top of our Polygon class:

```
import operator
from functools import reduce
```

Once imported, add the code in Listing 6-5 beneath the sides method.

```
import operator
from functools import reduce

from geom2d.point import Point
from geom2d.segment import Segment
from utils.pairs import make_round_pairs


class Polygon:
    --snip--

    @property
    def centroid(self):
 ❶     vtx_count = len(self.vertices)
 ❷     vtx_sum = reduce(operator.add, self.vertices)
 ❸     return Point(
            vtx_sum.x / vtx_count,
            vtx_sum.y / vtx_count
        )
```

Listing 6-5: Calculating a centroid of a polygon

We first store the length of the list of vertices in the variable vtx_count ❶. Then, we reduce the list of vertices by summing them into a resulting point called vtx_sum ❷. You may want to read "Filter, Map, and Reduce" on page 29 to review the reduce function and how we use operator. Note that the operator operator.add works for the reduce function because our Point class overloads the + operator.

The last thing we do is construct the resulting point by dividing each of the projections of vtx_sum by vtx_count ❸.

Testing the Centroid

Let's write a unit test to make sure the centroid is properly computed. In your file *polygon_test.py* enter the code in Listing 6-6.

```
class TestPolygon(unittest.TestCase):
    --snip--

    def test_centroid(self):
        expected = Point(10, 10)
        actual = self.polygon.centroid
        self.assertEqual(expected, actual)
```

Listing 6-6: Testing the centroid center of a polygon

Using Equation 6.1, we can calculate the centroid by hand to see where the projections in (10, 10) come from. Knowing that the vertices of our polygon test subject are $(0, 0)$, $(30, 0)$, and $(0, 30)$, we have this:

$$G = \frac{1}{3} \begin{pmatrix} 0 + 30 + 0 \\ 0 + 0 + 30 \end{pmatrix} = \begin{pmatrix} 10 \\ 10 \end{pmatrix}$$

You can inspect this visually in Figure 6-3.

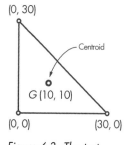

Figure 6-3: The test polygon's centroid

Run all tests in file *polygon_test.py* to make sure everything is working as expected. To run them from the shell, you can use the following:

```
$ python3 -m unittest geom2d/polygon_test.py
```

If both tests pass, you should get the following output:

```
Ran 2 tests in 0.000s
```

```
OK
```

Let's try one thing before moving on. Remember that to compute the centroid we reduced the list of vertices like so,

```
vtx_sum = reduce(operator.add, self.vertices)
```

We said that this reduction using the operator.add works because our Point class overloads the + operator? Let's see what would have happened if we hadn't overloaded this operator. Open *point.py* and comment out the __add__ method:

```
class Point:
    --snip--

    # def __add__(self, other):
    #     return Point(
    #         self.x + other.x,
    #         self.y + other.y
    #     )
```

Run the tests again. This time you'll see an error in the shell:

```
========================================================
ERROR: test_centroid (geom2d.polygon_test.TestPolygon)
--------------------------------------------------------
Traceback (most recent call last):
  --snip--
    vtx_sum = reduce(operator.add, self.vertices)
TypeError: unsupported operand type(s) for +: 'Point' and 'Point'


--------------------------------------------------------
Ran 2 tests in 0.020s
```

The TypeError with its message (unsupported operand type(s)...) is very descriptive about what the error is. Two Point instances cannot be added if they don't implement the __add__ method. Uncomment the __add__ method we commented for the experiment and rerun the tests just to make sure it's all back to how it was.

Contains Point

Now comes an interesting problem: How do we determine whether a given point is inside a polygon? A widely used procedure is the *ray casting algorithm*, which counts how many sides of the polygon are intersected by a ray going through the point in any direction. An even number of intersections (including zero) means the point is outside of the polygon, whereas an odd number means the point is inside. Take a look at Figure 6-4.

The drawing on the left depicts a complex polygon and a point *P* outside of it. Every ray cast from that point in any direction intersects zero or an even number of sides. The case on the right depicts the point P inside the polygon. This time, the ray always intersects an odd number of sides.

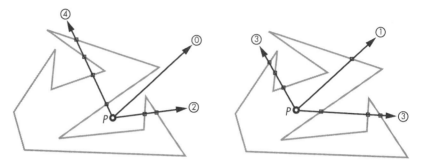

Figure 6-4: The ray casting algorithm

Another commonly used algorithm, and the one we'll be using, is the *winding number algorithm*. This algorithm works by summing angles between vectors that go from the point under test to the vertices of the polygon. This is how it works. To know whether a point P is inside a polygon with vertices $V_1, V_2, \ldots, V_n$, our algorithm looks like this:

1. Create a vector going from P to each of the vertices:
   $\vec{r}_1 = \overline{PV_1}$: Vector from P to vertex V_1
   $\vec{r}_2 = \overline{PV_2}$: Vector from P to vertex V_2
   ...
   $\vec{r}_n = \overline{PV_n}$: Vector from P to vertex V_n

2. Compute the angle from each vector $\vec{r}_i$ to the next $\vec{r}_{i+1}$, wrapping around and computing the angle between the last vector and the first:
   $\alpha|_{r_1 \to r_2}$: Angle from $\vec{r}_1$ to $\vec{r}_2$
   $\alpha|_{r_2 \to r_3}$: Angle from $\vec{r}_2$ to $\vec{r}_3$
   ...
   $\alpha|_{r_n \to r_1}$: Angle from $\vec{r}_n$ to $\vec{r}_1$

3. Sum all angles computed in the previous step.

4. The point P is inside the polygon if the angle is 2π, outside if 0.

Take a look at Figure 6-5 to better understand how this algorithm works. It's easy to see how the sum of angles is 2π in the case where the point is inside the polygon.

Although we could just as well implement the *ray casting algorithm*, I chose the *winding number algorithm* because it makes good use of three key functions we've created in this book: the make_vector_between factory function, make_round_pairs, and the angle_to method from the Vector class. Let's implement it.

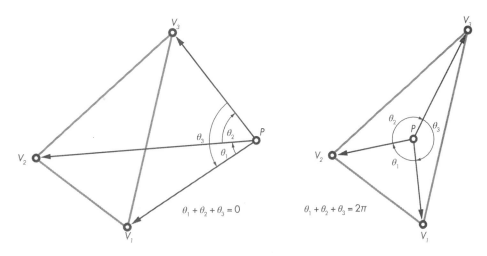

Figure 6-5: Testing whether a polygon contains a point

Implementing the Winding Number Algorithm

There are a few modules we need to import. Your imports at the top of file *polygon.py* should look like this:

```
import math
import operator
from functools import reduce

from geom2d.nums import are_close_enough
from geom2d.point import Point
from geom2d.vectors import make_vector_between
from geom2d.segment import Segment
from utils.pairs import make_round_pairs
```

Once you've imported everything, enter the code in Listing 6-7 as a new method for the Polygon class.

```
import math
import operator
from functools import reduce

from geom2d.nums import are_close_enough
from geom2d.point import Point
from geom2d.vectors import make_vector_between
from geom2d.segment import Segment
from utils.pairs import make_round_pairs

class Polygon:
    --snip--

    def contains_point(self, point: Point):
    ❶ vecs = [make_vector_between(point, vertex)
```

```
            for vertex in self.vertices]
❷   paired_vecs = make_round_pairs(vecs)
❸   angle_sum = reduce(
        operator.add,
❹     [v1.angle_to(v2) for v1, v2 in paired_vecs]
    )

❺   return are_close_enough(angle_sum, 2 * math.pi)
```

Listing 6-7: Polygon contains_point algorithm

We first compute the list of $\vec{r}$ vectors ❶ using a list comprehension, which maps each of the vertices of the polygon into a vector going from point to the vertex. Then, using make_round_pairs, we pair the vectors and store the result in paired_vecs ❷.

We map paired vectors to the angle each pair forms using another list comprehension ❹. We reduce the resulting list by adding together each of the computed angles ❸, and finally, we check whether the computed angle sum (angle_sum) is close enough to 2π ❺, in which case the point is inside the polygon. We'll consider any other value of the angle to mean the point is outside the polygon.

Testing contains_point

Let's make sure this algorithm works by adding two unit tests in file *polygon_test.py* (see Listing 6-8).

```
class TestPolygon(unittest.TestCase):
    --snip--

    def test_doesnt_contain_point(self):
        point = Point(15, 20)
        self.assertFalse(self.polygon.contains_point(point))

    def test_contains_point(self):
        point = Point(15, 10)
        self.assertTrue(self.polygon.contains_point(point))
```

Listing 6-8: Testing whether the polygon contains point

You can run the tests using the green play button in the IDE or from the shell:

```
$ python3 -m unittest geom2d/polygon_test.py
```

In the first test, we take a point we know is outside the triangular polygon and assert that it's actually outside. The second test asserts the point (15, 10) is inside the triangle.

Testing an Edge Case

Let's try one more test, just to see what happens. What about vertices of the polygon? Are they considered to be inside or outside the polygon? This is what we know as an *edge case*, a situation that requires special treatment in our code.

Enter the innocent-looking test in Listing 6-9 and run all the tests in file *rect_test.py*.

```
class TestPolygon(unittest.TestCase):
    --snip--

    def test_contains_vertex(self):
        self.assertTrue(
            self.polygon.contains_point(self.vertices[0])
        )
```

Listing 6-9: Proposed test of whether a polygon contains one of its vertices

The output from running the test is as follows:

```
Error
Traceback (most recent call last):
  --snip--
  File ".../geom2d/polygon.py", line 36, in <listcomp>
    [v1.angle_to(v2) for v1, v2 in paired_vecs]
  File ".../geom2d/vector.py", line 69, in angle_to
    value = self.angle_value_to(other)
  File ".../geom2d/vector.py", line 66, in angle_value_to
    return math.acos(dot_product / norm_product)
ZeroDivisionError: float division by zero
```

Oops! We must have done something wrong. Can you guess what by reading the traceback? Starting from the last line we find the originator: `ZeroDivisionError`. Apparently we attempted to divide by zero in method `angle_value_to`. To be specific, we did so in this line:

```
return math.acos(dot_product / norm_product)
```

This means `norm_product` was zero; hence, the norm of at least one of the vectors used to compute the angle had a length of 0. Going a bit up in the traceback we find the line where the angle method was being used before the error happened:

```
[v1.angle_to(v2) for v1, v2 in paired_vecs]
```

So, it appears that when we attempted to compute the angle between two of the vectors, one of them had a length of 0. The vector going from point P, this time a vertex of the polygon, to itself is obviously a zero vector.

To handle this particular edge case, we can consider vertices to be inside the polygon as a convention. At the beginning of method `contains_point`, let's check whether the point passed as an argument is a vertex of the polygon, in which case we simply return `True`. Modify the method to accommodate this new condition (Listing 6-10).

```
class Polygon:
    --snip--

    def contains_point(self, point: Point):
        if point in self.vertices:
            return True

        vecs = [make_vector_between(point, vertex)
                for vertex in self.vertices]
        paired_vecs = make_round_pairs(vecs)
        angle_sum = reduce(
            operator.add,
            [v1.angle_to(v2) for v1, v2 in paired_vecs]
        )

        return are_close_enough(angle_sum, 2 * math.pi)
```

Listing 6-10: Corrected algorithm to check whether a point is inside a polygon

As you see, dealing with edge cases requires individualized pieces of code. Run all the tests to make sure they all succeed now:

```
$ python3 -m unittest geom2d/polygon_test.py
```

The output this time should be as follows:

```
Ran 5 tests in 0.001s
```

```
OK
```

Polygon Factory

In practice, we commonly need to construct polygons from a list of numbers representing the coordinates of its vertices. This is done, for example, when reading a polygon from a text file, which we'll see in Chapter 12. To do this, we first need to pair up the numbers and map them into instances of `Point`.

For instance, the list

```
[0, 0, 50, 0, 0, 50]
```

could be used to define the three vertices of a triangle:

```
[(0, 0), (50, 0), (0, 50)]
```

Let's implement a factory function to create polygons given a sequence of floating-point numbers. Create a new file named *polygons.py*. Our project's structure currently looks like this:

```
Mechanics
|- geom2d
|    |- __init__.py
|    |- line.py
|    |- line_test.py
|    |- nums.py
|    |- point.py
|    |- point_test.py
|    |- polygon.py
|    |- polygon_test.py
|    |- polygons.py
|    |- segment.py
|    |- segment_test.py
|    |- vector.py
|    |- vector_test.py
|    |- vectors.py
|- utils
|    |- __init__.py
|    |- pairs.py
```

Inside the new file, enter the code in Listing 6-11.

```python
from geom2d import Point, Polygon


def make_polygon_from_coords(coords: [float]):
    if len(coords) % 2 != 0:
        raise ValueError('Need an even number of coordinates')

    indices = range(0, len(coords), 2)
    return Polygon(
        [Point(coords[i], coords[i + 1]) for i in indices]
    )
```

Listing 6-11: Polygon factory function

The function make_polygon_from_coords takes in a list of coordinates and first checks that there are an even number of them (otherwise, they can't be paired up). If the length of the list of coordinates is divisible by 2 with a remainder of 0, we have an even number of coordinates.

If the number of coordinates is found to be uneven, we raise a ValueError. If not, we then construct a list of the indices at which we'll find the x-coordinate of the vertices in the coords list. We achieve this with a range going from 0 to len(coords) (noninclusive) with a step of 2.

To better understand how we're doing this, try the following in Python's shell:

```
>>> list(range(0, 10, 2))
[0, 2, 4, 6, 8]
```

With these indices we can easily obtain a list of vertices using a list comprehension. Recall that Python's range function returns a half-open interval that doesn't include the upper bound, which is why we didn't get the number 10 in the resulting list. The list comprehension maps each index to an instance of Point class. We create the polygon passing this list to its constructor. As you can see from the code, the x-coordinate is the number from the input list at each index i, whereas the y-coordinate is the number to the right of it, that is, i + 1.

With that out of the way, let's take a look at how to compare polygons for equality.

Polygon Equality

To make sure we can check whether polygons are equal, let's implement the _eq_ method inside the Polygon class (see Listing 6-12).

```
class Polygon:
    --snip--

    def __eq__(self, other):
        if self is other:
            return True

        if not isinstance(other, Polygon):
            return False

        return self.vertices == other.vertices
```

Listing 6-12: Polygon equality

We first check whether the passed-in other is the same instance as self, in which case we return True. Second, if other is not an instance of Polygon, there's not much we can compare; we already know the equality is impossible.

Since Point already implements the _eq_ method, we just need to compare the list of vertices from both polygons if the two previous checks haven't returned anything yet. Python will check whether both lists contain the same vertices in the same order. Lists are ordered collections; thus, ordering is important when checking for equality. Try the following experiment in the shell:

```
>>> l1 = [1, 2, 3]
>>> l2 = [3, 2, 1]
>>> l3 = [3, 2, 1]
```

```
>>> l1 == l2
False

>>> l2 == l3
true
```

Even though l1 and l2 contain the same numbers, they are considered different by Python as they appear in a different order (don't forget that order matters for lists and tuples). By contrast, l2 and l3 do contain the numbers in the same order and hence are considered equal. Polygons are made of an ordered collection of vertices: different orderings of the same set of vertices would result in unequal polygons. This is the reason why we used a list, which is a collection where the order is a key factor.

If you followed along, your *polygon.py* file should look like Listing 6-13.

```python
import math
import operator
from functools import reduce

from geom2d.nums import are_close_enough
from geom2d.point import Point
from geom2d.vectors import make_vector_between
from geom2d.segment import Segment
from utils.pairs import make_round_pairs


class Polygon:
    def __init__(self, vertices: [Point]):
        if len(vertices) < 3:
            raise ValueError('Need 3 or more vertices')
        self.vertices = vertices

    def sides(self):
        vertex_pairs = make_round_pairs(self.vertices)
        return [Segment(pair[0], pair[1]) for pair in vertex_pairs]

    @property
    def centroid(self):
        vtx_count = len(self.vertices)
        vtx_sum = reduce(operator.add, self.vertices)
        return Point(
            vtx_sum.x / vtx_count,
            vtx_sum.y / vtx_count
        )

    def contains_point(self, point: Point):
        if point in self.vertices:
            return True
```

```
    vecs = [make_vector_between(point, vertex)
            for vertex in self.vertices]
    paired_vecs = make_round_pairs(vecs)
    angle_sum = reduce(
        operator.add,
        [v1.angle_to(v2) for v1, v2 in paired_vecs]
    )

    return are_close_enough(angle_sum, 2 * math.pi)

def __eq__(self, other):
    if self is other:
        return True

    if not isinstance(other, Polygon):
        return False

    return self.vertices == other.vertices
```

Listing 6-13: Polygon class

Now let's take a look at circles.

Circle Class

A *circle* is the set of all points in the plane a given distance (the *radius*) from a single point called the *center*. A circle is therefore defined by the position of its center C and the value of its radius r (see Figure 6-6).

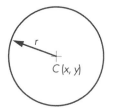

Figure 6-6: A circle defined by a center point C and radius r

As you may remember from high school, the area of a circle is calculated as follows:

$$A = \pi \cdot r^2$$

And a circle's circumference is calculated as follows:

$$l_c = 2\pi \cdot r$$

Create a new file named *circle.py* in the package *geom2d*. In the file, enter the code in Listing 6-14.

```
import math

from geom2d.point import Point


class Circle:
    def __init__(self, center: Point, radius: float):
        self.center = center
        self.radius = radius

    @property
    def area(self):
        return math.pi * self.radius ** 2

    @property
    def circumference(self):
        return 2 * math.pi * self.radius
```

Listing 6-14: Circle class initialization

Great! We now have a class to represent circles with the properties center and radius. We've also defined properties named area and circumference.

NOTE   *To keep the length of the chapter reasonable, we won't include any more unit testing sections. The accompanying code does include unit tests, and I encourage you to come up with them yourself.*

Contains Point

Testing whether a point *P* was inside a generic polygon required a few steps, but in the case of a circle, the logic is extremely simple. We compute the distance from the center *C* to point *P*: $d(C, P)$. If this distance is smaller than the radius, $d(C, P) < r$, the point is inside the circle. For values of $d(C, P)$ greater than *r*, the point is farther from the center than the radius and thus outside the circle. Inside Circle, enter the code in Listing 6-15.

```
class Circle:
    --snip--

    def contains_point(self, point: Point):
        return point.distance_to(self.center) < self.radius
```

Listing 6-15: Checking whether a circle contains a point

Can you come up with test cases to ensure method contains_point is bug free?

Circle to Polygon

In Chapter 7 we'll be transforming a polygon's geometry by rotating, scaling, and skewing it. After such transformations, circles may not be circles anymore, and the mathematical representation for the result can become complex.

Because accounting for all possible shapes using a specific geometry class would be arduous, and because our generic polygons work the same no matter their shape, why not try approximating the circle using a polygon with enough sides?

To convert a circle to a polygon, a number of divisions have to be chosen, say n. The entire 2π angle is divided into n subangles $\theta = 2\pi/n$. Starting at angle 0 and incrementing it by θ each time, we can compute n points in the circumference, which will then become the vertices of a polygon inscribed in the circle. We can compute a vertex V at a given angle α using Equation 6.2,

$$V(\alpha) = \begin{pmatrix} C_x \\ C_y \end{pmatrix} + r \cdot \begin{pmatrix} \cos \alpha \\ \sin \alpha \end{pmatrix} \tag{6.2}$$

where C is the center of the circle and r is the radius. Figure 6-7 shows the result of choosing $n = 8$, which converts the circle into an octagon with vertices $V_1, V_2, \ldots, V_8$.

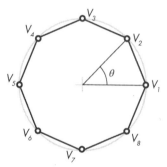

Figure 6-7: Converting a circle
to a polygon

Also note how for small numbers of n the resulting polygon poorly approximates the circle. In Figure 6-8, for example, n was chosen to be 3, 4, and 5, respectively. As you can see, the inscribed polygons only look remotely like the circles they approximate. We'll typically choose n values ranging from 30 to 200 to yield an acceptable result.

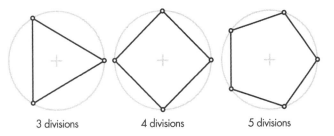

3 divisions   4 divisions   5 divisions

Figure 6-8: Number of divisions when converting a circle to a polygon

Inside `Circle`, implement to_polygon as in Listing 6-16.

```python
import math

from geom2d.point import Point
from geom2d.polygon import Polygon


class Circle:
    --snip--

    def to_polygon(self, divisions: int):
    ❶  angle_delta = 2 * math.pi / divisions
        return Polygon(
        ❷  [self.__point_at_angle(angle_delta * i)
            for i in range(divisions)]
        )

    def __point_at_angle(self, angle: float):
    ❸  return Point(
            self.center.x + self.radius * math.cos(angle),
            self.center.y + self.radius * math.sin(angle)
        )
```

Listing 6-16: Creating a polygon from a circle

This time we divided the algorithm in two: the main logic handled by to_polygon and a private method __point_at_angle, which, given an angle, returns the point in the circumference at that angle ❸. Such a point is computed according to Equation 6.2.

The to_polygon method first computes the angle delta (or angle increment) for the given number of divisions ❶. Then, using a list comprehension, it maps each integer number in the range $[0, n)$ to a point in the circumference at incremental angles ❷. This list of points is passed as the vertices for the initialization of a polygon. Note how we convert the range $[0, n)$ into an angle by multiplying the current number in the range by the angle increment.

Equality and String Representation

Let's implement equality comparison and string representation methods in our Circle class. Enter the code in Listing 6-17.

```
import math

from geom2d.nums import are_close_enough
from geom2d.point import Point
from geom2d.polygon import Polygon


class Circle:
    --snip--

    def __eq__(self, other):
        if self is other:
            return True

        if not isinstance(other, Circle):
            return False

        return self.center == other.center \
                and are_close_enough(self.radius, other.radius)

    def __str__(self):
        return f'circle c = {self.center}, r = {self.radius}'
```

Listing 6-17: Circle equality and string representation

If you followed along, your *circle.py* file should look like Listing 6-18.

```
import math

from geom2d.nums import are_close_enough
from geom2d.point import Point
from geom2d.polygon import Polygon


class Circle:
    def __init__(self, center: Point, radius: float):
        self.center = center
        self.radius = radius

    @property
    def area(self):
        return math.pi * self.radius ** 2

    @property
    def circumference(self):
```

```
        return 2 * math.pi * self.radius

    def contains_point(self, point: Point):
        return point.distance_to(self.center) < self.radius

    def to_polygon(self, divisions: int):
        angle_delta = 2 * math.pi / divisions
        return Polygon(
            [self.__point_at_angle(angle_delta * i)
             for i in range(divisions)]
        )

    def __point_at_angle(self, angle: float):
        return Point(
            self.center.x + self.radius * math.cos(angle),
            self.center.y + self.radius * math.sin(angle)
        )

    def __eq__(self, other):
        if self is other:
            return True

        if not isinstance(other, Circle):
            return False

        return self.center == other.center \
            and are_close_enough(self.radius, other.radius)

    def __str__(self):
        return f'circle c = {self.center}, r = {self.radius}'
```

Listing 6-18: The Circle class

Circle Factories

We'll typically construct circles from a center point and a radius, but there are a few more ways we can construct them. In this section, we'll look at one such case: generating a circle out of three points. We'll do this mostly for fun, but it also gives a sense of how powerful the geometrical primitives we're building are.

So, say we're given three non-collinear points, namely, A, B, and C. As you can see in Figure 6-9, you can find a circle such that it passes through all three points.

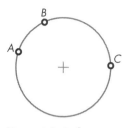

Figure 6-9: Defining a
circle with three points

To solve the problem, we need to find the center and radius, but the latter is straightforward since if we know where the center is, the distance of any of the three points to it yields the radius. So, the problem boils down to finding the center of a circle passing through the given points. Here's one way we can find it:

1. Compute the segment going from A to B; let's call it *seg*₁.
2. Compute the segment going from B to C; let's call it *seg*₂.
3. Find the intersection between bisectors of *seg*₁ and *seg*₂.

The intersection point O is the center of the circle (see Figure 6-10). And, as previously stated, finding the radius of the circle is as simple as measuring the distance between O and A, B, or C.

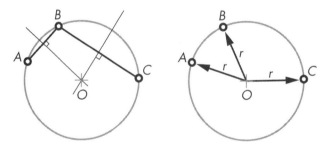

Figure 6-10: The center and radius of a circle defined by
three points

We're ready to implement the logic. Create a new file in the *geom2d* package and name it *circles.py*. In the file, enter the code in Listing 6-19.

```
from geom2d import Point
from geom2d.circle import Circle
from geom2d.segment import Segment


def make_circle_from_points(a: Point, b: Point, c: Point):
    chord_one_bisec = Segment(a, b).bisector
    chord_two_bisec = Segment(b, c).bisector
    center = chord_one_bisec.intersection_with(chord_two_bisec)
    radius = center.distance_to(a)
```

```
    return Circle(center, radius)
```

Listing 6-19: Circle from three points

NOTE *Recall that the chord of a circle is a segment whose endpoints lie on the circumference and cut across the circle.*

If you were asked to simplify the function, could you? Each line tells you exactly what it's doing; you can read the lines one by one and match them with the description of the algorithm. Self-explanatory code that clearly states its intent is commonly referred to as *clean code*, which is such a celebrated concept in the software industry that there are several books devoted to the topic. Two of my all-time favorites include [6] and [1], which I recommend you also read if you want to write truly readable code.

Rect Class

The last geometric primitive we'll implement in this chapter is a rectangle, but it's not any sort of rectangle—it's the kind whose sides are always horizontal and vertical. Rotated rectangles can be represented using the Polygon primitive from earlier in the chapter. The reason behind this seemingly restrictive rule has to do with what this primitive is typically used for.

Rectangles like this are often used in two-dimensional graphic applications for things like the following:

- Representing a portion of the screen that needs to be redrawn
- Determining the position on the screen where something needs to be drawn
- Determining the size of the geometry that has to be drawn
- Testing whether two objects are likely to collide
- Testing whether the mouse cursor is over a region of the screen

A *rectangle* can be defined by a point (called the *origin*) and a size, which in turn has two properties: width and height (see Figure 6-11). By convention, the origin point will be located at the bottom-left corner of the rectangle, assuming a coordinate system with an y-axis that points upward.

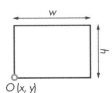

Figure 6-11: A rectangle defined by an origin point O, width w, and height h

Let's start with a class to represent sizes. Inside package *geom2d*, create a new file named *size.py* including the definition in Listing 6-20.

```python
from geom2d.nums import are_close_enough


class Size:
    def __init__(self, width: float, height: float):
        self.width = width
        self.height = height

    def __eq__(self, other):
        if self is other:
            return True

        if not isinstance(other, Size):
            return False

        return are_close_enough(self.width, other.width) \
            and are_close_enough(self.height, other.height)
```

Listing 6-20: The Size class

Using this representation of a size, let's create the initial definition of Rect. Create a new file named *rect.py* and enter the code in Listing 6-21.

```python
from geom2d.point import Point
from geom2d.size import Size


class Rect:
    def __init__(self, origin: Point, size: Size):
        self.origin = origin
        self.size = size

    @property
    def left(self):
        return self.origin.x

    @property
    def right(self):
        return self.origin.x + self.size.width

    @property
    def bottom(self):
        return self.origin.y

    @property
    def top(self):
```

```
        return self.origin.y + self.size.height

    @property
    def area(self):
        return self.size.width * self.size.height

    @property
    def perimeter(self):
        return 2 * self.size.width + 2 * self.size.height
```

Listing 6-21: The Rect class

The class stores a `Point` instance for the origin point and a `Size` instance encoding its width and length. We defined some interesting properties in the class, namely:

left   The x-coordinate of the left-most side of the rectangle

right   The x-coordinate of the right-most side of the rectangle

bottom   The y-coordinate of the bottom-most side of the rectangle

top   The y-coordinate of the top-most side of the rectangle

area   The area of the rectangle

perimeter   The perimeter of the rectangle

Let's create one of our rectangles in the shell:

```
>>> from geom2d.point import Point
>>> from geom2d.size import Size
>>> from geom2d.rect import Rect

>>> origin = Point(10, 20)
>>> size = Size(100, 150)
>>> rect = Rect(origin, size)
```

And let's inspect some of its properties:

```
>>> rect.right
110

>>> rect.area
15000

>>> rect.perimeter
500
```

Contains Point

The next logical step is implementing a method to test whether a point is inside the rectangle. To test whether a point *P* lies inside a rectangle, we'll use the following two conditions:

$$\begin{cases} \text{left} < P_x < \text{right} \\ \text{bottom} < P_y < \text{top} \end{cases}$$

Thanks to the attributes we added to the class, this is a piece of cake (see Listing 6-22).

```
class Rect:
    --snip--

    def contains_point(self, point: Point):
        return self.left < point.x < self.right \
                and self.bottom < point.y < self.top
```

Listing 6-22: Testing whether a rectangle contains a point

Notice Python's beautiful syntax for compound inequalities,

```
left < point.x < right
```

which in most other languages would have to be expressed as two different conditions:

```
left < point.x && point.x < right
```

Intersections

Suppose we have two rectangles and we want to know if they overlap. Since Rect represents rectangles with sides that are always horizontal and vertical, the problem simplifies a lot. Testing whether two Rects overlap is the same as testing whether their projections in both the x- and y-axes overlap. By *projections*, we mean the shadows they cast on the axis lines. Each shadow is an interval starting in the position of the value of the rectangle's origin, with a length that's either its width or its height (see Figure 6-12).

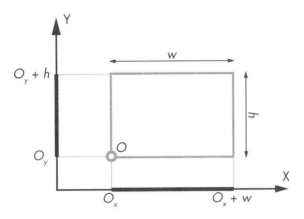

Figure 6-12: Projections of a rectangle

For example, the shadow in the horizontal axis of Figure 6-12 can be represented as the following interval,

$$(O_x, O_x + w)$$

where O is the origin point and w is the width of the rectangle. Similarly, the vertical shadow or projection would be:

$$(O_y, O_y + h)$$

where h is the height this time. Note that the result of $O_x + w$ is exactly the right property as we've defined it in our Rect class, and $O_y + h$ is top.

Figure 6-13 depicts two rectangles whose vertical projections overlap but whose horizontal projections don't. Thus, the rectangles don't overlap.

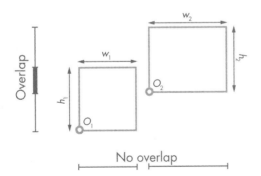

Figure 6-13: Two nonintersecting rectangles

Figure 6-14, on the other hand, depicts two rectangles with vertical and horizontal projections that overlap. As you can see, this layout does generate an overlapping region, shaded in gray. We can observe that overlapping rectangles always result in rectangular overlapping regions.

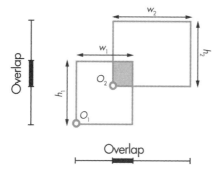

Figure 6-14: Two intersecting rectangles

Using the nomenclature from the previous figures, we can numerically define the condition using *open intervals*, intervals where the end points are excluded. Two rectangles overlap if

$$\begin{cases} (\underbrace{O_{1x}}_{\text{left}}, \underbrace{O_{1x}+w_1}_{\text{right}}) \cap (\underbrace{O_{2x}}_{\text{left}}, \underbrace{O_{2x}+w_2}_{\text{right}}) \\ (\underbrace{O_{1y}}_{\text{bottom}}, \underbrace{O_{1y}+h_1}_{\text{top}}) \cap (\underbrace{O_{2y}}_{\text{bottom}}, \underbrace{O_{2y}+h_2}_{\text{top}}) \end{cases}$$

where $\cap$ is the intersection binary operator.

Open Intervals

Now that we've reduced the problem to computing the intersection between intervals, let's create a new class OpenInterval to implement this logic. Note that writing the implementation of the algorithm to find the intersection between two intervals inside the Rect class would be conceptually wrong. Each class must only contain logic related to its domain of knowledge, and it seems obvious that interval intersection is not specifically about rectangles. A rectangle should know nothing about how the intersection of two intervals is performed; it's not part of its domain of knowledge. If it needs to compute one, like in our case, it should delegate it to the subject's expert: OpenRange.

If you respect this simple guideline, your code will be much easier to reason about and extend. Every piece of knowledge in your code should live exactly where it's supposed to, and only there. One of the worst enemies of software is *knowledge duplication*, a phenomenon where one piece of knowledge (call it an algorithm if you prefer) is written in more than one place. When the core of such logic needs to change, you need to remember to change it everywhere. Trust me when I say this problem is much worse than it sounds.

NOTE   *Most authors use the phrase duplication of code, but I prefer to call it duplication of knowledge. The choice of words is intentional as I've noticed some developers tend to misinterpret the concept, probably because the word code is quite generic. It's the knowledge expressed by the code that should not be duplicated.*

Create a new file named *open_interval.py* in *geom2d*, and inside, define the OpenInterval class as in Listing 6-23.

```
class OpenInterval:
    def __init__(self, start: float, end: float):
        if start > end:
            raise ValueError('start should be smaller than end')
        self.start = start
        self.end = end

    @property
    def length(self):
    ❶ return self.end - self.start

    def contains(self, value):
    ❷ return self.start < value < self.end
```

Listing 6-23: The OpenInterval class

An OpenInterval is created with start and end properties. We make sure that start is smaller than end; otherwise, we raise a ValueError exception. Recall our failing fast convention; we don't want an ill-constructed interval lying around. Next, we define the length of the interval as a property ❶ and a method to test whether a given value is inside the range ❷.

Let's now include two more methods: one for checking whether intervals overlap and another one for actually computing the resulting overlap (see Listing 6-24).

```
from geom2d.nums import are_close_enough


class OpenInterval:
    --snip--

    def overlaps_interval(self, other):
    ❶ if are_close_enough(self.start, other.start) and \
            are_close_enough(self.end, other.end):
        return True

    ❷ return self.contains(other.start) \
            or self.contains(other.end) \
            or other.contains(self.start) \
            or other.contains(self.end)

    def compute_overlap_with(self, other):
    ❸ if not self.overlaps_interval(other):
        return None

    ❹ return OpenInterval(
```

```
            max(self.start, other.start),
            min(self.end, other.end)
        )
```

Listing 6-24: Open interval overlapping

The first method, overlaps_interval, returns a boolean that will be True if the interval overlaps with other passed as an argument. To do this, we first check whether the two intervals have the same start and end values ❶, in which case we return True. Then we check whether any of the four ends is contained in the other interval ❷. If you're confused by this piece of logic, take a pen and some paper and draw every possible combination of two overlapping intervals (I've done this for you in Figure 6-15, excluding the case where the two intervals have the same start and end values).

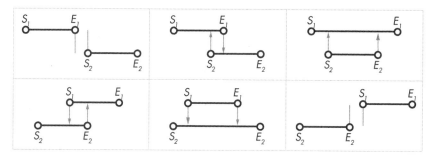

Figure 6-15: The possible cases for interval positions

The second method, compute_overlap_with, starts by making sure there's actually an overlap, returning None if there isn't ❸. The overlap is simply a new interval where the start is the maximum between both start values, and the end is the minimum between the two end values ❹.

I encourage you to write unit tests for this overlapping logic. It's a wonderful opportunity to develop your testing skills. There are a bunch of combinations of overlapping intervals; try to cover them all.

Computing Intersections

With the help of OpenInterval, rectangle intersections become simple to solve. Go back to *rect.py* and import the OpenInterval class:

```
from geom2d.open_interval import OpenInterval
```

Now, underneath the contains_point method, enter the code from Listing 6-25.

```
from geom2d.open_interval import OpenInterval
from geom2d.point import Point
from geom2d.size import Size


class Rect:
```

```
--snip--

    def intersection_with(self, other):
❶    h_overlap = self.__horizontal_overlap_with(other)
        if h_overlap is None:
            return None

❷    v_overlap = self.__vertical_overlap_with(other)
        if v_overlap is None:
            return None

❸    return Rect(
            Point(h_overlap.start, v_overlap.start),
            Size(h_overlap.length, v_overlap.length)
        )
```

Listing 6-25: Intersection between two rectangles

There are two private helper methods that compute both the horizontal and vertical overlaps; we'll take a look at those in a moment. The method first computes the horizontal overlap between self and other ❶. If it finds it to be None, there's no horizontal overlap; therefore, the rectangles don't intersect. None is returned. The same procedure goes for the vertical overlap ❷. Only if both are not None, which means we found both horizontal and vertical projections overlapping, will we reach the last return where the resulting rectangle is computed ❸. How do we go about finding the origin and size of such a rectangle? It's easy: the origin coordinates are the start values from both horizontal and vertical overlap intervals, the width is the length of the horizontal overlap, and the height is the length of the vertical overlap.

So, the only missing part is the implementation of the private methods that finds the horizontal and vertical interval overlaps, if they exist. The code for that is in Listing 6-26.

```
class Rect:
    --snip--

    def __horizontal_overlap_with(self, other):
        self_interval = OpenInterval(self.left, self.right)
        other_interval = OpenInterval(other.left, other.right)

        return self_interval.compute_overlap_with(other_interval)

    def __vertical_overlap_with(self, other):
        self_interval = OpenInterval(self.bottom, self.top)
        other_interval = OpenInterval(other.bottom, other.top)

        return self_interval.compute_overlap_with(other_interval)
```

Listing 6-26: Intersection private methods

Let's now take a look at how to build a generic polygon based on the rectangle.

Convert to Polygon

As with circles, applying an affine transformation to a rectangle may result in some nonrectangular shape. In fact, after a generic affine transformation, a rectangle gets transformed into a parallelogram, as depicted in Figure 6-16, and these shapes can't be described by our Rect class.

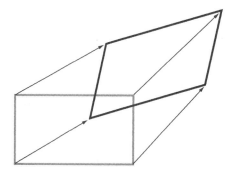

Figure 6-16: A rectangle after an affine transformation

Implementing a method to create a polygon from a rectangle is straightforward, as the vertices of such polygons are the four corners of the rectangle. In Rect class, add the method in Listing 6-27. Don't forget to import the Polygon class.

```
from geom2d.open_interval import OpenInterval
from geom2d.point import Point
from geom2d.polygon import Polygon
from geom2d.size import Size


class Rect:
    --snip--

    def to_polygon(self):
        return Polygon([
            self.origin,
            Point(self.right, self.bottom),
            Point(self.right, self.top),
            Point(self.left, self.top)
        ])
```

Listing 6-27: Creating a polygon from a rectangle

Needless to say, vertices should be given in order, clockwise or counterclockwise, but respecting the order nevertheless. It's really easy to mess up the order of vertices and end up with crossing sides. To make sure this never happens, we should write a test, which is left for you as an exercise.

Equality

You're already an expert at implementing __eq__ methods, aren't you? Listing 6-28 shows the code for it.

```
class Rect:
    --snip--

    def __eq__(self, other):
        if self is other:
            return True

        if not isinstance(other, Rect):
            return False

        return self.origin == other.origin \
                and self.size == other.size
```

Listing 6-28: Rectangle equality

The only thing to note is that we were able to directly compare sizes using == because we also implemented __eq__ on class Size.

Note that implementing __eq__ in *Rect* like are_close_enough(self.size.width, other.size.width) ... would not be ideal. Remember the law of Demeter? That knowledge belongs to class *Size* and should be implemented there and only there.

For reference, Listing 6-29 shows how your *rect.py* file should look.

```
from geom2d.open_interval import OpenInterval
from geom2d.point import Point
from geom2d.polygon import Polygon
from geom2d.size import Size


class Rect:

    def __init__(self, origin: Point, size: Size):
        self.origin = origin
        self.size = size

    @property
    def left(self):
        return self.origin.x

    @property
    def right(self):
```

```python
        return self.origin.x + self.size.width

    @property
    def bottom(self):
        return self.origin.y

    @property
    def top(self):
        return self.origin.y + self.size.height

    @property
    def area(self):
        return self.size.width * self.size.height

    @property
    def perimeter(self):
        return 2 * self.size.width + 2 * self.size.height

    def contains_point(self, point: Point):
        return self.left < point.x < self.right \
                and self.bottom < point.y < self.top

    def intersection_with(self, other):
        h_overlap = self.__horizontal_overlap_with(other)
        if h_overlap is None:
            return None

        v_overlap = self.__vertical_overlap_with(other)
        if v_overlap is None:
            return None

        return Rect(
            Point(h_overlap.start, v_overlap.start),
            Size(h_overlap.length, v_overlap.length)
        )

    def __horizontal_overlap_with(self, other):
        self_interval = OpenInterval(self.left, self.right)
        other_interval = OpenInterval(other.left, other.right)

        return self_interval.compute_overlap_with(other_interval)

    def __vertical_overlap_with(self, other):
        self_interval = OpenInterval(self.bottom, self.top)
        other_interval = OpenInterval(other.bottom, other.top)

        return self_interval.compute_overlap_with(other_interval)
```

```
    def to_polygon(self):
        return Polygon([
            self.origin,
            Point(self.right, self.bottom),
            Point(self.right, self.top),
            Point(self.left, self.top)
        ])

    def __eq__(self, other):
        if self is other:
            return True

        if not isinstance(other, Rect):
            return False

        return self.origin == other.origin \
            and self.size == other.size
```

Listing 6-29: The Rect implementation

Rectangle Factories

We'll often use rectangles to approximate the outside bounds of a set of geometries. In future chapters of the book, for example, we'll be generating diagrams as part of the solution for mechanics problems. To fit the diagrams inside an image of the right size, we'll create a rectangle that can contain everything. To do this, we'll create a factory function that returns a rectangle that contains a given list of points.

For example, if we're given the list of points $[A, B, C, D, E]$, the rectangle will look like the left illustration from Figure 6-17. We'll also need another factory function that does something similar but also adds some margin to the rectangle.

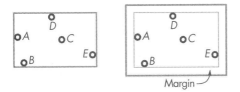

Figure 6-17: A rectangle containing points

Inside package *geom2d*, create a new file and name it *rects.py*. Add the first factory function (in Listing 6-30).

```
from geom2d.point import Point
from geom2d.rect import Rect
from geom2d.size import Size
```

```
def make_rect_containing(points: [Point]):
❶ if not points:
        raise ValueError('Expected at least one point')

    first_point = points[0]
❷ min_x, max_x = first_point.x, first_point.x
❸ min_y, max_y = first_point.y, first_point.y

    for point in points[1:]:
❹     min_x, max_x = min(min_x, point.x), max(max_x, point.x)
❺     min_y, max_y = min(min_y, point.y), max(max_y, point.y)

❻ return Rect(
        Point(min_x, min_y),
        Size(max_x - min_x, max_y - min_x)
    )
```

Listing 6-30: Creating a rectangle containing a list of points

The first step is checking that the list `points` contains at least one point ❶. You may be surprised about the syntax; the trick here is that Python evaluates empty lists as `False` in boolean contexts. In fact, that's a Pythonic idiom used to check whether a list is empty.

Next, we need to look for the bounds of the rectangle: the minimum and maximum x and y projections. Four variables store those values ❷ ❸ initialized with the coordinates of the first point in the list. Then we iterate through all points except for this first one, as it was already used to initialize the aforementioned variables. To avoid passing through the first point, we slice the `points` list starting at index 1 and going all the way to the end of the list: `points[1:]`. (You can refer to "Lists" on page 15 for a refresher on slicing lists.) For each point, the minimum and maximum x ❹ and y ❺ projections are compared to the values currently stored.

Once we have these four values, we construct the resulting rectangle ❻ using the minimum x and y projections for the origin and the difference between each maximum and minimum for the size.

Let's now implement a similar function with the addition of a margin around the points. After `make_rect_containing`, enter the code in Listing 6-31.

```
--snip--

def make_rect_containing_with_margin(points: [Point], margin: float):
❶ rect = make_rect_containing(points)
    return Rect(
❷     Point(
            rect.origin.x - margin,
            rect.origin.y - margin
        ),
❸     Size(
```

```
        2 * margin + rect.size.width,
        2 * margin + rect.size.height
    )
)
```

Listing 6-31: Creating a rectangle containing a list of points and a given margin

This function starts with a rectangle computed by the previous function ❶. The new rectangle is then computed by displacing rect's origin by the width of the margin to the left and downward ❷ and increasing the size by two times the width of the margin ❸. Recall that the margin is added to the left and to the right, which is why we add it twice to the width—the same goes for the height.

There's one last way we may want to build a rectangle: using its center and size. The implementation is straightforward, as you can see in Listing 6-32.

```
--snip--

def make_rect_centered(center: Point, width: float, height: float):
    origin = Point(
        center.x - width / 2,
        center.y - height / 2
    )
    return Rect(origin, Size(width, height))
```

Listing 6-32: Creating a rectangle given its center and size

With these three factory methods we have convenient ways of creating rectangles. We'll be using these in further chapters, so we want to make sure they yield the expected rectangle with some automated unit tests. I'll leave this as an exercise for you. You'll find the tests I wrote in *rects_test.py* in the source code accompanying the book.

Summary

We started the chapter implementing a generic polygon, described by a sequence of at least three vertices. We wrote an algorithm to pair sequences of objects such that the last and first elements are also paired up and used this logic to generate the sides of the polygon. We also implemented the winding number algorithm to check whether the polygon contains a point.

The second geometric primitive we created in this chapter was the circle. As you saw, checking whether a point is inside a circle was much simpler to implement than in the case of generic polygons. We came up with a way of constructing a generic polygon that approximates the geometry of the circle using a given number of divisions or sides. We'll make use of this method in the next chapter.

Lastly, we implemented a rectangle. To compute intersection between rectangles, we needed a way of figuring out the overlap between two intervals; thus, we created an abstraction of an open interval to handle this logic.

Our geometry library is almost complete. We have all the primitives that we need for the book; the only thing missing is a way of transforming them, which is the topic of the next chapter.

7

AFFINE TRANSFORMATIONS

If I had to choose my favorite topic from this book, it would be affine transformations. There's something oddly beautiful about affine transformations, as you'll see for yourself in Chapter 12 when we animate them.

Affine transformations are crucial to 2D graphic applications; they determine how to pan, zoom, and rotate what you see on the screen. If you've used AutoCAD, you're pretty much used to zooming in to a portion of the drawing, which is done with an affine transformation. Whenever you scale and rotate your pics in Instagram, an affine transformation does the trick. Mastering this topic is essential for writing any piece of software involving graphics, even more so for those where the user is allowed to interact with them.

The math behind affine transformations is quite simple, yet the concept is stunningly powerful. By the end of this chapter, you'll have a class representing these transformations with methods to apply them to geometric primitives. We'll also learn how to combine transformations to compute compound transformations and take a look at some useful transformations, such as one that zooms a drawing around a concrete point.

Affine Transformations

Since affine transformations apply to affine spaces, let's first try to understand what an affine space is. You can think of an *affine space* as being a vector space where the origin point can be moved around. The linear transformations used in vector spaces preserve the position of the space's origin, whereas in an affine space, as we stop caring about a fixed origin, translations are allowed.

An *affine transformation*, then, is a mapping between two affine spaces that preserves points, straight lines, and planes. Points after an affine transformation stay as points, straight lines continue to be straight, and planes remain plane. One interesting property of these transformations is that parallelism between lines is preserved. We'll see this in action in Chapter 12 when we animate affine transformations. In that exercise, we'll see how the sides of polygons that were originally parallel remain parallel during the whole simulation.

Affine transformations are similar to *linear transformations*. The only difference is that the latter preserves the origin; that is, the point $(0, 0)$ doesn't move. Affine transformations can alter the position of the origin. Figure 7-1 depicts both a linear transformation and an affine transformation.

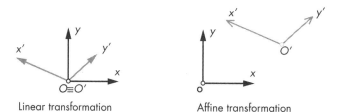

Figure 7-1: Linear versus affine transformation

Each pair of axes x, y in Figure 7-1 shows how the space was before the transformation; each x', y' pair shows what the space looks like after the transformation. In the case of the linear transformation, the origin of coordinates O is preserved; the affine transformation, in addition to scaling and rotating the axes, translated the origin O to O'.

Given a point P, we can define an affine transformation using the expression

$$P' = [M]P + \vec{t}$$

where M is a linear transformation, $\vec{t}$ is a translation vector, and P' is the resulting point after applying the transformation. An affine transformation is thus a linear transformation M plus a translation $\vec{t}$. This expression can be written with all its terms as shown in Equation 7.1.

$$\underbrace{\begin{pmatrix} x' \\ y' \end{pmatrix}}_{P'} = \underbrace{\begin{bmatrix} s_x & sh_x \\ sh_y & s_y \end{bmatrix}}_{[M]} \underbrace{\begin{pmatrix} x \\ y \end{pmatrix}}_{P} + \underbrace{\left\{ \begin{matrix} t_x \\ t_y \end{matrix} \right\}}_{\vec{t}} \tag{7.1}$$

The linear transformation matrix M has the items

s_x Scale in the x direction

s_y Scale in the y direction

sh_x Shear in the x direction

sh_y Shear in the y direction

and the translation $\vec{t}$ has the terms

t_x Translation in the x direction

t_y Translation in the y direction

Equation 7.2 shows an equivalent form using what is known as the *augmented matrix*.

$$\begin{pmatrix} x' \\ y' \\ 1 \end{pmatrix} = \begin{bmatrix} s_x & sh_x & t_x \\ sh_y & s_y & t_y \\ 0 & 0 & 1 \end{bmatrix} \begin{pmatrix} x \\ y \\ 1 \end{pmatrix} \tag{7.2}$$

This version reduces the transformation to one matrix multiplication by extending the size of the input and output vectors, appending a 1, which serves as an auxiliary value and can be discarded once the transformation has taken place. It's usually preferred as it requires only one step compared to the extra addition involved in the former. You can observe how in both cases, Equations 7.1 and 7.2, the resulting coordinates are as shown in Equation 7.3.

$$\begin{cases} x' = s_x \cdot x + sh_x \cdot y + t_x \\ y' = sh_y \cdot x + s_y \cdot y + t_y \end{cases} \tag{7.3}$$

Each of the values in the matrix from Equation 7.2 contributes differently in the transformation process. Figure 7-2 showcases the transformation that each of the components produces. A generic affine transformation is therefore a combination of those unitary transformations.

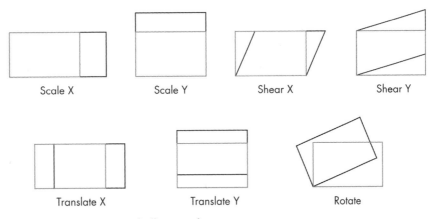

Figure 7-2: Components of affine transformations

There is a special affine transformation that maps each point to itself, the *identity transformation*.

$$\begin{bmatrix} 1 & 0 & 0 \\ 0 & 1 & 0 \\ 0 & 0 & 1 \end{bmatrix}$$

As you can observe, this is an identity matrix: whatever point you multiply this matrix by will stay the same.

Examples of Affine Transformations

Let's look at a few examples of affine transformations in action. For this section, leave your computer aside and take out your pen and paper. If you can work through the operations to transform spaces using affine transformations by hand, coding them will be straightforward.

Example 1: Scaling

Given a point $(2, 3)$, what point results after applying a horizontal scale of 2 and a vertical scale of 5?

In this case, the terms in the affine transformation matrix are all zero except for $s_x = 2$ and $s_y = 5$. Plugging these values into Equation 7.2, we get the following:

$$\begin{pmatrix} x' \\ y' \\ 1 \end{pmatrix} = \begin{bmatrix} 2 & 0 & 0 \\ 0 & 5 & 0 \\ 0 & 0 & 1 \end{bmatrix} \begin{pmatrix} 2 \\ 3 \\ 1 \end{pmatrix} = \begin{pmatrix} 4 \\ 15 \\ 1 \end{pmatrix}$$

The resulting point is therefore $(4, 15)$. Figure 7-3 depicts this transformation's effect on the point.

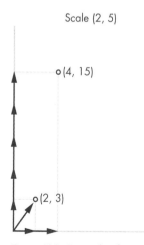

Figure 7-3: Example of a scale transformation

Example 2: Scaling and Translating

Given a point $(2, 3)$, what point results after applying a horizontal scale of 2, vertical scale of 5, and translation of $\langle 10, 15 \rangle$?

This case has the same values for the scale as the previous one, plus a displacement vector. Let's plug those values into our affine transformation equation:

$$\begin{pmatrix} x' \\ y' \\ 1 \end{pmatrix} = \begin{bmatrix} 2 & 0 & 10 \\ 0 & 5 & 15 \\ 0 & 0 & 1 \end{bmatrix} \begin{pmatrix} 2 \\ 3 \\ 1 \end{pmatrix} = \begin{pmatrix} 14 \\ 30 \\ 1 \end{pmatrix}$$

This time, the resulting point is $(14, 30)$. We'll take a look at this later, but it's interesting to note how we could achieve the same effect with two sequential affine transformations, the first one scaling the point and the second one translating it:

$$\begin{pmatrix} x' \\ y' \\ 1 \end{pmatrix} = \underbrace{\begin{bmatrix} 1 & 0 & 10 \\ 0 & 1 & 15 \\ 0 & 0 & 1 \end{bmatrix}}_{\text{translation}} \left(\underbrace{\begin{bmatrix} 2 & 0 & 0 \\ 0 & 5 & 0 \\ 0 & 0 & 1 \end{bmatrix}}_{\text{scale}} \begin{pmatrix} 2 \\ 3 \\ 1 \end{pmatrix} \right) = \begin{pmatrix} 14 \\ 30 \\ 1 \end{pmatrix}$$

Note that transformations are applied from right to left. In the previous case, the scaling goes first and then the translation. If you were to switch the order of transformations, the result would be different, which we can check by multiplying both transformation matrices in both directions and comparing the results. This yields our original matrix:

$$\underbrace{\begin{bmatrix} 1 & 0 & 10 \\ 0 & 1 & 15 \\ 0 & 0 & 1 \end{bmatrix}}_{\text{translation}} \underbrace{\begin{bmatrix} 2 & 0 & 0 \\ 0 & 5 & 0 \\ 0 & 0 & 1 \end{bmatrix}}_{\text{scale}} = \begin{bmatrix} 2 & 0 & 10 \\ 0 & 5 & 15 \\ 0 & 0 & 1 \end{bmatrix}$$

But switching the order yields:

$$\underbrace{\begin{bmatrix} 2 & 0 & 0 \\ 0 & 5 & 0 \\ 0 & 0 & 1 \end{bmatrix}}_{\text{scale}} \underbrace{\begin{bmatrix} 1 & 0 & 10 \\ 0 & 1 & 15 \\ 0 & 0 & 1 \end{bmatrix}}_{\text{translation}} = \begin{bmatrix} 2 & 0 & 20 \\ 0 & 5 & 75 \\ 0 & 0 & 1 \end{bmatrix}$$

Figure 7-4 depicts the effect of applying the scale first and then the translation.

Scale (2,5) + Translate (10, 15)

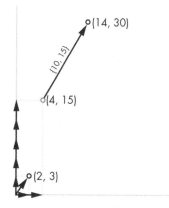

Figure 7-4: A scale plus a translation

Example 3: Vertical Reflection

Reflections can be achieved by using affine transformations with negative scale values. To reflect a point $(2, 3)$ in the vertical direction, use $s_y = -1$:

$$\begin{pmatrix} x' \\ y' \\ 1 \end{pmatrix} = \begin{bmatrix} 1 & 0 & 0 \\ 0 & -1 & 0 \\ 0 & 0 & 1 \end{bmatrix} \begin{pmatrix} 2 \\ 3 \\ 1 \end{pmatrix} = \begin{pmatrix} 2 \\ -3 \\ 1 \end{pmatrix}$$

This yields the vertical reflection of the original point: $(2, -3)$. Figure 7-5 represents this vertical reflection.

Scale (1, −1)

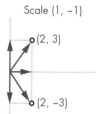

Figure 7-5: An example
of a vertical reflection

Example 4: Horizontal Shear

What is the result of applying a horizontal shear of $sh_x = 2$ to a rectangle with its lower-left point located at the origin, a width of 10 units, and a height of 5 units?

This time we'll have to apply the same transformation to all four vertices of the rectangle: $(0, 0)$, $(10, 0)$, $(10, 5)$, and $(0, 5)$. The affine transformation matrix is then as follows:

$$\begin{bmatrix} 1 & 2 & 0 \\ 0 & 1 & 0 \\ 0 & 0 & 1 \end{bmatrix}$$

Using Equation 7.2 with this matrix to transform the vertices yields the following: $(0, 0)$, $(10, 0)$, $(20, 5)$, and $(10, 5)$. Draw the resulting rectangle. It should look something like Figure 7-6.

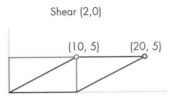

Figure 7-6: An example of a shear

The Affine Transformation Class

Without further ado, let's create a new class to represent affine transformations. We want to use a class so that the transformation scale, translation, and shear values are part of its inner state and don't need to be passed to every transformation method we use. If we used functions to transform geometric primitives instead, we'd need to pass all these values to every function, but that would be a lot of parameters.

In the *geom2d* package, create a new file named *affine_transf.py* and enter the code in Listing 7-1.

```
class AffineTransform:
    def __init__(self, sx=1, sy=1, tx=0, ty=0, shx=0, shy=0):
        self.sx = sx
        self.sy = sy
        self.tx = tx
        self.ty = ty
        self.shx = shx
        self.shy = shy
```

Listing 7-1: The AffineTransform class

The affine transformation stores values for the scales s_x and s_y, the translations t_x and t_y, and the shears sh_x and sh_y. All values are given a default value of zero, except for the scales, which are initialized to one, in case they are omitted in the initializer. This is for convenience, as we'll create many transformations where the shear or translation values are zero.

With these values at hand we can already implement a method to apply the transformation to a point with the help of Equation 7.3. Enter the code in Listing 7-2.

```
from geom2d.point import Point


class AffineTransform:
    --snip--
```

```
def apply_to_point(self, point: Point):
    return Point(
        (self.sx * point.x) + (self.shx * point.y) + self.tx,
        (self.shy * point.x) + (self.sy * point.y) + self.ty
    )
```

Listing 7-2: Applying an affine transformation to a point

To apply the affine transformation to a point, we create a new `Point` where the projections are calculated using Equation 7.3. Let's test this method using several different transformations.

Testing the Transformation of Points

Create a new file in the *geom2d* package named *affine_transf_test.py* and enter the code in Listing 7-3.

```
import unittest

from geom2d.point import Point
from geom2d.affine_transf import AffineTransform


class TestAffineTransform(unittest.TestCase):
    point = Point(2, 3)
    scale = AffineTransform(2, 5)
    trans = AffineTransform(1, 1, 10, 15)
    shear = AffineTransform(1, 1, 0, 0, 3, 4)

❶   def test_scale_point(self):
        expected = Point(4, 15)
        actual = self.scale.apply_to_point(self.point)
        self.assertEqual(expected, actual)

❷   def test_translate_point(self):
        expected = Point(12, 18)
        actual = self.trans.apply_to_point(self.point)
        self.assertEqual(expected, actual)

❸   def test_shear_point(self):
        expected = Point(11, 11)
        actual = self.shear.apply_to_point(self.point)
        self.assertEqual(expected, actual)
```

Listing 7-3: Testing the affine transformation application

The test file contains the `TestAffineTransform` class, inheriting from `unittest.TestCase` as usual. Inside the class we define a point that is used in all tests as well as all three affine transformations, namely:

scale   A scaling transformation

trans   A translation transformation

shear   A shear transformation

Then we have our first test ensure the scale is correctly applied to the point ❶. The second test applies the translation to the point and asserts that the result is as expected ❷. The third does the same with the shear transformation ❸. Run the tests. You can do so from the shell:

```
$ python3 -m unittest geom2d/affine_transf_test.py
```

This should produce the following:

```
Ran 3 tests in 0.001s
```

```
OK
```

Great! Now that we're confident we're correctly applying affine transformations to points, let's extend the logic to other more complex primitives.

Transform Segments and Polygons

We can harness the implementation for transforming `Points` to transform any shape as long as it's defined using points or vectors. The next logical step is implementing the transformation of segments, so after the `apply_to _point` method, enter the method in Listing 7-4.

```python
from geom2d.segment import Segment
from geom2d.point import Point


class AffineTransform:
    --snip--

    def apply_to_segment(self, segment: Segment):
        return Segment(
            self.apply_to_point(segment.start),
            self.apply_to_point(segment.end)
        )
```

Listing 7-4: Applying affine transformations to segments

That was easy, wasn't it? To transform a segment, we simply create a new segment with both end points transformed using the previous method. We can apply a similar logic to polygons (in Listing 7-5).

```
from geom2d.polygon import Polygon
from geom2d.segment import Segment
from geom2d.point import Point


class AffineTransform:
    --snip--



    def apply_to_polygon(self, polygon: Polygon):
        return Polygon(
            [self.apply_to_point(v) for v in polygon.vertices]
        )
```

Listing 7-5: Applying affine transformations to polygons

In this case, we return a new polygon where all vertices have been transformed. What about rectangles and circles? The idea is similar, with a caveat: after scaling, shearing, and rotating these primitives, the results may no longer be rectangles or circles. This is why, in the previous chapter, we provided Rect and Circle with a method to_polygon that creates a generic polygon representation for the primitive. The code is therefore quite simple. Enter the code from Listing 7-6:

```
from geom2d.rect import Rect
from geom2d.circle import Circle
from geom2d.polygon import Polygon
from geom2d.segment import Segment
from geom2d.point import Point

class AffineTransform:
    --snip--


    def apply_to_rect(self, rect: Rect):
        return self.apply_to_polygon(
            rect.to_polygon()
        )

    def apply_to_circle(self, circle: Circle, divisions=30):
        return self.apply_to_polygon(
            circle.to_polygon(divisions)
        )
```

Listing 7-6: Applying affine transformations to rectangles and circles

The procedure consists of obtaining the polygon representation of the rectangle or circle and delegating the rest of the process to `apply_to_polygon`. In the case of circles, the number of divisions must be chosen, which is given a value of 30 by default. Both methods return a `Polygon` instance, even if the affine transformation being applied is the identity, which wouldn't transform the geometries at all. Once a rectangle or a circle goes through an affine transformation, it turns into a generic polygon, no matter what transformation.

We won't do so here for space reasons, but feel free to add unit tests for these three new methods.

Concatenating Transformations

One interesting property of affine transformations is that any complex transformation can be expressed as a sequence of simpler transformations. In fact, when you work with a 2D graphics application such as Sketch or Photoshop, every zoom or pan on the canvas is a combination, or concatenation, of a new affine transformation with the current one, which defines the projection of what you see on your screen at that particular moment.

Given two affine transformations $[T_1]$ and $[T_2]$ and input point P, the result of applying $[T_1]$ to the point is as follows:

$$P' = [T_1]P$$

Then, applying the second transformation $[T_2]$ to the previous result, we get this:

$$P'' = [T_2]P'$$

If we substitute P' from the first expression into the second, we obtain the result of applying both transformations to input point P (Equation 7.4),

$$P'' = [T_2]([T_1]P) = \underbrace{[T_2][T_1]}_{[T_r]} P \qquad (7.4)$$

where $[T_r]$ is the affine transformation equivalent to applying $[T_1]$ first and $[T_2]$ second. Notice how the order of the original transformations appears in reverse if you read from left to right?

$$[T_r] = [T_2][T_1]$$

In the previous equation, reading from left to right $[T_2]$ appears first, but the effect of applying $[T_r]$ is equivalent to applying $[T_1]$ first and $[T_2]$ second. We need to be careful with the order, as matrix multiplication is noncommutative. If we swap the order of the operands, we obtain a different transformation, which was already proved in a previous exercise. The resulting transformation is then expressed mathematically as the product of matrices (see Equation 7.5).

$$[T_r] = [T_2][T_1] = \begin{bmatrix} s_{x2} & sh_{x2} & t_{x2} \\ sh_{y2} & s_{y2} & t_{y2} \\ 0 & 0 & 1 \end{bmatrix} \cdot \begin{bmatrix} s_{x1} & sh_{x1} & t_{x1} \\ sh_{y1} & s_{y1} & t_{y1} \\ 0 & 0 & 1 \end{bmatrix} =$$

$$\begin{bmatrix} s_{x2} \cdot s_{x1} + sh_{x2} \cdot sh_{y1} & s_{x2} \cdot sh_{x1} + sh_{x2} \cdot s_{y1} & s_{x2} \cdot t_{x1} + sh_{x2} \cdot t_{y1} + t_{x2} \\ sh_{y2} \cdot s_{x1} + s_{y2} \cdot sh_{y1} & sh_{y2} \cdot sh_{x1} + s_{y2} \cdot s_{y1} & sh_{y2} \cdot t_{x1} + s_{y2} \cdot t_{y1} + t_{y2} \\ 0 & 0 & 1 \end{bmatrix}$$

$$(7.5)$$

Let's provide the AffineTransform class with a method to concatenate affine transformations using Equation 7.5. We'll call the method then(), receiving parameters self and other. The first argument, self, is transformation $[T_1]$, and other is $[T_2]$. Inside *affine_transf.py*, toward the end of the class, enter the code in Listing 7-7.

```
class AffineTransform:
    --snip--



    def then(self, other):
        return AffineTransform(
            sx=other.sx * self.sx + other.shx * self.shy,
            sy=other.shy * self.shx + other.sy * self.sy,
            tx=other.sx * self.tx + other.shx * self.ty + other.tx,
            ty=other.shy * self.tx + other.sy * self.ty + other.ty,
            shx=other.sx * self.shx + other.shx * self.sy,
            shy=other.shy * self.sx + other.sy * self.shy
        )
```

Listing 7-7: Method to concatenate transformations

The name then is chosen so that it's absolutely clear that self is applied before other (the method's argument).

Since this is such an important method, we'll want it covered by unit tests; that means we need a way of knowing whether two given affine transformations are equal. Let's implement the special __eq__ method in AffineTransform (Listing 7-8).

```
from geom2d.nums import are_close_enough
from geom2d.rect import Rect
from geom2d.circle import Circle
from geom2d.polygon import Polygon
from geom2d.segment import Segment
from geom2d.point import Point



class AffineTransform:
    --snip--

    def __eq__(self, other):
```

```
    if self is other:
        return True

    if not isinstance(other, AffineTransform):
        return False

    return are_close_enough(self.sx, other.sx) \
            and are_close_enough(self.sy, other.sy) \
            and are_close_enough(self.tx, other.tx) \
            and are_close_enough(self.ty, other.ty) \
            and are_close_enough(self.shx, other.shx) \
            and are_close_enough(self.shy, other.shy)
```

Listing 7-8: Checking affine transformation equality

Testing the Concatenation of Transformations

Let's now enter two new tests in *affine_transf_test.py*; both are listed in Listing 7-9.

```
class TestAffineTransform(unittest.TestCase):
    --snip--

    def test_concatenate_scale_then_translate(self):
        expected = AffineTransform(2, 5, 10, 15)
        actual = self.scale.then(self.trans)
        self.assertEqual(expected, actual)

    def test_concatenate_translate_then_scale(self):
        expected = AffineTransform(2, 5, 20, 75)
        actual = self.trans.then(self.scale)
        self.assertEqual(expected, actual)
```

Listing 7-9: Testing affine transformation concatenation

As you've probably realized, these two tests are repeating the operations we did by hand in one of the exercises at the beginning of the chapter. Run them to make sure you have the implementation of then right.

```
$ python3 -m unittest geom2d/affine_transf_test.py
```

There is a lot of adding and multiplying between self and other, so it's easy to get the code wrong. If the tests aren't passing, well, that means they're doing their work by pointing out that something in the code is not right. Go back to your implementation and make sure you have everything right line by line.

Inverting Affine Transformations

To undo a transformation or apply the inverse of a known transformation $[T]$, we want to be able to compute a transformation $[T_I]$ such that

$$[T][T_I] = [T_I][T] = [I]$$

where $[I]$ is the identity matrix of size 3:

$$[I] = \begin{bmatrix} 1 & 0 & 0 \\ 0 & 1 & 0 \\ 0 & 0 & 1 \end{bmatrix}$$

An interesting property of these pairs of transformations $[T]$ and $[T_I]$ is that they cancel each other out. For example, here is the result of applying the transformations one after the other (in whichever order) to a point P:

$$[T_I]([T]P) = ([T_I][T])P = [I]P = P$$

Another reason the inverse affine transformation is interesting is that it maps a point on the screen back to our "model space," that is, the affine space where our model is defined. The direct transformation is used to compute how the geometry is projected onto the screen, that is, where each point of the model needs to be drawn—but what about the other way around? Knowing where a given point on the screen lies in the model requires the inverse transformation, the one that transforms the "screen space" into the model space. This is useful, for example, when trying to figure out whether the user's mouse pointer on the screen maps to something in the model that could potentially be selected.

Take a look at Figure 7-7. There's our model space with just a triangle defined in it. To draw the model to the user's screen, we have to apply an affine transformation that projects every point from model space to screen space. Now imagine the user has the mouse at point P' on the screen, and we want to know whether that point lies inside our triangle. Since the triangle is a geometry defined in the model space, we want to apply that point in the screen the inverse transformation: that which transforms screen space into model space. Recall that, to project our model geometry into the screen, we applied the direct affine transformation, so to map that geometry back into its original model space, the inverse of that transformation needs to be applied. With the point mapped to our model space (P), we can do the calculations to determine whether P is inside the triangle.

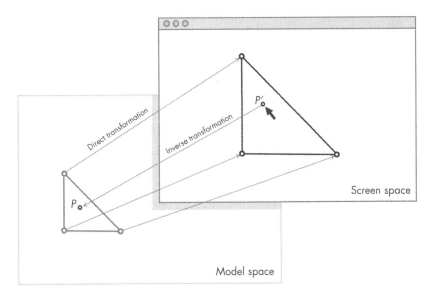

Figure 7-7: Model and screen spaces

You can try to compute the inverse affine transformation matrix by yourself, which is a great exercise, but inverting matrices by hand is a tedious task, so Equation 7.6 shows the result.

$$[T_I] = \frac{1}{s_x s_y - sh_x sh_y} \begin{bmatrix} s_y & -sh_x & t_y sh_x - s_y t_x \\ -sh_y & s_x & t_x sh_y - s_x t_y \\ 0 & 0 & s_x s_y - sh_x sh_y \end{bmatrix} \tag{7.6}$$

Using the transformation from Equation 7.6, computing the inverse requires only a few lines of code. In AffineTransform and after then, enter the code in Listing 7-10.

```
class AffineTransform:
    --snip--


    def inverse(self):
        denom = self.sx * self.sy - self.shx * self.shy
        return AffineTransform(
            sx=self.sy / denom,
            sy=self.sx / denom,
            tx=(self.ty * self.shx - self.sy * self.tx) / denom,
            ty=(self.tx * self.shy - self.sx * self.ty) / denom,
            shx=-self.shx / denom,
            shy=-self.shy / denom
        )
```

Listing 7-10: Inverse affine transformation

Let's also add a test to make sure the inverse is properly computed. In *affine_transf_test.py*, add a new method to class `TestAffineTransform` with the test in Listing 7-11.

```
class TestAffineTransform(unittest.TestCase):
    --snip--

    def test_inverse(self):
        transf = AffineTransform(1, 2, 3, 4, 5, 6)
        expected = AffineTransform()
        actual = transf.then(transf.inverse())
        self.assertEqual(expected, actual)
```

Listing 7-11: Testing the inverse affine transformation

In this test, we create a new affine transformation, `transf`, with all values set to nonzero values. Then we store the transformation result of concatenating `transf` and its inverse in `actual`, which, if you recall, should be the identity matrix if the inverse is properly constructed. Lastly, we compare the obtained result with the actual identity matrix. Run all tests in the file to make sure they succeed.

```
$ python3 -m unittest geom2d/affine_transf_test.py
```

Let's try an example. We'll apply a translation to a point and then apply the inverse translation to the resulting point, which should yield the original point. In the Python shell, write the following:

```
>>> from geom2d.affine_transf import AffineTransform
>>> from geom2d.point import Point
>>> trans = AffineTransform(tx=10, ty=20)
>>> original = Point(5, 7)
```

We know if we apply the $\langle 10, 20 \rangle$ translation to point $(5, 7)$, the resulting point should be $(15, 27)$. Let's test it.

```
>>> translated = trans.apply_to_point(original)
>>> str(translated)
'(15, 27)'
```

Using the `str` function, we get the string representation of `translated`, the point after applying the translation. Let's now apply the inverse translation transformation to that point.

```
>>> inverse = trans.inverse().apply_to_point(translated)
>>> str(inverse)
'(5.0, 7.0)'
```

Applying the inverse transformation to the translated point yields the original point, as expected.

Scaling

Whenever you zoom in or out using a graphics application such as Auto-CAD or Illustrator, a scaling affine transformation is applied to the geometric model so that it's drawn on your screen with a different size than the real one. Architects draw blueprints for buildings hundreds of meters tall that need to fit inside a laptop screen a few inches wide. Inside the computer's memory lives the geometric model with the real dimensions, but to draw it to the screen, a scale is applied: a scaling affine transformation.

To get a visual intuition of what happens in this kind of affine transformation, let's look at Figure 7-8. Given a point P, let's imagine a vector $\vec{v}$ starting at the origin and with its tip on P. Applying scales S_x and S_y to point P transforms it into a point P' whose vector $\vec{v'}$ horizontal projection is $S_x \cdot v_x$ and vertical projection is $S_y \cdot v_y$. As you see, a scale is a measure of how far or close points get to the origin with respect to their original distance to it. The origin, in fact, doesn't move with pure scaling transformations. Scales with absolute value smaller than the unit pull points closer to the origin, whereas scales greater than one push points away from it.

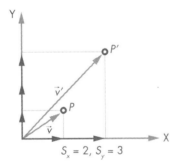

Figure 7-8: A scale affine transformation

This is useful, but often we want to apply a scale with respect to a point other than the origin. Imagine, for example, working with AutoCAD and wanting to zoom in to the drawing. If instead of zooming in around the center of your screen or mouse position it zoomed with respect to the origin (assuming it's located in the lower-left corner of the app's window), you'd feel like the drawing moved away, as depicted in the left diagram of Figure 7-9.

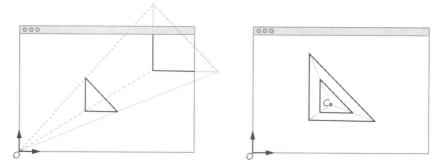

Figure 7-9: Zooming in around the origin (left) and around the center of the screen (right)

You're probably much more used to a zoom in function that scales the drawing around a point somewhere in the middle of your screen, or even the position of your mouse as it actually happens most of the time. Many graphic design programs work like this, and it makes things more convenient for the user, but the way we defined a pure scaling transformation, it can only happen with respect to the origin. So, how is this scaling around an arbitrary point achieved? Well, now that we know about constructing compound transformations, obtaining this transformation is actually a piece of cake.

NOTE *It took me quite some time to fully understand how to use affine transformations effectively and how to create compound transformations out of simpler ones. I had a really hard time trying to implement a proper "zoom in" option in my software InkStructure, and that's why the original versions felt a bit buggy when trying to zoom in to the drawing and not have it randomly move around the screen. So when I say "a piece of cake," I should probably qualify: it becomes easy only once you understand affine transformations.*

Let's quickly state the problem we want to solve: we want to find an affine transformation that applies scales S_x and S_y with respect to a center point C. Defining O as the origin of the coordinate system, we can build such a transformation by combining the following simpler transformations:

1. $[T_1]$: Translate so that C coincides with the origin O ($\vec{t} = \overline{CO} = \langle -C_x, -C_y \rangle$).

2. $[T_2]$: Scale with factors S_x and S_y.

3. $[T_3]$: Translate C back to where it was ($\vec{t'} = \overline{OC} = \langle C_x, C_y \rangle$).

Since scales can be applied only with respect to the origin, we move the whole space so that our point C lies exactly on the origin, and then we apply the scale and translate things back to where they were initially. Beautiful, isn't it? Thus, $[T_r]$ can be computed as shown in Equation 7.7.

$$[T_r] = \underbrace{\begin{bmatrix} 1 & 0 & C_x \\ 0 & 1 & C_y \\ 0 & 0 & 1 \end{bmatrix}}_{[T_3]} \underbrace{\begin{bmatrix} S_x & 0 & 0 \\ 0 & S_y & 0 \\ 0 & 0 & 1 \end{bmatrix}}_{[T_2]} \underbrace{\begin{bmatrix} 1 & 0 & -C_x \\ 0 & 1 & -C_y \\ 0 & 0 & 1 \end{bmatrix}}_{[T_1]} = \begin{bmatrix} S_x & 0 & C_x(1 - S_x) \\ 0 & S_y & C_y(1 - S_y) \\ 0 & 0 & 1 \end{bmatrix} \quad (7.7)$$

Let's create a factory function to generate these kinds of transformations. Start by creating a new file named *affine_transforms.py*; in it, enter the function in Listing 7-12.

```
from geom2d.affine_transf import AffineTransform
from geom2d.point import Point


def make_scale(sx: float, sy: float , center=Point(0, 0)):
    return AffineTransform(
        sx=sx,
        sy=sy,
        tx=center.x * (1.0 - sx),
        ty=center.y * (1.0 - sy)
    )
```

Listing 7-12: Creating a scale transformation

It is a good idea to add a few test cases checking the behavior of this function. For brevity, I'll leave that as an exercise for you.

Rotating

Similar to scales, rotations always take place around the origin. Just like before, by using a clever sequence of transformations, we can produce a rotation around any point we want. You may have rotated a drawing in Sketch, Illustrator, or a similar application, in which case you're used to choosing the *rotation pivot*, a point around which you then rotate using the square handles, something similar to Figure 7-10.

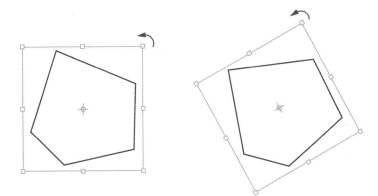

Figure 7-10: Rotation around the center

The pivot point can be moved so the rotation happens around a different point. For example, moving it near the bottom-left corner of the bounding box, the rotation may look like Figure 7-11.

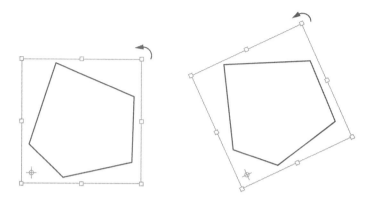

Figure 7-11: Rotation around a corner

Let's start by learning how to construct a rotation affine transformation around the origin; this will serve as the basis for constructing a more complex rotation around any point. Equation 7.8 shows how to rotate points θ radians around the origin.

$$[T_\theta] = \begin{bmatrix} \cos\theta & -\sin\theta & 0 \\ \sin\theta & \cos\theta & 0 \\ 0 & 0 & 1 \end{bmatrix} \tag{7.8}$$

With this in mind, let's find an affine transformation that rotates points θ radians around a center point C. With O as the origin of the coordinate system, the transformation is the combination of the following:

1. $[T_1]$: Translate C to the origin O so the rotation center is C ($\vec{t} = \overline{CO} = \langle -C_x, -C_y \rangle$).

2. $[T_2]$: Rotate θ radians.

3. $[T_3]$: Translate C back to where it was ($\vec{t'} = \overline{OC} = \langle C_x, C_y \rangle$).

It's the same algorithm as before, but this time we'll use a rotation instead of a scale. $[T_r]$ is now computed as follows:

$$[T_r] = \underbrace{\begin{bmatrix} 1 & 0 & C_x \\ 0 & 1 & C_y \\ 0 & 0 & 1 \end{bmatrix}}_{[T_3]} \underbrace{\begin{bmatrix} \cos\theta & -\sin\theta & 0 \\ \sin\theta & \cos\theta & 0 \\ 0 & 0 & 1 \end{bmatrix}}_{[T_2]} \underbrace{\begin{bmatrix} 1 & 0 & -C_x \\ 0 & 1 & -C_y \\ 0 & 0 & 1 \end{bmatrix}}_{[T_1]}$$

This yields the affine transformation in Equation 7.9.

$$[T_r] = \begin{bmatrix} \cos\theta & -\sin\theta & C_x(1 - \cos\theta) + C_y \cdot \sin\theta \\ \sin\theta & \cos\theta & C_y(1 - \cos\theta) - C_x \cdot \sin\theta \\ 0 & 0 & 1 \end{bmatrix} \tag{7.9}$$

Let's create a new factory function to generate rotations around a center point. In *affine_transforms.py*, with the help of Equation 7.9, implement the new function in Listing 7-13.

```
import math

from geom2d.affine_transf import AffineTransform
from geom2d.point import Point


--snip--

def make_rotation(radians: float, center=Point(0, 0)):
    cos = math.cos(radians)
    sin = math.sin(radians)
    one_minus_cos = 1.0 - cos

    return AffineTransform(
        sx=cos,
        sy=cos,
        tx=center.x * one_minus_cos + center.y * sin,
        ty=center.y * one_minus_cos - center.x * sin,
        shx=-sin,
        shy=sin
    )
```

Listing 7-13: Creating a rotation transformation

Once again, you want to come up with at least one unit test to make sure our implementation is bug free.

Let's give it a try in the shell: let's create two rotations of $\pi/4$ radians, one around the origin and another one around the point $(10, 10)$. Then, we'll apply both rotations to the point $(15, 15)$ to see where it lands in both cases. Reload the Python shell and write the following:

```
>>> from geom2d.affine_transforms import make_rotation
>>> from geom2d.point import Point
>>> import math
>>> point = Point(15, 15)
```

Let's now try with the rotation around the origin:

```
>>> rot_origin = make_rotation(math.pi / 4)
>>> str(rot_origin.apply_to_point(point))
'(1.7763568394002505e-15, 21.213203435596427)'
```

The resulting point has an x-coordinate that is effectively zero (note the exponent e-15) and a y-coordinate of 21.2132..., which is the length of the vector going from the origin to the original point ($\sqrt{15^2 + 15^2} = 21.2132...$).

Let's try the second rotation:

```
>>> rot_other = make_rotation(math.pi / 4, Point(10, 10))
>>> str(rot_other.apply_to_point(point))
'(10.000000000000002, 17.071067811865476)'
```

The resulting point is (10, 17.071...) this time. To help us make sense of the exercise we've just done, Figure 7-12 illustrates the two rotation transformations.

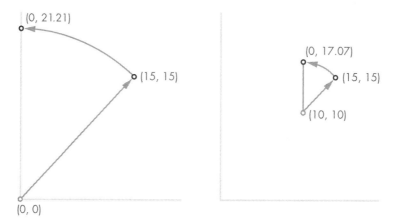

Figure 7-12: Example of a rotation around the origin (left) and around the point (10, 10) (right)

Interpolating Transformations

When you zoom in or out, most graphics programs don't apply the scale all at once, but they typically produce a quick and smooth animation of the zooming process. This helps you, the user, better understand how the drawing is being transformed. To achieve this, graphics programs typically use a transformation interpolation. Later in the book we'll animate affine transformations, that is, we'll create a kind of movie where we can appreciate how a given geometry is transformed one step at a time. Each frame in the animation will depict the geometry after applying a fraction of the affine transformation, and this is where we'll first use *interpolations*.

Motivating Interpolation

Before we dive into the concept of interpolating transformations, take a look at Figure 7-13.

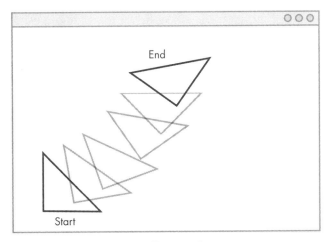

Figure 7-13: Animating an affine transformation

In the figure, there's a triangle originally in the bottom left of the window that ends up in the top middle after passing through some middle positions drawn in a lighter gray. Each of the triangles represents the result we'd see at a given point in time, a concrete frame in the animation.

If we want our animation to have n frames, where $n > 1$, there needs to be n affine transformations $[T_0], [T_1], \ldots, [T_{n-1}]$ such that each frame is the result of applying the corresponding transformation to the input geometry. It's clear that the last transformation, $[T_{n-1}]$, needs to be the target affine transformation, as the final frame should depict the geometry after applying such a transformation. What should $[T_0]$ be then? Let's give it some thought. What transformation applied to the input geometry results in the geometry itself? Well, there's only one such transformation that we know doesn't move things around, the identity transformation. So, our start and end transformations are as follows:

$$[T_0] = \begin{bmatrix} 1 & 0 & 0 \\ 0 & 1 & 0 \\ 0 & 0 & 1 \end{bmatrix} \quad \text{and} \quad [T_{n-1}] = \begin{bmatrix} s_x & sh_x & t_x \\ sh_y & s_y & t_y \\ 0 & 0 & 1 \end{bmatrix}$$

How do we go about computing $[T_1], \ldots, [T_{n-2}]$? It's easy: we can interpolate each of the start and end values to obtain as many intermediate values as we need. For example, a linear interpolation from 0 to 5 using five steps would yield $[0, 1, 2, 3, 4, 5]$. Note that five steps produce six values, so to obtain n frames, we'll use $n - 1$ steps.

To interpolate from a start value v_s to an end value v_e, we can use any function that passes through them. A straight line (linear function) is the simplest one, and the resulting values are uniformly spaced. This is a linear interpolation. If we used such interpolation to produce the frames of an animation, the result would move at constant speed from the beginning to the end (the slope of the interpolating function is constant), which looks unnatural to the eye. Why is that? Well, it's because we're not used to seeing things in real life abruptly accelerating, moving at the same speed, and stopping all of a sudden. This may look fine for projectiles or bullets, but it's strange for most real-life objects in motion. We can try a more natural-looking interpolating function such as an *ease-in-out*, plotted in the right-side graph of Figure 7-14.

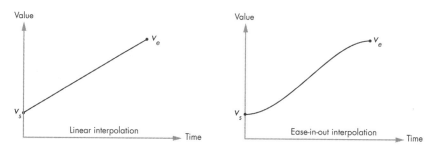

Figure 7-14: Two interpolation functions

In an ease-in-out function, values at the beginning and end vary slowly, which gives the sensation of things accelerating as they start to move and softly decelerating when reaching the end of their motion. This function defines motion in a much more natural way, and animations following this variation of the position with respect to time look nice to the human eye.

To obtain a value between v_s and v_e, we use a parameter t such that $0 \le t \le 1$ (see Equation 7.10).

$$v = v_s + t(v_e - v_s) \tag{7.10}$$

You can easily observe that Equation 7.10 yields a result of v_s for $t = 0$ and v_e for $t = 1$. For any intermediate value of t, the value varies between those two values. If we want to obtain a sequence of values starting with v_s all the way to v_e that follow a linear distribution, we just need to use equally spaced values for t, like, for example, $[0, 0.25, 0.5, 0.75, 1]$.

To produce an ease-in-out distribution of interpolated values, we need a sequence of t values from 0 to 1 with uneven spacing, with small steps near the extreme values and greater steps around the middle. If we represent the values of t by circles in a horizontal line starting at $t = 0$ and ending at $t = 1$, we can get a sense of how uniform and ease-in-out values are distributed from Figure 7-15.

$t = 0$ $t = 1$

Figure 7-15: Interpolating t values

To build the sequence of t values distributed according to the right-side plot in Figure 7-14, we can plug a sequence of evenly spaced t values into Equation 7.11.

$$f(t) = \frac{t^2}{t^2 + (1 - t)^2} \tag{7.11}$$

This alters their spacing so that more of them lie near the extremes 0 and 1 and fewer are located in the middle.

We have all the ingredients that we need; let's get our hands dirty!

Implementing Interpolation

Create a new file named *interpolation.py* inside *geom2d* and enter the code in Listing 7-14.

```
def uniform_t_sequence(steps: int):
    return [t / steps for t in range(steps + 1)]


def ease_in_out_t_sequence(steps: int):
    return [ease_in_out_t(t) for t in uniform_t_sequence(steps)]


def ease_in_out_t(t: float):
    return t ** 2 / (t ** 2 + (1 - t) ** 2)
```

Listing 7-14: Interpolated t values

Starting from the bottom, we have the function ease_in_out_t, which is simply the implementation of Equation 7.11. The first function builds a sequence of uniformly distributed *t* values using the given number of steps, thus producing as many values as steps plus one. We can test that in the shell. Reload it and try the following:

```
>>> from geom2d.interpolation import uniform_t_sequence
>>> uniform_t_sequence(10)
[0.0, 0.1, 0.2, 0.3, 0.4, 0.5, 0.6, 0.7, 0.8, 0.9, 1.0]
```

Function ease_in_out_t_sequence, on the other hand, creates sequences following an ease-in-out distribution. To do so, it applies Equation 7.11 to values of a uniform sequence. Let's try it as well in the shell:

```
>>> ease_in_out_t_sequence(10)
[0.0, 0.012195121951219514, 0.058823529411764705,
0.15517241379310345, 0.30769230769230776, 0.5,
0.6923076923076923, 0.8448275862068965,
0.9411764705882353, 0.9878048780487805, 1.0]
```

See how values near 0 and 1 are closer together while values in the middle (near 0.5) are farther apart? Great, so we're just missing a function to interpolate between two values for a given *t*, just as Equation 7.10 defines. Add Listing 7-15 in *interpolation.py*.

```
import geom2d.tparam as tparam


--snip--

def interpolate(vs: float, ve: float, t: float):
    tparam.ensure_valid(t)
    return vs + t * (ve - vs)
```

Listing 7-15: Interpolating between two values given t

If you recall from Chapter 5, when we operate using a passed-in *t* parameter value, we want to check that it's inside its expected range, for which the ensure_valid function is used. We're now ready for the last step, and I hope you followed along, because here's the actual interpolation of affine transformations we've been pursuing. Open your file *affine_transforms.py*, where we defined factory functions to create several special types of affine transformations, and enter the code in Listing 7-16.

```
import math

from geom2d.affine_transf import AffineTransform
from geom2d.interpolation import ease_in_out_t_sequence, interpolate
from geom2d.point import Point


--snip--

def ease_in_out_interpolation(start, end, steps):
❶   t_seq = ease_in_out_t_sequence(steps)
❷   return [__interpolated(start, end, t) for t in t_seq]


def __interpolated(s: AffineTransform, e: AffineTransform, t):
❸   return AffineTransform(
        sx=interpolate(s.sx, e.sx, t),
        sy=interpolate(s.sy, e.sy, t),
        tx=interpolate(s.tx, e.tx, t),
        ty=interpolate(s.ty, e.ty, t),
        shx=interpolate(s.shx, e.shx, t),
        shy=interpolate(s.shy, e.shy, t)
    )
```

Listing 7-16: Sequence of interpolated affine transformations

To help generate a sequence of interpolated affine transformations, we define a private function __interpolated, which, given two transformations and a value for *t*, returns the interpolation for that *t* ❸. Each value for the new transformation is the result of interpolating the values of both start and end transformations. Then we build a sequence of *t* values following the ease-in-out distribution ❶, each of which is mapped to the interpolated transformation using a list comprehension ❷.

We'll leave this for now until Chapter 12, where we'll be using the sequences of interpolated affine transformations to produce animations. Don't worry if the concepts explored in this last part of the chapter seem a little abstract. We'll build the foundations of animating motion in the next part of the book, and until then it may be hard to make sense out of this interpolation thing.

Geom2D Final Touches

Our *geom2d* package is tested and ready to be used throughout the rest of the book. We made it robust, but we can add a few small improvements before concluding this part of the book.

Test Files

The first thing we want to do is separate implementation and test files, which are all in the same folder at the moment. This is so that the *geom2d* package folder appears less cluttered and you can find implementation files easier. In the package, create a new folder named *tests*, and then select all test files, which we conveniently named ending in *_test.py*, and drag them to the folder. Your folder structure and files should look like the following:

```
Mechanics
 |- geom2d
 |    |- tests
 |    |    |- affine_transf_test.py
 |    |    |- affine_transforms_test.py
 |    |    |- circle_test.py
 |    |    |- ...
 |    |    |- vector_test.py
 |    |- __init__.py
 |    |- affine_transf.py
 |    |- affine_transforms.py
 |    |- circle.py
 |    |- ...
 |    |- vectors.py
```

Running All Tests

Now that all our test files live in the same folder, what about running all test cases at once? It may happen that you changed part of the code and want to make sure you didn't break anything, for which you decide to run every test in the package. The way we've been doing it would take you some time, as you'd have to open the test files one by one and click the green play button beside each of the class names. There's a better way!

Open the Terminal view inside PyCharm. If you can't see it, from the menu select **View ▶ Tool Windows ▶ Terminal**. By default, the shell opens right in the root directory of the project, which is exactly what we want. In the shell, run the following command:

```
$ python3 -m unittest discover -s geom2d/tests/ -p '*_test.py'
```

This command tells Python to discover and run all unit tests in *geom2d/tests/* inside files matching the pattern **_test.py*, that is, all files ending in *_test.py*. Running the command should result in something similar to the following:

```
Ran 58 tests in 0.004s

OK
```

You can save this command in a bash file at the project's root level so you can execute it whenever you want without needing to memorize it.

Package Imports

The last thing we want to do is include all modules in the package's exports so that they can be loaded like so:

```
from geom2d import Point, Polygon
```

Compare this to the following:

```
from geom2d.point import Point
from geom2d.polygon import Polygon
```

The latter requires the user to type the path where each module lives in *geom2d*, but the former doesn't: everything inside the package can be imported directly from the package itself. This style of exporting modules of a package is convenient for two reasons: (1) because it allows us to change the directory structure within the module without breaking the user's imports and (2) because users don't need to know where each module is located within the package and import everything from the package itself. As you can guess, this greatly reduces the cognitive load for using the package.

When PyCharm created the package *geom2d*, it included an empty file inside it named *__init__.py*. Can you spot it? Files with this name inside packages are loaded when the package itself is imported. We can use them to import what is defined inside the package.

NOTE *If for whatever reason the file __init__.py doesn't exist in your geom2d package, simply create it. Maybe you created the package as a normal directory inside PyCharm so the IDE didn't add it for you.*

So, open the file, which should be empty, and import all of the primitives we defined (see Listing 7-17).

```
from .point import Point
from .vector import Vector
from .vectors import *
from .circle import Circle
from .circles import *
from .interpolation import *
from .line import Line
from .nums import *
from .open_interval import OpenInterval
from .polygon import Polygon
from .rect import Rect
from .rects import *
from .segment import Segment
from .size import Size
from .tparam import *
from .affine_transf import *
from .affine_transforms import *
```

Listing 7-17: The geom2d *package* init *file*

That's all! To understand what we achieve with this change, you can try the following in the shell (Python's shell, not the shell we just used to run commands):

```
>>> from geom2d import Point, Size, Rect
>>> origin = Point(2, 3)
>>> size = Size(10, 15)
>>> rect = Rect(origin, size)
```

This will prove convenient in future chapters, as we can import any module from *geom2d* directly from the package.

Summary

In this chapter, we explored a core concept in computer graphics: affine transformations. They allow us to transform geometry by scaling, rotating, translating, and shearing it.

We started by taking a look at their mathematical definition and how they differ from linear transformations. The takeaway is that affine transformations can move the origin point, while linear transformations cannot. Affine transformations can be expressed as the combination of a linear transformation with a translation, but we saw a more convenient representation: the augmented matrix. Next, we implemented methods in the AffineTransform class to transform our geometric primitives: points, segments, and polygons.

We then learned how transformations can be concatenated to achieve complex transformations out of simpler ones. Thanks to that powerful idea, we were able to construct two essential affine transformations that happen in almost every graphics application we know: scaling and rotating around a point other than the origin.

Lastly, we implemented a function to interpolate between two affine transformations, yielding a couple intermediate transformations that we'll soon be using to produce animations.

PART III

GRAPHICS AND SIMULATIONS

8

DRAWING VECTOR IMAGES

We're about to start drawing images described by mathematical equations, a topic as fascinating as it is entertaining. We call images consisting of geometric primitives *vector images*, as opposed to *bitmap images*, which are sometimes also called *raster images*. Vector images are perfect for plotting the results of engineering problems that often come in the form of diagrams and simplified problem geometries.

In this chapter, we'll create our own Python package capable of creating SVG images out of the geometric primitives we created in Part II of the book: points, segments, circles, polygons, and so on. In later chapters, when we use code to solve actual mechanics problems, this package will help us produce graphical results.

There are good SVG packages out there (such as *svgwrite*, for instance), and we could just import them, but this book is about learning by doing, so we won't be using anything besides the Python Standard Library and our own code.

For the sake of brevity, we won't be writing unit tests in this chapter, but if you download the code, you'll see I wrote them to make sure everything works as it should. I encourage you to try to write your own unit tests for functions in this chapter and then compare them to the code I provided.

This chapter will introduce a powerful concept: *templating*. When templating, we have a piece of text, the *template*, that can be customized by filling in different placeholders. This technique is widely used in web development to produce the HTML document that gets rendered in your browser. Here again, there are many good templating libraries (such as *jinja2* or *mako*), but we want to learn how they work behind the scenes, so instead of using any of them, we'll write our own templating logic.

Bitmaps and Vector Images

There are two types of images: *bitmaps* and *vectors*. You've likely seen bitmap images before: *.jpeg*, *.gif*, and *.png* are all examples of bitmap image formats. A bitmap is an image defined over a grid of pixels where each individual pixel is assigned a particular color. These images look nice in their original size, but if you zoom in, you may start to distinguish those squares, the pixels.

Vector images, on the other hand, define their content by means of mathematical equations. This has the advantage of scaling smoothly without losing any quality. Let's explore *.svg*, the most widely used vector image format and the one we'll be using in this book.

The SVG Format

SVG stands for Scalable Vector Graphics. Its specification was developed by the *World Wide Web Consortium (W3C)* and is an open standard. I recommend that you open *https://developer.mozilla.org/en-US/docs/Web/SVG* and have it with you as a reference to look at; it'll provide more complete descriptions and examples that can complement the ones in this book. If you ever need to add something new to your SVG package, this page will be your ally.

Let's look at the following definition from the Mozilla website mentioned above for a quick reference on how these kinds of images are defined, as it beautifully describes the process:

> SVG images and their related behaviors are defined in XML text files, which means they can be searched, indexed, scripted, and compressed. Additionally, this means they can be created and edited with any text editor and with drawing software.

Note that SVG images are defined as plaintext, whereas most other image formats are binary encoded. This means we can readily automate the creation of SVG images and even inspect the contents of an existing image.

This chapter assumes you have a basic understanding of XML format, but if you don't, don't worry; it's quite simple to learn. Check the following resources to get started with it: https://www.w3schools.com/xml *and* https://www.xmlfiles.com/xml.

Let's try to create our first SVG image. Open your favorite plaintext editor such as Sublime Text, Visual Studio Code, Atom, or even PyCharm if you want, and write Listing 8-1.

```
<svg xmlns="http://www.w3.org/2000/svg" width="500" height="500">
    <circle cx="200" cy="200" r="100" fill="#ff000077" />
    <circle cx="300" cy="200" r="100" fill="#00ff0077" />
    <circle cx="250" cy="300" r="100" fill="#0000ff77" />
</svg>
```

Listing 8-1: SVG description of several circles

Note that you shouldn't create SVG files using a rich-text editor such as Word. These rich-text editors add their own markings into the raw file and break the SVG format.

Once you've copied what's in Listing 8-1, save the file as *circles.svg*, and open it using either Chrome or Firefox. Believe it or not, browsers are some of the best SVG image viewers. Using their *developer tools*, we can inspect the different parts that make up an image, something that will prove useful later when we build more complex images. You should see something like Figure 8-1 (there'll be colors on your screen, but the print version of the book is in grayscale). Zoom in on the image, and you'll see how it retains its crispness.

Figure 8-1: Examples of SVG circles

Let's break down the code in Listing 8-1. The first and most cryptic line contains the *XML namespace* (xmln) attribute.

```
xmlns="http://www.w3.org/2000/svg" width="500" height="500"
```

We have to include this namespace definition in every svg opening tag. The width and height attributes determine the size of the image in pixels. SVG *attributes* are modifiers that affect how a particular element is rendered. The width and height attributes, for example, determine the size of the drawing.

Then, between the svg open and close tags is the actual definition of what is drawn, in this case three circles:

```
<circle cx="200" cy="200" r="100" fill="#ff000077" />
<circle cx="300" cy="200" r="100" fill="#00ff0077" />
<circle cx="250" cy="300" r="100" fill="#0000ff77" />
```

As you may have guessed, cx and cy correspond to the coordinates of the center point; r is the radius of the circle. The attribute fill determines the fill color for the circles in hexadecimal format: #rrggbbaa, where rr is the red value, gg is the green value, bb is the blue value, and aa is the alpha or opacity value (see Figure 8-2).

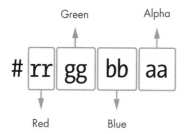

Figure 8-2: Hexadecimal color components

For example, the color #ff000077 has the following components:

red ff, the maximum value (255 in base 10)

green 00, the minimum value (0 in base 10)

blue 00, the minimum value (0 in base 10)

alpha 77, a value of 119 out of 255, which equals an alpha percentage of around 47%

This color is a perfect red with some transparency added to it.

You may not have realized, but the origin of coordinates for SVG images is located in the upper-left corner, with its y-axis pointing down. You may not be used to this orientation of the vertical axis, but don't worry: by using one of our affine transformations, we can easily transform space so that the y-axis points upward, as you'll see later in the chapter. Figure 8-3 shows the geometry and arrangement of coordinates for the image we created.

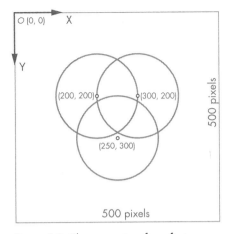

Figure 8-3: The geometry of our first
SVG image

The viewBox

A useful attribute that we can define for the svg tag is the viewBox. The viewBox
is the rectangular portion of the image the user sees. It's defined using four
numbers,

```
viewBox="x y w h"
```

where x and y are the coordinates of the rectangle's origin, and w and h are
the width and height of the rectangle.

Let's add a viewBox to our circles image to see its effect (see Listing 8-2).

```
<svg xmlns="http://www.w3.org/2000/svg"
    width="500"
    height="500"
    viewBox="100 100 300 300">
    <circle cx="200" cy="200" r="100" fill="#ff000077" />
    <circle cx="300" cy="200" r="100" fill="#00ff0077" />
    <circle cx="250" cy="300" r="100" fill="#0000ff77" />
</svg>
```

Listing 8-2: SVG viewBox

Save the changes we made in Listing 8-2 and reload the image in the
browser to see the change. To understand what's happened, take a look at
Figure 8-4.

We've defined a rectangle whose origin is at (100, 100), with a width of
300 and a height of 300: a rectangle that contains all three circles without
any margin. Notice the image retains its size of 500 by 500 pixels, as defined
by the width and height attributes. If the size of the viewBox is not the same as
the size of the SVG itself, the content is scaled.

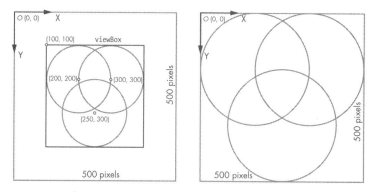

Figure 8-4: The viewBox of an SVG image

The viewBox is therefore the rectangular portion from the infinite canvas that's displayed to the user. It's optional, and it defaults to the rectangle with the size defined by width and height, with its origin at $(0, 0)$.

Space Transformation

Remember the concept of affine transformations from Chapter 7? SVG images use them to transform their content. The attribute transform can be used to define the affine transformation matrix as follows:

```
transform="matrix(sx shy shx sy tx ty)"
```

The confusing order of the matrix terms may seem surprising at first, but it actually makes sense, at least for the people behind the SVG standard. The SVG documentation defines the affine transformation matrix as follows:

$$[T] = \begin{bmatrix} a & c & e \\ b & d & f \\ 0 & 0 & 1 \end{bmatrix}$$

So these are the terms of the transform attribute:

```
transform="matrix(a b c d e f)"
```

Translated to our less cryptic language, the terms are $a = s_x$, $b = sh_y$, $c = sh_x$, $d = s_y$, $e = t_x$, and $f = t_y$:

$$[T] = \begin{bmatrix} s_x & sh_x & t_x \\ sh_y & s_y & t_y \\ 0 & 0 & 1 \end{bmatrix}$$

Let's see it in action. We'll apply a shear in the x direction by setting sh_x to be 1. Remember that both s_x and s_y have to be 1; otherwise, if set as zero, the image would collapse in a line or point, and we wouldn't see anything. Listing 8-3 has the added `transform` attribute.

```
<svg xmlns="http://www.w3.org/2000/svg"
    width="500"
    height="500"
    transform="matrix(1 0 1 1 0 0)"
    <circle cx="200" cy="200" r="100" fill="#ff000077" />
    <circle cx="300" cy="200" r="100" fill="#00ff0077" />
    <circle cx="250" cy="300" r="100" fill="#0000ff77" />
</svg>
```

Listing 8-3: Shear transformation in circles image

Remember to remove the `viewBox` attribute so the resulting geometry doesn't get cropped. You should see something like Figure 8-5.

Figure 8-5: Our circles once transformed

What about inverting the y-axis so that it points upward, like we're used to? Easy! Edit the transform matrix to the following:

```
transform="matrix(1 0 0 -1 0 0)"
```

The resulting geometry you should see is outlined in Figure 8-6. Compare it with Figure 8-1. See what happened? The picture flipped vertically.

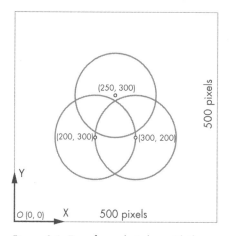

*Figure 8-6: Transformed circles, with the
y-axis inverted*

Now that you have a basic understanding of how to create SVG images,
let's do some Python coding. We'll create a package in our project to draw
SVG images.

The svg Package

Let's create a new package for graphics in our project, which will contain
a subpackage to produce SVG images. Later in the book we'll add other
subpackages for other kinds of graphical operations. Right-click the project
name in the **Project Tool** window and choose **New ▶ Python Package**. Name
it *graphic*. You can also create a new folder yourself, but don't forget to add
the __init__.py file to instruct Python this is a package.

You should have the package at the same level as *geom2d*, and it should
contain only an __init__.py file. Your project's directory structure should
look like this:

```
Mechanics
    |- geom2d
    |     |- tests
    |- graphic
    |- utils
```

Now let's add the *svg* subpackage: right-click the package you just created and choose **New ▶ Python Package** again, but this time name it *svg*.
Now we're ready to start adding our code.

Templates

A template is a document with some placeholders in it. By assigning values
to these placeholders we can produce a complete version of the document.
Think, for instance, about those email campaigns that greet you by your
name. The company sending them probably has a template like

```
Hello, {{name}}!
Here are some book recommendations we think you may like.
...
```

and an automatic process that substitutes the {{name}} placeholder with each of their clients' names and then sends the final composed email.

The placeholders in a template may also be called *variables*. Variables are given values in the process of rendering the template, which produces the final document with everything defined in it. Figure 8-7 illustrates the process of rendering the same template with two different sets of values. The template has the variables place-from, place-to, distance, and units, which we assign different values to produce different versions of the same template.

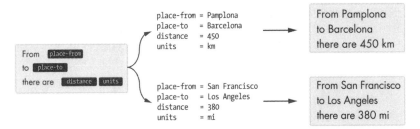

Figure 8-7: Template rendering process

Using templates is a powerful technique that solves a variety of problems where text of any shape and format needs to be generated. Most web frameworks, for instance, use some kind of templating to produce the rendered HTML document. We'll employ a template to generate our SVG images.

An Example Using Python's String Replacement

Let's work on a template example in code. Open Python's shell and enter the following template string:

```
>>> template = 'Hello, my name is {{name}}'
```

Now, let's create a greeting by substituting the {{name}} variable with a real name:

```
>>> template.replace('{{name}}', 'Angel')
'Hello, my name is Angel'
```

As you can see, we can use Python's replace string method to create a new string where {{name}} has been replaced by 'Angel'. Since replace returns a new instance, we can chain the calls like so:

```
>>> template.replace('{{name}}', 'Angel').replace('Hello', 'Hi there')
'Hi there, my name is Angel'
```

In this example, we first replaced the {{name}} variable with the string 'Angel'. Then, we called the replace method on the resulting string to substitute the word 'Hello' with 'Hi there'.

Note that we can substitute whatever sequence of characters we want using the `replace` method; there's no need for our replacement targets to appear between braces, like for instance we did with {{name}}. Using the double braces is a convention for us to quickly identify a variable inside a template. This convention also serves the purpose of preventing unwanted replacements: it's unlikely that our templates include anything inside two levels of braces, except for our variables.

Now that we know how to work with template strings in Python, let's see how we can define templates in separate files and load them into strings in our code.

Loading Templates

To avoid mixing XML and Python code, we want to separate the definitions of SVG tags into their own files. The files containing the XML need to have placeholders where the actual data will be inserted. For example, our circle definition file could look something like this:

```
<circle cx="{{cx}}" cy="{{cy}}" r="{{r}}" />
```

Here we've put placeholders using double braces. We'll use code to load this definition into a string and replace the placeholders with the actual coordinates of the center and the radius of the circle.

We'll be creating a few templates, so let's create a folder named *templates* inside the *svg* package by right-clicking the package name and choosing **New** ▶ **Directory**. We need a function that reads the templates inside this folder by their name and returns their content as a string. In the *svg* package, but not in the *templates* folder, create a new file named *read.py* and add the code in Listing 8-4.

```python
from os import path

import pkg_resources as res


def read_template(file_name: str):
    file_path = path.join('templates', file_name)
    bytes_str = res.resource_string(__name__, file_path)
    return bytes_str.decode('UTF-8')
```

Listing 8-4: Reading the content of a template file

Let's break Listing 8-4 down. The first thing we do in the function is obtain the path inside *templates* where the file lives. We do this using the `os.path` module's `join` function. This function computes the path by joining the parts passed as arguments and using the correct separator for your operating system. For instance, Unix-based operating systems use the / character.

Then, using `resource_string` from the *pkg_resources* module, we read the file as a *byte string*. A file is stored to disk as a sequence of bytes, so when we read it using the `resource_string` function, we get this byte string. To convert it to a Unicode character string, we need to *decode* it. For this, byte strings have the method `decode`, which accepts the encoding as an argument.

We return the result of decoding the string of bytes using UTF-8 encoding. This will give us a string version of the template we can easily work with.

Image Templates

The most important template we want to define is the template for the SVG image. Create a new text file named *img* (without an extension; we don't need one) in the *templates* folder and include the definition in Listing 8-5.

```
<svg xmlns="http://www.w3.org/2000/svg" version="1.1"
    width="{{width}}"
    height="{{height}}"
    viewBox="{{viewBox}}"
    transform="matrix({{transf}})">
    {{content}}
</svg>
```

Listing 8-5: SVG image template

This template includes five placeholders that need to be replaced with the actual values from the resulting image. We can try to load the template in Python's shell using the `read_template` function we defined earlier:

```
>>> from graphic.svg.read import read_template
>>> read_template('img')
'<svg xmlns="http://www.w3.org/2000/svg" version="1.1"\n  width="{{width}}"...'
```

Let's create a new file *image.py* in the *svg* directory (but outside the *templates* folder!) and define a function that reads in the file and does the replacement. In your *image.py* file, enter the code in Listing 8-6.

```
from geom2d import AffineTransform, Rect, Point, Size
from graphic.svg.read import read_template


def svg_content(
        size: Size,
        primitives: [str],
        viewbox_rect=None,
        transform=None
):
❶ viewbox_rect = viewbox_rect or __default_viewbox_rect(size)
❷ transform = transform or AffineTransform()
❸ template = read_template('img')
```

```
    return template \
        .replace('{{width}}', str(size.width)) \
        .replace('{{height}}', str(size.height)) \
    ❹ .replace('{{content}}', '\n\t'.join(primitives)) \
    ❺ .replace('{{viewBox}}', __viewbox_from_rect(viewbox_rect)) \
    ❻ .replace('{{transf}}', __transf_matrix_vals(transform))
```

Listing 8-6: SVG image

The `svg_content` function takes four parameters; the last two, `viewbox_rect` and `transform`, are given a default value of `None`. We can use `or` so that `viewbox_rect` keeps its value if it's not `None` and otherwise gets a default instance created by `__default_viewbox_rect` ❶ (we'll write this function next). We do the same with `transform` ❷, using an affine transformation constructed with the default values.

Then, using the function we prepared in the previous section, we load the template stored in *templates/img* ❸.

The last and most important step is to replace all placeholders in the loaded template string with the values we've been passed.

NOTE *One nice property of strings in Python, as in most programming languages, is that they're immutable; you can't take a string and change a character in it. What you do instead is create a new string with the desired change. This is how the `replace` string method works: it replaces a given sequence of characters with another and returns a new string with the result. Thanks to this nice property, we can beautifully chain several `replace` calls to the result of the call to `read_template`.*

The replacements for the `{{width}}` and `{{height}}` placeholders are straightforward; just keep in mind that the passed-in `size.width` and `size.height` properties are numbers, so we need to convert them to their string representation using `str`.

The `primitives` parameter contains a sequence of strings representing the content of the image. We need to collect these strings in a single string. The `join` string method joins all the elements in a list together into a single string using the string it was called on as a separator. To obtain a string including all the primitives, we'll use `join` ❹ on the list, with a new line and a tab character (`\n\t`) as the separator.

For `viewBox` we need to convert the `Rect` instance into the four numbers that define it ❺; this is done with `__viewbox_from_rect`, which we'll define in a minute. The same goes for `transf` ❻.

Let's write the missing helping functions after `svg_content`. The code is in Listing 8-7.

```
--snip--

def __default_viewbox_rect(size: Size):
    return Rect(Point(0, 0), size)
```

```
def __viewbox_from_rect(rect: Rect):
    x = rect.origin.x
    y = rect.origin.y
    width = rect.size.width
    height = rect.size.height

    return f'{x} {y} {width} {height}'


def __transf_matrix_vals(t: AffineTransform):
    return f'{t.sx} {t.shy} {t.shx} {t.sy} {t.tx} {t.ty}'
```

Listing 8-7: SVG image helper functions

The first function (`__default_viewbox_rect`) creates a rectangle for the viewBox using the point $(0, 0)$ as the origin and the provided size. This function, as its name indicates, is used to provide a default value for the viewbox _rect parameter in case it wasn't given by the user.

The `__viewbox_from_rect` function returns a string formatted to be used as viewBox inside the SVG definition. The last function, `__transf_matrix_vals`, does something similar: it converts an affine transformation into a string with the format expected by SVG.

Great! We now have a function that renders the SVG template into a string. Let's take a look at some attributes we'll add to almost all primitives.

Attributes

The appearance of SVG elements can be modified using *attributes*. SVG attributes are defined following the XML attribute syntax (don't forget that SVG images are defined following the XML format):

```
name="value"
```

For example, we can use the stroke attribute to set a primitive's stroke color:

```
<circle cx="10" cy="15" r="40" stroke="green" />
```

Note that, in the previous example, the circle's center coordinates (cx and cy) and radius (r) are also defined as attributes in the circle SVG element.

As we're about to see, many SVG geometry primitives have shared attributes to define things such as the color of their stroke, the stroke's width, the fill color, etc. To reuse this logic, we'll place it in a file that all primitive generation functions will use. As these attribute definitions are short, we won't include them in templates that need to be loaded; instead, we'll define them inside the function that replaces the placeholders.

Create a new file named *attributes.py* inside the *svg* directory. Your *graphic/svg* folder should look like the following:

```
svg
  |- templates
  |    |- img
  |- __init__.py
  |- attributes.py
  |- image.py
  |- read.py
```

Enter the functions in Listing 8-8.

```python
from geom2d.affine_transf import AffineTransform


def stroke_color(color: str):
    return f'stroke="{color}"'


def stroke_width(width: float):
    return f'stroke-width="{str(width)}"'


def fill_color(color: str):
    return f'fill="{color}"'


def fill_opacity(opacity: float):
    return f'fill-opacity="{str(opacity)}"'


def affine_transform(t: AffineTransform):
    values = f'{t.sx} {t.shy} {t.shx} {t.sy} {t.tx} {t.ty}'
    return f'transform="matrix({values})"'


def font_size(size: float):
    return f'font-size="{size}px"'


def font_family(font: str):
    return f'font-family="{font}"'


def attrs_to_str(attrs_list: [str]):
    return ' '.join(attrs_list)
```

Listing 8-8: SVG attributes

All the functions are quite straightforward; they receive a value and return a string with the definition of an SVG attribute. We use single quotes around the returned strings, and this allows us to use double quotes inside without the need of escaping them. The SVG attributes are defined using double quotes, like, for example, stroke="blue".

The last function takes some attributes and joins them into a string separating them with spaces. We achieve this using a single space (' ') as a separator for the join function. To fully understand how this works, give this a try in the shell:

```
>>> words = ['svg', 'is', 'a', 'nice', 'format']
>>> ' '.join(words)
'svg is a nice format'
```

The SVG Primitives

We've written the foundations of our *svg* package; we can now produce empty images, a process that involves reading the *img* template and replacing its variables. If we called our svg_content function from Python's shell,

```
>>> from graphic.svg.image import svg_content
>>> from geom2d import Size
>>> svg_content(Size(200, 150), [])
```

we'd get the following SVG content:

```
<svg xmlns="http://www.w3.org/2000/svg" version="1.1"
    width="200"
    height="150"
    viewBox="0 0 200 150"
    transform="matrix(1 0 0 1 0 0)">
</svg>
```

It's a great beginning, but who wants blank images?

In the next sections, we'll create a couple basic SVG primitives to add between the <svg></svg> tags: lines, rectangles, circles, polygons, and text labels, to name a few. As we'll see throughout the book, we don't need a lot of primitives to draw our engineering drawings; we can get pretty far with only straight lines, circles, and rectangles.

The strategy we'll follow to produce these SVG primitives is the same we used for the SVG content: we'll use a template to define the SVG code with variables that we'll replace inside a function.

Lines

The first primitive we'll implement in our *svg* package is the line segment, or line in SVG parlance. This may be a little unfortunate, as segments and lines are different concepts. (Recall that lines are infinite, but segments are not;

they have a finite length.) At any rate, we'll use the SVG terminology here, so let's create a new template file named *line* inside the *templates* folder and add the code in Listing 8-9:

```
<line x1="{{x1}}" y1="{{y1}}" x2="{{x2}}" y2="{{y2}}" {{attrs}}/>
```

Listing 8-9: Line template

The template for a line is simple. The placeholders define the following:

- x1 and y1, the coordinates of the start point
- x2 and y2, the coordinates of the end point
- attrs, where the attributes will be inserted

Figure 8-8 depicts the line with its attributes using the default coordinate system for SVG images.

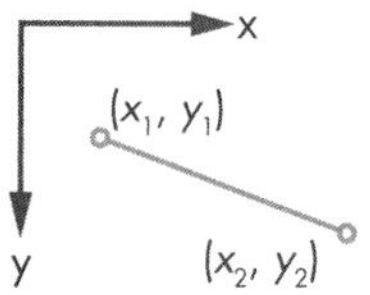

Figure 8-8: An example of an SVG line

Let's now create a function that reads the template and inserts the values of a segment. We need a new file; let's create it inside *svg* with the name *primitives.py*. Enter the function in Listing 8-10.

```
from geom2d import Segment
from graphic.svg.attributes import attrs_to_str
from graphic.svg.read import read_template


__segment_template = read_template('line')


def segment(seg: Segment, attributes=()):
    return __segment_template \
        .replace('{{x1}}', str(seg.start.x)) \
        .replace('{{y1}}', str(seg.start.y)) \
        .replace('{{x2}}', str(seg.end.x)) \
        .replace('{{y2}}', str(seg.end.y)) \
        .replace('{{attrs}}', attrs_to_str(attributes))
```

Listing 8-10: SVG line

One thing to note is that the parameter attributes has a default value of (), that is, an empty tuple. We could have also used an empty list [] as the default for the parameter, but there's an important difference between those two options: tuples are immutable, and lists are mutable. Function default arguments are evaluated only once when the file is loaded into the interpreter, so if a mutable default parameter is mutated, all subsequent calls to the same function would get the mutated value as the default, and that's something we want to avoid.

In the shell, try the code below to create an SVG line in order to see the result and make sure that all placeholders are properly replaced.

```
>>> from geom2d import Segment, make_point
>>> from graphic import svg
>>> seg = Segment(make_point(1, 4), make_point(2, 5))
>>> attrs = [svg.attributes.stroke_color('#cacaca')]
>>> svg.primitives.segment(seg, attrs)
'<line x1="1" y1="4" x2="2" y2="5" stroke="#cacaca"/>'
```

This line inside an SVG file would be drawn as in Figure 8-9.

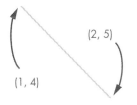

Figure 8-9: SVG line

Bear in mind the arrows and position captions are added in this figure for clarity but won't appear in the image itself.

Rectangles

Our next primitive is the rectangle, so inside *templates* create a new file named *rect* (remember, we're not using any extension in our template files) with the definition shown in Listing 8-11:

```
<rect x="{{x}}" y="{{y}}"
      width="{{width}}" height="{{height}}"
      {{attrs}}/>
```

Listing 8-11: The rectangle template

You can write the template in a single line; here we used several lines because in the print version, the code didn't fit in just one. The attributes that define a rectangle are, as expected, the coordinates of the origin x and y and its size given by width and height. In *primitives.py*, add the function in Listing 8-12.

```
from geom2d import Rect, Segment
from graphic.svg.attributes import attrs_to_str
from graphic.svg.read import read_template
```

```
__segment_template = read_template('line')
__rect_template = read_template('rect')

--snip--

def rectangle(rect: Rect, attributes=()):
    return __rect_template \
        .replace('{{x}}', str(rect.origin.x)) \
        .replace('{{y}}', str(rect.origin.y)) \
        .replace('{{width}}', str(rect.size.width)) \
        .replace('{{height}}', str(rect.size.height)) \
        .replace('{{attrs}}', attrs_to_str(attributes))
```

Listing 8-12: SVG rectangle

To gain a better understanding of the attributes that define a rectangle in the SVG format, take a look at Figure 8-10. The figure uses the default coordinate system from SVG: the y-axis pointing downward. This is why the origin of the rectangle is the upper-left corner. If we were using a coordinate system whose y-axis pointed upward, the origin would be the lower-left corner.

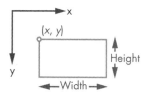

Figure 8-10: An example of an SVG rectangle

Give it a try in the shell, as we did with the segment, to check that all placeholders are properly replaced:

```
>>> from geom2d import Rect, Point, Size
>>> from graphic.svg.primitives import rectangle
>>> r = Rect(Point(3, 4), Size(10, 20))
>>> rectangle(r)
'<rect x="3" y="4" width="10" height="20" />'
```

It's a good idea to check that everything works as expected, since later in the book we'll be creating lots of diagrams using these simple primitives. Unit testing is the best option, much better than testing manually in the shell. If you downloaded the code for the book, you'll see all these primitive rendering functions are covered by tests. Try to write them yourself so you get used to writing unit tests and then compare them to the ones that I've provided you.

Circles

We'll take a similar approach to rectangles to create circles. Create the template in a file named *circle* (see Listing 8-13).

```
<circle cx="{{cx}}" cy="{{cy}}" r="{{r}}" {{attrs}}/>
```

Listing 8-13: The circle *template*

Then add the function to render the circle inside *primitives.py* (see Listing 8-14).

```
from geom2d import Circle, Rect, Segment
from graphic.svg.attributes import attrs_to_str
from graphic.svg.read import read_template


__segment_template = read_template('line')
__rect_template = read_template('rect')
__circle_template = read_template('circle')

--snip--

def circle(circ: Circle, attributes=()):
    return __circle_template \
        .replace('{{cx}}', str(circ.center.x)) \
        .replace('{{cy}}', str(circ.center.y)) \
        .replace('{{r}}', str(circ.radius)) \
        .replace('{{attrs}}', attrs_to_str(attributes))
```

Listing 8-14: SVG circle

Nothing unexpected here! You can take a look at Figure 8-11 to see the attributes we used to define the circle in the SVG format.

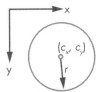

Figure 8-11: An example of an SVG circle

Let's give it a try in the shell:

```
>>> from geom2d import Circle, Point
>>> from graphic.svg.primitives import circle
>>> c = Circle(Point(3, 4), 10)
>>> circle(c)
'<circle cx="3" cy="4" r="10" />'
```

Polygons

Polygons are simple to define; we simply need to provide the list of vertex coordinates formatted in a specific way. Create the template file *polygon* in *templates* (see Listing 8-15).

```
<polygon points="{{points}}" {{attrs}}/>
```

Listing 8-15: The polygon *template*

Then inside *primitives.py* include the function in Listing 8-16.

```
from geom2d import Circle, Rect, Segment, Polygon
from graphic.svg.attributes import attrs_to_str
from graphic.svg.read import read_template


__segment_template = read_template('line')
__rect_template = read_template('rect')
__circle_template = read_template('circle')
__polygon_template = read_template('polygon')

--snip--

def polygon(pol: Polygon, attributes=()):
    return __polygon_template \
        .replace('{{points}}', __format_points(pol.vertices)) \
        .replace('{{attrs}}', attrs_to_str(attributes))
```

Listing 8-16: SVG polygon

The placeholder {{points}} is replaced with the result of applying __format_points to the list of vertices. Let's write that function here, inside the *primitives.py* file (see Listing 8-16):

```
--snip--

def __format_points(points: [Point]):
    return ' '.join([f'{p.x},{p.y}' for p in points])
```

Listing 8-17: Format points

As you can see, the list of vertices is converted into a string where each vertex is separated by a space,

```
' '.join(...)
```

and the two coordinates, x and y, are separated with a comma:

```
[f'\{p.x\},\{p.y\}' for p in points]
```

For example, a polygon with vertices $(1, 2)$, $(5, 6)$, and $(8, 9)$ would result in the following:

```
<polygon points="1,2 5,6 8,9" />
```

Polylines

Polylines are defined the same way as polygons—the only difference is that the last vertex isn't connected with the first one. Create the template in a file named *polyline* in *templates* (see Listing 8-18).

```
<polyline points="{{points}}" {{attrs}}/>
```

Listing 8-18: The polyline *template*

Include the rendering function inside file *primitives.py* (see Listing 8-19).

```
from geom2d import Circle, Rect, Segment, Polygon
from graphic.svg.attributes import attrs_to_str
from graphic.svg.read import read_template


__segment_template = read_template('line')
__rect_template = read_template('rect')
__circle_template = read_template('circle')
__polygon_template = read_template('polygon')
__polyline_template = read_template('polyline')

--snip--

def polyline(points: [Point], attributes=()):
    return __polyline_template \
        .replace('{{points}}', __format_points(points)) \
        .replace('{{attrs}}', attrs_to_str(attributes))
```

Listing 8-19: SVG polyline

Again, no surprises here. Figure 8-12 shows the difference between a polygon and a polyline. The definition for both is the same; the only difference is that last segment connecting vertex (x_4, y_4) back to (x_1, y_1) appears only in the case of a polygon.

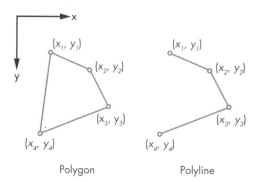

Figure 8-12: An SVG polygon and polyline

Let's try a polygon and a polyline in the shell to see the results:

```
>>> from geom2d import Polygon, Point
>>> from graphic.svg.primitives import polygon, polyline
>>> points = [Point(1, 2), Point(3, 4), Point(5, 6)]

>>> polygon(Polygon(points))
'<polygon points="1,2 3,4 5,6" />'

>>> polyline(points)
'<polyline points="1,2 3,4 5,6" />'
```

Both the polygon and the polyline have the same sequence of points, but in an SVG image, the polygon will have a segment connecting the first and last vertices, whereas the polyline will remain open.

Text

Our diagrams will contain captions (like the structural analysis result diagrams in Chapter 18), so we need to be able to include text in our images. Create a new template file named *text* in folder *templates* with the code in Listing 8-20.

```
<text x="{{x}}" y="{{y}}" dx="{{dx}}" dy="{{dy}}" {{attrs}}>
    {{text}}
</text>
```

Listing 8-20: The text template

The placeholder {{text}} has to be between the open and close tags <text> and </text>; this is where the actual text will be inserted. The attributes x and y define the position where the text will be located; then dx and dy displace that original position. We'll find this displacement handy when, for instance, we want to add the coordinates of a point next to it. We can choose the position of the point itself as the base, which we then displace a given amount so that the text and the drawing of the point don't overlap.

In *primitives.py* add the function shown in Listing 8-21 to render text:

```
from geom2d import Circle, Rect, Segment, Polygon, Vector
from graphic.svg.attributes import attrs_to_str
from graphic.svg.read import read_template


__segment_template = read_template('line')
__rect_template = read_template('rect')
__circle_template = read_template('circle')
__polygon_template = read_template('polygon')
__polyline_template = read_template('polyline')
__text_template = read_template('text')

--snip--

def text(txt: str, pos: Point, disp: Vector, attrs_list=()):
    return __text_template \
        .replace('{{x}}', str(pos.x)) \
        .replace('{{y}}', str(pos.y)) \
        .replace('{{dx}}', str(disp.u)) \
        .replace('{{dy}}', str(disp.v)) \
        .replace('{{text}}', txt) \
        .replace('{{attrs}}', attrs_to_str(attrs_list))
```

Listing 8-21: SVG text

Let's give it a try in the shell:

```
>>> from geom2d import Point, Vector
>>> from graphic.svg.primitives import text
>>> text('Hello, SVG', Point(10, 15), Vector(5, 6))
'<text x="10" y="15" dx="5" dy="6" >\n    Hello, SVG\n</text>'
```

If we format the result string, the result is as follows:

```
<text x="10" y="15" dx="5" dy="6" >
    Hello, SVG
</text>
```

Groups

Oftentimes we want to group a bunch of elements so we can add a common attribute to all of them, such as an affine transformation or fill color. This is what groups are for. They're nothing to be rendered by themselves, but they group a bunch of primitives in a neat way. Create the file *group* inside the *templates* folder (see Listing 8-22).

```
<g {{attrs}}>
    {{content}}
</g>
```

Listing 8-22: The group template

To render the group, we'll add the function shown in Listing 8-23 to file *primitives.py*.

```
from geom2d import Circle, Rect, Segment, Polygon, Vector
from graphic.svg.attributes import attrs_to_str
from graphic.svg.read import read_template


__segment_template = read_template('line')
__rect_template = read_template('rect')
__circle_template = read_template('circle')
__polygon_template = read_template('polygon')
__polyline_template = read_template('polyline')
__text_template = read_template('text')
__group_template = read_template('group')

--snip--

def group(primitives: [str], attributes=()):
    return __group_template \
        .replace('{{content}}', '\n'.join(primitives)) \
        .replace('{{attrs}}', attrs_to_str(attributes))
```

Listing 8-23: SVG group

This time, all primitives passed as a sequence are joined into a string separated by line breaks (\n). This is so that each primitive is inserted in a new line, which will make the file easier to read.

Arrows

In this section, we're going to add a different primitive, one that's built not by loading and rendering a template but by using other primitives: an arrow. In Chapter 18, when we draw structure diagrams, we'll use arrows to represent forces, so this is a good moment to implement them.

The arrow consists of a line segment with a small triangle at one of its ends, the arrow's head (see Figure 8-13).

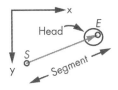

Figure 8-13: An SVG arrow

Drawing the arrow's segment is simple: we just need a line segment. Drawing the head is a bit more involved, because it needs to always be aligned with the segment. Using a bit of elementary geometry we can figure out the points that define the arrow's head. Take a look at Figure 8-14.

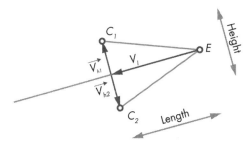

Figure 8-14: Key points in an arrow

Our arrow's head is a triangle defined between points C_1, E (the segment's end point), and C_2. The size of the arrow is given by a length and a height, sizes that we'll use to locate the C_1 and C_2 points.

The figure uses three vectors to position these two points.

$\vec{v}_l$ This is a vector in the direction opposite to the segment's direction vector and is the same length as the arrow.

$\vec{v}_{h1}$ This is a vector perpendicular to the segment, and the length is half the arrow's head height.

$\vec{v}_{h2}$ This is similar to $\vec{v}_{h1}$, but in the opposite direction.

Using these vectors, we can now compute the points as follows:

$$C_1 = E + (\vec{v}_l + \vec{v}_{h1})$$

and

$$C_2 = E + (\vec{v}_l + \vec{v}_{h2})$$

Without further ado, let's write the code to draw arrows. Inside *primitives.py*, enter the code in Listing 8-24.

```
--snip--

def arrow(
        _segment: Segment,
        length: float,
        height: float,
        attributes=()
):
    director = _segment.direction_vector
❶   v_l = director.opposite().with_length(length)
❷   v_h1 = director.perpendicular().with_length(height / 2.0)
❸   v_h2 = v_h1.opposite()

    return group(
        [

❹           segment(_segment),
❺           polyline([
                _segment.end.displaced(v_l + v_h1),
                _segment.end,
                _segment.end.displaced(v_l + v_h2)
            ])
        ],
        attributes
    )
```

Listing 8-24: SVG arrow

We've defined the `arrow` function that accepts as parameters a segment, the length and height of the arrow, and the SVG attributes. Note that the `_segment` parameter starts with an underscore. This is to avoid a clash with the file's `segment` function.

In this function we first store the segment's director vector in the variable `director`. We then compute the $\vec{v}_l$ vector taking director's opposite vector scaled to the passed-in length ❶. The $\vec{v}_{h1}$ vector is obtained by taking director's perpendicular vector scaled to the arrow's half-height ❷. Then, $\vec{v}_{h2}$ is simply the opposite of it ❸.

The function returns an SVG group including the arrow's segment ❹ and a polyline ❺. This polyline defines the arrow's head using the three points we discussed earlier.

The first point, C_1, is computed by displacing the segment's end point by the result of adding vectors $\vec{v}_l$ and $\vec{v}_{h1}$. Then comes the segment's end point. Lastly comes C_2, resulting from the displacement of the segment's end point by a vector that's the result of adding $\vec{v}_l$ and $\vec{v}_{h2}$.

Primitives Result

We've added a few functions to our *primitives.py* file. If you followed along, your file should look similar to Listing 8-25.

```
from geom2d import Circle, Rect, Segment, Point, Polygon, Vector
from graphic.svg.attributes import attrs_to_str
from graphic.svg.read import read_template


__segment_template = read_template('line')
__rect_template = read_template('rect')
__circle_template = read_template('circle')
__polygon_template = read_template('polygon')
__polyline_template = read_template('polyline')
__text_template = read_template('text')
__group_template = read_template('group')


def segment(seg: Segment, attributes=()):
    return __segment_template \
        .replace('{{x1}}', str(seg.start.x)) \
        .replace('{{y1}}', str(seg.start.y)) \
        .replace('{{x2}}', str(seg.end.x)) \
        .replace('{{y2}}', str(seg.end.y)) \
        .replace('{{attrs}}', attrs_to_str(attributes))


def rectangle(rect: Rect, attributes=()):
    return __rect_template \
        .replace('{{x}}', str(rect.origin.x)) \
        .replace('{{y}}', str(rect.origin.y)) \
        .replace('{{width}}', str(rect.size.width)) \
        .replace('{{height}}', str(rect.size.height)) \
        .replace('{{attrs}}', attrs_to_str(attributes))


def circle(circ: Circle, attributes=()):
    return __circle_template \
        .replace('{{cx}}', str(circ.center.x)) \
        .replace('{{cy}}', str(circ.center.y)) \
        .replace('{{r}}', str(circ.radius)) \
        .replace('{{attrs}}', attrs_to_str(attributes))


def polygon(pol: Polygon, attributes=()):
    return __polygon_template \
        .replace('{{points}}', __format_points(pol.vertices)) \
        .replace('{{attrs}}', attrs_to_str(attributes))
```

```
def polyline(points: [Point], attributes=()):
    return __polyline_template \
        .replace('{{points}}', __format_points(points)) \
        .replace('{{attrs}}', attrs_to_str(attributes))


def text(txt: str, pos: Point, disp: Vector, attrs_list=()):
    return __text_template \
        .replace('{{x}}', str(pos.x)) \
        .replace('{{y}}', str(pos.y)) \
        .replace('{{dx}}', str(disp.u)) \
        .replace('{{dy}}', str(disp.v)) \
        .replace('{{text}}', txt) \
        .replace('{{attrs}}', attrs_to_str(attrs_list))


def group(primitives: [str], attributes=()):
    return __group_template \
        .replace('{{content}}', '\n\t'.join(primitives)) \
        .replace('{{attrs}}', attrs_to_str(attributes))


def arrow(
        _segment: Segment,
        length: float,
        height: float,
        attributes=()
):
    director = _segment.direction_vector
    v_l = director.opposite().with_length(length)
    v_h1 = director.perpendicular().with_length(height / 2.0)
    v_h2 = v_h1.opposite()

    return group(
        [
            segment(_segment),
            polyline([
                _segment.end.displaced(v_l + v_h1),
                _segment.end,
                _segment.end.displaced(v_l + v_h2)
            ])
        ],
        attributes
    )
```

```
def __format_points(points: [Point]):
    return ' '.join([f'{p.x},{p.y}' for p in points])
```

Listing 8-25: SVG primitives result

We have everything we need to start drawing images. In the next chapter, we'll use our *svg* package to plot the result of a geometrical problem. But first, let's provide a convenient way of importing the contents of this package.

Package Imports

Similar to what we did with the *geom2d* package, we want to give the option of importing everything from *svg* with a single import line:

```
from graphic import svg
```

The only thing we have to do is import all relevant modules inside the *svg* package's *__init__.py* file file:

```
from .attributes import *
from .image import svg_content
from .primitives import *
```

Summary

Graphics are key to engineering applications. Many involve creating diagrams made of simple geometric primitives such as segments and rectangles. We created a geometry package in Part II of this book; in this chapter, we learned how to turn those primitives into vector images.

We started with a quick introduction to the SVG format and saw how easy it is to create SVG images using just a few lines of XML data. We then learned about templates, extensionless plaintext files that define the SVG structure using placeholders. The placeholders, which have the form of {{name}}, are replaced by concrete data using code. Templates are widely used, and there are some complex packages for rendering templates. Our use case was pretty simple, so we did the replacement using the replace method from Python strings.

Lastly, we created functions to obtain the SVG representation for our geometric primitives: line segments, circles, rectangles, and polygons. From now on, creating vector diagrams should be straightforward, something that we'll prove in the next chapter.

9

BUILDING A CIRCLE FROM THREE POINTS

In this chapter, we'll build an entire command line program to solve a well-known problem: finding a circle passing through three given points. You may have solved this problem graphically in high school using a ruler and compass; you may have even solved it numerically. This time, we'll be using the computer to solve it for us and produce an SVG image with the result. We already implemented the algorithm in Chapter 6; in this chapter, we'll use the algorithm inside an application.

It's a simple problem, but it is good for understanding how to code a complete application. We'll read the three input points from a file using regular expressions, which we'll learn about later in the chapter. We'll also read in a configuration file with the values for the colors and sizes for the program's output.

Then we'll build the *model*: a group of objects that implement what we call the *domain logic* of our application, that is, the knowledge needed to solve the problem. In this case, the model consists of three points and the factory function that creates a circle passing through the three of them.

Thanks to our previous work in Chapter 6, this shouldn't be complicated. We'll present the results graphically, with a vector image showing the input points and resulting circle.

This is our first complete command line program, and it has all the ingredients of an engineering application: reading from an input file, solving a problem, and outputting a result diagram. After building this program, you should feel empowered to build your own. The possibilities are endless!

Application Architecture

Most of the command line applications we'll build together in this book, and probably many others you may build on your own, will use a similar architecture. The concept of *software architecture* refers to the organization and design of the components that make up a software application. *Architecture* deals with both the design of each individual piece of the program and the system of communication and interaction between each piece.

To decide what components should make up the architecture of our application, let's think about what our program has to do. Our application will generally consist of three big phases, each performed by a different set of components or architectural building blocks:

Input parsing   We read the problem definition data from a file passed to our program. This phase may also include reading an external configuration file to tweak the program's behavior or outputs.

Problem resolution   Using the model we parse from the input definition data, we find a solution to the problem.

Output generation   We present the solution to the user. Depending on what kind of report we need, we may choose to produce diagrams, text files with data, simulations, or a combination of them. As important as solving the problem is, producing an output that is easy to understand and contains all the relevant pieces of information is crucial for our program to be of any use.

Since our problem for this chapter is fairly simple, we'll divide the three phases into three files: *input.py*, *main.py*, and *output.py*. Figure 9-1 shows the main architectural blocks of our application graphically.

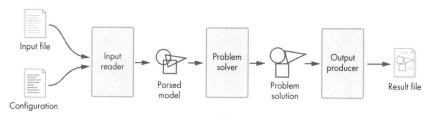

Figure 9-1: The application architecture diagram

The input file will contain the three points and should have the following format,

```
x y
x y
x y
```

where x and y are the coordinates of a point, separated by a space and each on a different line. An example input file could look like this:

```
300 300
700 400
300 500
```

This file defines three points: $A(300, 300)$, $B(700, 400)$, and $C(300, 500)$. We'll put a specification for the values of the coordinates and say they need to be positive integers. This simplifies the parsing logic a bit as there won't be decimal separators or minus signs in the numbers, which is good to get us started with regular expressions, but don't worry: we'll learn to identify floating-point numbers and minus signs in Chapter 12.

Using plaintext files as the input to our programs has a big advantage: we can write them by hand. Also, we can easily inspect and edit them. The downside is that plaintext files usually take up more space than their binary counterparts, but that won't be an issue for us. We'll go with ease of creation and manipulation over file size. Just remember, whenever you're working with plaintext files, always use a plaintext editor and never a rich-text editor. Rich-text editors (such as Word) have their own storage format that includes much more than you actually write to them, such as information about what goes in bold, what font face is used, or what size the font is. We need our input files to have in them only what we've written.

Setup

Since we'll be creating other applications throughout the book, let's create a new package at the top level of our Python project (the same level as the *geom2d*, *graphic*, and *utils* packages). Right-click the *Mechanics* folder, and from the menu choose **New ▸ Python Package**, name it *apps*, and click **OK**.

In *apps*, create a new package, this time named *circle_from_points*.

Your project's directory structure should look similar to the following:

```
Mechanics
  |- apps
  |    |- circle_from_points
  |- geom2d
  |    |- tests
  |- graphic
  |    |- svg
```

Let's create our main file. This is the file we'll execute from the command line to run the application. Create a file named *main.py* in *circle_from _points*. Enter the code in Listing 9-1.

```
if __name__ == '__main__':
    print('This is working')
```

Listing 9-1: Main file

If you recall from Chapter 1 (in the "Running Files" section), we're using the "if name is main" pattern to execute our main application script. We want to run this code only if we detect the file is being run by itself, and not when it's imported by some other file. For now we'll only print a message to the shell to make sure our setup works.

```
$ python3 apps/circle_from_points/main.py
```

This should print to the shell:

```
This is working
```

NOTE *This time, our main file doesn't define any function that could be imported and used by other files. But thanks to the "if name is main" pattern, if this file was imported (presumably by mistake), nothing would be exported, and no code would be run either. All of our "runnable" scripts will use this pattern.*

We'll need a file containing the definition of three points to test our progress. Create a new file inside *circle_from_points* named *test.txt*. In it, enter the following coordinates:

```
300 300
700 400
300 500
```

Next, we'll need to configure our IDE so we can test our application locally inside it.

Creating a Run Configuration

To test our application's code using the data in the *test.txt* file we just wrote, we need to create what's known as a *run configuration* inside PyCharm (refer to section "Creating Run Configurations" on page xxxvi for a refresher). Run configurations are a convenience that will save us time when we are developing.

NOTE *You may want to refer to the documentation online to better understand run configurations:* https://www.jetbrains.com/help/pycharm/run-debug-configuration.html. *If you happen to be using an IDE other than PyCharm, refer to its documentation. Most IDEs include a similar concept to run configurations to configure test runs for your programs.*

To create a run configuration, first make sure the navigation bar is visible by choosing **View ▶ Navigation Bar**. From the top menu, choose **Run ▶ Edit Configurations**. The dialog shown in Figure 9-2 will open.

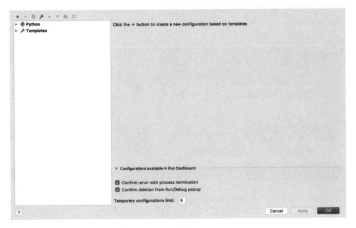

Figure 9-2: The run configuration dialog

Click the **+** icon on the top left, which opens the Add New Configuration drop-down, and choose **Python** (see Figure 9-3).

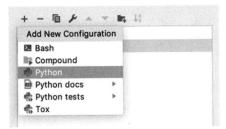

Figure 9-3: The new Python run configuration

The Run Configuration form should appear on the right side of the window. Enter the name *circle-three-points* in the Name field at the top. This will be the name you'll use to refer to the configuration. On the Configuration tab, you should see the Script path field. This is the path to our *main.py* file: our program's entry point. Click the folder icon inside the field and select *main.py*. Near the end of the Configuration tab, find the Execution section. Select the **Redirect input from** checkbox, and in the field click the folder icon and select our test file containing the definition of the points: *test.txt*. This way, the run configuration will always pass *test.txt* to the program's standard input. Your configuration dialog should look like Figure 9-4.

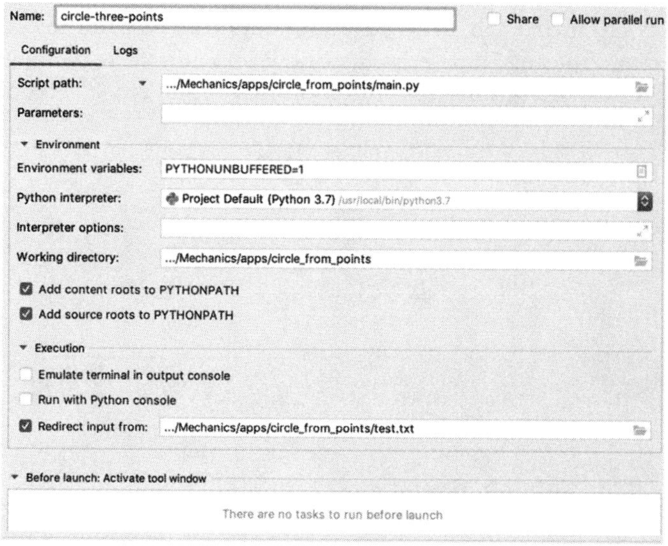

Figure 9-4: The run configuration data

We need to do one last thing. If we executed the run configuration as it is now, the output of the program would be printed to the shell (standard output). That is fine, but since we'll be outputting SVG code, we want to redirect the standard output to a file with the *.svg* extension.

Go to the Logs tab to the right of Configuration. Check **Save console output to file**; then click the folder icon, and select any file in *circle_from_points*. Once the file is selected, just change its name to *result.svg*. Alternatively, you can copy and paste the path to the package *circle_from_points* and then append the name of the *result.svg* file. You could also create an empty *result.svg* file and then select it here. Whatever way you choose, the result should look something like Figure 9-5.

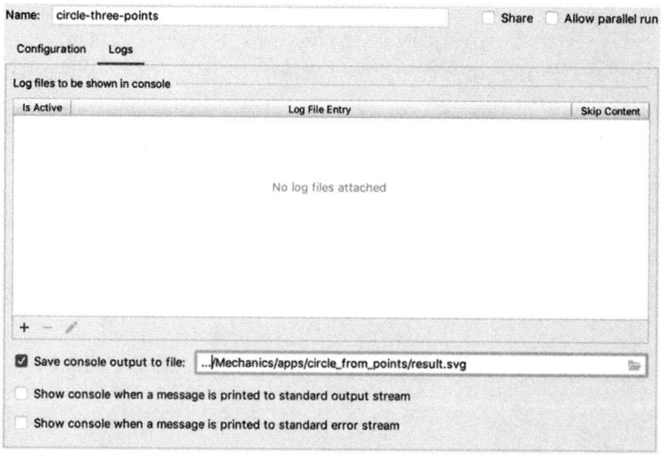

Figure 9-5: Redirecting output to a file

We're all set, so click **OK**. In your navigation bar you should see the newly created run configuration selected (see Figure 9-6). Click the green play button to its right. This executes the run configuration, which should result in the message "This is working" written in a file named *result.svg*.

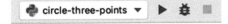

Figure 9-6: The run configuration in the navigation bar

Let's do a quick recap of what we've just done. We've created a configuration in PyCharm that instructs it on how to run our project. We told the configuration that *main.py* is the entry point to start executing our project. Then, we said we wanted the file *test.txt* containing our test data to be passed to the standard input of the program and the output of the program redirected to a file named *result.svg*.

Why Use a Run Configuration?

You may be asking yourself, why do we want to create a run configuration instead of just executing our script from the command line?

That's a good question. There are two good reasons why we use run configurations. The first is that we'll be much more productive during development. We won't need to enter commands into the shell to run the program, redirecting its standard input and output as necessary. Besides, this configuration allows us to debug the program, something that would be considerably harder from the shell. If you set a breakpoint somewhere in the code, you can click the bug-like button next to the green play button and the program should stop once the breakpoint is reached.

The second reason is that, as we'll see later in the chapter, if you try to run *main.py* from the shell, once we start importing our packages (such as *geom2d*) it simply won't work. Yes, that's kind of surprising, but we'll learn why this happens and, more importantly, how to fix it.

Reading the Input and Configuration Files

So far we have a *main.py* file and a run configuration that passes it *test.txt* using the standard input. Right now we're doing nothing with that file's contents, so a good next step would be reading the contents of the file and parsing each line as an instance of the Point class. How do we go about doing this? We need to use regular expressions, a powerful technology for reading and extracting information from a text.

Before we explore regular expressions, let's create a new file in our project to read both the input and configuration files. Let's also take some time to learn to read files passed to the standard input of our program.

In *circle_from_points*, create a new file named *input.py*. Your *circle_from _points* directory should look like the following:

```
circle_from_points
  |- __init__.py
  |- input.py
  |- main.py
  |- test.txt
```

Let's start small and go one step at a time. Enter the code in Listing 9-2 in the newly created file.

```python
def parse_points():
    return (
        input(),
        input(),
        input(),
    )
```

Listing 9-2: Reading lines from the input file

The parse_points function is not actually parsing points . . . yet. So far, it returns a tuple consisting of three strings, each of which corresponds to a line obtained from the standard input. Each line is read using Python's input function, which reads in one line of input at a time. Let's call parse_points from our main program to see how it reads the test file's contents. Go back to *main.py* and modify the code to make it match Listing 9-3.

```python
from apps.circle_from_points.input import parse_points

if __name__ == '__main__':
    (a, b, c) = parse_points()
    print(f'{a}\n{b}\n{c}')
```

Listing 9-3: Printing the points to the shell

You may be tempted to use Python's relative imports here like from .input import parse_points but that won't work properly when the file doing the imports is run from the command line. To get an idea of why that is, take a look at this excerpt from PEP 238:

> Relative imports use a module's __name__ attribute to determine that module's position in the package hierarchy. If the module's name does not contain any package information (e.g. it is set to '__main__') then relative imports are resolved as if the module were a top level module, regardless of where the module is actually located on the file system.

The first thing we do in Listing 9-3 is import parse_points from the *input.py* module. In the "if name is main" condition we call the parse_points function and assign its output to a tuple (a, b, c), which *destructures* its elements into the variables a, b, and c.

The following is the less elegant way of accomplishing the same result:

```
points = parse_points()
a = points[0]
b = points[1]
c = points[2]
```

But we'll go with the former, which is a little cleaner. The last line prints the contents of a, b, and c to the shell, each in its own line. Run the application by clicking the green play button beside the run configuration we created earlier. You should get the following printed to the shell in the IDE:

```
Input is being redirected from --snip--/test.txt
Console output is saving to: --snip--/result.svg
300 300
700 400
300 500

Process finished with exit code 0
```

The two first lines are pretty interesting. They tell us that the configuration used to run the file is receiving input from file *test.txt* and writing the output to file *result.svg*. If you open *result.svg*, you should see the three points the same way they're defined inside *test.txt*, and also the same way they were printed to the shell. We're making good progress here! The next step is to convert those space-separated coordinates into instances of our Point class. For that, we need regular expressions.

Regular Expressions

Regular expressions (*regex* for short) are powerful constructs when it comes to interpreting text. Because the input to most, if not all, applications we'll be creating in this book will be read from a plaintext file, we want to get acquainted with regular expressions.

NOTE   *If you want to learn more about regular expressions, take a look at this awesome interactive tutorial: https://regexone.com.*

Let's quickly review the problem we're trying to solve here: given a string of text containing two integer numbers separated by a space, extract them from the string, convert them to numbers, and use them as the coordinates of an instance of Point. How do regular expressions help us here?

A regular expression is a pattern defined as a string. It's used to search for matches inside other strings and, optionally, extract parts of them.

Let's try an example. Note that regular expressions are denoted by writing them between two slash characters. Imagine we're looking for this pattern,

```
/repeat 5 times/
```

and we're interested in knowing whether that pattern appears in any of the following sentences:

Repeat 5 times.

For each exercise, repeat 5 times.

For that particular exercise, repeat 7 times.

Let's repeat 3301 times.

The /repeat 5 times/ regular expression compares itself against these strings searching for exactly the text repeat 5 times and thus yielding only the single bold match:

Repeat 5 times.

For each exercise, **repeat 5 times**.

For that particular exercise, repeat 7 times.

Let's repeat 3301 times.

That's great, but not very flexible. The first sentence was not a match because the first letter, the *R*, is uppercase; our pattern is lowercased. We can tweak our pattern to accept both:

```
/[Rr]epeat 5 times/
```

This time the matches are as follows:

Repeat 5 times.

For each exercise, **repeat 5 times**.

For that particular exercise, repeat 7 times.

Let's repeat 3301 times.

To account for both kinds of *r*, we introduced a *character set*: a series of accepted characters in a given position of the text, any of which is considered valid. Character sets are defined between square brackets.

There's much more we can do with regular expressions. What about the number of repetitions specified in the sentence? Can we make it so any number of repetitions is considered a match? We sure can. If we modify our pattern to be

```
/[Rr]epeat \d times/
```

we'll get the following matches:

Repeat 5 times.

For each exercise, **repeat 5 times**.

For that particular exercise, **repeat 7 times**.

Let's repeat 3301 times.

The pattern \d matches a single digit, any number between 0 and 9. But what about that last sentence? If we wanted to match more than one digit, we'd need to add a *quantifier* to the \d pattern. In this case, the quantifier that makes the most sense is +, which is used to match one or more of the tokens it quantifies. The pattern

```
/[Rr]epeat \d+ times/
```

would then work with any number of repetitions and thus get us the full range of matches we've been after:

Repeat 5 times.

For each exercise, **repeat 5 times**.

For that particular exercise, **repeat 7 times**.

Let's **repeat 3301 times**.

Now that you're starting to see what regular expressions are about, let's explore some of their basic concepts.

Character Sets

As we've seen, we can include several different characters between square brackets to have our regular expression match any of them. For instance, we could use

```
/[mbg]ore/
```

to match **more**, **bore**, and **gore**. We can also include ranges like all lowercase letters from *a* to *z* like so:

```
/[a-z]ore/
```

This would produce a wide range of matches, for instance **more**, **core**, and exp**lore**. We can also include the range of uppercase letters,

```
/[a-zA-Z]ore/
```

to include matches like **More** or **Core**. One thing to keep an eye on is that consecutive ranges are not separated by a space. If you separated them using a space, the set would include the space as a valid character.

Character Classes

There are some special characters we can use to match common things such as digits, whitespace, or single letters. The first one is a dot (.). We use it to match anything except line breaks. It matches letters (both uppercase and lowercase), numbers, punctuation marks, and whitespace. As you can see, this is quite a powerful *matcher*. For example, the pattern

```
/the end./
```

would match **the end.**, **the end?**, **the end!**, and many more. To match a single dot, we need to escape the dot character using a backward slash,

```
/the end\./
```

which would produce only one match: **the end.**

We already learned about the class \d, which matches a digit. If we want to match everything *but* digits, we can use \D (uppercase). Similarly, to match letters, we can use the class \w, and we can use \W for nonletters. Lastly, for whitespace there's \s, and there's \S to match whatever isn't whitespace.

Now let's combine our knowledge on character classes into a regular expression:

```
/code\s\w-\d\d/
```

This regular expression matches strings like **code f-44**, **code M-81**, and **code p-29**.

Quantifiers

Quantifiers modify the number of matches expected for the token they quantify. There are five quantifiers:

?   Matches zero or one of the preceding tokens

*   Matches zero or more of the preceding tokens

+   Matches one or more of the preceding tokens

(n)   Matches exactly n of the preceding tokens

(n,m)   Matches from n to m of the preceding tokens

For example,

```
/o{2}m/
```

would match b**oom**, z**oom**, or kab**oom**. But, if instead we use

```
/o+m/
```

our matches could be any of the following: **nom**ad, b**oooom**, or **room**. We'll be using most of these quantifiers throughout the text, so there will be plenty more examples of them.

Capturing Groups

So far we've seen how to match text using regular expressions. But sometimes we also want to extract the text we've matched. Here's where groups come in. Groups are defined between parentheses. Let's try the following regular expression,

```
/it takes (\d+) hours to go from (\w+) to (\w+)/
```

which applied to the sentence "it takes 4 hours to go from Barcelona to Pamplona" would match it entirely and capture the following groups:

```
('4', 'Barcelona', 'Pamplona')
```

Let's try it in Python's shell. Python's standard library includes a powerful regular expression package: re. Open your IDE's shell and try entering the code in Listing 9-4.

```
>>> import re
>>> pattern = r'it takes (\d+) hours to go from (\w+) to (\w+)'
>>> target = 'it takes 4 hours to go from Barcelona to Pamplona'
>>> matches = re.match(pattern, target)
>>> matches.groups()
('4', 'Barcelona', 'Pamplona')
```

Listing 9-4: Capturing groups with regular expressions

We define the pattern using a *raw string literal*, which has the format r''. These strings treat the backslash (\) as a valid character instead of interpreting it as an escape sequence. Regular expressions need the backslash to define their structure.

In Listing 9-4, the result is stored in a variable named matches, which we can call the groups method on to yield the three captured groups: 4, Barcelona, and Pamplona.

A neat thing about groups is that they can be assigned a name that we can later use to retrieve the matched value. For instance, consider the following pattern:

```
/(?P<name>\w+), but they call me (?P<nick>\w+)/
```

Applied to a sentence like "my name is Nelson, but they call me Big Head," this would capture two groups, which we can retrieve by name:

```
name = matches.group('name')
nick = matches.group('nick')
```

As you can guess, the syntax used to assign a name to a group is as follows,

```
(?P<name><regex>)
```

where name is the name assigned to the group and regex is the actual pattern to match the group.

Regular Expressions Cheat Sheet

Table 9-1, Table 9-2, Table 9-3, and Table 9-4 summarize the concepts we've explored and can be used as references throughout the rest of the book.

Table 9-1: Regular Expressions Character Sets

[abc]	Matches 'a' or 'b' or 'c'
[^ab]	Matches every character except 'a' and 'b'
[a-z]	Matches every character between 'a' and 'z'

Table 9-2: Regular Expressions Character Classes

\s	Matches whitespace
\S	Matches every character but whitespace
\d	Matches digits
\D	Matches every character but digits
\w	Matches letters
\W	Matches every character but letters

Table 9-3: Regular Expressions Quantifiers

?	Zero or one
*	Zero or more
+	One or more
{n}	Exactly n
{n,m}	Between n and m (both included)

Table 9-4: Regular Expressions Capture Groups

(...)	A capture group goes between parentheses
(?P<name>...)	A named capture group

Matching Points

We already know everything we need to match the points defined as their space-separated coordinates and capture them by name. Because coordinates will be defined by integer numbers only, we can use the following regular expression:

```
/(?P<x>\d+)\s(?P<y>\d+)/
```

Let's break that down. There are three parts to it:

(?P<x>\d+)   Captures a group named x of one or more digits

\s   Matches a single space

(?P<y>\d+) Captures a group named y of one or more digits

Let's implement this matching pattern in our application's *input.py* file. Edit the code we wrote so that it looks like Listing 9-5.

```
❶ import re

from geom2d import Point


def parse_points():
    return (
        __point_from_string(input()),
        __point_from_string(input()),
        __point_from_string(input()),
    )


def __point_from_string(string: str):
❷  matches = re.match(r'(?P<x>\d+)\s(?P<y>\d+)', string)
    return Point(
❸      int(matches.group('x')),
❹      int(matches.group('y'))
    )
```

Listing 9-5: Parsing points

We start by importing re ❶. Then, we modify the parse_points function to map the line we read using input() on an instance of Point. This conversion is handled by the private __point_from_string function, which, using re.match, looks for matches of the pattern in the passed-in string ❷.

From matches we know there should be two groups named x and y, respectively. The function thus creates and returns an instance of Point whose x-coordinate is the result of parsing the string captured by the group with name x as an integer ❸. The y-coordinate is, in a similar fashion, the result of parsing the group named y ❹.

Run the application (using the *circle-three-points* configuration) by clicking the green play button. You should see something like this printed to the shell:

```
Input is being redirected from --snip--/test.txt
Console output is saving to: --snip--/result.svg
(300, 300)
(700, 400)
(300, 500)

Process finished with exit code 0
```

Congratulations! You just parsed three points from a file containing three lines of plaintext. From here on out, all the command line applications we'll create can expect the input data from a file, which you already know how to parse and interpret using the almighty regular expressions.

The Configuration File

Our application will produce a beautiful vector image of both the input points and the resulting circle. To do this, we'll use different colors and line thicknesses to help visually distinguish its parts. We could directly hard-code those colors and size values in our code, but that's not a great idea; our app will be easier to maintain if we separate the configuration values from the actual logic. Instead, we'll keep the configuration values in a separate JSON file. We'll use the JSON format because it's extremely easy to convert to a Python dictionary.

NOTE   *We say something is* hard-coded *into the code when there's no way of changing it without altering the program's source code. Configuration values, for instance, are often hard-coded into the main application's logic, making them impossible to change without the need of reading through the code and potentially recompiling the application. Don't do that. The fewer times you need to edit and recompile existing code, the better. Always move configuration values out of the program's logic into a file of its own.*

Inside *circle_from_points*, create a new file by right-clicking the package name and choosing **New ▶ File**. Enter the name *config.json*, and in it, write the contents in Listing 9-6.

```json
{
  "input": {
    "stroke-color": "#4A90E2",
    "stroke-width": 2,
    "fill-color": "#ffffffbb",
    "label-size": 16,
    "font-family": "Helvetica"
  },
  "output": {
    "stroke-color": "#50E3C2",
    "stroke-width": 4,
    "fill-color": "#ffffff",
    "label-size": 14,
    "font-family": "Helvetica"
  }
}
```

Listing 9-6: Application configuration inside a JSON file

This file is in JSON, a widely used format. If you happen to be new to it, you can read more about it at *www.json.org/*. It looks similar to Python dictionaries as it stores data in a key-value fashion. Luckily for us, Python has an easy way of reading in JSON files: the standard library includes the *json* package to handle JSON data.

In *input.py*, enter the function in Listing 9-7 (don't forget the imports).

```
import json
import re

import pkg_resources as res


def read_config():
    config = res.resource_string(__name__, 'config.json')
    return json.loads(config)

--snip--
```

Listing 9-7: Reading the configuration

Using the pkg_resources module, this process becomes a breeze. The contents of file *config.json* are read into a binary string using res.resource_string(), which, when passed to json.loads, gets us the resulting Python dictionary with everything parsed and ready to be used. We'll be using these values soon.

Problem Model and Resolution

We've already parsed the problem's model: the three instances of our Point class. Using these, our application should now compute the circle that passes through all of them. Our earlier work is about to pay off: we already have the code to do this (check out "Circle Factories" on page 153 for a refresher).

Open *main.py* and enter the code in Listing 9-8.

```
from apps.circle_from_points.input import parse_points
from geom2d import make_circle_from_points

if __name__ == '__main__':
    (a, b, c) = parse_points()
    circle = make_circle_from_points(a, b, c)
    print(circle)
```

Listing 9-8: Computing the circle passing through the three points

That was easy! We import make_circle_from_points from *geom2d* and simply pass it the three points: a, b, and c. To make sure the circle was correctly computed, we print the resulting circle. Run the application; you should expect the following string representation for the resulting circle:

```
circle c = (487.5, 400.0), r = 212.5
```

If you open *result.svg*, that should be its content. This file is where we're redirecting our program's output. There's only one thing missing from our program: plotting the output using the SVG format!

Generating Output

Now that the problem is solved, we need to draw an SVG with the resulting circle and input points. Start by creating a new file in *circle_from_points* named *output.py*. Your *circle_from_points* directory should look like the following:

```
circle_from_points
 |- __init__.py
 |- input.py
 |- main.py
 |- output.py
 |- test.txt
```

In it, enter the code in Listing 9-9.

```
from geom2d import Circle, Point


def draw_to_svg(points: [Point], circle: Circle, config):
    print("Almost there...")
```

Listing 9-9: First step to generating the output image

We defined a new function, draw_to_svg, which receives a sequence of points (the input points to the problem), the resulting circle, and a configuration dictionary. Note the type hint for a sequence of points: [Point]; it's declared by the Point class between square brackets. A sequence type hint defined like this accepts both lists and tuples.

For now, the function simply prints a message to the standard output, but we'll be updating it one step at a time until it finally draws everything. With this, you can go ahead and give *main.py* its final look. Modify your code so that it looks like Listing 9-10.

```
from apps.circle_from_points.input import parse_points, read_config
from apps.circle_from_points.output import draw_to_svg
from geom2d import make_circle_from_points

if __name__ == '__main__':
    (a, b, c) = parse_points()
    circle = make_circle_from_points(a, b, c)
    draw_to_svg((a, b, c), circle, read_config())
```

Listing 9-10: Main file

This code is concise. There are fundamentally three lines, which, respectively, read the input, solve the problem, and draw the output. With our main file all set up, let's fill out draw_to_svg.

Drawing the Output Circle

We'll start by drawing the circle. Open *output.py* and enter the code in Listing 9-11.

```
from geom2d import make_rect_centered, Circle, Point, Vector
from graphic import svg


def draw_to_svg(points: [Point], circle: Circle, config):
❶ svg_output = output_to_svg(circle, config['output'])

❷ viewbox = make_viewbox(circle)
❸ svg_img = svg.svg_content(
       viewbox.size, svg_output, viewbox
   )

   print(svg_img)


def output_to_svg(circle: Circle, config):
❹ style = style_from_config(config)
❺ label_style = label_style_from_config(config)

   return [
     ❻ svg.circle(circle, style),
     ❼ svg.text(
           f'O {circle.center}',
           circle.center,
           Vector(0, 0),
           label_style
       ),
     ❽ svg.text(
           f'r = {circle.radius}',
           circle.center,
           Vector(0, 20),
           label_style
       )
   ]
```

Listing 9-11: Drawing the resulting circle

That seems like a lot of code, but don't worry, we'll break it down. First, we update the `draw_to_svg` function. Using the `output_to_svg` function we define later in the code, we create the SVG representation for the circle ❶. Note that we're passing this function `config['output']`, the *output* part of the configuration dictionary.

Then, using `make_viewbox`, a function we've yet to define, we compute the `viewBox` for the image ❷. Using this `viewBox`, its size, and `svg_output`, we generate the image ❸ and print it to the standard output.

Now let's look at `output_to_svg`. This function stores the SVG attributes for the circle using another function we'll define shortly (`style_from_config`) in a variable named `style` ❹. The same happens for the styling attributes we'll use with the text, generated by `label_style_from_config` ❺. The function returns an array of three SVG primitives: the circle and two labels.

The circle is straightforward; we use our prewritten `circle` function ❻. Then comes the label indicating where the center of the circle is ❼, located with its origin at the center point. Lastly, there's the label with the information about the circle's radius. This label is located in the center of the circle but displaced $\langle 0, 20 \rangle$ so that it appears below the former ❽.

NOTE *You may remember we said that when displacing the label by a vector $\langle 0, 20 \rangle$, it appears below the other. A positive number in the y-coordinate of the vector should produce an upward displacement and hence move the label on top of the other. But remember that in SVG the y-axis points downward. We could fix that by applying an affine transformation, but we won't right now.*

To compute the `viewBox`, enter the code in Listing 9-12 under `output_to_svg`.

```
--snip--

def make_viewbox(circle: Circle):
    height = 2.5 * circle.radius
    width = 4 * circle.radius
    return make_rect_centered(circle.center, width, height)
```

Listing 9-12: Computing the `viewBox` for the image

This function computes the rectangle that defines the visible portion of the image. If you need a refresher, go back to section "The viewBox" on page 207. To construct the rectangle, we use the `make_rect_centered` factory function, which is pretty convenient now that we need a rectangle containing a circle. The height of the rectangle is 2.5 times the radius of the circle, that is, the diameter plus some margin. For the width, we use 4 times the radius (or 2 times the diameter), as we need some room for the labels we'll draw. I came up with these values by pure trial and error, but feel free to adjust them based on your experiments. They'll basically add more or less margin to your drawing; that's all.

Figure 9-7 describes the layout of the SVG image we're drawing for reference.

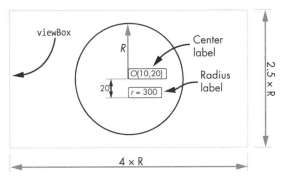

Figure 9-7: The SVG output layout

Let's implement the functions that generate the SVG styling attributes. Toward the end of your file *output.py*, enter the code in Listing 9-13.

```
--snip--

def style_from_config(config):
    return [
        svg.stroke_color(config['stroke-color']),
        svg.stroke_width(config['stroke-width']),
        svg.fill_color(config['fill-color'])
    ]
```

Listing 9-13: Creating styles from configuration

The style_from_config function creates a list of SVG attributes using the values from the configuration dictionary. Let's do the same for the label's style (see Listing 9-14).

```
--snip--

def label_style_from_config(config):
    return [
        svg.font_size(config['label-size']),
        svg.font_family(config['font-family']),
        svg.fill_color(config['stroke-color'])
    ]
```

Listing 9-14: Creating label styles from configuration

That's it! We have all the code needed to draw the resulting circle in a cyanish color. If you run the application now, you should see how the shell spits out some SVG code, the same that is written in the file *result.svg*. Open this file using your favorite browser. The result should be something similar to Figure 9-8.

O (487.5, 400.0)
r = 212.5

Figure 9-8: The SVG output circle

There you go! We solved our first geometry problem and plotted the result into a vector image. Isn't that super exciting? Go ahead and play with the configuration. Try changing the color for the output and rerunning the application.

Drawing the Input Points

It's nice that we drew the resulting circle with captions that indicate the position of the center and the radius, but the resulting image doesn't include information about the input points that generated the circle. Let's draw those so that one can get all the information from a single glance at the resulting image.

Let's create a new function that is similar to output_to_svg but produces the SVG primitives that represent the input points. We'll represent these points as circles as well. In *output.py* enter the code in Listing 9-15.

```
--snip--

def input_to_svg(points: [Point], point_radius: float, config):
    style = style_from_config(config)
    label_style = label_style_from_config(config)
❶ [a, b, c] = points
❷ disp = Vector(1.25 * point_radius, 0)

❸ return [
        svg.circle(Circle(a, point_radius), style),
        svg.circle(Circle(b, point_radius), style),
        svg.circle(Circle(c, point_radius), style),
        svg.text(f'A {a}', a, disp, label_style),
        svg.text(f'B {b}', b, disp, label_style),
```

```
        svg.text(f'C {c}', c, disp, label_style)
    ]
```

Listing 9-15: Drawing the input points

The input_to_svg function gets passed a list with the three input points, the radius to use for representing the points, and the input configuration dictionary.

As you'll see, we'll use a fraction of the size of the resulting circle as the radius for the input points. This is so that they look good no matter the size of the resulting image. Using a fixed number for their radius could result in tiny, almost invisible circles for certain inputs and monstrous circles bigger than the resulting one for others.

The styles for both the points and their labels are computed using the same functions we used before: style_from_config and label_style_from_config. The points in the sequence are destructured into variables a, b, and c so that we can conveniently use them ❶.

Because we'll need to move the labels a bit to the right so they don't overlap with their circle, we construct a displacement vector, disp ❷. The function returns the array of circles with their labels ❸.

Now update function draw_to_svg so that it also includes the three points in the resulting image (see Listing 9-16).

```
def draw_to_svg(points: [Point], circle: Circle, config):
❶  pt_radius = circle.radius / 20
    svg_output = output_to_svg(circle, config['output'])
❷  svg_input = input_to_svg(points, pt_radius, config['input'])

    viewbox = make_viewbox(circle)
    svg_img = svg.svg_content(
    ❸   viewbox.size, svg_output + svg_input, viewbox
    )

    print(svg_img)

--snip--
```

Listing 9-16: Drawing to SVG

As mentioned, the radius for the input points needs to be a fraction of that from the resulting circle, so we chose one-twentieth of its radius ❶. If you think the resulting circles are too big or too small, you can change that value and experiment until you're happy with the result. This value could be perfectly fine as part of the application's configuration, but we'll keep it as an implementation detail for the sake of simplicity.

After we compute pt_radius, we compute the SVG primitives for the output as before. Then we compute the SVG primitives for the input using the input_to_svg function and store the result in svg_input ❷.

After creating a viewBox, we update the contents of the SVG image by appending svg_input to svg_output ❸. It's important that svg_input goes after svg_output, as the image primitives are drawn in order. If you switched the order to this,

```
svg_input + svg_output
```

you'd see the input point circles behind the big circle.

You're now ready to run the application and then reload the *result.svg* file in the browser. The result should look like Figure 9-9.

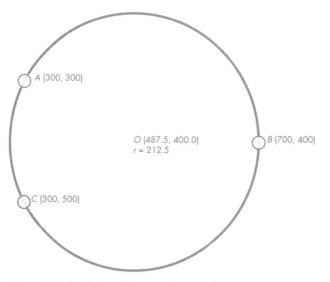

Figure 9-9: An SVG with the complete result

Result

For your reference, Listing 9-17 contains the finished version of *output.py*.

```
from geom2d import make_rect_centered, Circle, Point, Vector
from graphic import svg


def draw_to_svg(points: [Point], circle: Circle, config):
    pt_radius = circle.radius / 20
    svg_output = output_to_svg(circle, config['output'])
    svg_input = input_to_svg(points, pt_radius, config['input'])

    viewbox = make_viewbox(circle)
    svg_img = svg.svg_content(
        viewbox.size, svg_output + svg_input, viewbox
    )

    print(svg_img)
```

```python
def output_to_svg(circle: Circle, config):
    style = style_from_config(config)
    label_style = label_style_from_config(config)

    return [
        svg.circle(circle, style),
        svg.text(
            f'O {circle.center}',
            circle.center,
            Vector(0, 0),
            label_style
        ),
        svg.text(
            f'r = {circle.radius}',
            circle.center,
            Vector(0, 20),
            label_style
        )
    ]


def input_to_svg(points: [Point], point_radius: float, config):
    style = style_from_config(config)
    label_style = label_style_from_config(config)
    [a, b, c] = points
    disp = Vector(1.25 * point_radius, 0)

    return [
        svg.circle(Circle(a, point_radius), style),
        svg.circle(Circle(b, point_radius), style),
        svg.circle(Circle(c, point_radius), style),
        svg.text(f'A {a}', a, disp, label_style),
        svg.text(f'B {b}', b, disp, label_style),
        svg.text(f'C {c}', c, disp, label_style)
    ]


def style_from_config(config):
    return [
        svg.stroke_color(config['stroke-color']),
        svg.stroke_width(config['stroke-width']),
        svg.fill_color(config['fill-color'])
    ]


def label_style_from_config(config):
    return [
```

```
            svg.font_size(config['label-size']),
            svg.font_family(config['font-family']),
            svg.fill_color(config['stroke-color'])
        ]


def make_viewbox(circle: Circle):
    height = 2.5 * circle.radius
    width = 4 * circle.radius
    return make_rect_centered(circle.center, width, height)
```

Listing 9-17: Drawing to SVG result

Flip the Y-Axis

As you know by now, the SVG y-axis points downward. Point *C* at *y* = 500, for instance, is below *A* with *y* = 300. This isn't necessarily bad, but it may be the opposite of what you're used to.

Here's a challenge for you: modify *output.py* so that the SVG produced uses an affine transformation such that the y-axis is flipped and therefore points upward. If you need a clue, go back to the section "Space Transformation" from Chapter 8.

Note that if you choose to add an affine transformation that flips the y-axis of the entire SVG image, as follows,

```
<svg --snip-- transform="matrix(1 0 0 -1 0 0)">
    --snip--
</svg>
```

all of the text labels will also flip vertically, which makes them impossible to read. Try to address this problem by also adding an affine transformation to all captions so that you basically flip them twice.

This is challenging, but a great exercise for you to try. Don't worry, we'll explore this in depth in Part V.

Distributing Our Application

The word has spread among your friends, and they've all heard about your achievement: you developed an application that computes the circle passing through three points and plots a beautiful vector image with the result. They know you've accomplished this all by yourself, without using any third-party library. They are amazed; "That is so hardcore," you've even heard them say. They want to try it, and they've prepared a few input files to test your program. You share the code with them, and as they know Python, they open the shell and try to execute your *main.py* script, only to discover there's a strange error that won't let the program run.

It's unfortunate that to load all the modules that your application uses, there's a trick that PyCharm does and we need to account for. But don't worry, we'll explore why the error happens and give a solution to it. You can use what you'll learn here to distribute any application that we build in this book, or even those that you write yourself.

Understanding the Problem

Let's try to run our recently created program from the shell, without any change, to see whether we get the same result as from the IDE. In the bash shell (the one in your IDE or your system's), navigate to the app's directory,

```
$ cd apps/circle_from_points
```

and run this:

```
$ python3 main.py < test.txt
```

Surprisingly, it doesn't work:

```
Traceback (most recent call last):
  File "main.py", line 6, in <module>
    from apps.circle_from_points.input import --snip--
ModuleNotFoundError: No module named 'apps'
```

This is the error we get:

```
ModuleNotFoundError: No module named 'apps'
```

This is telling us that Python couldn't find the apps module when it tried to import it. But if that's the case, why was it running correctly from the IDE using the run configuration? Well, PyCharm's run configurations do a trick under the hood, a trick we now need to do ourselves.

When a script imports modules, Python looks for them in specific directories. To know what those directories are exactly, you can query them at runtime: Python stores them at sys.path, which is a list that contains all the paths where Python looks for libraries in your machine. Python also appends the path to the script itself; this path is known as the *working directory*.

The problem that we encountered is that sys.path doesn't get the parent path of our project appended. That is unfortunate because this is where it should go to find our *geom2d*, *graphic*, and *apps* packages. PyCharm's run configuration worked fine because it appends this path to sys.path. Let's check this fact by printing the contents of sys.path to the shell inside the main script and then run it again using the run configuration. Open the *main.py* file and at the top of the file add the following:

```
import sys
print(sys.path)

--snip--
```

Notice that the print statement goes right after importing sys and before the rest of the imports. You may get a PyCharm warning that doing this is conceptually wrong according to PEP-8 standards—ignore that warning. We want that `print` right before Python attempts to load anything else; otherwise, we'd get the same error as before when the script is run from the shell and never get to print `sys.path`. If you now rerun the project using the run configuration, the output you'll get should be similar to the following:

```
/usr/local/bin/python3.7 --snip--/main.py
Input is being redirected from --snip--/test.txt
Console output is saving to: --snip--/result.svg

['--snip--/Mechanics/apps/circle_from_points',
'--snip--/Mechanics',
'--snip--/Python.framework/Versions/3.7/lib/python37.zip',
'--snip--/Python.framework/Versions/3.7/lib/python3.7',
'--snip--/Python.framework/Versions/3.7/lib/python3.7/lib-dynload',
'--snip--/Python/3.7/lib/python/site-packages',
'/usr/local/lib/python3.7/site-packages']
```

Can you spot the second line (in bold) from the `sys.path` list? That line is the key to solving the problem of not finding the included modules inside our program. Let's run the script now from the shell to see what that list of paths contains. In the IDE's shell, navigate to the app's directory and run this:

```
$ python3 main.py < test.txt
```

This time the output is as follows:

```
['--snip--/Mechanics/apps/circle_from_points',
'--snip--/Python.framework/Versions/3.7/lib/python37.zip',
'--snip--/Python.framework/Versions/3.7/lib/python3.7',
'--snip--/Python.framework/Versions/3.7/lib/python3.7/lib-dynload',
'---snip--/Python/3.7/lib/python/site-packages',
'/usr/local/lib/python3.7/site-packages']
```

Can you see how the *Mechanics* directory isn't listed here as a search path? If that directory isn't included, Python won't be able to find any module from that route when running our application.

Delete the two lines you added to *main.py* so that the file looks like it did before, and let's explore some possible solutions.

Finding a Solution

The problem is clear: Python can't load our libraries since it doesn't have their parent directory listed as a search path. Let's see how we can solve this. We'll present two options, so we'll try to understand their pros and cons before we decide which one works best for us.

Appending to sys.path

One possible solution is to do what PyCharm's run configuration does: append the parent directory of our project to sys.path before Python attempts to import anything from it. We could modify *main.py* so that it looks like Listing 9-18.

```
import os
import sys

❶ parent_path = os.path.normpath(os.path.join(os.getcwd(), '..', '..'))
❷ sys.path.append(parent_path)

from apps.circle_from_points.input import parse_points, read_config
from apps.circle_from_points.output import draw_to_svg
from geom2d import make_circle_from_points


if __name__ == '__main__':
    (a, b, c) = parse_points()
    circle = make_circle_from_points(a, b, c)
    draw_to_svg((a, b, c), circle, read_config())
```

Listing 9-18: Appending to sys.path

We first import both the os and sys modules. We then compute the project's parent path by obtaining the current working directory (os.getcwd()) and navigating two steps back ('..', '..') ❶.

We're using the os.path.normpath function to normalize the path so that it doesn't contain the dots representing a backward movement in the directory tree. This function transforms a path like

```
/Documents/MechBook/code/Mechanics/../..
```

into the following:

```
/Documents/MechBook
```

That path is appended to sys.path before any other import attempts to load anything from our project ❷. If you run the app from the shell, it should run error free.

```
$ python3 main.py < test.txt
```

This solution works, but it still seems a bit awkward that we have to make users navigate into the *apps/circle_from_points* directory to run our script: it'd be more convenient if we could run the program from the parent directory of our project. Furthermore, the lines we added to *main.py* look a bit ugly and have nothing to do with solving the problem of finding the circle passing through three points. We don't want to add those lines to every application that we implement; that's unnecessary complexity we want to avoid.

Let's try a different approach that doesn't involve changing the code in our main script: let's create a bash script that appends the right working directory path to the Python script's execution. Start by undoing what we did in Listing 9-18 so your *main.py* file looks the same as in Listing 9-10.

Wrapping the App with a Script

For what we just saw in the previous section, every package that our *main.py* script needs to run should be accessible either from the working directory or from any other path listed in `sys.path`.

NOTE   *Remember that the working directory is where the executing file (in this case main.py) is located.*

Apart from appending paths to `sys.path` inside our Python code, we can also include paths in an *environment variable*: `PYTHONPATH`. When a Python script is run, it includes all paths defined in `PYTHONPATH` inside its `sys.path`.

We can therefore create a bash script at the project's top level, which sets the right paths in `PYTHONPATH` and then executes our app's *main.py*. Remember that we use bash scripts to group a set of command line statements and run them together by executing a single file (revisit Chapter 3 for a refresher).

At the top level of the project (at the same level as *geom2d* or *apps*), create a new file named *cifpts.sh* (an abbreviation of "circle from points"). In it, write the line in Listing 9-19.

```
PYTHONPATH=$PWD python3 apps/circle_from_points/main.py
```

Listing 9-19: Wrapper script

The first thing we do in this line is define an environment variable `PYTHONPATH` with a value set to the current directory; the current directory is stored inside another Unix environment variable: `PWD`.

Then, in the same line, we run *main.py* in *apps/circle_from_points*. Having the definition of `PYTHONPATH` in the same line where the script is run scopes the environment variable to the execution of the script only. This means that once the script is done, the variable doesn't exist anymore.

Let's try running the script from the shell passing the file *test.txt*:

```
$ bash cifpts.sh < apps/circle_from_points/test.txt
```

That should've printed the SVG output to the shell. We can even make the bash script appear as an executable by changing its user rights:

```
$ chmod +x cifpts.sh
```

This allows us to further simplify the execution:

```
$ ./cifpts.sh < apps/circle_from_points/test.txt
```

Remember that the output needs to be redirected to a file if we want the result written to it instead of being printed to the shell:

```
$ ./cifpts.sh < apps/circle_from_points/test.txt > result.svg
```

This looks more like something we want to share with our friends, all of whom have longed to have a script that computes the circle that passes through any three points.

Running the App Without an Input File

It's interesting to note that although we've been passing the script a file containing the definition of three points by their coordinates, our code just expects three lines from the standard input. This means we don't have to create a file to pass our script. We can simply execute the script and write the expected input. If you try this in the shell,

```
$ ./cifpts.sh > result.svg
$ 300 300
$ 700 400
$ 300 500
```

you'll get an image named *result.svg* with the result inside the current directory. As you see, you can directly give your program its input data from the shell.

Summary

In this chapter, we've developed our first application: a command line tool that reads a file, parses it using regular expressions, and produces a beautiful SVG vector image. This application has integrated a lot of knowledge that we've been acquiring throughout the past chapters and has taught us about regular expressions.

We also analyzed the problem that caused our modules to not be found by Python when the application was run from the shell. We learned that this happened because our project's root folder, *Mechanics*, wasn't part of the list of directories Python uses to resolve imports. You can now easily distribute your *Mechanics* project to your friends so that they can play with the applications that we'll be creating throughout the book, which will conveniently be wrapped into top-level bash scripts.

10

GRAPHICAL USER INTERFACES
AND THE CANVAS

Before we dive into simulations, we need to understand the basics of graphical user interfaces (GUIs). This is a massive topic, and we'll barely scratch the surface, but we'll see enough for us to present our simulations to the user.

GUIs typically consist of a parent window (or windows) containing *widgets* the user can interact with, such as buttons or text fields. For our goal of drawing simulations, the widget we're most interested in is the *canvas*. In a canvas we can draw geometric primitives, and we can redraw them many times per second, something that we'll use to create the perception of motion.

In this chapter, we'll cover how to lay out a GUI using Tkinter, a package shipped with Python's Standard Library. Once we've got that down, we'll implement a class that will make drawing our geometric primitives to the canvas convenient. This class will also include an affine transformation as part of its state. We'll use this to affect how all primitives are drawn to the canvas, which will allow us to do things such as flip the drawing vertically so that the y-axis points up.

Tkinter

Tkinter is a package that ships with Python's Standard Library. It's used for building graphical user interfaces. It provides the visual components, in other words, the widgets, such as buttons, text fields, and windows. It also provides the canvas, which we'll use to draw the frames of our simulations.

Tkinter is a feature-rich library; there are entire books written on it (see, for example, [7]). We'll only cover what we need for our purposes, but if you enjoy creating GUIs, I recommend you spend some time looking through Tkinter's documentation online; there's a lot you can learn that will help you build fancy GUIs for your programs.

Our First GUI Program

Let's create a new package in the *graphic* folder where we'll place our simulation code. Right-click *graphic*, choose **New ▶ Python Package**, name it *simulation*, and click **OK**. The folder structure in your project should look like this:

```
Mechanics
 |- apps
 |    |- circle_from_points
 |- geom2d
 |    |- tests
 |- graphic
 |    |- simulation
 |    |- svg
 |- utils
```

Let's now create our first GUI program to get acquainted with Tkinter. In the newly created *simulation* folder, add a new Python file named *hello_tkinter.py*. Enter the code in Listing 10-1.

```python
from tkinter import Tk

tk = Tk()
tk.title("Hello Tkinter")

tk.mainloop()
```

Listing 10-1: Hello Tkinter

To execute the code in the file, right-click it in the Project tree panel and choose **Run 'hello_tkinter'** from the menu that appears. When you execute the code, an empty window with the title "Hello Tkinter" opens, as shown in Figure 10-1.

Figure 10-1: The empty Tkinter window

Let's review the code we've just written. We start by importing the Tk class from tkinter. The tk variable holds an instance of Tk, which represents the main window in a Tkinter program. This window is also referred to as *root* in the documentation and examples online.

We then set the title of the window to Hello Tkinter and run the *main loop*. Notice that the main window won't appear on the screen until the main loop starts. In a GUI program, the main loop is an infinite loop: it runs the entire time the program is being executed; as it runs, it collects user events in its windows and reacts to them.

Graphical user interfaces are different than the other programs we've been writing so far in that they're *event driven*. This means that graphic components can be configured to run some code whenever they receive an event of the desired type. For example, we can tell a button to write a message when it receives a click event, that is, when it gets clicked. The code that reacts to an event is commonly known as an *event handler*.

Let's add a text field where the user can write their name, and let's add a button to greet them by name. Modify your *hello_tkinter.py* file to include the code in Listing 10-2. Pay attention to the new imports on top of the file.

```
from tkinter import Tk, Label, Entry, Button, StringVar

tk = Tk()
tk.title("Hello Tkinter")

❶ Label(tk, text='Enter your name:').grid(row=0, column=0)
❷ name = StringVar()
❸ Entry(tk, width=20, textvariable=name).grid(row=1, column=0)
❹ Button(tk, text='Greet me').grid(row=1, column=1)

tk.mainloop()
```

Listing 10-2: Hello Tkinter widgets

To add the label "Enter your name:" we've instantiated the `Label` class from tkinter ❶. We pass the constructor the reference to the program's main window (tk) and a named argument with the text to display: `text='Enter your name:'`. Before the label can appear in the window, we need to tell it where to place itself in the window.

On the created instance of `Label`, we call `grid` with the named arguments `row` and `column`. This method places the widget in an invisible grid in the window, in the given row and column indices. Cells in the grid adapt their size to fit their contents. As you can see in the code, we call this method on every widget to assign them a position in the window. Figure 10-2 shows our UI's grid. There are other ways of placing components in windows, but we'll use this one for now because it's flexible enough for us to easily arrange components.

Figure 10-2: Tkinter grid

The input field in Tkinter is known as `Entry` ❸. To have access to the contents of the field (the text written to it), we must first create a `StringVar`, which we'll call `name` ❷. This variable is passed to the `Entry` component using the `textvariable` argument. We can get the string written in the field by invoking `get` on the instance, as we'll do shortly. Lastly, we create a button with the text "Greet me" ❹; this button does nothing if clicked (we'll add that functionality shortly).

Run the file. You should now see a label, a text field, and a button, as in Figure 10-3.

```
● ● ●        Hello Tkinter
    Enter your name:

                                  Greet me
```

Figure 10-3: Some Tkinter widgets

Let's finish our program by adding an event handler to the button's click, which opens a new dialog with a greeting message. Modify your code so that it looks like Listing 10-3.

```python
from tkinter import Tk, Label, Entry, Button, StringVar, messagebox

tk = Tk()
tk.title("Hello Tkinter")
```

```
❶ def greet_user():
    messagebox.showinfo(
        'Greetings',
        f'Hello, {name.get()}'
    )


Label(tk, text='Enter your name:').grid(row=0, column=0)
name = StringVar()
Entry(tk, width=20, textvariable=name).grid(row=1, column=0)
Button(
    tk,
    text='Greet me',
❷   command=greet_user
).grid(row=1, column=1)

tk.mainloop()
```

Listing 10-3: Hello Tkinter that greets users

We've added a function named greet_user ❶. This function opens an information dialog with the title "Greetings" and a message saying hello to the name the user entered in the text field. Note that we import `messagebox` from `tkinter` to call the `showinfo` function. This function does the actual work of opening the dialog. To connect the button click event to our greet_user function, we need to pass it to Button's constructor in a parameter named command ❷.

Run the file now. Don't forget to close our application's window and rerun the program every time you want your new code to be executed. Enter your name in the text field and click the button. The program should open a new dialog with a personalized greeting, something similar to Figure 10-4.

Figure 10-4: Our Tkinter greeter program

There's much more Tkinter can do, but we won't need that much for this book. We're mostly interested in using its canvas component, which we'll explore in the next section. If you want to learn more about Tkinter, you have lots of great resources online. You can also refer to [7], as mentioned earlier.

The Canvas

A canvas is a surface to paint on. In Tkinter's digital world, it's the same. The canvas component is represented by the Canvas class in tkinter.

Let's create a new Tkinter application where we can experiment with drawing to the canvas. In the *simulation* folder, create a new file named *hello_canvas.py* and enter the code in Listing 10-4.

```
from tkinter import Tk, Canvas

tk = Tk()
tk.title("Hello Canvas")

canvas = Canvas(tk, width=600, height=600)
canvas.grid(row=0, column=0)

tk.mainloop()
```

Listing 10-4: Hello Canvas

The code creates a Tkinter application with its main window and a 600 by 600–pixel canvas. If you run the file, you should see an empty window with the title "Hello Canvas." The canvas is there; it's just that there's nothing drawn yet.

Drawing Lines

Let's start easy and draw a line on the canvas. Just between creating the canvas and starting the main loop, add the following line:

```
--snip--

canvas.create_line(0, 0, 300, 300)

tk.mainloop()
```

The arguments passed to create_line are, respectively, the x- and y-coordinates of the start point and the x- and y-coordinates of the end point.

Run the file again. There should be a line segment going from the upper-left corner, $(0, 0)$, to the center of the screen, $(300, 300)$. As you can guess, the origin of coordinates is in the upper-left corner of the screen with the y-axis pointing downward. Later when we're animating simulations, we'll use affine transformations to fix this.

By default, lines are drawn with a width of 1 pixel and painted in black, but we can change this. Try the following:

```
canvas.create_line(
    0, 0, 300, 300,
    width=3,
    fill='#aa3355'
)
```

The line is now thicker and has a reddish color. Your result should look like Figure 10-5.

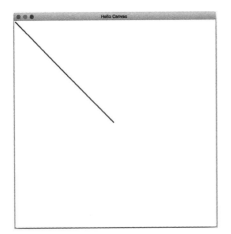

Figure 10-5: A line on a Tkinter canvas

Drawing Ovals

Let's draw a circle in the middle of our application's window using the same color as the previous line:

```
--snip--

canvas.create_oval(
    200, 200, 400, 400,
    width=3,
    outline='#aa3355'
)


tk.mainloop()
```

The arguments passed to create_oval are the x- and y-coordinates of the upper-left vertex of the rectangle that contains the oval, and the x- and y-coordinates of the lower-right vertex. These are followed by the named arguments used to determine the line's width and color: width and outline.

If you run the file, you'll see a circle in the center of the window. Let's turn it into a proper oval by making it 100 pixels wider, maintaining its height of 400 pixels:

```
canvas.create_oval(
    200, 200, 500, 400,
    width=3,
    outline='#aa3355'
)
```

By changing the x-coordinate of the lower-right corner from 400 to 500, the circle turns into an oval. The application now has a canvas with both a line and an oval, as in Figure 10-6.

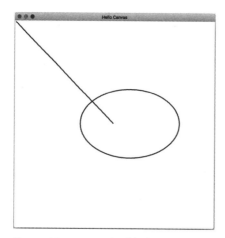

Figure 10-6: An oval added to our Tkinter canvas

If we wanted to add a fill color to the oval, we could do so using the named argument fill='...'. Here's an example:

```
canvas.create_oval(
    200, 200, 500, 400,
    width=3,
    outline='#aa3355',
    fill='#cc3355',
)
```

There's one limitation, though: Tkinter doesn't support transparency, which means all of our fills and strokes will be completely opaque. The color format #rrggbbaa where aa is the value for the *alpha* (transparency) is not supported in Tkinter.

Drawing Rectangles

Drawing rectangles is also pretty straightforward. Enter this code in the file:

```
--snip--

canvas.create_rectangle(
    40, 400, 500, 500,
    width=3,
    outline='#aa3355'
)

tk.mainloop()
```

The mandatory arguments to create_rectangle are the x- and y-coordinates of the upper-left corner of the rectangle and the x- and y-coordinates of the lower-right corner.

Run the file; the result should look like Figure 10-7.

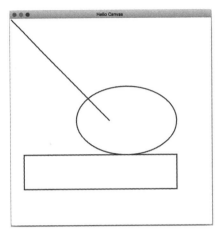

Figure 10-7: A rectangle added to our Tkinter canvas

Nice! The resulting image is getting weirder, but isn't it easy and fun to draw on the canvas?

Drawing Polygons

The last geometric primitive we need to know how to draw is a generic polygon. After the code you added to draw the rectangle, write the following:

```
--snip--

canvas.create_polygon(
    [40, 200, 300, 450, 600, 0],
    width=3,
    outline='#aa3355',
    fill=''
)

tk.mainloop()
```

The first parameter to create_polygon is a list of vertex coordinates. The rest are the named parameters that affect its style. Notice that we pass an empty string to the fill parameter; by default polygons get filled, but we want ours to be only an outline. Run the file to see the result. It should resemble Figure 10-8.

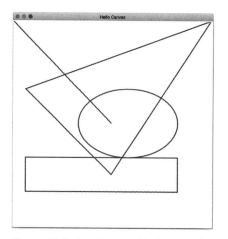

Figure 10-8: A polygon added to our Tkinter canvas

We created a triangle with vertices $(40, 200)$, $(300, 450)$, and $(600, 0)$. Try adding a fill color and seeing what results.

Drawing Text

It isn't a geometric primitive, but we may also need to draw some text to the canvas. Doing so is easy using the `create_text` method. Add the following to *hello_canvas.py*:

```
--snip--

canvas.create_text(
    300, 520,
    text='This is a weird drawing',
    fill='#aa3355',
    font='Helvetica 20 bold'
)

tk.mainloop()
```

The first two parameters are the x and y position for the center of the text. The named parameter text is where we set the actual text we want to draw; we can change its font using font. Run the file one last time to see the complete drawing, as shown in Figure 10-9.

If we can draw lines, circles, rectangles, generic polygons, and text, we can draw pretty much anything. We could also use arcs and splines, but we'll manage to do our simulations using only these simple primitives.

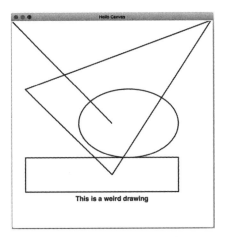

Figure 10-9: Text added to our Tkinter canvas

Your final code should look like Listing 10-5.

```
from tkinter import Tk, Canvas

tk = Tk()
tk.title("Hello Canvas")

canvas = Canvas(tk, width=600, height=600)
canvas.grid(row=0, column=0)

canvas.create_line(
    0, 0, 300, 300,
    width=3,
    fill='#aa3355'
)
canvas.create_oval(
    200, 200, 500, 400,
    width=3,
    outline='#aa3355'
)
canvas.create_rectangle(
    40, 400, 500, 500,
    width=3,
    outline='#aa3355'
)
canvas.create_polygon(
    [40, 200, 300, 450, 600, 0],
    width=3,
    outline='#aa3355',
    fill=''
)
canvas.create_text(
```

```
    300, 520,
    text='This is a weird drawing',
    fill='#aa3355',
    font='Helvetica 20 bold'
)

tk.mainloop()
```

Listing 10-5: Final drawing code

Now that we know how to draw simple primitives to the canvas, let's
come up with a way of drawing our *geom2d* library's geometric primitives
directly to the canvas.

Drawing Our Geometric Primitives

Drawing a circle to the canvas was easy using its create_oval method. This
method is, nevertheless, not convenient; to define the circle, you need to
pass the coordinates of two vertices that define a rectangle where the circle or oval is inscribed. On the other hand, our class Circle is defined by its
center point and radius, and it has some useful methods and can be transformed using instances of AffineTransform. It would be nice if we could directly draw our circles like so:

```
circle = Circle(Point(2, 5), 10)
canvas.draw_circle(circle)
```

We definitely want to work with our geometry primitives. Similar to how
we created SVG representations of them in Chapter 8, we'll need a way to
draw them to the canvas.

Here's the plan: we'll create a wrapper for Tkinter's Canvas widget. We'll
create a class that contains an instance of the canvas where we want to draw
but whose methods allow us to pass our own geometric primitives. To leverage our powerful affine transformation implementation, we'll associate
a transformation to our drawing so that all primitives we pass will first be
transformed.

The Canvas Wrapper Class

A wrapper class is simply a class that contains an instance of another class
(what it's wrapping) and is used to provide a similar functionality as the
wrapped class, but with a different interface and some added functionality.
It's a simple yet powerful concept.

In this case, we're wrapping a Tkinter canvas. Our canvas wrapper goal
is to allow us to draw our geometric primitives with a simple and clean interface: we want methods that directly accept instances of our primitives. This
wrapper will save us from the repetitive task of adapting the representation
of the geometric classes to the inputs expected by the Tkinter canvas's draw-

ing methods. Not only that, but we'll also apply an affine transformation to everything that we draw. Figure 10-10 depicts this process.

In the *simulation* package, create a new file named *draw.py*. Enter the code in Listing 10-6.

```
from tkinter import Canvas

from geom2d import AffineTransform


class CanvasDrawing:

    def __init__(self, canvas: Canvas, transform: AffineTransform):
        self.__canvas = canvas
        self.outline_color = '#aa3355'
        self.outline_width = 3
        self.fill_color = ''
        self.transform = transform

    def clear_drawing(self):
        self.__canvas.delete('all')
```

Listing 10-6: Canvas wrapper class

The class CanvasDrawing is defined as a wrapper to the Tkinter canvas. An instance of the canvas is passed to the initializer and stored in a private variable, __canvas. Making __canvas private means we don't want anyone using CanvasDrawing to access it directly. It now belongs to the wrapper class instance, and it should only be used with its methods.

An instance of AffineTransform is also passed to the initializer. We'll apply this affine transformation to all geometric primitives before we draw them to Tkinter's canvas. The transformation is stored in a public variable: transform. This means we're allowing users of CanvasDrawing instances to directly manipulate and edit this property, which is part of the state of the instance. We do this so that it's simple to alter the affine transformation applied to the drawing, by reassigning the transform property to a different transformation.

The state of an instance defines its behavior: if the state changes, the instance's behavior changes as well. In this case, it's clear that if the property transform is reassigned a different affine transformation, all subsequent drawing commands will produce results in accordance with it.

Figure 10-10 is a diagram representing the behavior of our canvas wrapper class. It'll receive draw requests for different geometric primitives, apply the affine transformation to them, and then call the Tkinter's canvas methods to draw into it.

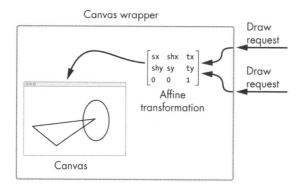

Figure 10-10: The canvas wrapper class

There are other state variables defined in the initializer: outline_color, which defines the color used for the outline of geometries, outline_width for the width of the outlines, and fill_color for the color used to fill the geometries. These are given default values in the initializer (those used in our example in the previous section) but are also public and accessible for users of the instance to change them. Like before, it should be clear that these properties are part of the state of the instance: if we edit outline_color, for example, all subsequent drawings will use that color for the outlines.

We've defined only one method in the class: clear_drawing. This method will clean the canvas for us before drawing each of the frames. Let's now focus on the drawing commands.

Drawing Segments

Let's start with the simplest primitive to draw: the segment. In the Canvas Drawing class, enter the method in Listing 10-7. For this code you first need to update the imports from *geom2d* to include the Segment class.

```
from tkinter import Canvas

from geom2d import Segment, AffineTransform


class CanvasDrawing:
    --snip--

    def draw_segment(self, segment: Segment):
        segment_t = self.transform.apply_to_segment(segment)
        self.__canvas.create_line(
            segment_t.start.x,
            segment_t.start.y,
            segment_t.end.x,
            segment_t.end.y,
            fill=self.outline_color,
            width=self.outline_width
```

```
)
```

Listing 10-7: Drawing a segment

NOTE   *Note how we're passing the* `self.outline_color` *value to the* `fill` *parameter. That looks like an error, but unfortunately, Tkinter picked a bad name. The* `fill` *attribute is used for the stroke's color in a* `create_line` *command. A better name would have been* `outline` *or, even better,* `stroke-color`*.*

The `draw_segment` method does two things: first it transforms the given segment using the current affine transformation and stores the result in `segment_t`. Then it calls the `create_line` method from the canvas instance. For the outline color and width, we use the state variables of the instance.

Let's move on to polygons, circles, and rectangles.

Drawing Polygons

If you recall from "Transform Segments and Polygons" on page 179, once an affine transformation is applied to a circle or rectangle, the result is a generic polygon. This means that all three polygons will be drawn using the `create_polygon` method from the canvas.

Let's create a private method that draws a polygon to the canvas, forgetting about the affine transformation; that part will be handled by each of the public drawing methods.

In your `CanvasDrawing` class, enter the private method in Listing 10-8.

```python
from functools import reduce
from tkinter import Canvas

from geom2d import Polygon, Segment, AffineTransform


class CanvasDrawing:
    --snip--

    def __draw_polygon(self, polygon: Polygon):
        vertices = reduce(
            list.__add__,
            [[v.x, v.y] for v in polygon.vertices]
        )

        self.__canvas.create_polygon(
            vertices,
            fill=self.fill_color,
            outline=self.outline_color,
            width=self.outline_width
        )
```

Listing 10-8: Drawing a polygon to the canvas

For this code you need to add the following import,

```
from functools import reduce
```

and update the imports from geom2d:

```
from geom2d import Polygon, Segment, AffineTransform
```

The _draw_polygon method first prepares the vertex coordinates of the polygon to meet the expectations of the canvas widget's create_polygon method. This is done by reducing a list of lists of vertex coordinates with Python's list _add_ method, which, if you recall, is the method that overloads the + operator.

Let's break this down. First, the polygon's vertices are mapped using a list comprehension:

```
[[v.x, v.y] for v in polygon.vertices]
```

This creates a list with the x- and y-coordinates from each vertex. If the vertices of the polygon were (0, 10), (10, 0), and (10, 10), the list comprehension shown earlier would result in the following list:

```
[[0, 10], [10, 0], [10, 10]]
```

This list then needs to be *flattened*: all values in the inner lists (the numeric coordinates) have to be concatenated into a single list. The result of flattening the previous list would be as follows:

```
[0, 10, 10, 0, 10, 10]
```

This is the list of vertex coordinates the method create_polygon expects. This final flattening step is achieved by the reduce function; we pass it the list ._add_ operator, and it produces a new list that results from concatenating both list operands. To see that in action, you can test the following in Python's shell:

```
>>> [1, 2] + [3, 4]
[1, 2, 3, 4]
```

Once the list of vertex coordinates is ready, drawing it to the canvas is straightforward: we simply pass the list to the canvas's create_polygon method. Now that the hardest part is done, drawing our polygons should be easier. Enter the code in Listing 10-9 to your class.

```
from functools import reduce
from tkinter import Canvas

from geom2d import Circle, Polygon, Segment, Rect, AffineTransform


class CanvasDrawing:
```

```
--snip--

    def draw_circle(self, circle: Circle, divisions=30):
        self.__draw_polygon(
            self.transform.apply_to_circle(circle, divisions)
        )

    def draw_rectangle(self, rect: Rect):
        self.__draw_polygon(
            self.transform.apply_to_rect(rect)
        )

    def draw_polygon(self, polygon: Polygon):
        self.__draw_polygon(
            self.transform.apply_to_polygon(polygon)
        )
```

Listing 10-9: Drawing circles, rectangles, and generic polygons

Don't forget to add the missing imports from *geom2d*:

```
from geom2d import Circle, Polygon, Segment, Rect, AffineTransform
```

In all three methods, the process is the same: call the private method __draw_polygon and pass it the result of applying the current affine transformation to the geometry. Don't forget that in the case of a circle, we need to pass the number of divisions we'll use to approximate it to the transform method.

Drawing Arrows

Let's now draw arrows following the same approach we used in Chapter 8 for SVG images.

The arrow's head will be drawn on the end point E of a segment and will be made of two segments at an angle meeting at such an end point. To allow some flexibility, we'll use two dimensions to define the arrow's geometry: a length and a height (see Figure 10-11).

As you can see in Figure 10-11 (repeated from Chapter 8), to draw the arrow's head, we need to figure out points C_1 and C_2. With those two points, we can easily draw the segments between C_1 and E and between C_2 and E.

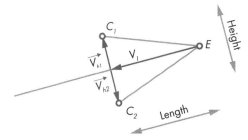

Figure 10-11: Key points in an arrow

To find out where those points lie in the plane, we'll be computing three vectors: $\vec{v}_l$, which has the same length as the arrow's head and is going in the opposite direction of the segment's direction vector, and $\vec{v}_{h1}$ and $\vec{v}_{h2}$, which are perpendicular to the segment and both have a length equal to half the arrow's head height. Figure 10-11 shows these vectors. The point C_1 can be computed by creating a displaced version of E (the segment's end point),

$$C_1 = E + (\vec{v}_l + \vec{v}_{h1})$$

and similarly, C_2:

$$C_2 = E + (\vec{v}_l + \vec{v}_{h2})$$

Let's write the method. In the `CanvasDrawing` class, enter the code in Listing 10-10.

```
class CanvasDrawing:
    --snip--

    def draw_arrow(
            self,
            segment: Segment,
            length: float,
            height: float
    ):
        director = segment.direction_vector
        v_l = director.opposite().with_length(length)
        v_h1 = director.perpendicular().with_length(height / 2.0)
        v_h2 = v_h1.opposite()

        self.draw_segment(segment)
        self.draw_segment(
            Segment(
                segment.end,
          ❶ segment.end.displaced(v_l + v_h1)
            )
        )
        self.draw_segment(
            Segment(
```

```
            segment.end,
    ❷   segment.end.displaced(v_l + v_h2)
        )
    )
```

Listing 10-10: Drawing an arrow

We start by computing the three vectors we need to figure out points C_1 and C_2 using the previous equations. As you can see, this is pretty straightforward thanks to the methods we implemented in our Vector class. For example, to obtain $\vec{v}_l$, we use the opposite vector of the segment's direction vector and scale it to have the desired length. We use similar operations to calculate the remaining elements of our equations.

Then we three segments: the base line, which is the segment passed as the argument; the segment going from E to C_1 ❶ ; and the one going from E to C_2 ❷.

For reference, your *drawing.py* file should look like Listing 10-11.

```
from functools import reduce
from tkinter import Canvas

from geom2d import Circle, Polygon, Segment, Rect, AffineTransform


class CanvasDrawing:

    def __init__(self, canvas: Canvas, transform: AffineTransform):
        self.__canvas = canvas
        self.outline_color = '#aa3355'
        self.outline_width = 3
        self.fill_color = ''
        self.transform = transform

    def clear_drawing(self):
        self.__canvas.delete('all')

    def draw_segment(self, segment: Segment):
        segment_t = self.transform.apply_to_segment(segment)
        self.__canvas.create_line(
            segment_t.start.x,
            segment_t.start.y,
            segment_t.end.x,
            segment_t.end.y,
            outline=self.outline_color,
            width=self.outline_width
        )

    def draw_circle(self, circle: Circle, divisions=30):
        self.__draw_polygon(
```

```python
            self.transform.apply_to_circle(circle, divisions)
        )

    def draw_rectangle(self, rect: Rect):
        self.__draw_polygon(
            self.transform.apply_to_rect(rect)
        )

    def draw_polygon(self, polygon: Polygon):
        self.__draw_polygon(
            self.transform.apply_to_polygon(polygon)
        )

    def __draw_polygon(self, polygon: Polygon):
        vertices = reduce(
            list.__add__,
            [[v.x, v.y] for v in polygon.vertices]
        )

        self.__canvas.create_polygon(
            vertices,
            fill=self.fill_color,
            outline=self.outline_color,
            width=self.outline_width
        )

    def draw_arrow(
            self,
            segment: Segment,
            length: float,
            height: float
    ):
        director = segment.direction_vector
        v_l = director.opposite().with_length(length)
        v_h1 = director.perpendicular().with_length(height / 2.0)
        v_h2 = v_h1.opposite()

        self.draw_segment(segment)
        self.draw_segment(
            Segment(
                segment.end,
                segment.end.displaced(v_l + v_h1)
            )
        )
        self.draw_segment(
            Segment(
                segment.end,
```

```
                segment.end.displaced(v_l + v_h2)
        )
    )
```

Listing 10-11: CanvasDrawing class result

We now have a convenient way of drawing our geometric primitives, but they're not moving at all, and we need motion to produce simulations. What's the missing ingredient to bring those geometries to life? That's the topic of the next chapter. Matters are getting more and more exciting!

Summary

In this chapter, we covered the basics of creating graphical user interfaces using Python's Tkinter package. We saw how to lay widgets on the main window using the grid system. We also learned how to make a button respond to being clicked and how to read the contents of a text field. Most importantly, we learned about the Canvas class and its methods that we can use to draw simple primitives to it.

We finished the chapter by creating a class of our own that wraps Tkinter's canvas and allows us to draw our geometric primitives directly. The class also includes an affine transformation that applies to the primitives before being drawn. The class has properties that define the stroke width and color as well as the fill color. These are the width and colors applied to the primitives we draw with it. Now it's time to put those static geometries into motion.

11

ANIMATIONS, SIMULATIONS, AND THE TIME LOOP

The same way vector images visualize static problems, animations help us build visual intuition for dynamic problems. A single image can show us only how things are at a specific point in time. When the properties of a system change over time, we'll need an animation to get the complete story.

Much like a static analysis presents a system in a moment, a *simulation* presents the evolution of a system over time. Animations are a good way of presenting the results of this evolution. There are two good reasons for engineers to simulate dynamic systems: it's a great exercise to solidify your understanding of these systems, and it's quite fun.

In this chapter, we'll start exploring the engaging world of animations, starting with a few definitions. We'll then learn how to make drawings move across the canvas. We'll use Tkinter's canvas and, more importantly, our CanvasDrawing wrapper class.

Defining Terms

Let's define a few of the terms we'll be using in this section.

What Is an Animation?

An *animation* is the sensation of motion generated by a rapid succession of images. Because the computer draws these images to the screen extremely quickly, our eyes perceive motion.

We'll make animations by drawing something to the canvas, clearing it, and then drawing something else. Each drawing, which remains on the screen for a fraction of a second, is called a *frame*.

Take, for example, Figure 11-1, which depicts each frame of an animation: a triangle moving right.

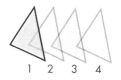

Figure 11-1: The animation frames of a triangle

Each of the four frames in the animation has the triangle in a slightly different position. If we draw them on the canvas, one after the other, clearing the previous drawing, the triangle will appear to move.

Simple, isn't it? We'll build our first animation in this chapter soon, but first let's define the terms *system* and *simulation*, as they'll appear frequently in our discussion.

What Is a System?

The word *system*, in our context, refers to whatever we're drawing to the canvas in an animation. It consists of a group of objects subject to some physical laws and interacting with one another. We'll use these laws to derive a mathematical model, often in the form of a system of differential equations. We'll resolve these equations using numerical methods, which yield the values that describe the system at discrete points in time. These values might be the system's position or velocity.

Now let's take a look at an example of a system and derive its equation. Let's suppose we have a body with mass m subject to an external force that is a function of time, $\vec{F}(t)$. Figure 11-2 depicts a *free body diagram*. There, you can see the external force and its weight force applied, where $\vec{g}$ is gravity's acceleration vector.

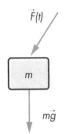

Figure 11-2: A mass
subject to external force

Using Newton's second law and denoting the position vector of the body by $\vec{p}$, we get the following:

$$\sum \vec{f} = m\ddot{\vec{p}} \quad \rightarrow \quad \vec{F}(t) + m\vec{g} = m\ddot{\vec{p}}$$

Solving for the acceleration $\ddot{\vec{p}}$,

$$\ddot{\vec{p}}(t) = \vec{g} + \frac{\vec{F}(t)}{m} = \left\{ \begin{array}{c} 0 \\ -g \end{array} \right\} + \frac{1}{m} \left\{ \begin{array}{c} F_x(t) \\ F_y(t) \end{array} \right\}$$

The previous vector equation can be broken down into its two scalar components:

$$\begin{cases} \ddot{x}(t) = \frac{F_x(t)}{m} \\ \ddot{y}(t) = -g + \frac{F_y(t)}{m} \end{cases}$$

These two equations express the acceleration of the body function of time. To simulate this simple system, we'd need to obtain a new value for the acceleration, velocity, and position of the body for each frame of the animation. We'll see what this means in a minute.

What Is a Simulation?

A *simulation* is the study of the evolution of a system whose behavior is mathematically described. Simulations harness the computation power of modern central processing units (CPUs) to understand how a given system would behave under real conditions.

Computer simulations are in general cheaper and simpler to set up than real-world experiments, so they're used to study and predict the behavior of many engineering designs.

Take the system whose equations we derived in the previous section. Given an expression of the external force with respect to time like

$$\vec{F}(t) = \left\{ \begin{array}{c} 10t \\ 5t^2 \end{array} \right\}$$

and the mass for the body is said to be $m = 5\text{kg}$, the acceleration equations become the following.

$$\begin{cases} \ddot{x}(t) = \frac{10t}{5} = 2t \\ \ddot{y}(t) = -g + \frac{5t^2}{5} = -g + t^2 \end{cases}$$

These scalar equations give us the acceleration components for the body at every moment in time. Since the equations are simple, we can integrate them to obtain the expression of the velocity components,

$$\begin{cases} \dot{x}(t) = \int 2t \cdot dt = t^2 + \dot{X}_0 \\ \dot{y}(t) = \int (-g + t^2) \cdot dt = -gt + \frac{t^3}{3} + \dot{Y}_0 \end{cases}$$

where $\dot{X}_0$ and $\dot{Y}_0$ are the components of the initial velocity: the velocity at time $t = 0$. We know the velocity of the mass for every moment in time. If we want to animate the movement of the mass, we need an expression for the position, which we can obtain by integrating the velocity equations,

$$\begin{cases} x(t) = \int (t^2 + \dot{X}_0) \cdot dt = \frac{t^3}{3} + \dot{X}_0 t + X_0 \\ y(t) = \int (-gt + \frac{t^3}{3} + \dot{Y}_0) \cdot dt = -g\frac{t^2}{2} + \frac{t^4}{12} + \dot{Y}_0 t + Y_0 \end{cases}$$

where X_0 and Y_0 are the initial position components for the mass. We can now create an animation to understand how the body moves under the effect of the external force by simply creating a sequence of time values, obtaining the position for each of them, and then drawing a rectangle to the screen at that position.

The *differential equations* relating how the acceleration of the system varies with respect to time for this example were straightforward, which allowed us to obtain an analytic solution using integration. We usually don't get an analytic solution for the system under simulation, so we tend to resort to numerical methods.

The *analytic solution* is the exact solution, whereas a *numerical solution* is obtained using computer algorithms that look for an approximation of the solution. A common numerical method, although not the most precise, is *Euler's method*.

Drawing the simulation in real time means we need to solve the equations as often as we draw frames. For example, if we want to simulate at a rate of 50 frames per second (fps), then we need to both draw the frames and solve the equations 50 times per second.

At 50 fps, the time between frames is 20 milliseconds. Taking into account the fact that your computer requires some of those milliseconds to redraw the screen with the current frame, we're left with little time for the math.

Simulations can also be computed ahead of time and later played back. This way solving the equations can take as long as required; the animation takes place only when all frames are ready.

Video game engines use real-time simulations as they need to simulate the world around the player as they interact with it, something that can't be determined ahead of time. These engines tend to trade accuracy for speed; their results are not physically accurate but look realistic to the naked eye.

Complex engineering systems require an ahead-of-time simulation since the governing equations for these problems are complex and require a much more exact solution.

What Is the Time Loop?

Real-time simulations happen inside a loop, which we'll refer to as the *time loop* or *main loop*. This loop executes as many times per second as frames are drawn to the screen. Here's some pseudocode showing what a time loop might look like:

```
while current_time < end_time:
    solve_system_equations()
    draw_system()
    sleep(time_delta - time_taken)
    current_time += time_delta
```

To make the animations look smooth, we want a steady frame rate. This means the drawing phase of the simulation should take place at evenly spaced points in time. (While not strictly necessary, there are techniques to adapt the frame rate to the processor and GPU's throughput, but we won't be getting that advanced in this book.)

The time elapsed between consecutive frames is referred to as the *time delta*, or δt; it's inversely proportional to the frame rate (fps) and typically measured in seconds or milliseconds: $FPS = \frac{1}{\delta t}$. As a consequence, everything happening in our time loop should take less than a single time delta to complete.

The first step in the loop is solving the equations to figure out how the system has evolved during the elapsed time delta. Then, we draw the system's new configuration to the screen. We need to measure the time taken so far in the loop and store the result in the time_taken variable.

At this point, the program is paused or put to sleep until an entire time delta has elapsed. The time we sleep can be figured out by subtracting time _taken from time_delta. The last step before ending the loop is to advance the current time by a time delta; the loop then starts over again. Figure 11-3 shows the time line with the events in the time loop drawn.

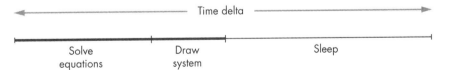

Figure 11-3: The time loop events

Now that we have those definitions out of the way, let's implement a time loop and start animating.

Our First Animation

At the beginning of the chapter, we explained how we can achieve the sensation of motion by drawing something many times per second. The time loop is in charge of keeping these drawings at a steady rate. Let's implement our first time loop.

Setup

We'll start by creating a new file where we can experiment. In the *simulation* package, create a new file and name it *hello_motion.py*. Enter the code in Listing 11-1.

```python
import time
from tkinter import Tk, Canvas

tk = Tk()
tk.title("Hello Motion")

canvas = Canvas(tk, width=600, height=600)
canvas.grid(row=0, column=0)

frame_rate_s = 1.0 / 30.0
frame_count = 1
max_frames = 100


def update_system():
    pass


def redraw():
    pass


❶ while frame_count <= max_frames:
      update_start = time.time()
❷     update_system()
❸     redraw()
❹     tk.update()
      update_end = time.time()

❺     elapsed_s = update_end - update_start
      remaining_time_s = frame_rate_s - elapsed_s

      if remaining_time_s > 0:
❻         time.sleep(remaining_time_s)
```

```
    frame_count += 1

tk.mainloop()
```

Listing 11-1: The hello_motion.py *file*

In the code in Listing 11-1, we start by creating a 600×600-pixel canvas and adding it to the grid of the main window. Then we initialize some variables: frame_rate_s holds the time between two consecutive frames, in seconds; frame_count is the count of how many frames have already been drawn; and max_frames is the number of total frames we'll draw.

NOTE   *Note that the variables storing time-related quantities include information in their name about the unit they use. The* s *in* frame_rate_s *or* elapsed_s *indicates seconds. It's good practice to do this, as it helps the developer understand what units the code is working with without needing to read comments or pick through all the code. When you spend many hours a day coding, these small details end up saving you a lot of time and frustration.*

Then comes the time loop ❶, which executes max_frames times at a rate of frame_rate_s, at least in principle (as you'll see in a minute). Note that we chose to limit the simulation using a maximum number of frames, but we could also limit it by time, that is, keep running the loop until a given amount of time has elapsed, just like we did in the pseudocode shown earlier. Both approaches work fine.

In the loop we start by storing the current time in update_start. After the updates to the system and the drawing have taken place, we store the time again, this time in update_end. The time elapsed is then computed by subtracting update_start from update_end and stored in elapsed_s ❺. We use this quantity to calculate how long the loop needs to sleep to keep the frame rate steady, subtracting elapsed_s from frame_rate_s. That amount is stored in remaining_time_s, and if it's greater than zero, we sleep the loop ❻.

If remaining_time_s is less than zero, the loop took longer than the frame rate, meaning it can't keep up with the rhythm we imposed on it. If this happens often, the time loop will become unsteady, and animations may look chunky, in which case it's better to simply reduce the frame rate.

The magic happens (or will happen, to be more precise) in update _system ❷ and redraw ❸, which we call in the loop to update and redraw the system. Here's where we'll soon be writing our drawing code. The pass statement is used in Python as a placeholder: it doesn't do anything, but it allows us to have, for example, a valid function body.

There's also a call to update from main window tk ❹, which tells Tkinter to run the main loop until all pending events have been processed. This is necessary to force Tkinter to look for the events that may trigger changes in the user interface widgets, including our canvas.

You can run the file now; you'll see an empty window apparently doing nothing, but it's actually running the loop max_frames times.

Adding a Frame Count Label

Let's add a label under the canvas to let us know the current frame being drawn to the canvas and the total number of frames. We can update its value in update. First, add Label to the tkinter imports:

```
from tkinter import Tk, Canvas, StringVar, Label
```

Then, under the definition of the canvas, add the label (Listing 11-2).

```
label = StringVar()
label.set('Frame ? of ?')
Label(tk, textvariable=label).grid(row=1, column=0)
```

Listing 11-2: Adding a label *to the window*

Finally, update the label's text in update by setting the value of its text variable, label (Listing 11-3).

```
def update():
    label.set(f'Frame {frame_count} of {max_frames}')
```

Listing 11-3: Updating the label's text

Try to run the file now. The canvas is still blank, but the label below it now displays the current frame. Your program should look like Figure 11-4: a blank window with a frame count going from 1 to 100.

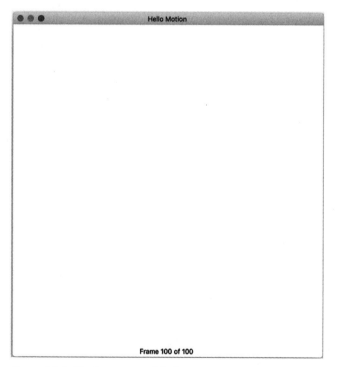

Figure 11-4: The frame count label

Just for reference, your code at this stage should look like Listing 11-4.

```python
import time
from tkinter import Tk, Canvas, StringVar, Label

tk = Tk()
tk.title("Hello Motion")

canvas = Canvas(tk, width=600, height=600)
canvas.grid(row=0, column=0)

label = StringVar()
label.set('Frame ? of ?')
Label(tk, textvariable=label).grid(row=1, column=0)

frame_rate_s = 1.0 / 30.0
frame_count = 1
max_frames = 100


def update_system():
    pass


def redraw():
    label.set(f'Frame {frame_count} of {max_frames}')


while frame_count <= max_frames:
    update_start = time.time()
    update_system()
    redraw()
    tk.update()
    update_end = time.time()

    elapsed_s = update_end - update_start
    remaining_time_s = frame_rate_s - elapsed_s

    if remaining_time_s > 0:
        time.sleep(remaining_time_s)

    frame_count += 1

tk.mainloop()
```

Listing 11-4: Hello canvas with label

To have anything drawn on the canvas, we need to have a system. Let's first take a look at how to add and update a system to our simulation.

Updating the System

For this example, we'll keep it simple and draw a circle whose center is always at the center of the canvas, point $(300, 300)$. Its radius will grow, starting with a value of zero. When the radius grows larger than the canvas and is no longer visible, we'll set it back to zero. This will generate a psychedelic tunnel-like effect.

We can represent our "system" with an instance of our Circle class. Since we'll be drawing the circle to the canvas, let's also create an instance of Canvas Drawing, using an identity affine transformation. Under the definition of variables frame_rate_s, frame_count, and max_frames, add the following:

```
transform = AffineTransform(sx=1, sy=1, tx=0, ty=0, shx=0, shy=0)
drawing = CanvasDrawing(canvas, transform)
circle = Circle(Point(300, 300), 0)
```

Don't forget to include the needed imports:

```
from geom2d import Point, Circle, AffineTransform
from graphic.simulation.draw import CanvasDrawing
```

We need to update the value of the radius every frame in update_system so that when redraw does its thing, the circle gets drawn with the updated value for the radius. In update_system, enter the code in Listing 11-5.

```
def update_system():
    circle.radius = (circle.radius + 15) % 450
    tk.update()
```

Listing 11-5: Updating the circle's radius

The value for the radius is updated by adding 15 to the current value. Using the modulo operator (%), whenever the radius becomes greater than 450, the value wraps around and goes back to zero.

NOTE   *Quick reminder: the modulo operator % returns the remainder of dividing its two operands. For instance, 5 % 3 yields 2.*

You've probably realized that we mutated the circle's radius property instead of creating a new circle with the value for the new radius; it's the first time in the book we mutate the properties of our geometric primitives. The reason is that, for simulations, maintaining the throughput of the loop is crucial, and creating a new instance of the system for each frame would have a high performance impact.

We now have the system defined in each of the frames: a circle whose center point is kept centered in the window while the radius gradually increases in size. Let's draw it to the screen!

Creating Motion

To create the effect of motion, the canvas has to be cleared and the system redrawn in each and every frame. Before `redraw` is invoked in the main loop, `update_system` has already updated the circle. In `redraw`, we simply need to clear whatever is drawn on the canvas and draw the circle again. Update `redraw` using the code in Listing 11-6.

```
def redraw():
    label.set(f'Frame {frame_count} of {max_frames}')
    drawing.clear_drawing()
    drawing.draw_circle(circle, 50)
```

Listing 11-6: Redrawing the circle every frame

You've probably been waiting for this grand moment for the whole chapter, so go ahead and execute the file. You should see a circle growing in size until it disappears from the screen and then starting over again.

Just for your reference, at this point, your *hello_motion.py* code should look like Listing 11-7.

```
import time
from tkinter import Tk, Canvas, StringVar, Label

from geom2d import Point, AffineTransform, Circle
from graphic.simulation import CanvasDrawing

tk = Tk()
tk.title("Hello Motion")

canvas = Canvas(tk, width=600, height=600)
canvas.grid(row=0, column=0)

label = StringVar()
label.set('Frame ? of ?')
Label(tk, textvariable=label).grid(row=1, column=0)

frame_rate_s = 1.0 / 30.0
frame_count = 1
max_frames = 100

transform = AffineTransform(sx=1, sy=1, tx=0, ty=0, shx=0, shy=0)
drawing = CanvasDrawing(canvas, transform)
circle = Circle(Point(300, 300), 0)


def update_system():
    circle.radius = (circle.radius + 15) % 450
    tk.update()
```

```
def redraw():
    label.set(f'Frame {frame_count} of {max_frames}')
    drawing.clear_drawing()
    drawing.draw_circle(circle, 50)


while frame_count <= max_frames:
    update_start = time.time()
    update_system()
    redraw()
    tk.update()
    update_end = time.time()

    elapsed_s = update_end - update_start
    remaining_time_s = frame_rate_s - elapsed_s

    if remaining_time_s > 0:
        time.sleep(remaining_time_s)

    frame_count += 1

tk.mainloop()
```

Listing 11-7: Resulting simulation

Note that before drawing anything, the redraw function clears the canvas. Can you guess what would happen if we forgot to do so? Comment that line out and run the simulation.

```
def redraw():
    label.set(f'Frame {frame_count} of {max_frames}')
    # drawing.clear_drawing()
    drawing.draw_circle(circle, 50)
```

All circles drawn should remain on the canvas, as you see in Figure 11-5.

We've drawn our first animation on the canvas, and it looks fantastic. If we were to write another, though, we'd have to copy and paste the code for the main loop. To avoid this needless duplication, let's move the main loop code into a function that can be easily reused.

Figure 11-5: What it'd look like if we forgot to clean the canvas

Abstracting the Main Loop Function

The main loop we just wrote had a fair amount of logic that will be the same for all simulations. Copying and pasting this code over and over again would not only be bad practice, but if we found an improvement or wanted to make a change to our implementation, we'd need to edit the code of all our simulations. We don't want to duplicate knowledge: we should define the logic for a main simulation loop in just one place.

To implement a generic version of the main loop, we need to do an abstraction exercise. Let's ask ourselves the following questions regarding the implementation of the main loop: Is there something that's never going to change in it, and is there anything simulation-specific? The while loop, the order of the operations inside of it, and the time calculations are the same for every simulation. Conversely, there are three pieces of logic that vary from simulation to simulation, namely, the decision that keeps the loop running, the updating, and the drawing.

If we encapsulate those in functions that the simulations implement, they can be passed to our main loop abstraction. The main loop we implement only needs to care about the timing, that is, trying to keep the frame rate stable.

Create a new file named *loop.py* in the *simulation* package. Enter the code in Listing 11-8.

```
import time


def main_loop(
        update_fn,
        redraw_fn,
        should_continue_fn,
        frame_rate_s=0.03
):
    frame = 1
    time_s = 0
    last_elapsed_s = frame_rate_s

❶ while should_continue_fn(frame, time_s):
        update_start = time.time()
    ❷ update_fn(last_elapsed_s, time_s, frame)
    ❸ redraw_fn()
        update_end = time.time()

        elapsed_s = update_end - update_start
        remaining_time_s = frame_rate_s - elapsed_s

        if remaining_time_s > 0:
            time.sleep(remaining_time_s)
            last_elapsed_s = frame_rate_s
        else:
            last_elapsed_s = elapsed_s

        frame += 1
        time_s += last_elapsed_s
```

Listing 11-8: Simulation's main loop function

The first thing you should notice is that three of the arguments to the main_loop function are also functions: update_fn, redraw_fn, and should_continue _fn. These functions contain the logic that's simulation-specific, so our main loop simply needs to call them as needed.

NOTE   *Passing functions as arguments to other functions was covered in Chapter 1, on page 27. You may want to refer to this section for a quick refresher.*

The main_loop function starts by declaring three variables: frame, which holds the current frame index; time_s, which holds the total time elapsed; and last_elapsed_s, which holds the number of seconds it took the last frame to complete. The condition to keep the loop running is now delegated to the should_continue_fn function ❶. The loop will continue as long as this function returns true. It accepts two arguments: the frame count and the total time elapsed in seconds. If you recall, most of our simulations will be limited by one of these values, so we pass them to the function so that it has the information required to decide whether the loop should keep running.

Next, the update_fn function ❷ updates the system under simulation and the user interface. This function receives three parameters: the time elapsed since the last frame, last_elapsed_s; the total elapsed time for the simulation, time_s; and the current frame number, frame. As we'll see later in the book, when we introduce physics to our simulations, the amount of time elapsed since the last frame is an important piece of data. Lastly comes redraw_fn ❸, which draws the system to the screen.

Thanks to our abstraction of the simulation's main loop, we won't need to write this logic anymore. Let's try to refactor our simulation from the previous section using this definition of the main loop.

Refactoring Our Simulation

Now that we've created an abstraction of the main loop, let's take a look at how our simulation could be refactored to include the main loop function.

Create a new file named *hello_motion_refactor.py* and enter the code from Listing 11-9. You may want to copy and paste the first lines from *hello_motion.py*, those that define the UI. Note that to make the code a bit shorter, I've removed the frame count label from the UI.

```
from tkinter import Tk, Canvas

from geom2d import Point, Circle, AffineTransform
from graphic.simulation.draw import CanvasDrawing
from graphic.simulation.loop import main_loop

tk = Tk()
tk.title("Hello Motion")

canvas = Canvas(tk, width=600, height=600)
canvas.grid(row=0, column=0)

max_frames = 100

transform = AffineTransform(sx=1, sy=1, tx=0, ty=0, shx=0, shy=0)
drawing = CanvasDrawing(canvas, transform)
circle = Circle(Point(300, 300), 0)


def update_system(time_delta_s, time_s, frame):
    circle.radius = (circle.radius + 15) % 450
    tk.update()


def redraw():
    drawing.clear_drawing()
```

```
    drawing.draw_circle(circle, 50)


def should_continue(frame, time_s):
    return frame <= max_frames


main_loop(update_system, redraw, should_continue)
tk.mainloop()
```

Listing 11-9: Refactored version of hello_motion.py

If we go toward the end of the code, we find the call to main_loop. We're passing in the functions that we previously defined, with the sole difference being that now those functions must declare the proper parameters to match the functions main_loop expects.

This code is much simpler to follow. All the logic to keep a steady frame rate has been moved away to its own function, so we can focus our attention on the simulation itself without needing to deal with those details. Let's now take some time to play with some of the parameters of the simulation and understand how they affect the final result.

Playing with the Circle Divisions

Remember that the CanvasDrawing class includes an affine transformation as part of its state, and every geometric primitive gets transformed by it before being drawn. Remember also that this is the reason a circle is converted to a generic polygon using a number of divisions high enough to approximate the circumference. The transformation happens in the drawing command; hence, the number of divisions has to be passed in, or else the default of 30 is used.

Going back to function redraw from Listing 11-9,

```
def redraw():
    drawing.clear_drawing()
    drawing.draw_circle(circle, 50)
```

you can see we used 50 divisions, but we could have used any other number. Let's try with 10, for example:

```
def redraw():
    drawing.clear_drawing()
    drawing.draw_circle(circle, 10)
```

Rerun the file. Can you see the difference? What about if you try with 6 divisions? Figure 11-6 shows the simulation using 50, 10, and 6 divisions for the circle.

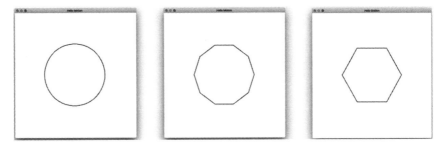

Figure 11-6: Circles drawn using 50, 10, and 6 divisions

After this interesting experiment we can clearly see the influence of the divisions used to approximate a circle. Let's now experiment with the affine transformation used to transform the geometric primitives before they're drawn to the canvas.

Playing with the Affine Transformation

The affine transformation applied to the drawing in our simulation is an identity transformation: it keeps points exactly where they are. But we could use this transformation to do something different, such as invert the y-axis so that it points upward, for example. Go back to *hello_motion_refactor.py* and locate the line where the transformation is defined:

```
transform = AffineTransform(sx=1, sy=1, tx=0, ty=0, shx=0, shy=0)
```

Then, edit it so that it inverts the y-axis:

```
transform = AffineTransform(
    sx=1, sy=-1, tx=0, ty=0, shx=0, shy=0
)
```

Run the simulation again. What do you see? Just a little rim coming from the top of the canvas, right? What's happening is that we inverted the y-axis, but the origin of coordinates is still in the upper-left corner; thus, the circle we're trying to draw is outside the window, as depicted by Figure 11-7.

Figure 11-7: Simulation with
the y-axis inverted

We can easily fix this problem by translating the origin of the coordinates all the way down to the lower-left corner of the canvas. Since the canvas height is 600 pixels, we can set the transformation to be as follows:

```
transform = AffineTransform(
    sx=1, sy=-1, tx=0, ty=600, shx=0, shy=0
)
```

It may surprise you that the value for the vertical translation is 600 and not −600, but remember that in the original system of coordinates, the y direction points downward, and this affine transformation refers to that system.

If you prefer, it may be easier to understand the process of obtaining that transformation by concatenating two simpler ones, the first moving the origin downward 600 pixels and the second flipping the y-axis,

```
>>> t1 = AffineTransform(sx=1, sy=1, tx=0, ty=-600, shx=0, shy=0)
>>> t2 = AffineTransform(sx=1, sy=-1, tx=0, ty=0, shx=0, shy=0)
>>> t1.then(t2).__dict__
{'sx': 1, 'sy': -1, 'tx': 0, 'ty': 600, 'shx': 0, 'shy': 0}
```

which yields the same transformation, as you can see.

Now, let's add some shear in the horizontal direction to see how the circle gets deformed. Try the following values for the transformation,

```
transform = AffineTransform(
    sx=1, sy=-1, tx=150, ty=600, shx=-0.5, shy=0
)
```

and run the simulation again. You should see a shape similar to that in Figure 11-8.

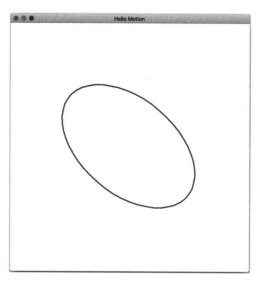

Figure 11-8: A circle drawn using a horizontal shear

Now it's your turn to play with the values and see whether you can build a better intuition for how the animations, drawings, and transformations are working. You've created something beautiful from scratch, so take your time to experiment with it. Try to change the circle primitive using a triangle or a rectangle. You can update the geometric primitive by moving it instead of changing its size. Play around with the affine transformation values and try to reason about how the drawing should look before you actually run the simulation. Use this exercise to reinforce your affine transformation intuition.

Cleaning Up the Module

Let's do two small refactors to the module to clean it up a bit. First, create a new folder in the *simulation* package and name it *examples*. We'll use it to house all the files that are not part of the simulation and drawing logic, but rather examples we wrote in this chapter. So, basically, move all the files except for *draw.py* and *loop.py* there. Your folder structure in *simulation* should look like this:

```
simulation
  |- examples
  |     |- hello_canvas.py
  |     |- hello_motion.py
  |     |- ...
  |
  |- __init__.py
  |- draw.py
  |- loop.py
```

The second thing we want to do is add both the CanvasDrawing class and the main_loop function to the default exports of the *simulation* package. Open file *__init__.py* in *simulation* and add the following imports:

```
from .draw import CanvasDrawing
from .loop import main_loop
```

That's it! From now on we'll be able to import both using a shorter syntax.

Summary

In this chapter, we learned about the time loop. The time loop keeps executing while a condition is met, and its main job is to keep the frame rate steady. In this loop two things take place: the updating of the system under simulation and the redrawing of the screen. Those operations are timed so that when they're done, we know how much more time remains to complete a cycle.

Because the time loop will appear in all of our simulations, we decided to implement it as a function. This function gets passed other functions:

one that updates the system, another that draws it to the screen, and a last one that decides whether the simulation is over or not.

In the next chapter, we'll use this time loop function to animate affine transformations.

12

ANIMATING AFFINE TRANSFORMATIONS

You just learned the basics of animation and GUI design. In this chapter, we'll combine the two and build an application that animates affine transformations. This will help build your visual intuition for this potentially confusing topic and strengthen your programming skills.

The application will first read a text file defining the affine transformation and the geometries to transform. Then, it'll compute a sequence of affine transformations, interpolating from the identity to the given transformation. Each of the transformations in this sequence will be used to draw a frame of the animation.

As with the circle building application we built in Chapter 9, we'll use regular expressions to read the primitives from the text file. We'll be using some more advanced ones here, which we'll analyze in detail. There will be a lot of code in this chapter. We're building a larger application, and it's a great opportunity to learn about how to distribute responsibilities in your code.

As always, we'll try to keep the architecture and design as clean as possible, explaining the reasoning behind each decision we encounter. Let's get started!

Application Architecture and Visibility Diagrams

To discuss this application's architecture, we'll introduce a new kind of diagram: a *visibility diagram*. Visibility diagrams display the components of an application using arrows to indicate what each part of the program knows—in other words, who can see whom. Take a look at the diagram from Figure 12-1.

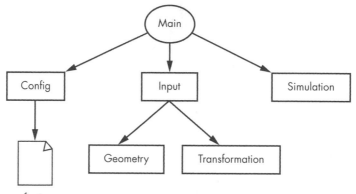

Figure 12-1: Our application architecture

At the top of the diagram is *Main*, the executing script. The circle around it signifies that it's the entry point to the application. There are three arrows starting from *Main*, which means *Main* knows about three other modules: *Config*, *Input*, and *Simulation*. Modules are represented with rectangles.

Note the arrows go one way. *Main* knows these modules exist, and depends on them, but these modules know nothing about the existence of *Main*. This is critical: we want to minimize what the components of our application know about each other. This ensures the modules are as *decoupled* as possible, meaning that they can live on their own.

The benefits of a decoupled design are mainly simplicity, which allows us to easily grow and maintain our software, and reusability. The fewer dependencies a module has, the easier it is to use it somewhere else.

Going back to the diagram in Figure 12-1, we said that *Main* uses three modules: *Config*, *Input*, and *Simulation*. The *Config* module will be in charge of loading the configuration for the application stored in *config.json*—indicated by the arrow.

The *Input* module will read the input file given by the user and define both an affine transformation and geometric primitives. Thus, this module will use two more modules: *Geometry*, to parse the primitives, and *Transformation*, to parse the affine transformation. Again, the fact that the arrows go from *Input* toward the other two modules means these other two modules have no clue about *Input*: they could be used perfectly by another module.

Lastly, we have the *Simulation* module, which will be in charge of performing the actual simulation.

NOTE   *I can't stress the importance of decoupled architectures enough. Applications should be made of small submodules that expose a straightforward, concise interface and hide their inner working from the rest of the world. These modules are simpler to maintain when they have as few dependencies of their own as possible. Applications that don't respect this simple principle end up doomed more often than not, and trust me when I say that you'll feel hopeless when you fix a small bug in a module and it breaks some apparently unrelated piece of another module.*

Let's move on and set up the project.

Setting Up

In the *apps* folder, create a new Python package named *aff_transf_motion*. In it, add all the files shown in the following tree. If you created the new package by right-clicking *apps* and choosing **New ▸ Python Package**, *__init__.py* will already be in the directory; the IDE created it for us. If you created the package in another way, don't forget to add this file.

```
apps
 |- aff_transf_motion
        |- __init__.py
        |- config.json
        |- config.py
        |- input.py
        |- main.py
        |- parse_geom.py
        |- parse_transform.py
        |- simulation.py
        |- test.txt
```

All your files are empty for now, but we'll be filling them with code soon.

Before we do that, though, we want to have a run configuration or bash script to run the project as we develop, just like we did in Chapter 9. We first need to define the script it will execute in *main.py*. For now, we'll simply print a message to the shell to make sure things are working properly. Open the file and enter the code in Listing 12-1.

```
if __name__ == '__main__':
    print('Ready!')
```

Listing 12-1: Main file

Let's now explore our two options for executing the project: a run configuration and a bash script. You don't need to set up both; you can choose the one that works best for you and skip the other.

Creating a Run Configuration

In the menu choose **Run ▶ Edit Configurations**. Click the **+** icon at the top left and choose **Python** to create the run configuration. Name it *aff-transf-motion*. Similar to what we did in Chapter 9, choose *main.py* as the script path and *aff_transform_motion* as the working directory. Lastly, check the **Redirect input from** option, and choose *test.txt*. Your configuration should look similar to Figure 12-2.

| Name: | aff-transf-motion | | Allow parallel run | Store as project file |

Configuration   Logs

| Script path: | /Mechanics/apps/aff_transf_motion/main.py |

Parameters: + ↗

⌄ Environment

Environment variables: PYTHONUNBUFFERED=1 $

Python interpreter: 🌐 Project Default (Python 3.8) /usr/local/opt/python@3.8/bin/python3.8   ▾

Interpreter options: ↗

| Working directory: | /Mechanics/apps/aff_transf_motion |

☑ Add content roots to PYTHONPATH
☑ Add source roots to PYTHONPATH

⌄ Execution

　　Emulate terminal in output console

　　Run with Python Console

| ☑ Redirect input from: | /Mechanics/apps/aff_transf_motion/test.txt |

⌄ Before launch

There are no tasks to run before launch

+ − ⌕ ⌃ ⌄

Show this page ☑ Activate tool window

CANCEL   APPLY   OK

Figure 12-2: The run configuration

To make sure the run configuration is properly set up, choose it from the run configuration navigation bar and click the green play button. The shell should display the message Ready!. If you had any trouble setting this up, refer to Chapter 9 where we covered this process in detail.

Creating a Bash Script

To run the app from the command line, we'll use the technique we explored in Chapter 9: creating a bash script wrapper that uses our project root as the workspace for Python to resolve our dependencies. Create a new file in the root of the project (under *Mechanics*): *aff_motion.sh*. In the file, enter the code in Listing 12-2.

```
#!/usr/bin/env bash
PYTHONPATH=$PWD python3 apps/aff_transf_motion/main.py
```

Listing 12-2: Bash script to execute the project

Using this bash script, we can now execute the application from the command line like so:

```
$ bash ./aff_motion.sh < apps/aff_transf_motion/test.txt
```

We can make this bash script executable:

```
$ chmod +x aff_motion.sh
```

then run it like so:

```
$ ./aff_motion.sh < apps/aff_transf_motion/test.txt
```

Reading the Configuration File

Because we want to separate configuration values from the code, we'll keep them in a JSON file. This allows us to change the behavior of our application without needing to touch the code. Open *config.json* and enter the content in Listing 12-3.

```
{
  "frames": 200,
  "axes": {
    "length": 100,
    "arrow-length": 20,
    "arrow-height": 15,
    "stroke-width": 2,
    "x-color": "#D53636",
    "y-color": "#33FF86"
  },
  "geometry": {
    "stroke-color": "#3F4783",
    "stroke-width": 3
  }
}
```

Listing 12-3: Configuration JSON file

This configuration first defines the number of frames to use for the simulation. Then comes the dimensions and the color of the coordinate axes, which we'll draw to help us visualize how the space is transformed. Lastly, we have configuration values for the geometry that will be transformed. Here we're defining stroke color and width.

We now need a way to read this configuration JSON file and transform its contents into a Python dictionary. Let's use the same approach we used in Chapter 9. In *config.py*, enter the code in Listing 12-4.

```
import json

import pkg_resources as res


def read_config():
    config = res.resource_string(__name__, 'config.json')
    return json.loads(config)
```

Listing 12-4: Reading the configuration file

That's it for the configuration; let's turn our attention to reading and parsing input.

Reading Input

We're expecting the user to pass our program a file containing the definition of an affine transformation and a list of the geometric primitives to transform. Let's define how these files should be formatted. We can start by reading the affine transformation values since we know beforehand how many values we're expecting. Because there can be any number of geometric primitives, we'll put those at the end.

Formatting the Input

Here's a nice way of formatting the affine transformation values:

```
sx <value>
sy <value>
shx <value>
shy <value>
tx <value>
ty <value>
```

Here each value is defined in its own line and has a tag indicating which term it is. We could use a more condensed format and simply have all those values in a single line, like so:

```
transformation: <value> <value> <value> <value> <value> <value>
```

But this has the downside of being less clear for the user. What's the order of the values? Was the third number the shear in the x direction or the translation in the y direction? To answer this question, you'd need to open the source code and find out how those values are parsed. I tend to favor clarity over compactness in cases where the size of the input isn't too big, so we'll stick to the first approach.

So what about the geometric primitives? For each kind of geometric primitive, we'll use a different four-letter code: circ for circle, for example. This code will be followed by a bunch of numbers that define the primitive's properties.

For a circle, the definition will look like

```
circ <cx> <cy> <r>
```

where <cx> and <cy> are the coordinates of the center point and <r> is the value for the radius.

A rectangle will look like

```
rect <ox> <oy> <w> <h>
```

with <ox> and <oy> defining the coordinates of its origin, <w> its width, and <h> its height.

A polygon will look like

```
poly [<x1> <y1> <x2> <y2> <x3> <y3> ...]
```

where [<x> <y>] means a sequence of x and y values representing the coordinates of a vertex. Bear in mind that the minimum number of vertices to build a polygon is three; therefore, we need at least six values here.

Lastly, a segment is defined like

```
segm <sx> <sy> <ex> <ey>
```

where <sx> and <sy> are the coordinates of the start point, and <ex> and <ey> are the coordinates of the end point.

Adding Example Input

Let's fill our *test.txt* file with an example input. Remember that we redirected the standard input in our program to read from *test.txt*, so we'll be using it to test our code. Open the file and enter the definition in Listing 12-5.

```
sx 1.2
sy 1.4
shx 2.0
shy 3.0
tx 50.0
ty 25.0

circ 150 40 20
rect 70 60 40 100
rect 100 90 40 100
poly 30 10 80 10 30 90
segm 10 20 200 240
```

Listing 12-5: Input test file

This file first defines an affine transformation as follows:

$$[T] = \begin{bmatrix} 1.2 & 2.0 & 50.0 \\ 3.0 & 1.4 & 25.0 \\ 0 & 0 & 1 \end{bmatrix}$$

It also defines a circle, two rectangles, a polygon, and a segment. Figure 12-3 depicts the approximate layout of these geometric primitives before we apply the affine transformation.

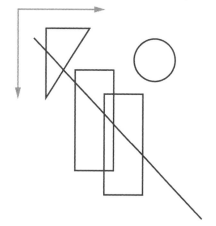

Figure 12-3: The geometric primitives in our test file

Now that *test.txt* has these definitions, let's write the outline of the code we need to read and parse the input. Open *input.py* and enter the code in Listing 12-6.

```
def read_input():
    transform = __read_transform()
    primitives = __read_primitives()
    return transform, primitives


def __read_transform():
    return None


def __read_primitives():
    return None
```

Listing 12-6: Parsing the input file starting point

We first define a function, read_input, which will read both the affine transformation and the geometric primitives and return a tuple containing both. To do its work, it delegates each of the two tasks to private functions: __read_transform and __read_primitives. These functions return None for now. We'll implement them in the next two sections.

Parsing the Affine Transformation

The affine transformation in the input file will always span six lines, one line per term. We can simplify the parsing by requiring that the terms always appear in the same, predefined order. We'll double-check that each of the terms has the appropriate name tag, just to make sure the user wrote the terms in the right order, but we won't include that bit in our regular expression, which should make things a bit simpler.

The first thing we need is a regular expression that can match the floating-point numbers in the components of the transformation. It's important to design this regular expression so that it also matches integer numbers; the decimal part should be optional. We also want to accept negative numbers. A regular expression combining all these characteristics could look like this:

```
/-?\d+(\.\d+)?/
```

The regular expression has three parts. The first, -?, matches zero or one instances of the minus symbol. The second, \d+, matches one or more digits before the decimal separator: the integer part. Lastly comes (\.\d+)?, which matches zero or one sequence made of a dot and one or more digits. Note that we've used ? to handle our optional components.

Using the regular expression shown earlier, we can prepare another regular expression that matches all of the term values:

```
/(?P<val>-?\d+(\.\d+)?)/
```

This defines a group named val that will capture the term's value using the previous expression.

Let's open *parse_transform.py* (empty at the moment) and implement the logic for reading and parsing the affine transformation terms. Enter the code in Listing 12-7.

```
import re

__TRANSF_VAL_RE = r'(?P<val>-?\d+(\.\d+)?)'


def parse_transform_term(term, line):
    __ensure_term_name(term, line)
    return __parse_transform_term(line)


def __ensure_term_name(name, line):
    if name not in line:
        raise ValueError(f'Expected {name} term')


def __parse_transform_term(line):
    matches = re.search(__TRANSF_VAL_RE, line)
    if not matches:
```

```
            raise ValueError('Couldn\'t read transform term')

        return float(matches.group('val'))
```

Listing 12-7: Parsing the affine transformation terms

We first define the regular expression to parse the affine transformation term values: __TRANSF_VAL_RE. Then comes the main function: parse_transform _term, which takes two parameters: the name of the term to validate and the line to parse. Each of these operations is handled by two private functions.

The function __ensure_term_name checks whether the given name is present in line. If it's not, the function raises a ValueError with a helpful message to let the user know which term couldn't be properly interpreted. Then, __parse_transform_term applies the regular expression __TRANSF_VAL_RE to match the term's value. If it succeeds, the matched group val is converted to a float value and returned. An error is raised in the case that the string doesn't match the regular expression.

Let's now use this parse function in the *Input* module (as depicted by Figure 12-1). Open your *input.py* file and add the following imports at the top:

```
from apps.aff_transf_motion.parse_transform import parse_transform_term
from geom2d import AffineTransform
```

Then, refactor the __read_transform function as in Listing 12-8.

```
--snip--

def __read_transform():
    return AffineTransform(
        sx=parse_transform_term('sx', input()),
        sy=parse_transform_term('sy', input()),
        shx=parse_transform_term('shx', input()),
        shy=parse_transform_term('shy', input()),
        tx=parse_transform_term('tx', input()),
        ty=parse_transform_term('ty', input())
    )
```

Listing 12-8: Parsing the affine transformation

We can easily test that our code works by editing the contents of our *main.py* file to match Listing 12-9.

```
from apps.aff_transf_motion.input import read_input

if __name__ == '__main__':
    (transform, primitives) = read_input()
    print(transform)
```

Listing 12-9: Main file: reading transformation test

If you run the application using the run configuration or the bash script we created before, the output in your shell should be the following:

```
Input is being redirected from .../test.txt
(sx: 1.2, sy: 1.4, shx: 2.0, shy: 3.0, tx: 50.0, ty: 25.0)

Process finished with exit code 0
```

You want to make sure all of the values in the affine transformation we defined in *test.txt* are properly parsed. If you recall, those were as follows:

```
sx 1.2
sy 1.4
shx 2.0
shy 3.0
tx 50.0
ty 25.0
```

Double-check that the output you got from the program matches these values. If you got it all right, congratulations! If you got any unexpected value, debug your program until you find the culprit and fix the bug.

Parsing the Geometric Primitives

The geometric primitives can come in any order, and there can be any number of them, so we'll need a different parsing strategy. We need to tackle two separate problems: we need to read an unknown number of lines from the input and then figure out the the type of geometric primitive for each line. Let's solve these problems separately, starting with the first one.

Reading an Unknown Number of Lines

To read an unknown number of lines, we can keep reading from the standard input until an EOFError (end of file error) is raised, signaling that we've exhausted all the available lines. Open *input.py* and refactor __read_primitives by entering the code in Listing 12-10.

```
--snip--

def __read_primitives():
    has_more_lines = True

    while has_more_lines:
        try:
            line = input()
            print('got line -->', line)

        except EOFError:
            has_more_lines = False
```

Listing 12-10: Reading lines from standard input

We declare a variable has_more_lines and assign it a value of True. Then, in a while loop that keeps looping provided the variable remains True, we try to read another line from the standard input. If the operation succeeds, we print the line to the output; otherwise, we catch the EOFError and set has_more _lines to False.

Run the program again to make sure all the lines from the input file are processed by __read_primitives and appear in the shell output. The output of your program should include the following lines:

```
got line -->
got line --> circ 150 40 20
got line --> rect 70 60 40 100
got line --> rect 100 90 40 100
got line --> poly 30 10 80 10 30 90
got line --> segm 10 20 200 240
```

The first problem is solved: our *input.py* module knows how to read all the lines from the input file. Notice that empty lines are also processed by the __read_primitives function; we'll handle that in the next section. Now that we know how to read in the lines, let's turn our focus to our second problem: identifying the primitive type for each of the read-in lines.

Parsing the Right Primitive

Let's start with one thing we know for sure: we need to have regular expressions for each of the geometric primitives our program understands. Earlier in the chapter, we defined the input format we expect for each of the primitives. We just need to turn that into a regular expression. We'll accept either an integer or floating-point number for the properties of each of the primitives. We saw how to do this before. Let's call the regex that captures a property value NUM_RE and use the following definition:

```
/\d+(\.\d+)?/
```

Using this regex, we could have the regular expression for a circle as follows:

```
/circ (?P<cx>NUM_RE) (?P<cy>NUM_RE) (?P<r>NUM_RE)/
```

Here we've included three capture groups: cx, cy, and r. These groups coincide with the properties we defined for the input representation of the previous circle. In a similar fashion, a rectangle can be matched by the regular expression:

```
/rect (?P<ox>NUM_RE) (?P<oy>NUM_RE) (?P<w>NUM_RE) (?P<h>NUM_RE)/
```

A regular expression to match segments can be as follows:

```
/segm (?P<sx>NUM_RE) (?P<sy>NUM_RE) (?P<ex>NUM_RE) (?P<ey>NUM_RE)/
```

Lastly, for the polygon, we use a slightly different approach that simplifies its parsing process a bit, as we'll see now. The following is the regular expression we'll use:

```
/poly (?P<coords>[\d\s\.]+)/
```

This regex matches strings starting with the word *poly* followed by a space and a sequence of digits, spaces, or dots (used as decimal separator). With it, we'll match polygon definitions, as follows,

```
poly 30 10 80.5 10 30 90.5
```

which we'll parse as a polygon defined by the vertices $(30, 10)$, $(80.5, 10)$, and $(30, 90.5)$.

Let's include these definitions in our *parse_geom.py* file, along with some imports that we'll need to create the geometric primitives. Enter the code in Listing 12-11.

```
import re

from geom2d import Circle, Point, Rect, Size, Segment
from geom2d import make_polygon_from_coords

__NUM_RE = r'\d+(\.\d+)?'

__CIRC_RE = rf'circ (?P<cx>{__NUM_RE}) (?P<cy>{__NUM_RE}) ' \
    rf'(?P<r>{__NUM_RE})'

__RECT_RE = rf'rect (?P<ox>{__NUM_RE}) (?P<oy>{__NUM_RE}) ' \
    rf'(?P<w>{__NUM_RE}) (?P<h>{__NUM_RE})'

__POLY_RE = rf'poly (?P<coords>[\d\s\.]+)'

__SEGM_RE = rf'segm (?P<sx>{__NUM_RE}) (?P<sy>{__NUM_RE}) ' \
    rf'(?P<ex>{__NUM_RE}) (?P<ey>{__NUM_RE})'
```

Listing 12-11: Geometric primitives, regex definitions

We have all the regular expressions we need, so our next goal is for the appropriate primitive for each line we read. To solve this problem, we'll follow the "if can <verb> then <verb>" pattern, in our case "if can parse then parse." Let's see how this works. We have a sequence of parser functions, each of which expects a string formatted in a specific way. These functions would fail if they tried to parse a geometric primitive out of a string with a wrong format. So before putting them to work, we want to make sure they'll understand the string we pass them in. We'll accompany each of the parse functions with a can_parse function. This second function should determine whether all of the parts the parse function expects are in the string: the pattern's "can parse" part.

For each of our geometric primitives we need a pair of functions: one to determine whether the given line of text can be parsed to this primitive (the "can parse" part) and another to actually parse it (the "then parse" part). The code for this algorithm is as follows:

```
if can_parse_circle(line):
    parse_circle(line)

elif can_parse_rect(line):
    parse_rect(line)

elif can_parse_polygon(line):
    parse_polygon(line)

elif can_parse_segment(line):
    parse_segment(line)

else:
    handle_unknown_line(line)
```

We first check whether the given line can be parsed to a circle. If the test passes, we proceed to parse the circle; otherwise, we continue with the next comparison, repeating this pattern. It may happen that none of these comparisons passes, and we reach the last else statement; we handle this situation in the handle_unknown_line function. Think, for example, about those empty lines we read from the input file; those won't match against any known primitive. There are a couple of ways we could handle these problem lines. We could, for example, print them to the shell with a warning message, thus letting the user know there were lines the program didn't understand. To keep things simple, we'll just ignore unknown lines.

Let's now implement the "can parse" and "parse" functions for each of our primitives. In *parse_geom.py*, after the regular expressions we just defined, enter the code in Listing 12-12. This code handles the circle case.

```
--snip--

def can_parse_circle(line):
    return re.match(__CIRC_RE, line)


def parse_circle(line):
    match = re.match(__CIRC_RE, line)
    return Circle(
        center=Point(
            float(match.group('cx')),
            float(match.group('cy'))
        ),
        radius=float(match.group('r'))
```

```
    )
```

Listing 12-12: Parsing a circle

As you can see, the can_parse_circle function simply checks for a match between the passed-in line and the regular expression for a circle: _CIRC_RE. The parse_circle function goes one step further and, assuming the line matches the regular expression, extracts the cx and cy group values, the center of the circle. It does the same with the r group, the radius.

Don't forget that the values we extract from the regular expression capture groups are always strings. Since we're expecting floating-point numbers, we need to do the conversion using the float function.

Let's now implement the same functions for the case of a rectangle. After the code you just wrote, enter the code in Listing 12-13.

```
--snip--

def can_parse_rect(line):
    return re.match(__RECT_RE, line)


def parse_rect(line):
    match = re.match(__RECT_RE, line)
    return Rect(
        origin=Point(
            float(match.group('ox')),
            float(match.group('oy'))
        ),
        size=Size(
            float(match.group('w')),
            float(match.group('h'))
        )
    )
```

Listing 12-13: Parsing a rectangle

No surprises here. We applied the same procedure, this time extracting groups named ox, oy, w, and h, which define the origin point and the size of the rectangle. Let's do the same for the case of a polygon. Enter the code in Listing 12-14.

```
--snip--

def can_parse_polygon(line):
    return re.match(__POLY_RE, line)


def parse_polygon(line):
    match = re.match(__POLY_RE, line)
    coords = [float(n) for n in match.group('coords').split(' ')]
```

```
    return make_polygon_from_coords(coords)
```

Listing 12-14: Parsing a polygon

In this case, the mechanics are a bit different. Remember we had a slightly different regular expression for the case of a polygon. Since polygons are defined by an unknown number of vertices, the regex to match these numbers by pairs had to be more complicated. We also had to use a list comprehension to properly parse the coordinates.

First, the string captured by the group named coords is split using a space as the separator. Thus, the string of numbers

```
'10 20 30 40 50 60'
```

would be converted to an array of strings like so:

```
['10', '20', '30', '40', '50', '60']
```

Then each of the strings is converted into a floating-point number:

```
[10.0, 20.0, 30.0, 40.0, 50.0, 60.0]
```

With this array of numbers we can easily create an instance of our Polygon class using the factory function make_polygon_from_coords. Don't forget to add the import at the top of the file:

```
from geom2d import make_polygon_from_coords
```

The last pair of "can parse" and "parse" functions we need are for segments. Enter the code in Listing 12-15.

```
--snip--

def can_parse_segment(line):
    return re.match(__SEGM_RE, line)


def parse_segment(line):
    match = re.match(__SEGM_RE, line)
    return Segment(
        start=Point(
            float(match.group('sx')),
            float(match.group('sy'))
        ),
        end=Point(
            float(match.group('ex')),
            float(match.group('ey'))
        )
    )
```

Listing 12-15: Parsing a segment

Great! We now have the functions we need to apply our "if can parse then parse" strategy. Open *input.py* and import these functions:

```
from apps.aff_transf_motion.parse_geom import *
```

We use the asterisk import to bring all the defined functions in the *parse _geom* module without writing all of their names. Now let's refactor the __read _primitives function (Listing 12-16).

```
--snip--

def __read_primitives():
    prims = {'circs': [], 'rects': [], 'polys': [], 'segs': []}
    has_more_lines = True

    while has_more_lines:
        try:
            line = input()

            if can_parse_circle(line):
                prims['circs'].append(parse_circle(line))

            elif can_parse_rect(line):
                prims['rects'].append(parse_rect(line))

            elif can_parse_polygon(line):
                prims['polys'].append(parse_polygon(line))

            elif can_parse_segment(line):
                prims['segs'].append(parse_segment(line))

        except EOFError:
            has_more_lines = False

    return prims
```

Listing 12-16: Reading the primitives from the input

We start defining a dictionary named prims with an array for each type of geometric primitive. Each of the arrays in the dictionary is identified by a name: circs, rects, polys, and segs. Then comes the while loop, which iterates through all the read-in lines. Instead of printing them to the shell, we added our parsing functions, similar to what we did in pseudocode before. This time, whenever a primitive is parsed, the result is appended to the corresponding array of the prims dictionary. The function ends by returning prims.

Listing 12-17 contains the final result for *input.py*. Make sure yours looks similar.

```python
from apps.aff_transf_motion.parse_geom import *
from apps.aff_transf_motion.parse_transform import parse_transform_term
from geom2d import AffineTransform


def read_input():
    transform = __read_transform()
    primitives = __read_primitives()
    return transform, primitives


def __read_transform():
    return AffineTransform(
        sx=parse_transform_term('sx', input()),
        sy=parse_transform_term('sy', input()),
        shx=parse_transform_term('shx', input()),
        shy=parse_transform_term('shy', input()),
        tx=parse_transform_term('tx', input()),
        ty=parse_transform_term('ty', input())
    )


def __read_primitives():
    prims = {'circs': [], 'rects': [], 'polys': [], 'segs': []}
    has_more_lines = True

    while has_more_lines:
        try:
            line = input()

            if can_parse_circle(line):
                prims['circs'].append(parse_circle(line))

            elif can_parse_rect(line):
                prims['rects'].append(parse_rect(line))

            elif can_parse_polygon(line):
                prims['polys'].append(parse_polygon(line))

            elif can_parse_segment(line):
                prims['segs'].append(parse_segment(line))

        except EOFError:
            has_more_lines = False
```

```
    return prims
```

Listing 12-17: Complete input-reading code

Now that we can fully parse the input, let's move on and implement the simulation.

Running the Simulation

Once the configuration and input are completely read and parsed, they're both passed to a simulation function that we'll write shortly. This function will also define the user interface: a canvas to draw the shapes and a button to start the animation. Figure 12-4 shows how these components will be laid out.

The simulation won't start until the user clicks the play button. This way we prevent the simulation from starting too soon; otherwise, the user may miss the first part of it. Furthermore, thanks to the button, we'll be able to rerun the simulation without needing to relaunch the application.

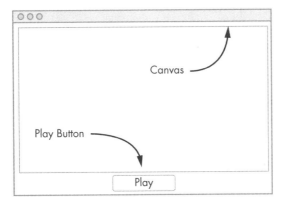

Figure 12-4: The simulation's user interface

Building the User Interface

Open the empty *simulation.py* and enter the code in Listing 12-18.

```python
from tkinter import Tk, Canvas, Button


def simulate(transform, primitives, config):
    # ---------- UI DEFINITION ---------- #
    tk = Tk()
    tk.title("Affine Transformations")

    canvas = Canvas(tk, width=800, height=800)
    canvas.grid(row=0, column=0)

    def start_simulation():
```

```
    tk.update()
    print('Starting Simulation...')

Button(tk, text='Play', command=start_simulation) \
    .grid(row=1, column=0)


# ---------- UPDATE, DRAW & CONTINUE ---------- #
def update_system(time_delta_s, time_s, frame):
    pass


def redraw():
    pass


def should_continue(frame, time_s):
    pass


# ---------- MAIN LOOP ---------- #
redraw()
tk.mainloop()
```

Listing 12-18: Simulation function

We've defined a function simulate, which takes in the target transform, the geometric primitives, and the configuration for the application. Recall that the configuration JSON file contains the number of frames to use for the simulation and the sizes and colors of everything we'll draw to the screen. Since the function will get a bit long, we've added three header comments to easily locate each of the sections: the user interface definition; the update, draw, and should_continue functions; and the main loop.

The first section of the function builds the user interface. We instantiate the Tk class and add a Canvas and a Button to it. Using the grid system, we place the canvas in the first row (row=0) and the button in the second one (row=1). We've also created a function, start_simulation, which is executed when the button is pressed. This function doesn't do much for now; all it does is tell Tkinter to process all pending events (tk.update()) and print a message to the shell. We'll add the simulation's updating logic here shortly.

Then we define the templates for the key simulation functions: update _system, redraw, and should_continue. Don't forget to declare the appropriate input parameters for each of them; otherwise, Python will complain once we hand them to our main_loop function. We'll fill in these functions shortly.

Lastly, we call redraw to render the initial state of the geometric primitives to the screen and start Tkinter's main loop. To test our progress, let's edit *main.py* so that it shows the user interface. Open that file and modify it so that it looks like Listing 12-19.

```
from apps.aff_transf_motion.config import read_config
from apps.aff_transf_motion.input import read_input
from apps.aff_transf_motion.simulation import import simulate
```

```
if __name__ == '__main__':
    (transform, primitives) = read_input()
    config = read_config()
    simulate(transform, primitives, config)
```

Listing 12-19: Execution entry point

Our *main.py* file is now ready. Let's work on the simulation code.

Implementing the Simulation Logic

Let's move on to the simulation logic. If you recall from Chapter 7, to draw the different frames of the animation, we need to generate a sequence of interpolated affine transformations going from the identity transformation to the target transformation that we parsed from the input. If you need a refresher on the topic, refer to "Interpolating Transformations" on page 192. Thanks to the affine-transformation interpolation function we implemented in Chapter 7, ease_in_out_interpolation, this piece of logic is a breeze. In *simulation.py* make the changes shown in Listing 12-20.

```
from tkinter import Tk, Canvas, Button

from geom2d import affine_transforms as tf


def simulate(transform, primitives, config):
    # ---------- UI DEFINITION ---------- #
    --snip--

    # ---------- UPDATE, DRAW & CONTINUE ---------- #
    frames = config['frames']
    transform_seq = __make_transform_sequence(transform, frames)

    --snip--


def __make_transform_sequence(end_transform, frames):
    start_transform = tf.AffineTransform(sx=1, sy=1, tx=20, ty=20)
    return tf.ease_in_out_interpolation(
        start_transform, end_transform, frames
    )
```

Listing 12-20: Computing the transformation sequence

The first thing that we need is the number of steps for the interpolation. This is just the number of frames, a value that we read from the configuration and stored in variable frames. To compute the interpolated sequence, we've defined a private function in the file: __make_transform_sequence. This function takes the target affine transformation and the number of frames and computes the sequence using the following transformation as the starting point:

$$[T] = \begin{bmatrix} 1 & 0 & 20 \\ 0 & 1 & 20 \\ 0 & 0 & 1 \end{bmatrix}$$

Notice the translation of 20 pixels in both the horizontal and vertical axes. This small offset separates the axes from the canvas's upper and left sides. The resulting sequence of transformations is stored in transform_seq.

Let's now dive into the key functions for the simulation: update_system, redraw, and should_continue. Edit *simulation.py* to look like the code in Listing 12-21.

```
from tkinter import Tk, Canvas, Button

from geom2d import affine_transforms as tf
from graphic.simulation import CanvasDrawing


def simulate(transform, primitives, config):
    # ---------- UI DEFINITION ---------- #
    --snip--

    # ---------- UPDATE, DRAW & CONTINUE ---------- #
    frames = config['frames']
    transform_seq = __make_transform_sequence(transform, frames)
❶ drawing = CanvasDrawing(canvas, transform_seq[0])

    def update_system(time_delta_s, time_s, frame):
❷     drawing.transform = transform_seq[frame - 1]
        tk.update()

❸ def redraw():
        drawing.clear_drawing()

        drawing.outline_width = config['geometry']['stroke-width']
        drawing.outline_color = config['geometry']['stroke-color']

        for circle in primitives['circs']:
            drawing.draw_circle(circle)

        for rect in primitives['rects']:
            drawing.draw_rectangle(rect)

        for polygon in primitives['polys']:
            drawing.draw_polygon(polygon)

        for segment in primitives['segs']:
```

```
        drawing.draw_segment(segment)

def should_continue(frame, time_s):
❹ return frame <= frames


# ---------- MAIN LOOP ---------- #
redraw()
tk.mainloop()
```

--snip--

Listing 12-21: Implementing drawing and updating

After the sequence of transformations we recently computed, we instantiate our CanvasDrawing class, passing in the Tkinter canvas and the first affine transformations ❶. Note that we imported the class at the top of the file and that the first transformation on the sequence is the initial transformation for the geometric primitives.

Then, we implement the update_system function. This function updates the drawing's transformation according to the current frame number ❷ and invokes tk's update method. To compute the index used to obtain the corresponding transformation, we subtract 1 from the frame number. Recall that the frames are counted from 1, while a Python list's first index is 0. It's important to realize that, in this particular simulation, it's not the system (made up of the geometric primitives) that gets updated every frame but rather the affine transformation, a property of the CanvasDrawing class, that gets a new value.

Next is the redraw function ❸. It first clears the canvas and sets the size and color for the outlines of the shapes we're drawing. These two values come from the configuration file. Then, it iterates through all the primitives in the dictionary, calling the corresponding draw command from the CanvasDrawing class. Thanks to our previous work on that class, drawing to the canvas is that simple.

Last is the implementation of should_continue that simply compares the current frame number to the total number of frames for the animation ❹.

Drawing the Axes

We're almost there! Let's add some code to draw the x- and y-axes as well as a call to the simulation's main loop (not to be confused with Tkinter's mainloop function). The axes will provide a good visual reference for how the space is transformed. Include the changes in Listing 12-22.

```
from tkinter import Tk, Canvas, Button

from geom2d import affine_transforms as tf, Segment, Point
from graphic.simulation import CanvasDrawing, main_loop
```

```
def simulate(transform, primitives, config):
    # ---------- UI DEFINITION ---------- #
    --snip--

    def start_simulation():
        tk.update()
    ❶  main_loop(update_system, redraw, should_continue)

    Button(tk, text='Play', command=start_simulation) \
        .grid(row=1, column=0)

    # ---------- UPDATE, DRAW & CONTINUE ---------- #
    frames = config['frames']
    transform_seq = __make_transform_sequence(transform, frames)
    axis_length = config['axes']['length']
❷  x_axis = Segment(Point(0, 0), Point(axis_length, 0))
❸  y_axis = Segment(Point(0, 0), Point(0, axis_length))
    drawing = CanvasDrawing(canvas, transform_seq[0])

    def update_system(time_delta_s, time_s, frame):
        drawing.transform = transform_seq[frame - 1]
        tk.update()

    def redraw():
        drawing.clear_drawing()

        drawing.outline_width = config['axes']['stroke-width']
        drawing.outline_color = config['axes']['x-color']
    ❹  drawing.draw_arrow(
            x_axis,
            config['axes']['arrow-length'],
            config['axes']['arrow-height']
        )

        drawing.outline_color = config['axes']['y-color']
    ❺  drawing.draw_arrow(
            y_axis,
            config['axes']['arrow-length'],
            config['axes']['arrow-height']
        )

        --snip--

    def should_continue(frame, time_s):
        return frame <= frames
```

```
# ---------- MAIN LOOP ---------- #
redraw()
tk.mainloop()
```

--snip--

Listing 12-22: Drawing the axes and main loop

First comes the most important addition: the inclusion of a call to the
main_loop function ❶. We pass in the functions defined next to take care of
the updating, redrawing, and continuation of the simulation. Make sure you
import the main_loop function at the top of the file.

Next come the definitions of x_axis ❷ and y_axis ❸, both defined as
segments. Each length is a parameter we read from the configuration file
and store in axis_length. To draw the axes, we need to take into account that
they have a different stroke width and color than the other geometry. We've
added the code for these properties in the redraw function, just below the call
to clear_drawing.

After setting the corresponding outline width and color, we use our
CanvasDrawing class's draw_arrow method, passing it the segment that defines
the x_axis geometry and the size of the arrow ❹. The size of the arrow, once
again, comes from the configuration. We have to add the same code to draw
y_axis ❺, but this time only the stroke color needs to be updated: the axes
are drawn using the same stroke width.

Well, we've been incrementally writing a lot of code. Just for reference,
Listing 12-23 shows the final *simulation.py* file. Take a look and make sure
you got it all.

```
from tkinter import Tk, Canvas, Button

from geom2d import affine_transforms as tf, Segment, Point
from graphic.simulation import CanvasDrawing, main_loop


def simulate(transform, primitives, config):
    # ---------- UI DEFINITION ---------- #
    tk = Tk()
    tk.title("Affine Transformations")

    canvas = Canvas(tk, width=800, height=800)
    canvas.grid(row=0, column=0)

    def start_simulation():
        tk.update()
        main_loop(update_system, redraw, should_continue)

    Button(tk, text='Play', command=start_simulation) \
        .grid(row=1, column=0)
```

```
# ---------- UPDATE, DRAW & CONTINUE ---------- #
frames = config['frames']
transform_seq = __make_transform_sequence(transform, frames)
axis_length = config['axes']['length']
x_axis = Segment(Point(0, 0), Point(axis_length, 0))
y_axis = Segment(Point(0, 0), Point(0, axis_length))
drawing = CanvasDrawing(canvas, transform_seq[0])

def update_system(time_delta_s, time_s, frame):
    drawing.transform = transform_seq[frame - 1]
    tk.update()

def redraw():
    drawing.clear_drawing()

    drawing.outline_width = config['axes']['stroke-width']
    drawing.outline_color = config['axes']['x-color']
    drawing.draw_arrow(
        x_axis,
        config['axes']['arrow-length'],
        config['axes']['arrow-height']
    )

    drawing.outline_color = config['axes']['y-color']
    drawing.draw_arrow(
        y_axis,
        config['axes']['arrow-length'],
        config['axes']['arrow-height']
    )

    drawing.outline_width = config['geometry']['stroke-width']
    drawing.outline_color = config['geometry']['stroke-color']

    for circle in primitives['circs']:
        drawing.draw_circle(circle)

    for rect in primitives['rects']:
        drawing.draw_rectangle(rect)

    for polygon in primitives['polys']:
        drawing.draw_polygon(polygon)

    for segment in primitives['segs']:
        drawing.draw_segment(segment)

def should_continue(frame, time_s):
```

```
        return frame <= frames

    # ---------- MAIN LOOP ---------- #
    redraw()
    tk.mainloop()


def __make_transform_sequence(end_transform, frames):
    start_transform = tf.AffineTransform(sx=1, sy=1, tx=20, ty=20)
    return tf.ease_in_out_interpolation(
        start_transform, end_transform, frames
    )
```

Listing 12-23: Complete simulation code

At last! We're now ready to see the result, so execute the application using the run configuration or the bash script. A window with the geometric primitives as they were defined in the input file should appear (see the left image in Figure 12-5). Notice also the x- and y-axes, which we drew as arrows; can you spot the 20 pixels of separation we gave the origin?

Now click **Play** and watch the result. The simulation should start slow, then build some speed, and finally decelerate toward its end. We achieved this effect using ease-in-out interpolation, which makes the animation look smooth and realistic.

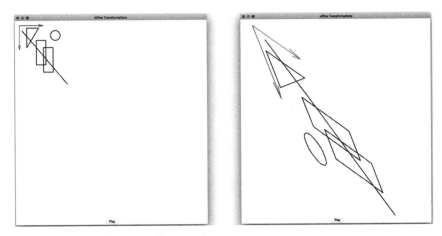

Figure 12-5: Simulating an affine transformation

Now is a good time to go back to "Interpolating Transformations" on page 192 and give it a second read. After seeing the ease-in-out effect in action, you can build a solid visual intuition for Equation 7.11 (page 194), which defines the pace for the animation you just witnessed.

Take some time to play with your application. Change some parameters to see the effect on the resulting simulation. For example, try to change the offset of the initial affine transformation (the translation components tx and ty). Play with the stroke widths and colors in the configuration file, and edit the number of frames. Another interesting exercise is editing the affine transformation and the geometric primitives defined in the input file *test.txt*.

Summary

In this chapter, we developed our second application, one that animates the effect of affine transformations. Like before, we used regular expressions to parse the input and used our geometry library for the heavy lifting. This time the output was an animation, which, thanks to the work we did in the previous chapters, was straightforward to implement.

This chapter concludes Part III of the book. In this part, we learned to create SVG vector graphics and animated simulations from our geometric primitives, key skills for building good engineering software. We used that knowledge to build two simple applications: one that determines a circle passing through three given points and one that animates geometric primitives under an affine transformation. Those were simple applications, but they illustrate how powerful geometric and visual primitives really are.

In the next part of the book, we'll look at how to solve systems of equations, another key piece for any engineering application. That is the last tool our *Mechanics* package needs. After exploring that topic, the rest of the book will be focused on solving mechanics problems using only the powerful primitives we coded ourselves.

PART IV

SYSTEMS OF EQUATIONS

13

MATRICES AND VECTORS

This part of the book will deal with solving systems of equations. We can conveniently represent a set of equations using its *matrix form*, where we store the unknown coefficients in a matrix and the free terms in a vector.

We've been working with matrices and vectors with our affine transformations, but for the sake of completeness, let's define them here. A *matrix* is a two-dimensional array of numbers arranged in rows and columns. Matrices are subject to some mathematical operations, including addition, subtraction, multiplication, and a few more. A *vector*, in this context, is a matrix with only one row or column (typically one column).

Consider the following system of equations:

$$
\begin{aligned}
7x &- 3y + 4z = 1 \\
2x &+ 5y - z = -3
\end{aligned}
$$

We can conveniently write this in matrix form as follows:

$$
\begin{bmatrix} 7 & -3 & 4 \\ 2 & 5 & -1 \end{bmatrix}
\begin{bmatrix} x \\ y \\ z \end{bmatrix}
=
\begin{bmatrix} 1 \\ -3 \end{bmatrix}
$$

Note how the coefficients of the equation are represented in the 2 (rows) by 3 (columns) matrix. According to the matrix multiplication rules, these coefficients multiplied by the unknowns x, y, and z yield our two equations, each of which needs to equal its corresponding right-side term stored in the $\langle 1, -3 \rangle$ vector.

It may not be obvious now, but matrices, and by extension vectors, will greatly simplify working with systems of equations. To use them, however, we'll need to implement new classes for both matrices and vectors.

The new Vector class will represent a uni-dimensional array of numbers (a sequence) of any length. This type of vector should not be confused with the geometric vector we implemented in Chapter 4, which was made up of two coordinates (u and v). An instance of our new Vector class with a size of 2 could look similar to the geometric vector, but they are distinct: the numbers don't necessarily represent coordinates that define a direction. We'll have to deal with having two classes named the same: Vector. As you'll see, since they're defined in different modules, it shouldn't be any problem to disambiguate them.

There are quite a few operations we could implement for these two new classes, but we'll be pragmatic and implement only those we need in the next chapter for solving systems of equations. For instance, we won't need to implement the addition, subtraction, or multiplication operations, even though these are common.

Let's begin by implementing two simple functions to help us fill newly instantiated vectors and matrices with zeros. We'll use these functions when we instantiate a vector or matrix.

List Utils

Internally, an instance of this new Vector class will use a list of numbers to store its data. When an instance of the class is instantiated, we want to fill its internal list with zeros. This way, values that haven't been explicitly set to some other value will be zero by default. Similarly, the Matrix class will store its data in a list of lists. We also want every position in the matrix initialized to zero.

Create a new Python file inside the *utils* package, name it *lists.py*, and enter the code in Listing 13-1.

```
def list_of_zeros(length: int):
    return [0] * length


def list_of_list_of_zeros(rows: int, cols: int):
    return [list_of_zeros(cols) for _ in range(rows)]
```

Listing 13-1: Lists of zeros

We've defined two functions. The first one, list_of_zeros, takes in a length argument and creates a list of that size filled with zeros. The second, list_of_list_of_zeros, creates as many lists of zeros of size cols as the parameter rows instructs.

The funny syntax for [0] * length can be read as follows: "Create a list made up of zeros with the given length." Give it a try in the Python console:

```
>>> [0] * 5
[0, 0, 0, 0, 0]
```

This is a neat way of initializing a list that contains the same repeating value.

The list_of_list_of_zeros function uses a list comprehension to create a list of size rows where each item is another list of size cols. The index in each iteration isn't used, so an underscore is used:

```
from _ in range(rows)
```

Let's try this function in the shell:

```
>>> from utils.lists import list_of_list_of_zeros
>>> list_of_list_of_zeros(2, 3)
[[0, 0, 0], [0, 0, 0]]
```

Let's now set up the new package where we'll add the new Matrix and Vector classes.

Setup

Let's now create a new package in our project where we'll add the Vector and Matrix implementations. This package will also contain the equation-solving functions that we'll implement in the next chapters and generally in any math or equation resolution algorithm we write. Create the new package at the project's top level and name it *eqs*. Add another package inside it, and name it *tests*. Your project's structure should now look something like this:

```
Mechanics
  |- apps
  |    |- circle_from_points
  |- eqs
  |    |- tests
  |- geom2d
  |    |- tests
  |- graphic
  |    |- simulation
  |    |- svg
  |- utils
```

You should just have added the *eqs* directory and its *tests* subdirectory:

```
Mechanics
  | ...
  |- eqs
  |    |- tests
  | ...
```

Vectors

As we saw in the introduction of the chapter, a vector inside the *eqs* package will represent a sequence of numbers stored together in a list. We won't confuse it with the Vector implementation from the *geom2d* package; it's unfortunate they share a name, but remember that they are two different (although arguably related) concepts. Vectors here are a special kind of matrix; specifically, they are matrices with only one row or column. For instance, we may refer to a vector like

$$\begin{bmatrix} 2 \\ -1 \\ 3 \end{bmatrix}$$

as a *column vector*, highlighting the fact that it's a matrix with only one column. Similarly, we call a vector like

$$\begin{bmatrix} 2 & -1 & 3 \end{bmatrix}$$

a *row vector*, as it's nothing more than a matrix with only one row.

We'll implement matrices and vectors as separate classes (instead of using the Matrix class to represent both) just for the sake of readability. For example, to get a value from a matrix we indicate both the row and column indices. For a vector, we require just one index, so using the Matrix class to store a vector could make sense but would force us to pass two indices to get or set values when, conceptually, just one should be enough. Thus, when reading code like

```
m.value_at(2, 4)
v.value_at(3)
```

we can quickly identify that m is a matrix and v is a vector.

Implementing the Vector Class

We'll use a list to store the vector's data. We won't be giving users access to this private list of numbers but instead will provide methods in the class to work with the vector. Create a new file, *vector.py*, inside *eqs* and enter the code in Listing 13-2.

```
from utils.lists import list_of_zeros


class Vector:

    def __init__(self, length: int):
        self.__length = length
        self.__data = list_of_zeros(length)

    @property
```

```
    def length(self):
        return self.__length
```

Listing 13-2: Vector class

When an instance of the Vector class is initialized, we pass in a length. This length is kept in a private attribute called __length of the class and is exposed as a property using the @property decorator. This ensures the length property won't be modified once the Vector class has been instantiated. Recall that properties are read-only attributes.

The vector's data is stored in the __data attribute, which is initialized using our list_of_zeros function from before.

Let's implement methods to set values in the vector. In the class, enter the new code in Listing 13-3.

```
class Vector:
    --snip--

    def set_value(self, value: float, index: int):
        self.__data[index] = value
        return self

    def add_to_value(self, amount: float, index: int):
        self.__data[index] += amount
        return self

    def set_data(self, data: [float]):
        if len(data) != self.__length:
            raise ValueError('Cannot set data: length mismatch')

        for i in range(self.__length):
            self.__data[i] = data[i]

        return self
```

Listing 13-3: Setting vector values

We've added three new methods. The first one, set_value, is the simplest of all: it sets a value at the specified index inside the vector. Note that if the given index is either greater than or equal to the vector's length, or smaller than zero, we raise what we commonly refer to as an *out of bounds* error, namely, an IndexError. We don't need to check for this condition ourselves as long as we're happy with how Python handles it. Note as well that the method returns self, that is, the instance of the class itself. We'll keep using this pattern where we return the instance when setting values in our class. This is so that we can chain "set" operations or do things like

```
vec = Vector(5).set_value(3, 2)
```

instead of having to do this less pretty equivalent:

```
vec = Vector(5)
vec.set_value(3, 2)
```

The second method we've defined is add_to_value, which adds the given amount to a value inside the vector. This method will be convenient when working with structures in Part V of the book, as you'll see.

Lastly, we have set_data, which sets all the values in the vector from a source data list. To do so, it first checks that the provided list has the same length as the vector; then it copies each of the values to the private list __data.

Let's now implement a method to retrieve values from the vector at given indices. In the *vector.py* file, enter the code in Listing 13-4.

```
class Vector:
    --snip--

    def value_at(self, index: int):
        return self.__data[index]
```

Listing 13-4: Getting vector values

We're almost done with the Vector class. We could implement many more methods to do things such as add or subtract vectors, but we won't need them for the purposes of this book. The only method we'll need and we haven't implemented (or overridden) yet is __eq__, which we can use to check whether two Vector instances are equal. Let's do so now. Start by adding the following import in *vector.py*:

```
from geom2d import are_close_enough
```

Then enter the new code in Listing 13-5.

```
from geom2d import are_close_enough
from utils.lists import import list_of_zeros


class Vector:
    --snip--

    def __eq__(self, other):
        if self is other:
            return True

        if not isinstance(other, Vector):
            return False

        if self.__length != other.__length:
            return False
```

```
        for i in range(self.length):
            if not are_close_enough(
                    self.value_at(i),
                    other.value_at(i)
            ):
                return False

    return True
```

Listing 13-5: Vector class equality

We first check whether we're comparing the same instance against itself, in which case the result is True and we don't need to compare anything else. Then, if the passed-in other is not an instance of the Vector class, we know the comparison can't succeed, so we return False. If we find out we're comparing two instances of the Vector class, we start the actual check. First we make sure the lengths of the vectors are the same (vectors with different sizes cannot be equal). If the length check succeeds, we finally check the values one by one using our are_close_enough function.

When we implement potentially computationally expensive __eq__ methods, it's important to check the less computationally intensive conditions first. Here, for example, we do a fast check on the lengths of the vectors before checking every pair of values for equality. Whereas the pairwise value comparison needs to perform n comparisons (where n is the length of the vectors), the length comparison requires only one comparison.

Our finished Vector class should look like the one in Listing 13-6.

```
from geom2d import are_close_enough
from utils.lists import list_of_zeros


class Vector:

    def __init__(self, length: int):
        self.__length = length
        self.__data = list_of_zeros(length)

    @property
    def length(self):
        return self.__length

    def set_value(self, value: float, index: int):
        self.__data[index] = value
        return self

    def add_to_value(self, amount: float, index: int):
        self.__data[index] += amount
        return self
```

```
    def set_data(self, data: [float]):
        if len(data) != self.__length:
            raise ValueError('Cannot set data: length mismatch')

        for i in range(self.__length):
            self.__data[i] = data[i]

        return self

    def value_at(self, index: int):
        return self.__data[index]

    def __eq__(self, other):
        if self is other:
            return True

        if not isinstance(other, Vector):
            return False

        if self.__length != other.__length:
            return False

        for i in range(self.length):
            if not are_close_enough(
                    self.value_at(i),
                    other.value_at(i)
            ):
                return False

        return True
```

Listing 13-6: Vector class result

Because this class will serve as the base for the resolution of systems of linear equations, we can't afford to have any bugs in its implementation: that would render the resolution of such systems useless. Let's add a few tests to make sure the class is bug-free.

Testing the Vector Class

At the beginning of the chapter we created a *test* directory inside the *eqs* package. Inside that directory, create a new file named *vector_test.py* and enter the code in Listing 13-7.

```
import unittest

from eqs.vector import Vector
```

```
class VectorTest(unittest.TestCase):

    def test_length(self):
        self.assertEqual(5, Vector(5).length)

    def test_unset_value_is_zero(self):
        vector = Vector(2)
        self.assertEqual(0.0, vector.value_at(0))
        self.assertEqual(0.0, vector.value_at(1))

    def test_set_get_value(self):
        value = 10.0
        vector = Vector(2).set_value(value, 1)
        self.assertEqual(0.0, vector.value_at(0))
        self.assertEqual(value, vector.value_at(1))

    def test_add_to_value(self):
        vector = Vector(2).set_data([1, 2]).add_to_value(10, 0)
        self.assertEqual(11, vector.value_at(0))
        self.assertEqual(2, vector.value_at(1))
```

Listing 13-7: Vector class unit tests

This code defines a new test class, VectorTest, with four unit tests. Run all the tests to make sure they pass and our implementation is right. You can do so from the bash shell:

```
$ python3 -m unittest eqs/tests/vector_test.py
```

The first test, test_length, checks that the vector's length property returns the right number. Then comes test_unset_value_is_zero, which ensures that we properly initialize the vector, filling it with zeros. The test_set_get _value sets the value 10.0 at index 1 and checks that the vector returns that same value when asked for the item at index 1. We also assert that the vector returns a zero for the item at index 0, just to make sure that set_value doesn't modify any value other than the one it's supposed to. Last, we have test_add_to_value to test the add_to_value method. The test initializes the vector with values [1, 2], adds 10 units to the item at index 0, and asserts that the value at that index is updated correctly.

You may have noticed that the test_set_get_value test may actually fail for two different reasons: an error in the implementation of the vector's (1) set_value method or (2) value_at method. That's mostly true, and you'd be right to point out that we broke our first rule for good testing here (see "Three Golden Rules for Unit Testing" on page 97). But it's hard to test set_value without using the value_at method in the assertion. We could get the value by somehow accessing the vector's private __data instead of using value_at, but it's preferable to test a class through its public API and not access its implementation details. We want to be able to change the internal implementation of our classes without altering their behavior, and that shouldn't break any test. If we rely on the internals of a class to test it, we couple the test to the class's implementation.

As a rule of thumb, the private implementation of a class should always be kept secret to the outside world; only the class itself should know about it. This is called *encapsulation* in object-oriented parlance.

Our Vector class is now ready and tested. Let's implement a class to represent matrices.

Matrices

Matrices add an extra dimension to vectors. Matrices are an array of numbers distributed in rows and columns.

Let's create a new file *matrix.py* inside the *eqs* directory. Enter the initial definition for the Matrix class, as in Listing 13-8.

```
from utils.lists import list_of_list_of_zeros


class Matrix:

    def __init__(self, rows_count: int, cols_count: int):
        self.__rows_count = rows_count
        self.__cols_count = cols_count
        self.__is_square = rows_count == cols_count
        self.__data = list_of_list_of_zeros(rows_count, cols_count)

    @property
    def rows_count(self):
        return self.__rows_count

    @property
    def cols_count(self):
        return self.__cols_count

    @property
    def is_square(self):
        return self.__is_square
```

Listing 13-8: Matrix class

The Matrix class is initialized with the number of rows and columns. These values are saved as private attributes of the class: __rows_count and __cols_count. They are exposed as public properties: rows_count and cols_count. A matrix is square if it has the same number of rows and columns. We exposed this as a property as well: is_square. Last, we initialize the private attribute __data with a list of lists of zeros using the function that we created at the beginning of the chapter.

Setting Values

Let's add the methods to set the matrix's values. In the Matrix class, enter the two methods in Listing 13-9.

```
class Matrix:
    --snip--

    def set_value(self, value: float, row: int, col: int):
        self.__data[row][col] = value
        return self

    def add_to_value(self, amount: float, row: int, col: int):
        self.__data[row][col] += amount
        return self
```

Listing 13-9: Setting matrix values

Like we did with our Vector class, we've implemented one method to set a value in the matrix given its position (given by row and col) and one method to add a given amount to an existing value in the matrix. Following our convention of returning the instance when a value is set, both set_value and add_to_value return self.

It'll also be handy to have a way to fill the matrix given a list of values, so after what we've just written, enter the method in Listing 13-10.

```
class Matrix:
    --snip--

    def set_data(self, data: [float]):
    ❶ if len(data) != self.__cols_count * self.__rows_count:
            raise ValueError('Cannot set data: size mismatch')

        for row in range(self.__rows_count):
        ❷ offset = self.__cols_count * row
            for col in range(self.__cols_count):
            ❸ self.__data[row][col] = data[offset + col]

        return self
```

Listing 13-10: Setting data to the matrix

As you can already tell, using the values in a list to set the matrix data is not as straightforward as it was for vectors. There's a check we need to perform to make sure the data fits inside the matrix: the given data should have the same length as the number of rows times the number of columns ❶, the total number of values the matrix holds. If it doesn't, we raise a ValueError.

Then, we iterate through the matrix's row indices. In the offset variable we store the offset to the beginning of the current's row data inside the input list ❷. For the row at index 0, the offset is 0 as well. For the row at index 1, the offset will be the length of a row: the number of columns in the matrix, and so forth. Figure 13-1 shows this offset. We iterate through the column's indices and set each of the values in __data from the input data ❸.

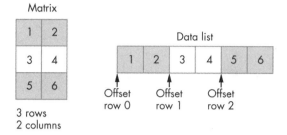

Matrix

3 rows
2 columns

Data list

Offset row 0   Offset row 1   Offset row 2

Figure 13-1: Setting matrix data from a list

As we'll see in Part V of the book, when we're working with truss structures, one of the steps for computing the structure's system of equations is accounting for the external constraints on nodes. We'll get into all the details later, but for now it's enough to know that this modification requires that we set a row and a column of the matrix as identity vectors. For example, if we had the following matrix,

$$\begin{bmatrix} 1 & 2 & 3 \\ 4 & 5 & 6 \\ 7 & 8 & 9 \end{bmatrix}$$

setting the row and column with indices 0 and 1, respectively, as identity vectors would result in the following:

$$\begin{bmatrix} 1 & 0 & 0 \\ 4 & 1 & 6 \\ 7 & 0 & 9 \end{bmatrix}$$

Let's write two methods to do this in our Matrix class. Enter the code in Listing 13-11.

```
class Matrix:
    --snip--

    def set_identity_row(self, row: int):
        for col in range(self.__cols_count):
            self.__data[row][col] = 1 if row == col else 0

        return self

    def set_identity_col(self, col: int):
        for row in range(self.__rows_count):
            self.__data[row][col] = 1 if row == col else 0

        return self
```

Listing 13-11: Setting identity rows and columns

We implemented two new methods: set_identity_row and set_identity_col. Both are similar in implementation: they set all values in the row or column as 0 except for the position in the main diagonal, which is set to 1.

In this code, we've used a compact condition expression: a ternary operator. This operator's syntax is as follows:

`<expression>` if `<condition>` else `<expression>`

It returns one of the two expressions depending on the condition value. In this particular case, our condition is `row == col`, which is `True` if the row and column indices are equal.

Note that if the matrix is not square, it can happen that we set a row or column as the identity vector and it ends up filled with all zeros. For example, see Figure 13-2. We have a matrix with three rows and two columns, and we set the third row (the row at index 2) as the identity. Since the matrix has only two columns, the value 1 would be outside the matrix, in the nonexistent third column.

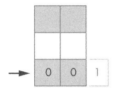

Figure 13-2: Setting an identity row in a nonsquare matrix

Let's now add two methods to get values from the matrix.

Getting Values

We need to implement value_at to get a value at the given row and column indices. We also want another method, value_transposed_at, which pulls a value from the matrix as if the matrix had been transposed. Quick reminder: the transpose of a matrix $[M]$ is another matrix $[M]'$ where $[M]$'s rows are swapped with its columns:

$$[M] = \begin{bmatrix} 1 & 2 \\ 3 & 4 \\ 5 & 6 \end{bmatrix} \quad \rightarrow \quad [M]' = \begin{bmatrix} 1 & 3 & 5 \\ 2 & 4 & 6 \end{bmatrix}$$

We'll use this second method in Chapter 14 in our implementation of Cholesky's factorization algorithm to solve linear systems of equations. We could also implement a method in our Matrix class that returned a new matrix resulting from transposing the current one and then withdraw the values from this matrix. That would be a good option indeed, but as matrices representing systems of equations are often enough very big, copying all the values into a new matrix is a computationally expensive operation. Being able to get values from the matrix as if it were transposed is a performance optimization we'll use in our Cholesky implementation.

In *matrix.py*, enter the code in Listing 13-12.

```
class Matrix:
    --snip--

    def value_at(self, row: int, col: int):
        return self.__data[row][col]

    def value_transposed_at(self, row: int, col: int):
        return self.__data[col][row]
```

Listing 13-12: Getting matrix values

First we implement value_at. This method returns a value in the given row and column indices from the private data storage. Then we have value _transposed_at. As you can see, this method is similar to value_at. The only difference is that instead of being

```
self.__data[row][col]
```

this time the value pulled from the matrix is

```
self.__data[col][row]
```

This retrieves the value of that matrix as if it were transposed simply by swapping the row and col indices. This method will bring us a big performance improvement later.

One thing to keep in mind when using this method is that the row index we pass in should be no greater than the number of columns, and the column index should be no greater than the number of rows. Since we're accessing the matrix's data as if it were transposed, the actual number or rows is the number of columns from the original matrix. The same goes for the number of columns.

Scaling Values

Let's implement one last useful method: scaling the matrix. The same way we can scale a vector, we can scale a matrix by multiplying all of its values by a scalar. Enter the method in Listing 13-13.

```
class Matrix:
    --snip--

    def scale(self, factor: float):
        for i in range(self.__rows_count):
            for j in range(self.__cols_count):
                self.__data[i][j] *= factor

        return self
```

Listing 13-13: Scaling a matrix

This method iterates through all the row and column indices and multiplies the value stored in every position by the passed-in factor. We return self, as this is a method that sets data.

Matrix Equality

To finish the implementation for our Matrix class, let's include the __eq__ method to compare matrices for equality. Start by adding the following import at the top of *matrix.py*:

```
from geom2d import are_close_enough
```

Then enter the implementation for the __eq__ method in Listing 13-14.

```
from geom2d import are_close_enough
from utils.lists import list_of_list_of_zeros


class Matrix:
    --snip--

    def __eq__(self, other):
        if self is other:
            return True

        if not isinstance(other, Matrix):
            return False

        if self.__rows_count != other.rows_count:
            return False

        if self.__cols_count != other.cols_count:
            return False

        for i in range(self.__rows_count):
            for j in range(self.__cols_count):
                if not are_close_enough(
                        self.__data[i][j],
                        other.__data[i][j]
                ):
                    return False

        return True
```

Listing 13-14: Matrix class equality

As usual, we start by checking the references for self and other, because if we're comparing an instance against itself, there's no need to compare anything else, and the comparison can safely return True. Then, we make sure the passed-in object is an instance of the `Matrix` class; otherwise, there's not much we can compare.

Before we start comparing values from the matrices one by one, we want to make sure we have matrices of the same size. If we detect that either the row or column lengths don't match, we return `False`.

Finally, if all the previous checks haven't returned a value, we compare the values of both matrices. As soon as we find a pair of values that aren't equal (according to our are_close_enough function), we return `False`. If all values are equal, we exit the for loops and finally return `True`.

For reference, your *matrix.py* file should look like Listing 13-15.

```
from geom2d import are_close_enough
from utils.lists import list_of_list_of_zeros


class Matrix:

    def __init__(self, rows_count: int, cols_count: int):
        self.__rows_count = rows_count
        self.__cols_count = cols_count
        self.__is_square = rows_count == cols_count
        self.__data = list_of_list_of_zeros(rows_count, cols_count)

    @property
    def rows_count(self):
        return self.__rows_count

    @property
    def cols_count(self):
        return self.__cols_count

    @property
    def is_square(self):
        return self.__is_square

    def set_value(self, value: float, row: int, col: int):
        self.__data[row][col] = value
        return self

    def add_to_value(self, amount: float, row: int, col: int):
        self.__data[row][col] += amount
        return self

    def set_data(self, data: [float]):
        if len(data) != self.__cols_count * self.__rows_count:
            raise ValueError('Cannot set data: size mismatch')

        for row in range(self.__rows_count):
```

```python
            offset = self.__cols_count * row
            for col in range(self.__cols_count):
                self.__data[row][col] = data[offset + col]

        return self

    def set_identity_row(self, row: int):
        for col in range(self.__cols_count):
            self.__data[row][col] = 1 if row == col else 0

        return self

    def set_identity_col(self, col: int):
        for row in range(self.__rows_count):
            self.__data[row][col] = 1 if row == col else 0

        return self

    def value_at(self, row: int, col: int):
        return self.__data[row][col]

    def value_transposed_at(self, row: int, col: int):
        return self.__data[col][row]

    def scale(self, factor: float):
        for i in range(self.__rows_count):
            for j in range(self.__cols_count):
                self.__data[i][j] *= factor

        return self

    def __eq__(self, other):
        if self is other:
            return True

        if not isinstance(other, Matrix):
            return False

        if self.__rows_count != other.rows_count:
            return False

        if self.__cols_count != other.cols_count:
            return False

        for i in range(self.__rows_count):
            for j in range(self.__cols_count):
                if not are_close_enough(
```

```
                    self.__data[i][j],
                    other.__data[i][j]
        ):
                return False

        return True
```

Listing 13-15: Matrix class result

Our `Matrix` class is almost ready! We need to check for bugs. We may have made some small mistakes when writing the code. This could be problematic once we start using this class to solve systems of equations. These kinds of calculations are usually mission-critical in engineering applications. Thus, we can't afford a single bug in our implementation. But that's no problem for us. We know how to tackle this: let's add some automated unit tests.

Testing the Matrix Class

In the *tests* folder, create a new file named *matrix_test.py*. Enter the initial code for the test in Listing 13-16.

```
import unittest

from eqs.matrix import Matrix


class MatrixTest(unittest.TestCase):

    def test_is_square(self):
        self.assertTrue(
            Matrix(2, 2).is_square
        )

    def test_is_not_square(self):
        self.assertFalse(
            Matrix(2, 3).is_square
        )
```

Listing 13-16: Matrix unit tests

In this file we define a new test class called `MatrixTest`, which inherits from `TestCase`. We created two tests for the `is_square` property, one to check if a matrix is actually square, and another to check if a matrix is not square. Run the tests; ideally they both pass, but if not, go back to the implementation of the property and ensure you have the implementation right. You can run the tests from the shell using the following command:

```
$ python3 -m unittest eqs/tests/matrix_test.py
```

You should get output similar to the following:

```
Ran 2 tests in 0.001s

OK
```

Let's now check the methods that set or get values. After the two tests we just wrote, enter the tests in Listing 13-17.

```
class MatrixTest(unittest.TestCase):
    --snip--

    def test_unset_value_is_zero(self):
        matrix = Matrix(2, 2)
        self.assertEqual(0.0, matrix.value_at(0, 1))

    def test_set_get_value(self):
        value = 10.0
        matrix = Matrix(2, 2).set_value(value, 0, 1)
        self.assertEqual(value, matrix.value_at(0, 1))

    def test_add_to_value(self):
        expected = [1, 12, 3, 4]
        matrix = Matrix(2, 2) \
            .set_data([1, 2, 3, 4]) \
            .add_to_value(10, 0, 1)
        self.assert_matrix_has_data(matrix, expected)
```

Listing 13-17: Testing setting and getting values

The first test ensures that values in the matrix that haven't been set are zero upon instantiation. Then we test that both the set_value and value_at methods actually set and get matrix values. Lastly, we test the add_to_value method, making sure that it adds a given amount to an already set value.

In this last test, we've used an assertion method that doesn't exist: assert _matrix_has_data. We need to implement this method ourselves inside the MatrixTest class, and we'll use it when we need to ensure all values inside a matrix are as expected. By doing this, we can use only one assertion to check that the values in a matrix are the same as the values in a list passed in as the second parameter. Inside the test class, toward the end, enter the method definition shown in Listing 13-18.

```
class MatrixTest(unittest.TestCase):
    --snip--


    def assert_matrix_has_data(self, matrix, data):
        for row in range(matrix.rows_count):
            offset = matrix.cols_count * row
            for col in range(matrix.cols_count):
```

```
            self.assertEqual(
                data[offset + col],
                matrix.value_at(row, col)
            )
```

Listing 13-18: Custom assertion for matrix values

This assertion method has the same structure as `set_data` inside the `Matrix` class. This time, instead of setting values, we use `assertEqual` to test for equality.

We have to note that, by including an assertion method that has some logic of its own (the `offset` computation in this case), we introduce one more possible reason for the tests to fail: the assertion method itself being wrongly implemented. As always, if we want to be practical, we need to make trade-offs. We can use our engineering common sense to analyze the pros, cons, and alternatives. In this case, having a custom assertion to check matrix values is worth it: it facilitates the simple assertion of matrix values and makes writing new tests and checking matrix values painless. We just have to be extra sure that our logic in the assertion method is correct.

Let's now test the `set_data` method. The test is in Listing 13-19.

```
class MatrixTest(unittest.TestCase):
    --snip--

    def test_set_data(self):
        data = [1, 2, 3, 4, 5, 6]
        matrix = Matrix(2, 3).set_data(data)
        self.assert_matrix_has_data(matrix, data)
```

Listing 13-19: Testing setting data from a list

In this test we're using our custom assertion method, which makes the test quite short and concise. We create a matrix with two rows and three columns, set its data using a list with the numbers between 1 and 6, and then assert they've been correctly placed in their respective slots.

Moving on, our next tests should be for the methods that set identity rows and columns. Enter the tests in Listing 13-20.

```
class MatrixTest(unittest.TestCase):
    --snip--

    def test_set_identity_row(self):
        expected = [1, 0, 4, 5]
        matrix = Matrix(2, 2) \
            .set_data([2, 3, 4, 5]) \
            .set_identity_row(0)
        self.assert_matrix_has_data(matrix, expected)

    def test_set_identity_col(self):
        expected = [2, 0, 4, 1]
```

```
matrix = Matrix(2, 2) \
    .set_data([2, 3, 4, 5]) \
    .set_identity_col(1)
self.assert_matrix_has_data(matrix, expected)
```

Listing 13-20: Testing setting identity rows and columns

In these two tests we start by specifying the expected values for the resulting matrix. Then, we create a new 2×2 matrix and set its values to the list of numbers between 2 and 5. We set the identity row or column and assert that the values are as expected.

We avoided using 1 for any of the initial values in the matrix: the methods we're testing will set one of the values inside the matrix with a 1. Imagine that our implementation of the set_identity_row method wrongly set a value in the matrix as a 1 and that it chose to set the same value that we already initialized as 1. Our tests wouldn't be able to detect such an error because there's no way to tell whether that 1 is the one we set ourselves in the beginning of the test or a value that the set_identity_row method set. By not using 1 as an input value, we avoid exposing our test to such a problem.

There's one last method we implemented in our Matrix class that needs to be tested: scale. Enter the test in Listing 13-21.

```
class MatrixTest(unittest.TestCase):
    --snip--

    def test_scale(self):
        expected = [2, 4, 6, 8, 10, 12]
        matrix = Matrix(2, 3) \
            .set_data([1, 2, 3, 4, 5, 6]) \
            .scale(2)
        self.assert_matrix_has_data(matrix, expected)
```

Listing 13-21: Testing scaling matrices

This test creates a 2×3 matrix, sets its data using the numbers from 1 to 6, and then scales everything by 2. Using the custom assert_matrix_has_data assertion we check that all values have been scaled correctly. Make sure to run the tests in the test class. From the shell, this would be as follows:

```
$ python3 -m unittest eqs/tests/matrix_test.py
```

You should get an output similar to the following:

```
Ran 9 tests in 0.001s
```

```
OK
```

Summary

In this chapter, we implemented two classes that we'll need to work with systems of equations: Vector and Matrix. In the next chapter, we'll use these two classes to represent systems of equations that we'll solve using numerical methods.

14

LINEAR EQUATIONS

Many engineering problems require resolving a system of linear equations. These
equations arise in structural analysis, electric
circuits, statistics, and optimization problems,
just to name a few. Implementing algorithms to solve
these ubiquitous systems of equations is key for our
Mechanics project to deal with real-world engineering
problems.

In this chapter, we'll explore the concept of *numerical methods*: existing
algorithms that use computers to solve systems of equations. We'll implement a powerful method to solve systems of linear equations: the Cholesky
decomposition. We'll use this method when we need to solve the big systems
of equations from the structural analysis problems in Part V of the book.

Systems of Linear Equations

A linear equation with n unknowns $x_1, x_2, \ldots, x_n$ can be expressed as shown
in Equation 14.1.

$$m_1 x_1 + m_2 x_2 + \cdots + m_n x_n = b \tag{14.1}$$

Here, $m_1, m_2, \ldots, m_n$ are the equation's coefficients, known numbers that multiply each of the unknowns, and b is a known number that doesn't multiply any unknown. We call this last number b the *free term*.

If the unknowns are only multiplied by a scalar, added, or subtracted, then we say the equation is *linear*. The coefficients are always known quantities. An alternative way of expressing a linear equation is shown here,

$$\sum_i^n m_i x_i = b$$

where m_i is the coefficients, x_i is the unknowns, and b is the free term.

By contrast, a nonlinear equation includes things like unknowns with an exponent (x^3), trigonometric functions ($\sin(x)$), or the product of several unknowns ($x_1 \cdot x_2$). These equations are considerably harder to solve than linear ones, so we'll stay focused on linear equations.

A system of linear equations has the form shown in Equation 14.2.

$$
\begin{array}{ccccccccc}
m_{1,1}x_1 & + & m_{1,2}x_2 & + & \ldots & + & m_{1,n}x_n & = & b_1 \\
m_{2,1}x_1 & + & m_{2,2}x_2 & + & \ldots & + & m_{2,n}x_n & = & b_2 \\
\multicolumn{9}{c}{\ldots\ldots\ldots\ldots\ldots\ldots} \\
m_{n,1}x_1 & + & m_{n,2}x_2 & + & \ldots & + & m_{n,n}x_n & = & b_n
\end{array}
\tag{14.2}
$$

Here, a coefficient $m_{i,j}$ is the term that multiplies the jth unknown in the ith equation. These systems can be conveniently expressed in their matrix form as shown in Equation 14.3.

$$[M][x] = [b] \tag{14.3}$$

Here, $[M]$ is the matrix of coefficients,

$$
[M] = \begin{bmatrix}
m_{1,1} & m_{1,2} & \ldots & m_{1,n} \\
m_{2,1} & m_{2,2} & \ldots & m_{2,n} \\
\multicolumn{4}{c}{\ldots\ldots\ldots\ldots} \\
m_{n,1} & m_{n,2} & \ldots & m_{n,n}
\end{bmatrix}
$$

and $[x]$ and $[b]$ are the unknown and the free-term column vectors:

$$
[x] = \begin{bmatrix} x_1 \\ x_2 \\ \vdots \\ x_n \end{bmatrix}
\qquad
[b] = \begin{bmatrix} b_1 \\ b_2 \\ \vdots \\ b_n \end{bmatrix}
$$

A solution for Equation 14.3 is a set of numbers $x_1, x_2, \ldots, x_n$ that satisfies all n equations. Finding solutions for big systems of equations by hand can take a long time, but don't worry: there are plenty of algorithms for solving systems like this using a computer.

A quick note on nomenclature. We'll use uppercase letters inside square brackets to denote matrices: $[M]$. The items in a matrix will be named using the same letter used for the matrix but lowercase. Items will include as a subscript two comma-separated numbers, which are the row and column indices of their position inside the matrix. For example, the number in row 3 and column 5 of the matrix $[M]$ will be referred to as $m_{3,5}$. Column and row vectors are denoted as lowercase letters inside square brackets: $[x]$. Remember that column and row vectors are also matrices.

Numerical Methods

Numerical methods are algorithms that find an approximate solution for a system of equations using the computational power of a computer.

There are numerical methods designed to solve systems of linear, nonlinear, and differential systems of equations. Most numerical methods, nevertheless, are limited to solving specific types of systems. For instance, the Cholesky decomposition works only with linear systems whose coefficient matrix is symmetric and positive definite (we'll see what this means in a bit). If we need to solve a nonlinear system of equations, or even one that is linear but with a nonsymmetric coefficient matrix, Cholesky decomposition simply won't work.

There are two big families of numerical methods: *direct* and *iterative*. Direct methods use algebraic modifications on the original system to solve it. Iterative methods, on the other hand, start with an approximate solution for the system and improve it step-by-step until the solution has the desired accuracy. The Cholesky decomposition is a direct numerical method.

Numerical methods are a big topic: entire books have been written about it. There are many technical details about numerical methods that we won't be covering here. But this isn't a theory book; we're much more interested in the practice, so we'll implement an algorithm that solves the kinds of systems of equations that'll arise in the structural analysis application we'll create in the next part of the book. In this case, that means we'll be working with linear systems with symmetric, positive-definite coefficient matrices.

Cholesky Decomposition

The *Cholesky decomposition* is a direct (noniterative) method that solves linear systems of equations provided their $[M]$ (the coefficient matrix) is *symmetric* and *positive definite*.

A symmetric matrix $[M]$ is one that is equal to its transpose: $[M] = [M]'$. That is the same as saying that the values in the matrix are symmetric with respect to the main diagonal. In a symmetric matrix, every row contains the same values as the column with the same index, and vice versa. Note that to be symmetric, a matrix needs to be square. The following is an example of a symmetric matrix:

$$\begin{bmatrix} 4 & -2 & 4 \\ -2 & 10 & -2 \\ 4 & -2 & 8 \end{bmatrix}$$

A square matrix [M] with n rows and columns is *positive definite* if for any column vector [x] made of n real numbers (with the exception of a vector filled with zeros), the expression in Equation 14.4 is satisfied.

$$[x]'[M][x] > 0 \qquad (14.4)$$

If you find a nonzero vector [x] that doesn't satisfy the previous equation, then the matrix [M] is not positive definite.

We can also say that a matrix is positive definite if it's symmetric and all its eigenvalues are positive. If you remember the process of obtaining the eigenvalues of a matrix, you might agree that it's painful and a bit boring. In either case, proving that $[x]'[M][x] > 0$ for every possible [x] or obtaining all eigenvalues of the matrix and making sure all are positive is an involved process.

We are going to skip all that technical complexity and won't be demonstrating that the matrices we'll work with are positive definite. We'll apply the Cholesky factorization to a problem that is well-known for yielding systems of equations with a symmetric and positive-definite matrix: truss structure analysis using the direct stiffness method. If you ever need to apply this algorithm to any another problem, you'll first need to figure out whether the system of equations derived for it has a matrix that Cholesky can work with. If it's not the case, don't worry: there are plenty of other numerical methods that you can use.

After we implement Cholesky's algorithm together, I hope you feel empowered to implement any other numerical method on your own. As you'll see, the most powerful resource we have at our disposal to make sure we get these tricky algorithms right is unit testing.

LU Factorization Methods

Cholesky is a computation method from the family of so-called *LU* factorization or decomposition methods. An *LU* factorization of a given square matrix [M] has the form shown in Equation 14.5.

$$[M] = [L][U] \qquad (14.5)$$

Here, [L] is a *lower-triangular matrix*, and [U] is an *upper-triangular matrix*. A lower-triangular matrix is one where all nonzero values are on and below the main diagonal. Conversely, an upper-triangular matrix has the nonzero values on and above the main diagonal. Here's an example of a lower- and an upper-triangular matrix:

$$[L] = \begin{bmatrix} 2 & 0 & 0 \\ 1 & 3 & 0 \\ 4 & 1 & 2 \end{bmatrix} \quad [U] = \begin{bmatrix} 2 & 1 & 5 \\ 0 & 3 & 4 \\ 0 & 0 & 7 \end{bmatrix}$$

Every *nonsingular matrix* (a matrix that has an inverse) always has an *LU* factorization. For example, the matrices from the previous example are the *LU* factorization for the matrix

$$\begin{bmatrix} 4 & 2 & 10 \\ 2 & 10 & 17 \\ 8 & 7 & 38 \end{bmatrix}$$

which you can verify by multiplying the following:

$$\begin{bmatrix} 4 & 2 & 10 \\ 2 & 10 & 17 \\ 8 & 7 & 38 \end{bmatrix} = \begin{bmatrix} 2 & 0 & 0 \\ 1 & 3 & 0 \\ 4 & 1 & 2 \end{bmatrix} \begin{bmatrix} 2 & 1 & 5 \\ 0 & 3 & 4 \\ 0 & 0 & 7 \end{bmatrix}$$

The Cholesky algorithm will provide us with a lower- and an upper-triangular matrix. Besides Cholesky, there are two well-known methods for obtaining the factorization of any nonsingular matrix: the Doolittle and Crout algorithms. These algorithms define the formulas necessary to compute the $l_{i,j}$ and $u_{i,j}$ values for the lower- and upper-triangular matrices. The benefit of these methods is that they work for any kind of matrix, not just symmetric, positive-definite matrices. We won't be covering them here, but I encourage you to take a look and try to implement one of them yourself in our *Mechanics* project. You may want to try that as an exercise after we've implemented Cholesky's algorithm.

It's fair to ask, why not use the Doolittle or Crout algorithms that work with every nonsingular matrix instead of the more restrictive Cholesky? For symmetric and positive-definite matrices, Cholesky's decomposition is about twice as fast as these other algorithms. Since we'll use the method with the type of matrices required, we'll want to benefit from the execution speed offered by Cholesky's method.

Once we obtain the *LU* factorization for the matrix, we can solve our system of equations in two steps. Suppose our original system was as follows:

$$[M][x] = [b]$$

After factorizing [*M*], we have Equation 14.6.

$$[L][U][x] = [b] \tag{14.6}$$

We can extract two systems from Equation 14.6 if we take the product [*U*][*x*] and substitute it with a new unknown vector [*y*]:

$$[L]\underbrace{[U][x]}_{[y]} = [b]$$

We now have a lower-triangular matrix system, as shown in Equation 14.7,

$$[L][y] = [b] \tag{14.7}$$

and an upper-triangular matrix system, as shown in Equation 14.8.

$$[U][x] = [y] \qquad (14.8)$$

By first solving Equation 14.7, we find $[y]$, which plugged into Equation 14.8 allows us to compute the unknown vector $[x]$: the system's solution. Both Equation 14.7 and Equation 14.8 are systems with a triangular matrix, and they can be easily solved by forward and backward substitution.

Take this system of equations whose coefficient matrix is lower triangular:

$$\begin{bmatrix} l_{1,1} & 0 & 0 \\ l_{2,1} & l_{2,2} & 0 \\ l_{3,1} & l_{3,2} & l_{3,3} \end{bmatrix} \begin{bmatrix} y_1 \\ y_2 \\ y_3 \end{bmatrix} = \begin{bmatrix} b_1 \\ b_2 \\ b_3 \end{bmatrix}$$

The first unknown y_1 can be computed from the first equation as follows:

$$y_1 = \frac{b_1}{l_{1,1}}$$

From the second equation we have the following,

$$y_2 = \frac{b_2 - l_{2,1} y_1}{l_{2,2}}$$

which can be solved, as we already computed the value for y_1 in the previous step. We do the same for the third equation:

$$y_3 = \frac{b_3 - l_{3,1} y_1 - l_{3,2} y_2}{l_{3,3}}$$

We have the values for y_1 and y_2, so the value for y_3 can be computed. This process is known as *forward substitution*. A formula to obtain the y^{ith} solution term using forward substitution is shown in Equation 14.9 (using zero-based indices).

$$y_i = \frac{b_i - \sum_{j=0}^{j<i} l_{i,j} y_j}{l_{i,i}} \qquad (14.9)$$

In a system whose coefficient matrix is upper triangular, we can use a similar substitution process, but starting from the bottom this time. The process is called *backward substitution*. This time we have the following:

$$\begin{bmatrix} u_{1,1} & u_{1,2} & u_{1,3} \\ 0 & u_{2,2} & u_{2,3} \\ 0 & 0 & u_{3,3} \end{bmatrix} \begin{bmatrix} x_1 \\ x_2 \\ x_3 \end{bmatrix} = \begin{bmatrix} y_1 \\ y_2 \\ y_3 \end{bmatrix}$$

Starting from the last equation, we can compute x_3:

$$x_3 = \frac{y_3}{u_{3,3}}$$

With this value we can move to the second equation to obtain x_2:

$$x_2 = \frac{y_2 - u_{2,3}x_3}{u_{2,2}}$$

Lastly, from the first equation in the system, we have this:

$$x_1 = \frac{y_1 - u_{1,2}x_2 - u_{1,3}x_3}{u_{1,1}}$$

For the backward substitution, the formula to compute the x^{ith} term is described by Equation 14.10, with n being the size of the system.

$$x_i = \frac{y_i - \sum_{j=i+1}^{j \leq n} u_{i,j}x_j}{u_{i,i}} \tag{14.10}$$

We'll need to implement these formulas in our code soon. You'll see that it's actually simpler than it looks.

Understanding Cholesky

As we discussed, the Cholesky decomposition is an LU method that works with symmetric, positive-definite matrices. Thanks to those properties, a matrix $[M]$ can be decomposed into an $[L][U]$ form where the upper-triangular matrix is the transpose of the lower-triangular one: $[U] = [L]'$. This means we only need to compute the lower-triangular matrix $[L]$: $[U]$ is just its transpose. Using the Cholesky method, the $[M]$ matrix factorization has the form shown in Equation 14.11.

$$[M] = [L][L]' \tag{14.11}$$

So, the system of equations now looks like Equation 14.12.

$$[L][L]'[x] = [b] \tag{14.12}$$

In this case, we obtain the two systems we need to solve by substituting $[L]'[x]$ with $[y]$:

$$[L]\underbrace{[L]'[x]}_{[y]} = [b]$$

As we already know, this transformation yields a lower system, which we'll solve first using forward substitution (see Equation 14.13),

$$[L][y] = [b] \tag{14.13}$$

and then using an upper system that we'll solve by backward substitution to obtain the solution vector $[x]$ (see Equation 14.14).

$$[L]'[x] = [y] \tag{14.14}$$

Given a symmetric, positive-definite matrix $[M]$, we can compute the lower-triangular matrix terms of its Cholesky decomposition, the $l_{i,j}$ terms, using the formulas in Equation 14.15.

$$l_{i,j} = \begin{cases} \sqrt{m_{i,i} - \sum_{k=0}^{i-1} l_{i,k}^2} & \text{if } i = j \\ \dfrac{1}{l_{j,j}} \left(m_{i,j} - \sum_{k=0}^{j-1} l_{i,k} l_{j,k} \right) & \text{if } i > j \end{cases}$$

(14.15)

Equation 14.15 may look intimidating, but it's actually not that complicated. The best way to see this is by doing an exercise by hand. Grab a pen and some paper and let's factor a matrix together.

A Factorization by Hand

Given the symmetric and positive-definite matrix

$$[M] = \begin{bmatrix} 4 & -2 & 4 \\ -2 & 10 & -2 \\ 4 & -2 & 8 \end{bmatrix}$$

let's find its Cholesky factorization, a lower-triangular matrix $[L]$,

$$[L] = \begin{bmatrix} l_{0,0} & 0 & 0 \\ l_{1,0} & l_{1,1} & 0 \\ l_{2,0} & l_{2,1} & l_{2,2} \end{bmatrix}$$

such that $[M] = [L][L]'$. To compute the $l_{i,j}$ terms, we use Equation 14.15. Don't forget that index i represents the rows of the matrix, and j represents its columns. Let's do it step-by-step.

Step 1: $i = 0, j = 0$. Since $i = j$, we use the first formula:

$$l_{0,0} = \sqrt{m_{0,0} - \cancel{\sum_{k=0}^{-1} l_{0,k}^2}} = \sqrt{4} = 2$$

Note that the summation is struck through because it doesn't yield any term. This is because the summation's end value $k = -1$ is smaller than the start one $k = 0$. As you probably know, for the summation to yield any term, the end value for k (the iterating variable) needs to be equal to or greater than the start value.

Step 2: $i = 1, j = 0$. In this case, $i \neq j$, so we use the second formula:

$$l_{1,0} = \frac{1}{l_{0,0}} \left(m_{1,0} - \cancel{\sum_{k=0}^{-1} l_{1,k} l_{0,k}} \right) = \frac{-2}{2} = -1$$

Step 3: $i = 1, j = 1$.

$$l_{1,1} = \sqrt{m_{1,1} - \sum_{k=0}^{0} l_{1,k}^2} = \sqrt{m_{1,1} - l_{1,0}^2} = \sqrt{10 - 1} = 3$$

Step 4: $i = 2, j = 0$.

$$l_{2,0} = \frac{1}{l_{0,0}} \left(m_{2,0} - \sum_{k=0}^{-1} l_{2,k} l_{0,k} \right) = \frac{4}{2} = 2$$

Step 5: $i = 2, j = 1$.

$$l_{2,1} = \frac{1}{l_{1,1}} \left(m_{2,0} - \sum_{k=0}^{0} l_{2,k} l_{1,k} \right) = \frac{1}{l_{1,1}} \left(m_{2,0} - l_{2,0} l_{1,0} \right) = \frac{1}{3} (-2 + 2) = 0$$

Step 6: $i = 2, j = 2$.

$$l_{2,2} = \sqrt{m_{2,2} - \sum_{k=0}^{1} l_{2,k}^2} = \sqrt{m_{2,2} - \left(l_{2,0}^2 + l_{2,1}^2 \right)} = \sqrt{8 - \left(2^2 + 0^2 \right)} = 2$$

If we combine all the computed $l_{i,j}$ values, the resulting matrix is as follows:

$$[L] = \begin{bmatrix} 2 & 0 & 0 \\ -1 & 3 & 0 \\ 2 & 0 & 2 \end{bmatrix}$$

This means that the original system's matrix $[M]$ can be factorized as follows:

$$\begin{bmatrix} 4 & -2 & 4 \\ -2 & 10 & -2 \\ 4 & -2 & 8 \end{bmatrix} = \begin{bmatrix} 2 & 0 & 0 \\ -1 & 3 & 0 \\ 2 & 0 & 2 \end{bmatrix} \begin{bmatrix} 2 & -1 & 2 \\ 0 & 3 & 0 \\ 0 & 0 & 2 \end{bmatrix}$$

You can do the matrix multiplication to verify that the product $[L][L]'$ is actually equal to $[M]$. To complete the exercise, let's suppose this matrix is the coefficient matrix of a system of equations and solve it using the forward and backward substitutions.

A Resolution by Hand

Let's suppose the matrix we decomposed earlier into its $[L][L]'$ form is part of the following system of equations:

$$\begin{bmatrix} 4 & -2 & 4 \\ -2 & 10 & -2 \\ 4 & -2 & 8 \end{bmatrix} \begin{bmatrix} x_1 \\ x_2 \\ x_3 \end{bmatrix} = \begin{bmatrix} 0 \\ -3 \\ -15 \end{bmatrix}$$

We need to find the values of x_1, x_2, and x_3 that satisfy all three equations. Using the Cholesky factorization we just obtained, we can rewrite the system as follows:

$$\begin{bmatrix} 2 & 0 & 0 \\ -1 & 3 & 0 \\ 2 & 0 & 2 \end{bmatrix} \begin{bmatrix} 2 & -1 & 2 \\ 0 & 3 & 0 \\ 0 & 0 & 2 \end{bmatrix} \begin{bmatrix} x_1 \\ x_2 \\ x_3 \end{bmatrix} = \begin{bmatrix} 0 \\ -3 \\ -15 \end{bmatrix}$$

The first of the two subsystems we have to solve, $[L][y] = [b]$, results from substituting $[L]'[x]$ with a new unknown vector $[y]$:

$$\begin{bmatrix} 2 & 0 & 0 \\ -1 & 3 & 0 \\ 2 & 0 & 2 \end{bmatrix} \underbrace{\begin{bmatrix} 2 & -1 & 2 \\ 0 & 3 & 0 \\ 0 & 0 & 2 \end{bmatrix} \begin{bmatrix} x_1 \\ x_2 \\ x_3 \end{bmatrix}}_{\begin{bmatrix} y_1 & y_2 & y_3 \end{bmatrix}'} = \begin{bmatrix} 0 \\ -3 \\ -15 \end{bmatrix}$$

This results in the first system (the lower system):

$$\begin{bmatrix} 2 & 0 & 0 \\ -1 & 3 & 0 \\ 2 & 0 & 2 \end{bmatrix} \begin{bmatrix} y_1 \\ y_2 \\ y_3 \end{bmatrix} = \begin{bmatrix} 0 \\ -3 \\ -15 \end{bmatrix}$$

We have to solve this system using the forward-substitution formula from Equation 14.9.

Lower System: Forward Substitution

Let's apply Equation 14.9 step-by-step:

Step 1: $i = 0$.

$$y_0 = \frac{b_0 - \overset{j<0}{\underset{j\neq 0}{\sum}} l_{0,j} y_j}{l_{0,0}} = \frac{0}{2} = 0$$

Step 2: $i = 1$.

$$y_1 = \frac{b_1 - \overset{j<1}{\underset{j=0}{\sum}} l_{1,j} y_j}{l_{1,1}} = \frac{b_1 - l_{1,0} y_0}{l_{1,1}} = \frac{-3 + 1 \cdot 0}{3} = -1$$

Step 3: $i = 2$.

$$y_2 = \frac{b_2 - \overset{j<2}{\underset{j=0}{\sum}} l_{2,j} y_j}{l_{2,2}} = \frac{b_2 - (l_{2,0} y_0 + l_{2,1} y_1)}{l_{2,2}} = \frac{-15 - (2 \cdot 0 - 0 \cdot 1)}{2} = \frac{-15}{2} = -7.5$$

Thus, the solution for the first system is as follows:

$$[y] = \begin{bmatrix} 0 \\ -1 \\ -7.5 \end{bmatrix}$$

With this solution, we can use backward substitution to compute $[x]$: the solution to our system of equations.

Upper System: Backward Substitution

Let's use Equation 14.10 to compute the solution vector step-by-step. This time we have to solve the following system using the backward-substitution process:

$$\begin{bmatrix} 2 & -1 & 2 \\ 0 & 3 & 0 \\ 0 & 0 & 2 \end{bmatrix} \begin{bmatrix} x_1 \\ x_2 \\ x_3 \end{bmatrix} = \begin{bmatrix} 0 \\ -1 \\ -7.5 \end{bmatrix}$$

Since the substitution is backward, we have to start from the last row ($i = 2$) and go up to the first one ($i = 0$).

Step 1: $i = 2$.

$$x_2 = \frac{y_2 - \sum_{j=3}^{j \le 2} u_{2,j}x_j}{u_{2,2}} = \frac{-7.5}{2} = -\frac{15}{4}$$

Step 2: $i = 1$.

$$x_1 = \frac{y_1 - \sum_{j=2}^{j \le 2} u_{1,j}x_j}{u_{1,1}} = \frac{y_1 - u_{1,2}x_2}{u_{1,1}} = \frac{-1 + 0 \cdot \frac{15}{4}}{3} = -\frac{1}{3}$$

Step 3: $i = 0$.

$$x_0 = \frac{y_0 - \sum_{j=1}^{j \le 2} u_{0,j}x_j}{u_{0,0}} = \frac{y_0 - (u_{0,1}x_1 + u_{0,2}x_2)}{u_{0,0}} = \frac{0 - (\frac{1}{3} - \frac{15}{2})}{2} = \frac{43}{12}$$

Then, the solution to the initial system is as follows:

$$[x] = \begin{bmatrix} 43/12 \\ -1/3 \\ -15/4 \end{bmatrix}$$

You can test if the solution is correct by checking if the equality holds:

$$\begin{bmatrix} 4 & -2 & 4 \\ -2 & 10 & -2 \\ 4 & -2 & 8 \end{bmatrix} \begin{bmatrix} 43/12 \\ -1/3 \\ -15/4 \end{bmatrix} = \begin{bmatrix} 0 \\ -3 \\ -15 \end{bmatrix}$$

Now that we know how the Cholesky algorithm works and we've worked out an example by hand, let's implement the algorithm in our code.

Implementing Cholesky

Start by creating a new file in the *eqs* package named *cholesky.py*. In it, include the cholesky_solve function in Listing 14-1.

```
import math

from eqs.matrix import Matrix
from eqs.vector import Vector


def cholesky_solve(sys_mat: Matrix, sys_vec: Vector):
    validate_system(sys_mat, sys_vec)

    low_matrix = lower_matrix_decomposition(sys_mat)
    low_solution = solve_lower_sys(low_matrix, sys_vec)
    return solve_upper_sys(low_matrix, low_solution)
```

Listing 14-1: Cholesky decomposition algorithm

This function takes a Matrix and a Vector as inputs. These are the coefficient matrix and free vector of a system: the $[M]$ and the $[b]$ from the system of equations $[M][x] = [b]$. The returned Vector is $[x]$, the solution to the system found applying Cholesky's method.

This cholesky_solve function defines the highest-level algorithm, which has three main steps plus a validation of the input system. We haven't implemented any of these functions yet; we'll get to this shortly. The following are the three main steps to the algorithm:

lower_matrix_decomposition   Obtain $[L]$, the lower-triangular matrix, by applying Equation 14.15.

solve_lower_sys   Solve the first subsystem, the lower-triangular system, by applying the forward-substitution technique (see Equation 14.9).

solve_upper_sys   Solve the second subsystem, the upper-triangular system, by applying the backward-substitution technique (see Equation 14.10).

From the function names, it's easy enough to see what the code in cholesky _solve is doing. Note that we broke the function into several smaller functions. If we had thrown all the code for the Cholesky resolution into the cholesky_solve function, the result would be a long pile of source code with no readily identifiable structure. This code would be extremely hard to understand.

As a general rule, you want to divide your big algorithms into smaller subalgorithms, each contained in a small function with a descriptive name.

Notice the visibility of the subfunctions used by cholesky_solve. All the subfunctions are public. This is so that they can be unit tested individually.

The resolution algorithm is a bit complex; we're safer if we know that each of its subparts does its job without errors.

Validating the System

Let's implement a function that validates that the system is square and has a number of columns equal to the size of the vector. Enter the code for the validate_system function, found in Listing 14-2.

```
--snip--

def validate_system(sys_matrix: Matrix, sys_vector: Vector):
    if sys_matrix.cols_count != sys_vector.length:
        raise ValueError('Size mismatch between matrix and vector')

    if not sys_matrix.is_square:
        raise ValueError('System matrix must be square')
```

Listing 14-2: System validation

We first check that the matrix has the same number columns as the vector's length. If this condition isn't satisfied, the system can't be solved, so we raise an error. The same applies if the system's matrix is not square.

We're not doing any check to ensure the matrix is symmetric or positive definite; if the matrix passed to our function isn't, the function will simply fail at some point with a by-zero division error or something similar. It'd be a nice idea to add those guards, at least the check for symmetry, but checking that the system's matrix is positive definite may be more challenging. The symmetry check is easy to implement, but it has the downside of being computationally expensive. I encourage you to think about ways of doing these checks and maybe add them in your code.

Now we're going to do something a little backward. We're going to start with a unit test instead of the code itself. This is so that we know when our code is ready: once the tests pass. We can keep running the test to check whether the logic we're writing is ready or not; we can refactor it until it looks readable, with the safety net of the test that will warn us if we did something wrong. This technique where the test is written before the code is known as *test-driven development*, or TDD for short.

We'll start by looking at the system of equations we'll use in the unit tests.

System of Equations for Testing

To make sure we implement all the logic without bugs, we're going to use tests for each of the subfunctions in the Cholesky algorithm. We'll also implement a test to check that all the subfunctions work together to compute the final solution. For these tests we want to use a system of equations whose solution we know in advance.

Let's use the following size 4 system:

$$
\begin{bmatrix} 4 & -2 & 4 & 2 \\ -2 & 10 & -2 & -7 \\ 4 & -2 & 8 & 4 \\ 2 & -7 & 4 & 7 \end{bmatrix} \begin{bmatrix} x_1 \\ x_2 \\ x_3 \\ x_4 \end{bmatrix} = \begin{bmatrix} 20 \\ -16 \\ 40 \\ 28 \end{bmatrix}
$$

For this system's matrix $[M]$, the Cholesky $[L][L]'$ factorization is as follows:

$$
\begin{bmatrix} 4 & -2 & 4 & 2 \\ -2 & 10 & -2 & -7 \\ 4 & -2 & 8 & 4 \\ 2 & -7 & 4 & 7 \end{bmatrix} = \begin{bmatrix} 2 & 0 & 0 & 0 \\ -1 & 3 & 0 & 0 \\ 2 & 0 & 2 & 0 \\ 1 & -2 & 1 & 1 \end{bmatrix} \begin{bmatrix} 2 & -1 & 2 & 1 \\ 0 & 3 & 0 & -2 \\ 0 & 0 & 2 & 1 \\ 0 & 0 & 0 & 1 \end{bmatrix}
$$

The solution of the lower system,

$$
\begin{bmatrix} 2 & 0 & 0 & 0 \\ -1 & 3 & 0 & 0 \\ 2 & 0 & 2 & 0 \\ 1 & -2 & 1 & 1 \end{bmatrix} \begin{bmatrix} y_1 \\ y_2 \\ y_3 \\ y_4 \end{bmatrix} = \begin{bmatrix} 20 \\ -16 \\ 40 \\ 28 \end{bmatrix}
$$

is the following vector:

$$
[y] = \begin{bmatrix} 10 \\ -2 \\ 10 \\ 4 \end{bmatrix}
$$

The final solution, resulting from the resolution of the upper system,

$$
\begin{bmatrix} 2 & -1 & 2 & 1 \\ 0 & 3 & 0 & -2 \\ 0 & 0 & 2 & 1 \\ 0 & 0 & 0 & 1 \end{bmatrix} \begin{bmatrix} x_1 \\ x_2 \\ x_3 \\ x_4 \end{bmatrix} = \begin{bmatrix} 10 \\ -2 \\ 10 \\ 4 \end{bmatrix}
$$

is the following vector:

$$
[x] = \begin{bmatrix} 1 \\ 2 \\ 3 \\ 4 \end{bmatrix}
$$

It's a good idea to take some time to check all those numbers and make sure you understand the resolution process. Once you're solid on the fundamentals of the process, let's code it up, starting with a unit test.

Lower Matrix Factorization

As we're about to implement the most complex algorithm in the book so far, let's first write a unit test. We'll know our factorization logic is well implemented once the test passes. Chances are we'll need to debug our code, and having a test will help.

Create a new file for our test, *cholesky_test.py*, and place it inside the *eqs/tests* directory. Then enter the test code in Listing 14-3.

```
import unittest

from eqs.cholesky import lower_matrix_decomposition
from eqs.matrix import Matrix


class CholeskyTest(unittest.TestCase):
    sys_matrix = Matrix(4, 4).set_data([
        4, -2, 4, 2,
        -2, 10, -2, -7,
        4, -2, 8, 4,
        2, -7, 4, 7
    ])
    low_matrix = Matrix(4, 4).set_data([
        2, 0, 0, 0,
        -1, 3, 0, 0,
        2, 0, 2, 0,
        1, -2, 1, 1
    ])

    def test_lower_matrix_decomposition(self):
        actual = lower_matrix_decomposition(self.sys_matrix)
        self.assertEqual(self.low_matrix, actual)
```

Listing 14-3: Testing the lower matrix factorization

This test defines both the original matrix, sys_matrix, and the expected decomposition, low_matrix. Using a function we haven't defined yet, lower _matrix_decomposition, we compute the decomposition matrix and compare it against the known solution. Your IDE should complain that you're trying to import a function it can't find in the *eqs.cholesky* module:

```
Cannot find reference 'lower_matrix_decomposition' in 'cholesky.py'
```

Let's implement the function. Go back to the *cholesky.py* file, and after validate_system, enter the code in Listing 14-4.

```
--snip--

def lower_matrix_decomposition(sys_mat: Matrix):
    size = sys_mat.rows_count
    low_mat = Matrix(size, size)

    for i in range(size):
        sq_sum = 0

        for j in range(i + 1):
```

```
❶ m_ij = sys_mat.value_at(i, j)

    if i == j:
        # main diagonal value
❷       diag_val = math.sqrt(m_ij - sq_sum)
❸       low_mat.set_value(diag_val, i, j)

    else:
        # value under main diagonal
        non_diag_sum = 0
❹       for k in range(j):
            l_ik = low_mat.value_at(i, k)
            l_jk = low_mat.value_at(j, k)
            non_diag_sum += l_ik * l_jk

        l_jj = low_mat.value_at(j, j)
❺       non_diag_val = (m_ij - non_diag_sum) / l_jj
❻       sq_sum += non_diag_val * non_diag_val

❼       low_mat.set_value(non_diag_val, i, j)

return low_mat
```

Listing 14-4: Lower matrix decomposition

We start by storing the size of the system in a variable named size. The size is the number of rows or columns—it doesn't matter which since the matrix is square. Then we create a new square matrix, low_mat, of that same size. Recall that our matrices are filled with zeros when they're instantiated.

The algorithm has two main nested loops. These loops iterate through all the positions in the matrix that are in the main diagonal and below it, that is, all $m_{i,j}$ where $i \geq j$.

NOTE *Don't forget that Python's range(n) function generates a sequence starting from 0 up to n − 1, not n.*

Inside the j loop, we store the value of the system's matrix at position (i, j) in m_ij ❶. Then, we distinguish between the case where we're on the main diagonal (i == j) or below it using an if else statement. Recall that the formula to compute a term in the main diagonal of the decomposition matrix is as follows:

$$l_{i,i} = \sqrt{m_{i,i} - \sum_{k=0}^{i-1} l_{i,k}^2}$$

We used that expression to compute the value, which we store in diag _val ❷ and set in the matrix ❸. In the calculation we used the m_ij value and sq_sum. The latter is initialized as 0 for every new iteration of i (for each row) and updated for every new value below the main diagonal ❻.

For the case where we're under the main diagonal (i > j, the else branch), the formula to compute the $l_{i,j}$ term is as follows:

$$l_{i,j} = \frac{1}{l_{j,j}} \left(m_{i,j} - \sum_{k=0}^{j-1} l_{i,k} l_{j,k} \right)$$

Note that to compute this $l_{i,j}$ value, we need to have $l_{j,j}$, which is a value from a previous row since $i > j$. The first term that we compute is the sum of $l_{i,k} l_{j,k}$ with k going from 0 to $j - 1$. The loop in ❹ does exactly this. Before entering the loop, we initialize a variable non_diag_sum to zero. Inside the loop this variable gets added to the product of l_ik and l_jk for every value of k.

With non_diag_sum computed, we have everything we need. The value of $l_{j,j}$ is extracted from low_mat and stored in variable l_jj. Then the value for the decomposition is computed and stored in variable non_diag_val ❺. This value is first used to update the sq_sum ❻ and then stored in the decomposition matrix ❼.

That's it. Run the test we wrote earlier and make sure your code passes it. Don't worry if it doesn't; in fact, it's a bit hard to get this algorithm right the first time you write it, but that's exactly why we implemented the test first. Use the test to debug the code and carefully compare what you wrote with the printed version of the code in this book. You can also refer to the code distributed with the book.

To run the test in the shell, use this:

```
$ python3 -m unittest eqs/tests/cholesky_test.py
```

We've obtained the [L] decomposition matrix using Cholesky's algorithm. Let's now implement the resolution of the lower and upper systems.

Lower System Resolution

To solve the lower-triangular system using forward substitution, we need to implement the algorithm in Equation 14.9. We'll repeat the formula here for convenience:

$$y_i = \frac{b_i - \sum_{j=0}^{j<i} l_{i,j} y_j}{l_{i,i}}$$

We're going to follow the same approach as before and write the test before we write the main code. In the *cholesky_test.py* file, enter the new test in Listing 14-5.

```
import unittest

from eqs.cholesky import lower_matrix_decomposition, \
    solve_lower_sys
from eqs.matrix import Matrix
from eqs.vector import Vector
```

```
class CholeskyTest(unittest.TestCase):
    --snip--
❶  sys_vec = Vector(4).set_data([20, -16, 40, 28])
❷  low_solution = Vector(4).set_data([10, -2, 10, 4])

    def test_lower_matrix_decomposition(self):
        actual = lower_matrix_decomposition(self.sys_matrix)
        self.assertEqual(self.low_matrix, actual)

❸  def test_lower_system_resolution(self):
        actual = solve_lower_sys(self.low_matrix, self.sys_vec)
        self.assertEqual(self.low_solution, actual)
```

Listing 14-5: Testing the lower system resolution

We've first imported the Vector class from eqs.vector. Then we've added two new vectors that we need for the new test: sys_vec ❶, which is the free vector of the system of equations, and low_solution ❷, the expected solution for the lower-triangular system.

With the test in place ❸, let's now implement the missing solve_lower_sys function. After the factorization function in the *cholesky.py* file, enter the code in Listing 14-6.

```
--snip--

def solve_lower_sys(low_mat: Matrix, vector: Vector):
    size = vector.length
    solution = Vector(size)

❶  for i in range(size):
        _sum = 0.0

❷      for j in range(i):
            l_ij = low_mat.value_at(i, j)
            y_j = solution.value_at(j)
            _sum += l_ij * y_j

        b_i = vector.value_at(i)
        l_ii = low_mat.value_at(i, i)
❸      solution_val = (b_i - _sum) / l_ii
        solution.set_value(solution_val, i)

    return solution
```

Listing 14-6: Solving the lower system

The first thing we do is save the size of the system in a variable size and create the solution vector of that size. The main loop that iterates through all values in the `sys_vector` is the i loop ❶. In it, we start by initializing a sum to zero. The j loop ❷ iterates through all values from 0 to $i - 1$, updating the sum for each iteration.

Having obtained the sum part of the equation, we can compute the solution value, which is stored in `solution_val` ❸. Then we set in the `solution` vector in the next line.

Run the two tests in *cholesky_test.py* to make sure both pass. It seems reasonable that the first one will pass: we haven't modified the factorization function in any way, but it's good practice to run all tests in the file, just in case we modified something that we shouldn't have. I hope the second test also passes for you, in which case you got the new function right! You'll need to debug your code otherwise. Take your time to do so; it's a great exercise.

To run the tests from the shell, use this:

```
$ python3 -m unittest eqs/tests/cholesky_test.py
```

Let's now work out the upper system resolution.

Upper System Resolution

The resolution of the upper-triangular system using backward substitution can be carried out using Equation 14.10. As a reminder, the formula is as follows:

$$x_i = \frac{y_i - \sum_{j=i+1}^{j \le n} u_{i,j} x_j}{u_{i,i}}$$

One important thing to recall is that the upper-triangular matrix $[U]$, with values $u_{i,j}$, is the transpose of Cholesky's lower-triangular decomposition: $[L]'$.

Once again we'll start with the test. Open your *cholesky_test.py* file and enter the new test in Listing 14-7.

```
import unittest

from eqs.cholesky import lower_matrix_decomposition, \
    solve_lower_sys, solve_upper_sys
from eqs.matrix import Matrix
from eqs.vector import Vector


class CholeskyTest(unittest.TestCase):
    --snip--
❶  solution = Vector(4).set_data([1, 2, 3, 4])

    def test_lower_matrix_decomposition(self):
        actual = lower_matrix_decomposition(self.sys_matrix)
        self.assertEqual(self.low_matrix, actual)
```

```
      def test_lower_system_resolution(self):
          actual = solve_lower_sys(self.low_matrix, self.sys_vec)
          self.assertEqual(self.low_solution, actual)

❷ def test_upper_system_resolution(self):
          actual = solve_upper_sys(
              self.low_matrix,
              self.low_solution
          )
          self.assertEqual(self.solution, actual)
```

Listing 14-7: Testing the upper system resolution

In this new test ❷, we call solve_upper_sys (still to be written), passing it in both the factorized matrix low_matrix and the lower system solution low_solution. Then, we assert that the vector we get returned is the one we expect, which we've defined as part of the test's data in the solution variable ❶.

We're now ready to implement the last part to complete Cholesky's method: the resolution of the upper system. Open the *cholesky.py* file again and enter the solve_upper_sys function in Listing 14-8.

```
--snip--

def solve_upper_sys(up_matrix: Matrix, vector: Vector):
    size = vector.length
    last_index = size - 1
    solution = Vector(size)

❶  for i in range(last_index, -1, -1):
        _sum = 0.0

❷      for j in range(i + 1, size):
❸          u_ij = up_matrix.value_transposed_at(i, j)
            x_j = solution.value_at(j)
            _sum += u_ij * x_j

        y_i = vector.value_at(i)
❹      u_ii = up_matrix.value_transposed_at(i, i)
❺      solution_val = (y_i - _sum) / u_ii
        solution.set_value(solution_val, i)

    return solution
```

Listing 14-8: Solving the upper system

This function is similar to the previous solve_lower_sys function. We start by initializing the solution vector, solution, with the same size as the passed-in `low_vector`. This time, as we'll iterate starting from the last row, we save its index in the `last_index` variable.

The loop that iterates through all row indices goes from `last_index` all the way down to −1 (noninclusive) ❶. The inner loop going from $i + 1$ to size (again, noninclusive) computes the sum of the $u_{i,j}x_j$ products ❷. To obtain `u_ij`, we ask the lower-triangular matrix for the value as if it were transposed ❸. Thanks to this neat trick, we avoid transposing $[L]$, a process that is computationally expensive. This is the optimization we talked about in the previous chapter.

To get the divisor in Equation 14.10, we use the `value_transposed_at` function again ❹. With this value we can already compute the solution at each row ❺ and store it in the result vector.

Run all the tests in the file to check whether the implementation is bug-free. Just for your reference, Listing 14-9 is the complete *cholesky.py*.

```python
import math

from eqs.matrix import Matrix
from eqs.vector import Vector


def cholesky_solve(sys_mat: Matrix, sys_vec: Vector) -> Vector:
    validate_system(sys_mat, sys_vec)

    low_matrix = lower_matrix_decomposition(sys_mat)
    low_solution = solve_lower_sys(low_matrix, sys_vec)
    return solve_upper_sys(low_matrix, low_solution)


def validate_system(sys_matrix: Matrix, sys_vector: Vector):
    if sys_matrix.cols_count != sys_vector.length:
        raise ValueError('Size mismatch between matrix and vector')

    if not sys_matrix.is_square:
        raise ValueError('System matrix must be square')


def lower_matrix_decomposition(sys_mat: Matrix) -> Matrix:
    size = sys_mat.rows_count
    low_mat = Matrix(size, size)

    for i in range(size):
        sq_sum = 0

        for j in range(i + 1):
            m_ij = sys_mat.value_at(i, j)

            if i == j:
```

```
                    # main diagonal value
                    diag_val = math.sqrt(m_ij - sq_sum)
                    low_mat.set_value(diag_val, i, j)

                else:
                    # value under main diagonal
                    non_diag_sum = 0
                    for k in range(j):
                        l_ik = low_mat.value_at(i, k)
                        l_jk = low_mat.value_at(j, k)
                        non_diag_sum += l_ik * l_jk

                    l_jj = low_mat.value_at(j, j)
                    non_diag_val = (m_ij - non_diag_sum) / l_jj
                    sq_sum += non_diag_val * non_diag_val

                    low_mat.set_value(non_diag_val, i, j)

        return low_mat


def solve_lower_sys(low_mat: Matrix, vector: Vector):
    size = vector.length
    solution = Vector(size)

    for i in range(size):
        _sum = 0.0

        for j in range(i):
            l_ij = low_mat.value_at(i, j)
            y_j = solution.value_at(j)
            _sum += l_ij * y_j

        b_i = vector.value_at(i)
        l_ii = low_mat.value_at(i, i)
        solution_val = (b_i - _sum) / l_ii
        solution.set_value(solution_val, i)

    return solution


def solve_upper_sys(up_matrix: Matrix, vector: Vector):
    size = vector.length
    last_index = size - 1
    solution = Vector(size)

    for i in range(last_index, -1, -1):
```

```
        _sum = 0.0

        for j in range(i + 1, size):
            u_ij = up_matrix.value_transposed_at(i, j)
            x_j = solution.value_at(j)
            _sum += u_ij * x_j

        y_i = vector.value_at(i)
        u_ii = up_matrix.value_transposed_at(i, i)
        solution_val = (y_i - _sum) / u_ii
        solution.set_value(solution_val, i)

    return solution
```

Listing 14-9: Cholesky method result

Each of the three subfunctions that take part in the resolution of a system of equations using Cholesky's method has been tested separately: we can be sure those work properly. Does this mean that the cholesky_solve function is free of bugs itself? Not necessarily. We may still make mistakes when putting all those well-tested functions together.

Checking that the cholesky_solve function works as a whole requires one more test. This a test that ensures that each of the subfunctions behaves well when combined; it's called an *integration test*.

Testing Cholesky: An Integration Test

Open your *cholesky_test.py* file one last time. Let's add a final test (shown in Listing 14-10).

```
import unittest

from eqs.cholesky import lower_matrix_decomposition, \
    solve_lower_sys, solve_upper_sys, cholesky_solve
from eqs.matrix import Matrix
from eqs.vector import Vector


class CholeskyTest(unittest.TestCase):
    sys_matrix = Matrix(4, 4).set_data([
        4, -2, 4, 2,
        -2, 10, -2, -7,
        4, -2, 8, 4,
        2, -7, 4, 7
    ])
    low_matrix = Matrix(4, 4).set_data([
        2, 0, 0, 0,
        -1, 3, 0, 0,
        2, 0, 2, 0,
```

```
        1, -2, 1, 1
    ])
    sys_vec = Vector(4).set_data([20, -16, 40, 28])
    low_solution = Vector(4).set_data([10, -2, 10, 4])
    solution = Vector(4).set_data([1, 2, 3, 4])

    def test_lower_matrix_decomposition(self):
        actual = lower_matrix_decomposition(self.sys_matrix)
        self.assertEqual(self.low_matrix, actual)

    def test_lower_system_resolution(self):
        actual = solve_lower_sys(self.low_matrix, self.sys_vec)
        self.assertEqual(self.low_solution, actual)

    def test_upper_system_resolution(self):
        actual = solve_upper_sys(
            self.low_matrix,
            self.low_solution
        )
        self.assertEqual(self.solution, actual)

    def test_solve_system(self):
        actual = cholesky_solve(self.sys_matrix, self.sys_vec)
        self.assertEqual(self.solution, actual)
```

Listing 14-10: Testing the Cholesky decomposition method

Listing 14-10 is the resulting test file. We included the last test: test_solve
_system. This test exercises the Cholesky algorithm as a whole by calling
cholesky_solve.

Run all the tests in the file. If all four tests pass, you got all the code
right. You should be proud of yourself for following along with the code in
this long chapter. Congratulations!

If you want to run the tests from the command line, use this:

```
$ python3 -m unittest eqs/tests/cholesky_test.py
```

Summary

In this chapter, we discussed numerical methods and then centered the discussion around those that solve linear systems of equations. In particular, we
analyzed the Cholesky decomposition method. This $[L][U]$ decomposition
algorithm works with symmetric, positive-definite matrices and can be twice
as fast as other $[L][U]$ alternatives.

We paid special attention to the code's readability. To make the algorithm easy to follow, we broke it down into smaller functions, each of which
was tested separately. We started writing the test before the main algorithm's

logic, a technique referred to as test-driven development. We included one last test integrating the complete resolution of a system of equations.

We've implemented a powerful resolution algorithm, and we'll put it to work in Part V of the book.

PART V

TRUSS STRUCTURES

15

STRUCTURAL MODELS

In this part of the book, we'll focus on solving truss structures. Truss structures are used to support the roof of industrial warehouses (see Figure 15-1) and long-span bridges. This is a real engineering problem that is a good example of building an application that reads data from a file, builds a model out of that data, solves a system of linear equations, and presents the results graphically in a diagram.

Since solving truss structures is a big topic, we'll break it down into several chapters. This first one will give you a rough introduction to the basics of mechanics of materials; it's not meant to explain the concepts from scratch but should serve as a refresher. Once we've gone through the basics, we'll implement two classes to model truss structures: nodes and bars. As we've seen in earlier chapters, the first step of solving a problem in code is to have a set of primitives that represent the entities involved in the solution.

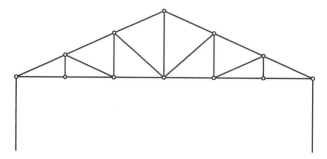

Figure 15-1: A warehouse roof is a good example
of a truss structure.

Solving Structural Problems

Let's begin with a few definitions. A *structure* is a set of resistant elements
built to withstand the external application of loads, as well as their own weight.
A *truss structure* is a structure in which the resistant elements are bars joined
by pins in both ends, and the external forces are applied only where those
bars join: at the nodes.

When working out a structural problem, we're most interested in two
things. First, can the bars of the structure handle the forces acting on them
and avoid collapse? Second, how big are the displacements of the structure
once it's deformed under the action of the external loads? The first is an
obvious concern: if any of the bars in the structure break, the structure
may collapse, which could have catastrophic consequences (think: collaps-
ing warehouse roofs or bridges). Our analysis should make sure this never
happens.

The second concern is less obvious, but important nevertheless. If a
structure is deformed enough for the naked eye to notice, even if the structure is safe and won't collapse, people around or below it may get anxious.
Think about how you would feel if you saw your living room's ceiling noticeably curved. Keeping the deformation of the structure between some limits
impacts the comfort of its users.

The solution we're after should include the amount of stress on each
bar, as well as the global displacements of the structure. We'll code up the
actual solution in the next chapter; here, we'll define the solution model.
We can expect our solution model to include these two quantities: the
amount of mechanical stress on each bar and the node displacements.

Before we can do that, though, we'll need to dive into the world of structural analysis. Be prepared to write lots of code. We're about to solve a serious engineering problem, so the payoff for our hard work will be high.

Structural Member Internal Forces

Let's begin by quickly recapping how elastic bodies respond to the application of external forces. This is a topic typically taught in mechanics of materials, a classic subject in mechanical engineering courses. If you've exten-

sively studied this subject, feel free to skip this section or browse through it as a refresher. If not, this section is for you. Your mechanics knowledge should be enough to follow the text, but we can't possibly cover everything in detail. You can refer to [3], one of my all-time favorites on the subject. Books on statics also cover this topic with some detail. I recommend you take a look at [9] or [11].

Elastic Bodies Subject to External Forces

Let's use an I beam as an example of an elastic body and apply an external system of balanced forces to it. These are forces whose sum equals zero: $\sum \vec{F}_i = 0$. Figure 15-2 shows the beam.

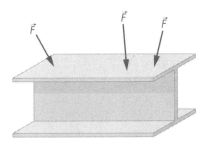

Figure 15-2: A beam subject to external forces

When external forces are applied to this elastic body, its atoms will fight back in an attempt to preserve the relative distances between themselves. If the external loads want to separate the atoms, they'll try to hold each other tighter. If they're pushed together, they'll try not to get too close. This "fighting back" makes up the *internal forces*: forces inside the body itself that exist in response to the application of external forces.

To study the effects of these forces on the body, let's take our beam from Figure 15-2 and virtually cut it with a plane, like in Figure 15-3.

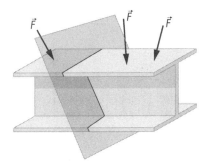

Figure 15-3: A section of a beam subject to external forces

Let's remove the right chunk of the beam and analyze what happens in the left part's cross section. Since the entire beam was in static equilibrium before we cut it, the left chunk should be in static equilibrium as well. To preserve this equilibrium, we must account for the distribution of internal forces that the now removed right chunk exerted on the left one. These forces appear because the atoms in the left chunk have been separated from their neighbors in the right chunk. The force that pulled them together needs to be added to the cut section so that the atoms stay in the same equilibrium state as before.

These forces are distributed over the whole cut surface and represented in Figure 15-4.

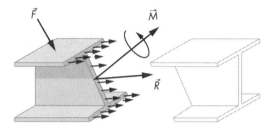

Figure 15-4: Analyzing equilibrium in a section

The distribution of forces over an area is referred to as *stress*. The net effect of the stress can be substituted with an equivalent system of a resulting force $\vec{R}$ and moment $\vec{M}$. Each of the components of this equivalent force and moment produces a different effect on the beam. Let's break the components down.

Axial and Shear Forces

The equivalent internal force $\vec{R}$ can be broken down into an equivalent system of two forces, one that is normal to the section, $\vec{R}_N$, and one tangent to it, $\vec{R}_T$ (see Figure 15-5).

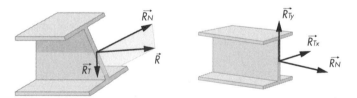

Figure 15-5: Equivalent internal forces in the section of a beam

If the elastic body has a prismatic shape (one of its sides is considerably longer than the other two) and we cut a section normal to its directrix, the resulting normal force $\vec{R}_N$ we obtain is referred to as the *axial force*. The name reflects the fact that this force is aligned with the prism's main axis or directrix. Prismatic bodies are common in structural analysis; beams and columns are good examples.

The axial force can either elongate or compress the body. An axial force that pulls the body apart is called a *tension force*, whereas one that compresses it is known as a *compression force*. Figure 15-6 shows two prismatic bodies subject to these forces.

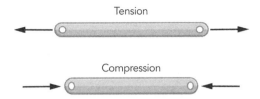

Figure 15-6: Tension and compression forces

The *shear force* is the force tangent to the cross section (see Figure 15-7) and thus can be further decomposed into two components: $\vec{R}_{Tx}$ and $\vec{R}_{Ty}$ (see the diagram on the right of Figure 15-5). These two components have the same effect: they try to shear the body apart. Figure 15-7 shows the effect of shearing forces applied to a prismatic body.

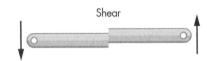

Figure 15-7: Shear force

In summary, the equivalent internal force in a cross section of the body may have a normal component that either elongates or compresses it; it may also have a tangent component that shears it. These are the two ways internal forces can produce deformations on a body.

Bending and Torsional Moments

We studied the possible effects of the resulting internal force on a given cross section. What effects does the resulting moment produce? As you can see in Figure 15-8, the resulting moment $\vec{M}$ can be decomposed into a moment normal to the cross section, $\vec{M}_N$, and a moment tangent to it, $\vec{M}_T$.

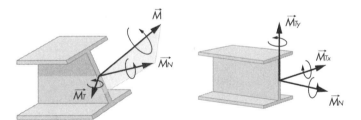

Figure 15-8: Equivalent internal moments in the section of a beam

These moments bend the body in arbitrary ways, but if we choose a prismatic body and cut it normal to its directrix (the same thing that we did with the forces), the moments we obtain have a predictable and well-defined effect. The moment normal to the surface, $\vec{M}_N$, generates a torsional (twisting) effect on the prism and thus receives the name of *torsional moment*.

Once again, the moment tangent to the section can be further broken down into two subcomponents: $\vec{M}_{Tx}$ and $\vec{M}_{Ty}$ (see the right illustration in

Figure 15-8). These two moments have a similar effect: they bend the prism and hence are called *bending moments*. Figure 15-9 illustrates this effect.

Figure 15-9: Bending moment

To summarize, the equivalent internal moment on a cross section of the body may have a normal component that tends to twist it around its directrix (the torsional moment) and may also have two tangent moments that tend to bend the prism (the bending moments).

Let's now analyze in detail how prismatic bars behave when subject to axial forces. Then, we'll see how, by using a group of these resistant prisms, we can build structures that can withstand the application of heavy loads.

Tension and Compression

Let's focus our analysis on axial forces: those aligned with the axis of a prismatic resistant body. As we'll see in the next section, the structures we'll solve are made of only prismatic elements (bars) subject to axial forces.

Hooke's Law

It's been experimentally proven that within some limits, the elongation of a prismatic bar is proportional to the axial force applied to it. This linear relation is known as *Hooke's law*. Let's suppose a bar with length l and cross section A is subject to a pair of external forces $\vec{F}$ and $-\vec{F}$, like in Figure 15-10.

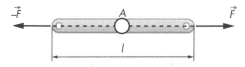

Figure 15-10: A bar subject to axial forces

Equation 15.1 gives Hooke's law.

$$\delta = \frac{Fl}{EA} \qquad (15.1)$$

In this equation,

δ is the total elongation of the bar.

F is the $\vec{F}$ force's magnitude.

E is the proportionality constant or Young's modulus, which is specific to the material.

Hooke's law states that the total elongation δ of a bar subject to a pair of external forces is (1) directly proportional to the magnitude of the forces and the bar's length and is (2) inversely proportional to its cross section and Young's modulus. The longer a bar or the stronger the force applied is, the greater the elongation produced will be. Conversely, the bigger the cross section values are or Young's modulus is, the smaller the elongation will be.

Recall that when a force is distributed over an area, the intensity of such force per unit area is known as *stress*. Stress is usually denoted by the Greek letter σ (see Equation 15.2).

$$\sigma = \frac{F}{A} \tag{15.2}$$

By convention, the stress is positive for tensile forces and negative for compression forces. The stress is a useful quantity in mechanical design; it's used to determine whether a given component (in a structure or machine, for example) will break down during operation. The stress values a given material can undergo before failure are well studied.

We define *strain* as the elongation per unit length, a dimensionless quantity denoted by the Greek letter ϵ (see Equation 15.3).

$$\epsilon = \frac{\delta}{l} \tag{15.3}$$

Using the equations for the stress and strain, Hooke's law from Equation 15.1 can be rewritten as shown in Equation 15.4.

$$\sigma = E\epsilon \tag{15.4}$$

Interestingly, by introducing stress and strain, the relation between the external actions applied to a resistant body (forces) and their effects (elongations) no longer depends on the area or length of the body. We've effectively removed all dimensional parameters from the equation. The proportionality constant in Equation 15.4 (E) is Young's modulus, which is a characteristic of materials. For structural steels, for example, E is around 200 GPa, that is, $200 \cdot 10^9 \ Pa$. We can therefore predict the mechanical behavior of bodies by applying experimental results obtained for the material in use. To do this, we use *stress-strain diagrams*, which plot the stress versus the strain for a given material.

Stress-Strain Diagrams

Stress-strain diagrams plot the stress versus the strain for a given material and are obtained by performing tension or compression tests (see [3] for more details). We use these diagrams to predict the behavior of resistant bodies made of the same material. Recall that since we introduced the quantities stress and strain, every dimensional term has disappeared from Hooke's equation, meaning that once we've experimentally determined the strain and stress a material undergoes under a given load, we can use those results for any bodies made of the same material, regardless of their shape or size.

Figure 15-11 is a plot of the approximate stress-strain diagram for structural steels. Note this graph is not to scale.

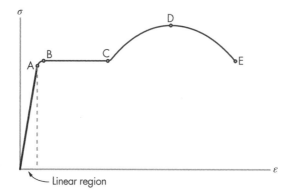

Figure 15-11: The stress-strain diagram for structural steel

This diagram has an initial linear region that holds up to a given stress value known as the *proportional limit*, depicted by point A. For stress values greater than the proportionality limit, the stress-strain relation is no longer linear. The proportional limit is typically between 210 MPa and 350 MPa for structural steels—three orders of magnitude smaller than Young's modulus. This region is modeled by Hooke's law and the linear relation $\sigma = E\epsilon$. We'll center our analysis here.

With a small stress increment after A, the proportional limit, we reach point B, the *yield stress* or *yield strength*. After the yield stress, big elongations happen without an increase in the stress. This phenomenon is called the *yielding* of the material.

After a noticeable amount of strain, we reach point C, and the material appears to harden. The stress must continue to increase to reach point D, which is the maximum amount of stress structural steel can withstand. We call this stress value the *ultimate stress* or *ultimate strength*. From this point, the material will acquire bigger strains with a reduction in the stress value.

The point E is where the material fractures. The amount of strain the material can take before it fractures can be called the *fracture strain*. This is the point of complete mechanical failure, but if you think about it, after the ultimate stress is reached (point D), it's likely that the material will fracture anyway. The ultimate stress is typically used as the maximum value of stress a given material can absorb before failure.

Now that we have a good understanding of how resistant bodies respond to tensile stresses, let's look at truss structures.

Plane Trusses

There are many structural typologies, but we'll focus our analysis on the simplest of them: plane trusses.

A *plane truss* structure is a structure contained in a plane whose resistant bodies are bars subject only to axial forces and whose own weight can be ignored. There are two conditions that allow this.

- Bars must be joined by pins at their ends.

- External loads must always be applied to nodes.

A *node* is the point where several bar ends meet. Nodes join bar ends together in frictionless unions, meaning the rotation of the bars around the node is not constrained.

Plane trusses are made of triangles: three bars pinned at their ends. The triangle is the simplest rigid frame; bars joined to form a polygon of four or more sides form nonrigid frames. Figure 15-12 shows how a plane truss made of four bars can be moved from its original position and thus isn't considered rigid. Simply by adding a new bar and creating two subtriangles, the structure becomes rigid.

Figure 15-12: Example of a polygonal plane truss

Figure 15-13 is an example of a plane truss. The structure is made of eight nodes (N1, N2, . . . , N8) and thirteen bars. Nodes 1 and 5 have external supports or constraints applied. Nodes 6, 7, and 8 have external loads applied to them.

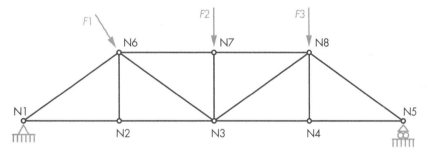

Figure 15-13: A plane truss structure

Figure 15-14 is the diagram resulting from the structural analysis of the plane truss described in Figure 15-13. It was produced by the very application we'll build in this part of the book.

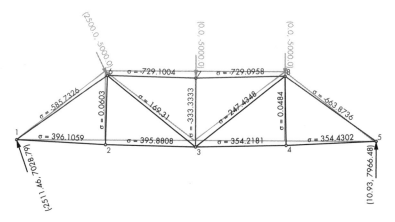

Figure 15-14: A plane truss structure solution diagram

In this diagram, we can appreciate the structure's deformed geometry because it has been scaled to be noticeable. Node displacements tend to be very small (around two orders of magnitude smaller than the dimension of the structural bars), so a diagram depicting the nonscaled node displacements may be hard to tell apart from the original geometry.

You'll notice there's a lot of information in Figure 15-14. Every bar is labeled with the stress it's subject to, though the font size of the labels in this figure is small, so the labels may not be easy to read. Positive numbers are tension stresses, and negative are compression. The bars are also colored in green or red depending on the load they're subject to: green for tension and red for compression. Since the book is printed in black and white, you won't be able to tell the colors apart, but once you've developed the complete application, you'll produce the figure with your own code and will be able to explore all the details in it.

Let's now study the mechanical response of the bars that make up plane trusses. They have an interesting particularity we've already mentioned: they develop axial stresses only.

Two-Force Members

As we've already discussed, plane truss bars are pinned at their ends, and loads are always applied at the nodes; because of this, the bars are subject only to axial forces. We can apply an external force only to the ends of the bar, using the contact of the pinned joint with the node. Because these unions are frictionless, they can only transmit forces to bars and just in the direction of the bar's directrix.

Figure 15-15 shows how an external force applied to a node is transferred to the bars. These forces are aligned with the bars' directrices and thus produce axial stresses only.

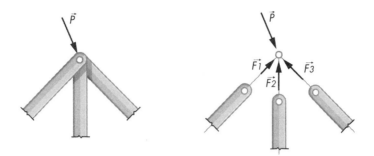

Figure 15-15: The transmission of forces in a node

Since bars have two pinned ends where external forces are applied, they are subject to two forces. To be in equilibrium, such a body requires the two forces to be collinear, equal in magnitude and with opposite directions. In the case of a bar (a long prismatic body), these two forces have to be in the direction of the bar's directrix (Figure 15-16) and, hence, produce axial stresses only. We call these bars with two collinear forces applied *two-force members* (see Figure 15-16).

Figure 15-16: A two-force member

The forces applied to the bar in Figure 15-16 are labeled $\vec{F}$ and $-\vec{F}$ to signify that the two forces must be equal in magnitude and point in opposite directions. In this case, the forces would produce tension stresses on the bar.

Thanks to Hooke's law, we know how materials respond to the external application of loads. We've also explored two-force members, and we've seen that the bars in plane trusses are two-force members. Let's now derive a set of equations to relate these two forces with the displacements they produce on such two-force members.

Stiffness Matrices in Global Coordinates

Going back to the original formulation of Hooke's law in Equation 15.1, we can isolate the force term to get the following:

$$F = \frac{EA}{l} \delta$$

Here, the term $\frac{EA}{l}$ is the bar's proportionality constant relating the force applied, F, with the elongation it produces, δ. This term also receives the name *stiffness*. As you can see, the stiffness depends on the bar's Young's modulus (E), which is material dependent, and geometry (A and l).

Now look at the bar in Figure 15-17. If we consider a local system of reference whose x-axis is aligned with the bar directrix, this bar has two *degrees of freedom (DOF)*, in other words, two different ways it can independently move. These are the displacements in the local x-axis of both nodes, denoted by u'_1 and u'_2. Each node has a force applied: F_1 and F_2.

NOTE

A note on the nomenclature: we'll use primes to label DOFs referred to by the bar's local system of coordinates. For example, u_1' refers to the x displacement of the node 1 referred to the bar's local system of reference: (x', y'). By contrast, nonprime values, such as u_1, are referred to the global system of reference: (x, y).

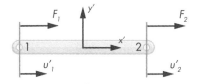

Figure 15-17: A bar with two degrees of freedom

Using the previous equation, we can relate the force in each node to the displacements u_1' and u_2' like so:

$$\begin{cases} F_1 = \frac{EA}{l}(u_1' - u_2') \\ F_2 = \frac{EA}{l}(u_2' - u_1') \end{cases}$$

The two equations above can be written in matrix notation (Equation 15.5),

$$\begin{bmatrix} F_1 \\ F_2 \end{bmatrix} = \underbrace{\frac{EA}{l} \begin{bmatrix} 1 & -1 \\ -1 & 1 \end{bmatrix}}_{[k']} \begin{bmatrix} u_1' \\ u_2' \end{bmatrix} \tag{15.5}$$

where $[k']$ is referred to as the local *stiffness matrix* for the bar. This stiffness matrix relates the displacements in the two nodes of the bar with the external forces applied to them, all in the bar's local system of reference. Using this local system of reference, the bar has only two degrees of freedom, which are the displacements of each of the two nodes in the local x-axis direction (u_1' and u_2').

Let's now consider a bar rotated with respect to the global system of coordinates. Take Figure 15-18 as an example. This bar has its own local system of reference (x', y'), which forms an angle of θ with respect to the global system of reference (x, y).

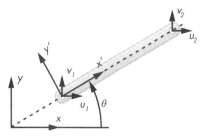

Figure 15-18: A bar's local reference frame

From the global system of reference's perspective, each node of the bar has two degrees of freedom: each node can move in both the x and y directions. Projected in this system of reference, the four DOFs are u_1, v_1, u_2, and v_2.

To transform the bar's local stiffness matrix $[k']$ into a global $[k]$ stiffness matrix, we have to apply a transformation matrix. We can find such a matrix by breaking down the local displacements u'_1 and u'_2 into their global components. Figure 15-19 shows this operation.

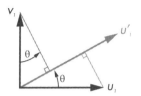

Figure 15-19: The local displacement projections

Let's find a mathematical expression to compute the global displacements based on their local counterparts:

$$\begin{cases} u'_1 = \cos\theta \cdot u_1 + \sin\theta \cdot v_1 \\ u'_2 = \cos\theta \cdot u_2 + \sin\theta \cdot v_2 \end{cases}$$

Written in its matrix form, it looks like

$$\begin{bmatrix} u'_1 \\ u'_2 \end{bmatrix} = \underbrace{\begin{bmatrix} \cos\theta & \sin\theta & 0 & 0 \\ 0 & 0 & \cos\theta & \sin\theta \end{bmatrix}}_{[L]} \begin{bmatrix} u_1 \\ v_1 \\ u_2 \\ v_2 \end{bmatrix}$$

where $[L]$ is the transformation matrix. To compute the global stiffness matrix from the local $[k']$, we can use the following equation (refer to [2] or [10] for the details on how to derive this expression),

$$[k] = [L]'[k'][L]$$

which, shortening the notation to $c = \cos\theta$ and $s = \sin\theta$, yields Equation 15.6.

$$[k] = \frac{EA}{l} \begin{bmatrix} c^2 & cs & -c^2 & -cs \\ cs & s^2 & -cs & -s^2 \\ -c^2 & -cs & c^2 & cs \\ -cs & -s^2 & cs & s^2 \end{bmatrix} \tag{15.6}$$

We now have a system of equations that relates the external forces applied to a bar's nodes to their displacements in global coordinates (see Equation 15.7).

$$\begin{bmatrix} F_{1x} \\ F_{1y} \\ F_{2x} \\ F_{2y} \end{bmatrix} = \frac{EA}{l} \begin{bmatrix} c^2 & cs & -c^2 & -cs \\ cs & s^2 & -cs & -s^2 \\ -c^2 & -cs & c^2 & cs \\ -cs & -s^2 & cs & s^2 \end{bmatrix} \begin{bmatrix} u_1 \\ v_1 \\ u_2 \\ v_2 \end{bmatrix} \tag{15.7}$$

Let's now use this knowledge to start building our structural model in code.

Original Structure Model

In our *Mechanics* project, create a new Python package named *structures*. In *structures*, create another package: *model*. Here's where we'll define the classes that make up the structural model. Create another package in *structures* named *solution*. This is where we'll have the classes that model the resolved structure. Also create a *tests* folder in *structures* to contain the unit tests we'll develop. Your project's structure should look something like this:

```
Mechanics
  |- apps
  |- eqs
  |- geom2d
  |- graphic
  |- structures
  |    |- model
  |    |    |- __init__.py
  |    |- solution
  |    |    |- __init__.py
  |    |- tests
  |    |    |- __init__.py
  |    |- __init__.py
  |- utils
```

The next step is to create a class that represents structural nodes.

The Node Class

Create a new file in *model* named *node.py* and enter the code in Listing 15-1. This is the basic definition for a structural node.

```python
import operator
from functools import reduce

from geom2d import Point, Vector


class StrNode:

    def __init__(
        self,
      ❶ _id: int,
        position: Point,
        loads=None,
        dx_constrained=False,
        dy_constrained=False
```

```
    ):
        self.id = _id
        self.position = position
❷     self.loads = loads or []
        self.dx_constrained = dx_constrained
        self.dy_constrained = dy_constrained

    @property
    def loads_count(self):
        return len(self.loads)

    @property
    def net_load(self):
❸     return reduce(
            operator.add,
            self.loads,
            Vector(0, 0)
        )
```

Listing 15-1: Structure node class

In this listing, we define the new class StrNode. This class defines an id, which will serve to identify each of its instances.

Note that the parameter passed to the constructor uses an underscore: _id ❶. Python already has an id global function defined, so if we named our parameter the same (instead of using the underscore), we'd be shadowing the global id function definition inside the constructor. This means id wouldn't refer to Python's function inside the constructor but to our passed-in value instead. Although we're not using Python's id function inside this class's constructor, we'll try to avoid shadowing global functions.

The StrNode also includes an instance of the Point class that determines the node's position and a list of loads applied to the node with a default value of None. The structure may have quite a few nodes without external loads applied to them; thus, we make the loads argument optional (and provide a default value of None). When the loads argument is None, we assign the self.loads attribute an empty list ([]) ❷.

You might be wondering how the or operator works in ❷:

```
self.loads = loads or []
```

The or operator returns the first "truthy" value from its operands or None. Take a look at the following examples:

```
>>> 'Hello' or 'Good bye'
'Hello'

>>> None or 'Good bye'
'Good bye'
```

```
>>> False or True
True

>>> False or 'Hello'
'Hello'

>>> False or None
# nothing returned here

>>> False or None or 'Hi'
'Hi'
```

As you might have guessed, in a boolean context, None is evaluated as "falsy."

There are two more attributes that we have to pass the constructor; these are given a default value in the constructor: dx_constrained and dy _constrained. These attributes determine whether the displacements in the x and y directions are externally constrained. We initialize them as False, which means the node isn't externally constrained unless we say otherwise.

We've defined two properties in the class: loads_count and net_load. The first, loads_count, simply returns the length of the loads list.

NOTE   *If you remember the law of Demeter from Chapter 5, anyone from outside the StrNode class who wants to know the number of loads applied to the node should be able to ask StrNode directly. But asking StrNode to return the list of loads and then use the len function to get its length would violate this important principle.*

The net_load property uses reduce to compute the sum of all the loads ❸. Note that we're passing in a third argument to the reduce function: Vector(0, 0). This third argument is the initial value for the reduction. In the perfectly valid case that the list of loads is empty, we'll return this initial value. Otherwise, the first step in the reduction process will combine this initial value with the list's first item. If we didn't provide an initial value, reducing the loads list would raise the following error:

```
TypeError: reduce() of empty sequence with no initial value
```

Next, we'll add a method to add loads to the node's list of loads; enter the method in Listing 15-2.

```
class StrNode:
    --snip--

    def add_load(self, load: Vector):
        self.loads.append(load)
```

Listing 15-2: Adding loads to the node

Lastly, let's implement the equality comparison for the StrNode class. There are a few attributes in the class, but we'll consider two nodes equal only if they are located at equal positions in the plane. This comparison deems overlapping nodes to be equal, regardless of their other attributes.

If we want nodes in a structure to be truly unique, we could rely on an equality comparison that compares all of the attributes of a node, including the list of loads and external constraints. In our case, we're interested only in making sure that we have no overlapping nodes, though. If we included more fields in the equality check, it could happen that two overlapping nodes (nodes with the same position) were evaluated as different because they have a different list of loads. We'd be allowing two overlapping nodes to exist in the structure.

Enter the __eq__ method implementation in Listing 15-3.

```
class StrNode:
    --snip--

    def __eq__(self, other):
        if self is other:
            return True

        if not isinstance(other, StrNode):
            return False

        return self.position == other.position
```

Listing 15-3: Nodes equality

Our StrNode class is now ready! Listing 15-4 contains the resulting StrNode class.

```
import operator
from functools import reduce

from geom2d import Point, Vector


class StrNode:

    def __init__(
            self,
            _id: int,
            position: Point,
            loads=None,
            dx_constrained=False,
            dy_constrained=False
    ):
        self.id = _id
        self.position = position
        self.loads = loads or []
        self.dx_constrained = dx_constrained
```

```
        self.dy_constrained = dy_constrained

    @property
    def loads_count(self):
        return len(self.loads)

    @property
    def net_load(self):
        return reduce(
            operator.add,
            self.loads,
            Vector(0, 0)
        )

    def add_load(self, load: Vector):
        self.loads.append(load)

    def __eq__(self, other):
        if self is other:
            return True

        if not isinstance(other, StrNode):
            return False

        return self.position == other.position
```

Listing 15-4: Node class result

Let's now implement a class to represent structural bars.

The Bar Class

Structural bars are defined between two nodes modeled by the StrNode class. Bars need to store values for the two resistant properties required for the stiffness matrix calculation (Equation 15.6): the Young's modulus and cross section.

Implementing the Bar Class

In *model* create a new file named *bar.py* and enter the initial definition for the StrBar class (Listing 15-5).

```
from geom2d import Segment
from .node import StrNode


class StrBar:

    def __init__(
            self,
```

```
        _id: int,
        start_node: StrNode,
        end_node: StrNode,
        cross_section: float,
        young_mod: float
    ):
        self.id = _id
        self.start_node = start_node
        self.end_node = end_node
        self.cross_section = cross_section
        self.young_mod = young_mod

    @property
    def geometry(self):
        return Segment(
            self.start_node.position,
            self.end_node.position
        )

    @property
    def length(self):
        return self.geometry.length
```

Listing 15-5: Structure bar class

In this listing we define the StrBar class with five attributes: the ID that serves as identifier, the start and end nodes, the cross section value, and the Young's modulus value. These are passed in to the constructor and stored inside the class.

We also define two properties using the @property decorator: geometry and length. The geometry of the bar is a segment going from the start node position to the end node position, and the length of the bar is this segment's length.

The last thing we need to implement is a method to compute the bar's stiffness matrix in global coordinates as defined in Equation 15.6. Enter the method in Listing 15-6.

```
from eqs import Matrix
from geom2d import Segment
from .node import StrNode


class StrBar:
    --snip--

    def global_stiffness_matrix(self) -> Matrix:
        direction = self.geometry.direction_vector
        eal = self.young_mod * self.cross_section / self.length
        c = direction.cosine
```

```
s = direction.sine

c2_eal = (c ** 2) * eal
s2_eal = (s ** 2) * eal
sc_eal = (s * c) * eal

return Matrix(4, 4).set_data([
    c2_eal, sc_eal, -c2_eal, -sc_eal,
    sc_eal, s2_eal, -sc_eal, -s2_eal,
    -c2_eal, -sc_eal, c2_eal, sc_eal,
    -sc_eal, -s2_eal, sc_eal, s2_eal
])
```

Listing 15-6: Bar stiffness matrix in global coordinates

Don't forget to import Matrix, shown here:

```
from eqs import Matrix
```

We've added the global_stiffness_matrix method. This method creates a 4×4 matrix and sets its values to the appropriate stiffness terms as given in Equation 15.6 and repeated here for convenience:

$$[k] = \frac{EA}{l} \begin{bmatrix} c^2 & cs & -c^2 & -cs \\ cs & s^2 & -cs & -s^2 \\ -c^2 & -cs & c^2 & cs \\ -cs & -s^2 & cs & s^2 \end{bmatrix}$$

To compute each of the values, we first get the bar geometry's direction vector and get its sine and cosine. Because every term in $[k]$ is multiplied by $\frac{EA}{l}$, we compute it and store the result in the eal variable. From the sixteen terms in the matrix, there are really only three different values we need to compute. These are stored in c2_eal, s2_eal, and sc_eal, and they are later referenced in the set_data method.

Testing the Bar Class

The stiffness matrix computation is core to our structural analysis problem; a bug in this code would result in completely incorrect results, like, for instance, huge deformations in the bars. Let's add a unit test to make sure all the terms in the stiffness matrix are computed correctly. We first need to create a new test file in the *structures/tests* directory named *bar_test.py*. In the file, enter the code in Listing 15-7.

```
import unittest
from math import sqrt

from eqs import Matrix
from geom2d import Point
from structures.model.node import StrNode
from structures.model.bar import StrBar
```

```
class BarTest(unittest.TestCase):
    section = sqrt(5)
    young = 5

    node_a = StrNode(1, Point(0, 0))
    node_b = StrNode(2, Point(2, 1))
    bar = StrBar(1, node_a, node_b, section, young)

    def test_global_stiffness_matrix(self):
        expected = Matrix(4, 4).set_data([
            4, 2, -4, -2,
            2, 1, -2, -1,
            -4, -2, 4, 2,
            -2, -1, 2, 1
        ])
        actual = self.bar.global_stiffness_matrix()
        self.assertEqual(expected, actual)
```

Listing 15-7: Testing the bar's stiffness matrix

In this test we create a bar with nodes located at $(0, 0)$ and $(2, 1)$, a section of $\sqrt{5}$, and a Young's modulus of 5. We chose these numbers so all the values in the expected stiffness matrix would be integers, which makes it convenient for us to write the assertion, particularly in this case: $\sin \theta = \frac{1}{\sqrt{5}}$, $\cos \theta = \frac{2}{\sqrt{5}}$, and $\frac{EA}{l} = \frac{5\sqrt{5}}{\sqrt{5}} = 5$.

You can run the test from the IDE by clicking the green play button or from the shell.

```
$ python3 -m unittest structures/tests/bar_test.py
```

This should produce the following output:

```
Ran 1 test in 0.000s
```

```
OK
```

Your StrBar class should look similar to Listing 15-8.

```
from eqs import Matrix
from geom2d import Segment
from .node import StrNode


class StrBar:

    def __init__(
            self,
```

```
                _id: int,
                start_node: StrNode,
                end_node: StrNode,
                cross_section: float,
                young_mod: float
        ):
            self.id = _id
            self.start_node = start_node
            self.end_node = end_node
            self.cross_section = cross_section
            self.young_mod = young_mod

        @property
        def geometry(self):
            return Segment(
                self.start_node.position,
                self.end_node.position
            )

        @property
        def length(self):
            return self.geometry.length

        def global_stiffness_matrix(self) -> Matrix:
            direction = self.geometry.direction_vector
            eal = self.young_mod * self.cross_section / self.length
            c = direction.cosine
            s = direction.sine

            c2_eal = (c ** 2) * eal
            s2_eal = (s ** 2) * eal
            sc_eal = (s * c) * eal

            return Matrix(4, 4).set_data([
                c2_eal, sc_eal, -c2_eal, -sc_eal,
                sc_eal, s2_eal, -sc_eal, -s2_eal,
                -c2_eal, -sc_eal, c2_eal, sc_eal,
                -sc_eal, -s2_eal, sc_eal, s2_eal
            ])
```

Listing 15-8: Bar class result

We need one last class to bundle nodes and bars together: the structure itself.

The Structure Class

Create a new Python file named *structure.py* in *structures/model* and enter the Structure class's code (Listing 15-9).

```
from functools import reduce

from .node import StrNode
from .bar import StrBar


class Structure:
    def __init__(self, nodes: [StrNode], bars: [StrBar]):
        self.__bars = bars
        self.__nodes = nodes

    @property
    def nodes_count(self):
        return len(self.__nodes)

    @property
    def bars_count(self):
        return len(self.__bars)

    @property
    def loads_count(self):
        return reduce(
            lambda count, node: count + node.loads_count,
            self.__nodes,
            0
        )
```

Listing 15-9: Structure class

This class is quite simple at the moment, but in a later chapter, we'll write the code responsible for assembling the structure's global stiffness matrix, generating the system of equations, solving it, and creating the solution. For now, all the class does is store a list of nodes and a list of bars passed in to the constructor, along with a few computations that deal with the number of items it holds.

The loads_count property sums the load count from every node. To accomplish this, we pass a lambda function as the first argument to the reduce function. This lambda takes two arguments: the current count of loads and the next node in the self.__nodes list. This reduction requires an initial value (which is the third argument, the 0), which we add the first node's count to. Without this initial value, the reduction couldn't take place, because the reduce function wouldn't know what value the lambda's first parameter, count, had for the first iteration.

We now have the complete model that defines the structure!

Creating a Structure from the Python Shell

Let's try to construct the truss structure in Figure 15-20 using our model classes.

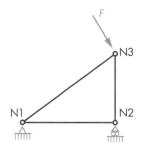

Figure 15-20: Example truss structure

To define the structure, first import the following classes in the Python shell:

```
>>> from geom2d import Point, Vector
>>> from structures.model.node import StrNode
>>> from structures.model.bar import StrBar
>>> from structures.model.structure import Structure
```

Then enter the following code:

```
>>> node_one = StrNode(1, Point(0, 0), None, True, True)
>>> node_two = StrNode(2, Point(100, 0), None, False, True)
>>> node_three = StrNode(3, Point(100, 100), (Vector(50, -100)))

>>> bar_one = (1, node_one, node_two, 20, 20000000)
>>> bar_two = (2, node_two, node_three, 20, 20000000)
>>> bar_three = (3, node_three, node_one, 20, 20000000)

>>> structure = Structure(
    (node_one, node_two, node_three),
    (bar_one, bar_two, bar_three)
)
```

As you can see, creating the model for a truss structure in code is a piece of cake. In any case, we'll most often load the model from an external definition file, as we'll learn in Chapter 17. Working an example by hand, nevertheless, is a great exercise to understand how our model classes work.

To finish this chapter, let's create the model for the structure's solution: the classes that will store the node displacements and bar stresses.

The Structure Solution Model

We'll tackle resolving the structure in the next chapter, but we'll prepare the classes to store the solution values here. For now, let's imagine we have the resolution algorithm ready and require the solution classes to store the solution's data.

When we resolve a structure, we first obtain the node displacements in global coordinates. From the new positions of the structure's nodes, we can compute all the rest (strains, stresses, and reaction values). We need a new class to represent displaced nodes, which are similar to the nodes we've just defined using the StrNode class, but with the addition of a displacement vector.

These node displacements will elongate or compress the structure's bars. Remember that bars develop strains and stresses, which are their mechanical response to being extended or compressed. The strain and stress values are important pieces of data in the structural solution: they'll determine whether the structure can withstand the loads applied to it.

We'll create a new class to represent the solution bars as well. This class will reference the displaced nodes and compute the strain and stress values.

The Solution Nodes

Let's create the class that represents nodes in the structure's solution. In the *structures/solution* package, create a new file named *node.py* and enter the code in Listing 15-10.

```
from geom2d import Vector
from structures.model.node import StrNode


class StrNodeSolution:
    def __init__(
            self,
            original_node: StrNode,
            global_disp: Vector
    ):
        self.__original_node = original_node
        self.global_disp = global_disp

    @property
❶ def id(self):
        return self.__original_node.id

    @property
❷ def original_pos(self):
        return self.__original_node.position

    @property
```

```
❸ def is_constrained(self):
        return self.__original_node.dx_constrained \
            or self.__original_node.dy_constrained

    @property
❹ def loads(self):
        return self.__original_node.loads

    @property
❺ def is_loaded(self):
        return self.__original_node.loads_count > 0

    @property
❻ def net_load(self):
        return self.__original_node.net_load
```

Listing 15-10: Solution node class

This listing declares the StrNodeSolution class. As you can see, this class's constructor gets passed the original node and its displacement vector in global coordinates—that's all we need. The original node is kept private to the class (__original_node), but some of its properties are exposed. For example, the id property ❶ simply returns the original node's ID, and the same goes for loads.

The original_pos property ❷ returns the original node's position: the position before applying the displacement obtained as part of the structure's resolution. The naming here is important, as we'll shortly add another property to expose the new position of the node after being displaced.

The is_constrained property ❸ checks whether the original node had any of its degrees of freedom (the displacement in x or y) externally constrained. We'll use this information to know whether a reaction force needs to be computed for the node or not. *Reaction forces* are those external forces exerted by the supports or constraints in a node. We want to know the magnitude of the force a support absorbs to properly design and dimension this support.

Lastly, we have three properties related to the external loads: loads ❹, is_loaded ❺, and net_load ❻. The first simply returns the original node's list of forces. We'll use this information when drawing the solution to a vector image like in Figure 15-14. Property is_loaded lets us know whether the node has any load applied. This property will be handy when we need to check which solution nodes have a load applied to them to draw those loads to the result diagram. Property net_load returns the original node's net load, which we'll use to compute the reaction force in the node.

Displaced Position

Let's include the displaced position as a property. Since displacements tend to be orders of magnitude smaller than the structure's dimensions, we'll want to include a method that scales the displacement vector to plot the resulting deformed geometry. This ensures that we'll be able to tell the deformed geometry apart from the original geometry in the resulting diagram.

Enter the code shown in Listing 15-11 in the StrNodeSolution class.

```
class StrNodeSolution:
    --snip--

    @property
    def displaced_pos(self):
        return self.original_pos.displaced(self.global_disp)

    def displaced_pos_scaled(self, scale=1):
        return self.original_pos.displaced(self.global_disp, scale)
```

Listing 15-11: Solution node displacement

The displaced_pos method returns the position of the original node after applying the global_disp vector to it. The displaced_pos_scaled method does something similar, but with a scale value that will allow us to increase the displacement's size.

The End Result

If you've followed along, your StrNodeSolution class should look like Listing 15-12.

```
from geom2d import Vector
from structures.model.node import StrNode


class StrNodeSolution:
    def __init__(
            self,
            original_node: StrNode,
            global_disp: Vector
    ):
        self.__original_node = original_node
        self.global_disp = global_disp

    @property
    def id(self):
        return self.__original_node.id

    @property
    def original_pos(self):
        return self.__original_node.position

    @property
    def is_constrained(self):
        return self.__original_node.dx_constrained \
```

```
            or self.__original_node.dy_constrained

    @property
    def loads(self):
        return self.__original_node.loads

    @property
    def is_loaded(self):
        return self.__original_node.loads_count > 0

    @property
    def displaced_pos(self):
        return self.original_pos.displaced(self.global_disp)

    def displaced_position_scaled(self, scale=1):
        return self.original_pos.displaced(self.global_disp, scale)
```

Listing 15-12: Solution node class result

Let's now implement the bar's solution class.

The Solution Bars

Knowing the displacements of a bar's nodes is all we need to compute its
strain and axial stress. We'll explain why this is as we develop the `StrBarSolution`
class.

Create a new file in *structures/solution* named *bar.py* and enter the code
in Listing 15-13.

```
from structures.model.bar import StrBar
from .node import StrNodeSolution


class StrBarSolution:
    def __init__(
            self,
            original_bar: StrBar,
            start_node: StrNodeSolution,
            end_node: StrNodeSolution
    ):
        if original_bar.start_node.id != start_node.id:
            raise ValueError('Wrong start node')

        if original_bar.end_node.id != end_node.id:
            raise ValueError('Wrong end node')

        self.__original_bar = original_bar
        self.start_node = start_node
        self.end_node = end_node
```

```
@property
def id(self):
    return self.__original_bar.id

@property
def cross_section(self):
    return self.__original_bar.cross_section

@property
def young_mod(self):
    return self.__original_bar.young_mod
```

Listing 15-13: Solution bar class

The StrBarSolution class is initialized with the original bar and the two solution nodes. In the constructor, we check that we got the correct solution nodes passed in by comparing their IDs with the original bar nodes' IDs. If we detect a wrong node is being passed, we raise a ValueError that will halt execution. If we continued executing the program, the results would be incorrect because the solution bar would be linked with nodes it wasn't connected to in the original definition of the structure. This will prevent us from making mistakes when constructing the structure's solution classes.

The class also defines the id, cross_section, and young_mod properties. These simply return the original bar's values.

Elongation, Stress, and Strain

Let's now work out the strain and stress values one step at a time. The stress can be derived from the strain (using Equation 15.4), so we'll start with the strain. The strain is the bar's elongation per unit of length (see Equation 15.3), so we need to find out this elongation value. For this, we first want to know both the bar's original and resulting geometries. Enter the properties shown in Listing 15-14.

```
from geom2d import Segment
from structures.model.bar import StrBar
from .node import StrNodeSolution


class StrBarSolution:
    --snip--

    @property
    def original_geometry(self):
        return self.__original_bar.geometry

    @property
    def final_geometry(self):
        return Segment(
```

```
        self.start_node.displaced_pos,
        self.end_node.displaced_pos
    )
```

Listing 15-14: Solution bar geometry

The original geometry was already a property in `StrBar`. The final geometry is also a segment, this time between the displaced start and end nodes. It's important to understand that since the bars of a truss structure are two-force members, they're only subject to axial forces. Thus, the directrix of the bars will always remain a straight segment. Figure 15-21 depicts the original bar and the deformed bar that results when displacing the position of the original nodes $\vec{u}_1$ and $\vec{u}_2$.

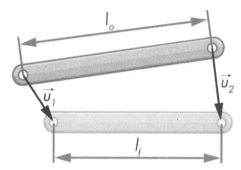

Figure 15-21: A bar's length increment

Assuming the original bar had a length of l_o and that l_f is the final length, the elongation of the bar is simply $\Delta l = l_f - l_o$. The elongation value will be positive if the bar stretches and negative if it compresses. Note that this agrees with our stress sign convention: positive for tension and negative for compression. Enter the properties in Listing 15-15.

```
class StrBarSolution:
    --snip--

    @property
    def original_length(self):
        return self.original_geometry.length

    @property
    def final_length(self):
        return self.final_geometry.length

    @property
    def elongation(self):
        return self.final_length - self.original_length
```

Listing 15-15: Solution bar length

Now that we know the bar's elongation, we can easily compute the strain and also the stress. Enter the strain and stress properties in the StrBarSolution class as in Listing 15-16.

```
class StrBarSolution:
    --snip--

    @property
    def strain(self):
        return self.elongation / self.original_length

    @property
    def stress(self):
        return self.young_mod * self.strain
```

Listing 15-16: Bar strain and stress

Finally! As you can see, the strain, given by Equation 15.3, is the quotient between the bar's elongation and the original length. With the strain value we can obtain the stress by simple multiplication with the material's Young's modulus. This is Hooke's law as formulated in Equation 15.4.

Internal Forces

To compute the reaction forces, we'll use the static equilibrium condition in each of the nodes: the net force in a node is always zero. In this sum of forces, every bar that is connected to the node exerts a force equal in value and opposite in direction to its internal force (this is illustrated in Figure 15-23). This internal force is computed as the bar's stress times its cross section (see Equation 15.2).

We need both the magnitude and the direction of the internal force in each of the bar's nodes, because, if you recall, for this two-force member to be in equilibrium, the forces in both ends need to have equal magnitude and opposite directions. Let's see how we'd go about doing this.

Enter the code in Listing 15-17.

```
from geom2d import Segment, make_vector_between
from structures.model.bar import StrBar
from .node import StrNodeSolution


class StrBarSolution:
    --snip--

    @property
    def internal_force_value(self):
        return self.stress * self.cross_section

    def force_in_node(self, node: StrNodeSolution):
      ❶ if node is self.start_node:
```

```
            return make_vector_between(
                self.end_node.displaced_pos,
                self.start_node.displaced_pos
            ).with_length(
                self.internal_force_value
            )
❷       elif node is self.end_node:
            return make_vector_between(
                self.start_node.displaced_pos,
                self.end_node.displaced_pos
            ).with_length(
                self.internal_force_value
            )

        raise ValueError(
            f'Bar {self.id} does not know about node {node.id}'
        )
```

Listing 15-17: Bar internal force

In this code, we first define the internal_force_value property, which yields the magnitude, positive or negative, of the internal force computed according to Equation 15.2.

Then comes the force_in_node method, which, given either the start or end node of the bar, returns the force vector in that node. The magnitude of the force vector is internal_force_value in both cases. It's the direction that changes depending on the passed-in node.

Our sign convention is that tension forces are considered positive and compression forces negative. If we choose the direction of the internal force to be positive in each of the nodes, the force vector will always have the correct direction. This is because later we'll give it a length of internal_force_value, which is negative for a compressing force, and, as you know, assigning a negative length to one of our Vector instances reverses its direction.

Look back at the code. If the passed-in node is the start node ❶, the force vector is created to go from the end node's final position to the start's. Then, the resulting vector is scaled according to internal_force_value.

Conversely, if the passed-in node is the end node ❷, the force vector is the opposite, but the scaling part remains the same.

Lastly, if the passed-in node is neither of the two bar nodes, we raise an error.

Bar Has Node?

We're almost done with the bar solution class; we just need two more methods, and our class will be ready. The first one checks whether any node in the structure is one of the end nodes in the bar. We'll use this method to draw the results. Enter the method in Listing 15-18.

```
class StrBarSolution:
    --snip--
```

```
    def has_node(self, node: StrNodeSolution):
        return node is self.start_node or node is self.end_node
```

Listing 15-18: Bar has node?

Lastly, we need a method to generate the bar's final geometry but with a scale applied to the displacements.

Scaled Final Geometry

If you remember, we already implemented a method in the StrNodeSolution class that yields its position with a scale applied to the displacement. Let's harness this implementation to build the segment representing the deformed bar's geometry with a scale applied. Enter the code in Listing 15-19.

```
class StrBarSolution:
    --snip--

    def final_geometry_scaling_displacement(self, scale: float):
        return Segment(
            self.start_node.displaced_pos_scaled(scale),
            self.end_node.displaced_pos_scaled(scale)
        )
```

Listing 15-19: Bar scaled geometry

The final_geometry_scaling_displacement method returns a segment whose end points are the bar nodes' final positions with a scale applied to the displacement vector. This is the segment we'll draw to the result plot to visualize how the original bar got displaced from its original position.

Again, because the displacements are fairly small compared to the size of the structure itself, we'll want to scale the node displacements so we can clearly see how the structure gets deformed in the solution diagram.

The End Result

If you followed along, your StrBarSolution should look like Listing 15-20.

```
from geom2d import Segment, make_vector_between
from structures.model.bar import StrBar
from .node import StrNodeSolution


class StrBarSolution:
    def __init__(
            self,
            original_bar: StrBar,
            start_node: StrNodeSolution,
            end_node: StrNodeSolution
    ):
        if original_bar.start_node.id != start_node.id:
```

```python
            raise ValueError('Wrong start node')

        if original_bar.end_node.id != end_node.id:
            raise ValueError('Wrong end node')

        self.__original_bar = original_bar
        self.start_node = start_node
        self.end_node = end_node

    @property
    def id(self):
        return self.__original_bar.id

    @property
    def cross_section(self):
        return self.__original_bar.cross_section

    @property
    def young_mod(self):
        return self.__original_bar.young_mod

    @property
    def original_geometry(self):
        return self.__original_bar.geometry

    @property
    def final_geometry(self):
        return Segment(
            self.start_node.displaced_pos,
            self.end_node.displaced_pos
        )

    @property
    def original_length(self):
        return self.original_geometry.length

    @property
    def final_length(self):
        return self.final_geometry.length

    @property
    def elongation(self):
        return self.final_length - self.original_length

    @property
    def strain(self):
        return self.elongation / self.original_length
```

```
@property
def stress(self):
    return self.young_mod * self.strain

@property
def internal_force_value(self):
    return self.stress * self.cross_section

def force_in_node(self, node: StrNodeSolution):
    if node is self.start_node:
        return make_vector_between(
            self.end_node.displaced_pos,
            self.start_node.displaced_pos
        ).with_length(
            self.internal_force_value
        )
    elif node is self.end_node:
        return make_vector_between(
            self.start_node.displaced_pos,
            self.end_node.displaced_pos
        ).with_length(
            self.internal_force_value
        )

    raise ValueError(
        f'Bar {self.id} does not know about node {node.id}'
    )

def has_node(self, node: StrNodeSolution):
    return node is self.start_node or node is self.end_node

def final_geometry_scaling_displacement(self, scale: float):
    return Segment(
        self.start_node.displaced_position_scaled(scale),
        self.end_node.displaced_position_scaled(scale)
    )
```

Listing 15-20: Solution bar class result

There's one last class we want to define: the structure solution.

The Structure Solution

Just as we had a class for the original structure model, we want a class representing the structure's solution. The goal of this class is to put the solution nodes and bars together.

Create a new file in the *structures/solution* folder named *structure.py*. In the file, enter the basic definition for the class (Listing 15-21).

```
from .bar import StrBarSolution
from .node import StrNodeSolution


class StructureSolution:
    def __init__(
            self,
            nodes: [StrNodeSolution],
            bars: [StrBarSolution]
    ):
        self.nodes = nodes
        self.bars = bars
```

Listing 15-21: Structure solution class

The StructureSolution class is initialized with the list of nodes and bars that make up the solution. This is similar to the original structure's definition. But because we're using this class to generate results—reports and diagrams—we'll need some additional attributes.

Structure Rectangular Bounds

When plotting the structural analysis results, we'll want to know how much space we need to draw the complete structure. Knowing the rectangular bounds of the entire structure will allow us to compute the viewBox for the SVG plot later. Let's compute these bounds and add in some margin as well (see Figure 15-22) so that there's some extra room for drawing things like the arrows that represent loads.

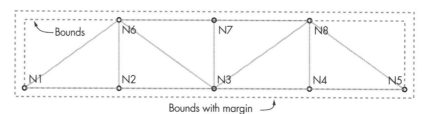

Figure 15-22: Bounding a structure

In the class, enter the bounds_rect method (Listing 15-22).

```
from geom2d import make_rect_containing_with_margin
from .bar import StrBarSolution
from .node import StrNodeSolution


class StructureSolution:
    --snip--

    def bounds_rect(self, margin: float, scale=1):
        d_pos = [
```

```
        node.displaced_pos_scaled(scale)
        for node in self.nodes
    ]
    return make_rect_containing_with_margin(d_pos, margin)
```

Listing 15-22: Structure graphical bounds

We first import the `make_rect_containing_with_margin` function. We implemented this function in Part II of the book; it creates a `Rect` primitive containing all the passed-in points, along with some margin.

The `bounds_rect` method we've written initializes the `d_pos` variable as a list with all the structure nodes' displaced positions and passes it to the function, which generates the rectangle. Note that we're using the scaled version of the displacements to make sure the rectangular bounds contain all the nodes in the positions where they'll be drawn.

Node Reaction Forces

Lastly, because the `StructureSolution` class has access to all the nodes and bars of the structure, it will be in charge of calculating the reaction forces for each of the nodes. The `StrNodeSolution` class couldn't do this computation itself, as it doesn't have access to the list of bars that meet in that node.

Now how do we go about computing the reaction force in a node? Let's suppose we have a node like that in Figure 15-23. Two bars, bar 1 and bar 2, meet in this node and are subject to internal forces $\vec{F}_1$ and $\vec{F}_2$, respectively. An external load $\vec{q}$ is applied to the node as well. This node is externally constrained, and $\vec{R}$ is the reaction force we're after.

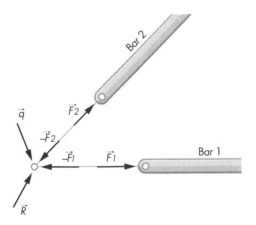

Figure 15-23: The reaction forces in a node

From these quantities, only $\vec{R}$ is unknown. The bar internal forces, $\vec{F}_1$ and $\vec{F}_2$, are computed using the `force_in_node` method we implemented in Listing 15-17, and the external load $\vec{q}$ is given as part of the problem's statement.

Provided the node is under static equilibrium, the following condition must be held.

$$\vec{R} + \vec{q} - \vec{F}_1 - \vec{F}_2 = \vec{0}$$

You may have noticed that in this condition the bar forces appear with a negative sign. Those are the reaction forces the node receives from the bars' forces, in accordance with Newton's third law. If a bar is subject to a pair of forces that compress it, the bar pulls the node toward itself. On the other hand, if a bar tends to expand, it'll push the nodes away from itself.

We can easily isolate $\vec{R}$ from the previous equation,

$$\vec{R} = \vec{F}_1 + \vec{F}_2 - \vec{q}$$

or in a more generic fashion (Equation 15.8),

$$\vec{R} = \sum \vec{F}_i - \sum \vec{q}_j \tag{15.8}$$

where $\sum \vec{F}_i$ is the sum of all bar forces, and $\sum \vec{q}_j$ is the sum of all external loads applied to the node (the node's net load).

Let's implement this in our class. Enter the code in Listing 15-23.

```
import operator
from functools import reduce

from geom2d import make_rect_containing_with_margin, Vector
from .bar import StrBarSolution
from .node import StrNodeSolution



class StructureSolution:
    --snip--

    def reaction_for_node(self, node: StrNodeSolution):
    ❶ if not node.is_constrained:
            return Vector(0, 0)

    ❷ forces = [
            bar.force_in_node(node)
            for bar in self.bars
            if bar.has_node(node)
        ]

        if node.is_loaded:
        ❸ forces.append(node.net_load.opposite())

    ❹ return reduce(operator.add, forces)
```

Listing 15-23: Node reaction force

We've defined the reaction_for_node method, which, given a node, computes its reaction force. Don't forget that reaction forces exist only for those nodes that have external supports or constraints. That's in fact the first thing we check ❶: if the node is not constrained, we return a zero vector (meaning no reaction force).

The second step is to search for all bars in the structure that are linked to the passed-in node and get their internal forces in that given node ❷. We do this using a list comprehension that iterates through all the bars in the structure, filtering those that pass the bar.has_node(node) test and finally mapping each of them to its internal force in the given node. This is the $\sum \vec{F_i}$ in Equation 15.8.

Next, we append the net external load to the forces list if the node is externally loaded ❸. Note that the net load received from the node appears with a negative sign in Equation 15.8, which is why we call the opposite method on it. Also note that we don't need to sum these loads (as the $\sum \vec{q_j}$ in Equation 15.8 suggests) because the StrNodeSolution class already does that for us and provides us with the net load.

Lastly, all the forces in the list are summed using the reduce function with the operator.add operator ❹.

The End Result

For your reference, Listing 15-24 shows the complete StructureSolution class implementation.

```
import operator
from functools import reduce

from geom2d import make_rect_containing_with_margin, Vector
from .bar import StrBarSolution
from .node import StrNodeSolution


class StructureSolution:
    def __init__(
            self,
            nodes: [StrNodeSolution],
            bars: [StrBarSolution]
    ):
        self.nodes = nodes
        self.bars = bars

    def bounds_rect(self, margin: float, scale=1):
        d_pos = [
            node.displaced_pos_scaled(scale)
            for node in self.nodes
        ]
        return make_rect_containing_with_margin(d_pos, margin)
```

```
def reaction_for_node(self, node: StrNodeSolution):
    if not node.is_constrained:
        return Vector(0, 0)

    forces = [
        bar.force_in_node(node)
        for bar in self.bars
        if bar.has_node(node)
    ]

    if node.is_loaded:
        forces.append(node.net_load.opposite())

    return reduce(operator.add, forces)
```

Listing 15-24: Structure solution class result

It's important to unit test this class to make sure we haven't made any mistakes. Nevertheless, to test it, we need to learn about an advanced testing technique: mocking. We'll be exploring this topic in the next chapter, so we'll come back to this implementation.

Summary

We started this chapter reviewing some mechanics of materials topics such as the internal forces developed by elastic bodies as a response to being externally loaded. We introduced the concepts of stress and strain, both central to structural analysis. We were particularly interested in the axial stresses developed in prismatic bodies, as those are crucial in plane truss structures, the focus of this part of the book.

We then took a look at plane trusses and their particularities and formulated the relation between forces and displacements on a bar using the concept of a stiffness matrix. As we'll see in the next chapter, these matrices play a crucial role in the resolution of the structure.

Lastly, we implemented the structure's modeling classes: StrNode, StrBar, and Structure. We implemented the structure's solution classes as well: StrNodeSolution, StrBarSolution, and StructureSolution. These two sets of classes represent the structure as originally designed and the structure solution, including the stress value for each bar and the displacements of every node. We'll cover how we go from the original definition to the solution in the next chapter.

16

STRUCTURE RESOLUTION

In the previous chapter, we defined the classes for the structure model: StrNode, StrBar, and Structure. We also wrote the classes for the structure's solution: StrNodeSolution, StrBarSolution, and StructureSolution. We use the first three to define a structure and the other three to model the solution, including the nodes' displacements and bars' stresses and strains. The question is, how do we go from the definition model to the solution model?

In this chapter, we'll answer that question by developing the resolution algorithm, the link between the original and solution structure models. We'll revise the structure's resolution process, where we assemble the structure's stiffness matrix $[k]$ based on the individual bar's matrices and assemble the load vector $\{\vec{F}\}$ based on the individual node's loads. Resolving the $\{\vec{F}\} = [k]\{\vec{x}\}$ system of equations yields the displacements of the nodes in the structure in global coordinates: $\{\vec{x}\}$. To solve the system of equations, we'll use our Cholesky's implementation.

This chapter will also introduce an advanced unit testing technique: test doubles. Test doubles help us isolate a piece of the code by replacing the functions or classes it relies on with "fake" implementations so that when we run the test, we're testing only one piece of the code.

Structure Resolution

In the previous chapter we studied the system of equations that relates the forces applied in each of the degrees of freedom of a bar with its displacements. A bar has two nodes, each with two degrees of freedom:

u The displacement in the x direction

v The displacement in the y direction

This makes a total of four degrees of freedom per bar: u_1 and v_1 for node 1 and u_2 and v_2 for node 2. The forces applied to the nodes—let's call them $\vec{F}_1$ and $\vec{F}_2$—can each be decomposed into their two projections. Thus, $\vec{F}_1$ can be decomposed into F_{1x} and F_{1y}, and the same goes for $\vec{F}_2$ (see Figure 16-1).

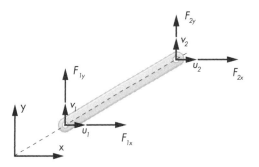

Figure 16-1: A bar's degrees of freedom

The system of equations relating these forces and the node displacements is repeated here from section "Stiffness Matrices in Global Coordinates" on page 397:

$$\begin{bmatrix} F_{1x} \\ F_{1y} \\ F_{2x} \\ F_{2y} \end{bmatrix} = \frac{EA}{l} \underbrace{\begin{bmatrix} c^2 & cs & -c^2 & -cs \\ cs & s^2 & -cs & -s^2 \\ -c^2 & -cs & c^2 & cs \\ -cs & -s^2 & cs & s^2 \end{bmatrix}}_{[k]} \begin{bmatrix} u_1 \\ v_1 \\ u_2 \\ v_2 \end{bmatrix}$$

It's important to note that these forces and displacements, as well as the stiffness matrix $[k]$, are all based on the global system of coordinates, which is the one represented on the bottom left of Figure 16-1. Each bar has its own local coordinate system, as you may recall from Figure 15-18, but to build the structure's global system of equations, we want the forces and displacements referred to this global coordinate system.

Before we move on, let's briefly touch on what each term in the stiffness matrix means.

Interpreting the Stiffness Matrix Terms

The stiffness matrix terms relate the force in a given degree of freedom with the displacement produced in another degree of freedom. They are ordered in a well-defined way:

$$[k] = \begin{bmatrix} F_x^1 \to \delta_x^1 & F_x^1 \to \delta_y^1 & F_x^1 \to \delta_x^2 & F_x^1 \to \delta_y^2 \\ F_y^1 \to \delta_x^1 & F_y^1 \to \delta_y^1 & F_y^1 \to \delta_x^2 & F_y^1 \to \delta_y^2 \\ F_x^2 \to \delta_x^1 & F_x^2 \to \delta_y^1 & F_x^2 \to \delta_x^2 & F_x^2 \to \delta_y^2 \\ F_y^2 \to \delta_x^1 & F_y^2 \to \delta_y^1 & F_y^2 \to \delta_x^2 & F_y^2 \to \delta_y^2 \end{bmatrix}$$

Here, for example, $F_x^1 \to \delta_y^2$ can be read as "the relation between the force in the first node's x direction (F_x^1) and the displacement it produces in the second node's y direction (δ_y^2)." With this is mind, we can discern a pattern.

Each row contains the stiffness terms relating the force in one degree of freedom with the displacements in every degree of freedom. For example, the first row includes the terms that relate the force in the x-axis of the start node F_x^1 with all possible displacements: δ_x^1, δ_y^1, δ_x^2, and δ_y^2.

Each of the columns contains the stiffness terms relating the forces in every degree of freedom with the displacement in a given degree of freedom. For example, the first column includes the terms that relate the forces in every degree of freedom—F_x^1, F_y^1, F_x^2, and F_y^2—with the start node's displacement in the x-axis.

Remember this interpretation of the stiffness terms; we'll use this knowledge later when we assemble the structure's global stiffness matrix. Let's continue revising the resolution process and write the code for it one step at a time.

Structure Initialization

As part of the structure's resolution process there will be some intermediate results we want to save in the Structure class as private attributes. Let's initialize these attributes before we dive into the main algorithm.

Open your *model/structure.py* file and edit the class so that it includes the new attributes we're adding in the __init__ method, as shown in Listing 16-1.

```
from functools import reduce

❶ from eqs import Matrix, Vector as EqVector
  from .node import StrNode
  from .bar import StrBar


  class Structure:
  ❷     __DOF_PER_NODE = 2

          def __init__(self, nodes: [StrNode], bars: [StrBar]):
```

```
        self.__bars = bars
        self.__nodes = nodes

 ❸ self.__dofs_dict = None
        self.__system_matrix: Matrix = None
        self.__system_vector: EqVector = None
        self.__global_displacements: EqVector = None

--snip--
```

Listing 16-1: Initializing the structure

We need to add two new imports, `Matrix` and `Vector`, from the eqs package ❶. Because we'll later need to import the other `Vector` class, the one defined in the geom2d package, we alias `Vector` from the eqs package to be named `EqVector` instead. Notice the aliasing syntax in Python:

```
from <module> import <identifier> as <alias>
```

Next, we define a constant called `__DOF_PER_NODE` ❷, which is set to 2. We'll use this constant in our code instead of directly using the number. Its clear name should give a good hint as to what the number actually means. We'll avoid using *magic numbers* in our code, that is, numbers that appear in the code where it isn't clear what they represent. Well-named constants tell the readers of our code what the number actually stands for.

Lastly, we define four new private attributes and initialize all of them to None ❸.

`__dofs_dict`   A dictionary where the keys are IDs of the nodes, and the values are the lists of degrees of freedom numbers assigned to the node. We'll see what this means in a minute.

`__system_matrix`   The stiffness matrix for the structure's global system of equations.

`__system_vector`   The load vector for the structure's global system of equations.

`__global_displacements`   The list of a node's global displacements, where the indices of each displacement are the same as their degrees of freedom numbers.

Don't worry if you don't fully understand what each of these new attributes mean; we'll explain each in detail in the following sections.

The Main Structure Resolution Algorithm

The structure resolution algorithm can be broken down into three big steps:

1. Assign each degree of freedom a number.
2. Assemble and resolve the structure's system of equations.

3. Use the system's resulting vector to build the solution model.

Let's try to quickly understand what each of these steps is about; we'll fill in the remaining details later. The first step, numbering the degrees of freedom, is a process that assigns every DOF in the structure a unique number. Let's take the structure in Figure 16-2 as an example.

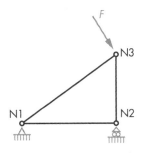

Figure 16-2: Our example structure

The structure in Figure 16-2 has three nodes (N1, N2, and N3), and each node has two degrees of freedom. Assigning numbers to the degrees of freedom is as simple as it sounds: we take each DOF and associate a unique number with it. Table 16-1 shows a possible DOF number assignment that uses the natural ordering of the nodes.

Table 16-1: Assigning
Degrees of Freedom
Numbers

Node	DOF numbers
N1	0, 1
N2	2, 3
N3	4, 5

As you can see, we assign DOF numbers starting from zero. We could have chosen any other set of numbers, including a numbering scheme starting at any number we like, but as we'll use these numbers to refer to positions in the system's matrix and vector, it'll be more convenient to have numbers that directly refer to indices. Otherwise, we'd need a mapping between the DOF numbers and indices in the system.

With the DOF numbers assigned, the next step is to assemble the global system of equations. This system has the same structure as the bar's system of equations: $\{\vec{F}\} = [k]\{\vec{u}\}$. When we solve this system of equations, we obtain the global displacements for all DOFs. Using these displacements, we can create the structure solution model using the classes we defined in Chapter 15.

Let's implement this three-step algorithm in a new method in the Structure class (from the *model* package). Enter the new method in Listing 16-2.

```
class Structure:
    --snip--

    def solve_structure(self):
        self.__assign_degrees_of_freedom()
        self.__solve_system_of_equations()
        return self.__make_structure_solution()
```

Listing 16-2: Structure resolution

The solve_structure method will compute the solution and return an instance of StructureSolution. This method outlines the three steps we just described. None of the three private methods exist yet, but we'll implement them in the following sections one by one.

Numbering Degrees of Freedom

The first step of the resolution process is to assign a number to each of the structure's degrees of freedom. Remember that each node has two degrees of freedom, so the __assign_degrees_of_freedom method will assign two numbers to each of the structure's nodes and save them in the __dofs_dict dictionary we initialized in Listing 16-1. With the DOF numbers assigned, the structure we saw in Figure 16-2 could now look like Figure 16-3.

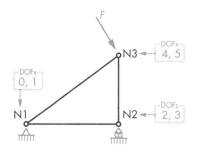

*Figure 16-3: Our structure nodes'
degrees of freedom, with number labels*

Let's implement the method. Enter the code in Listing 16-3.

```
class Structure:
    --snip--

    def __assign_degrees_of_freedom(self):
        self.__dofs_dict = {}
        for i, node in enumerate(self.__nodes):
            self.__dofs_dict[node.id] = (2 * i, 2 * i + 1)
```

Listing 16-3: Degrees of freedom assignment

The method first initializes the __dofs_dict attribute, setting it to an empty dictionary to make sure that we use a fresh new dictionary each time we run the method. Then, we iterate over the enumeration of all the nodes in the structure (self.__nodes), adding each node's id as the key in the dictionary associated with a tuple of two numbers: the node's DOFs.

The enumerate function in Python returns an iterable sequence of the elements that we pass the function, together with their indices. This function is convenient for when the logic of what we're doing requires the index of the items in a list. Here, we use the index of the node to compute its DOF numbers, which for a given index i are $2i$ and $2i + 1$.

The first node, at index 0, will therefore get the degrees of freedom 0 and 1. The node at index 1 will get 2 and 3, and so on and so forth.

For a structure with three nodes whose IDs are 1, 2, and 3, the degrees of freedom dictionary could look like the following:

```
dofs_dict = {
    1: (0, 1),
    2: (2, 3),
    3: (4, 5)
}
```

Let's move on to the next step, where the heavy lifting happens.

Assembling and Resolving the System of Equations

To find the displacements of the structure's nodes, we need to assemble and solve the structure's global $\{\vec{F}\} = [k]\{\vec{u}\}$ system of equations. This system consists of the bar's individual systems of equations assembled together. The same way a bar's $\{\vec{F}\} = [k]\{\vec{u}\}$ system relates the external forces and displacements on both its nodes, the structure's global system of equations relates the forces and displacements of every node in the structure.

Let's break this down a bit more so we understand all the details. As always, doing a small example by hand will help us understand the process better.

An Example by Hand

Before we begin, a quick note on nomenclature: we'll label each bar using the numbers of the nodes it lies on, separated with an arrow. So, $1 \rightarrow 2$ is the bar going from node 1 to node 2. The nomenclature

$$\frac{EA}{l}\bigg|_{1\rightarrow2}$$

refers to the $\frac{EA}{l}$ quantity for the bar $1 \rightarrow 2$: E refers to the bar's material Young's modulus, A is the bar's cross section, and l is the bar's length.

Now let's look at the structure in Figure 16-3. This structure has three nodes, three bars, and an external load applied to node 3. Let's derive the system of equations for each of the three bars using the degrees of freedom numbering we've defined (see Figure 16-4).

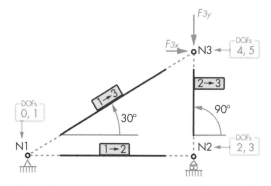

Figure 16-4: Our structure's nodes and bars, labeled

Bar $1 \to 2$ This horizontal bar goes from node 1 to node 2. Its local x- and y-axes are aligned with the global coordinate system; thus, in this case, $\theta = 0°$, and therefore $\cos 0° = 1$ and $\sin 0° = 0$. The bar's system of equations is as follows:

$$
\begin{bmatrix} 0 \\ 0 \\ 0 \\ 0 \end{bmatrix} = \left.\frac{EA}{l}\right|_{1\to2} \begin{bmatrix} 1 & 0 & -1 & 0 \\ 0 & 0 & 0 & 0 \\ -1 & 0 & 1 & 0 \\ 0 & 0 & 0 & 0 \end{bmatrix} \begin{bmatrix} u_1 \\ v_1 \\ u_2 \\ v_2 \end{bmatrix}
$$

If you need a refresher on how this system of equations is derived, refer to section "Stiffness Matrices in Global Coordinates" on page 397.

Bar $1 \to 3$ This bar going from node 1 to node 3 forms an angle of $30°$ with the global x-axis; therefore, $\sin 30° = \frac{1}{2}$ and $\cos 30° = \frac{\sqrt{3}}{2}$. The bar's system of equations is as follows:

$$
\begin{bmatrix} 0 \\ 0 \\ F_{3x} \\ F_{3y} \end{bmatrix} = \left.\frac{EA}{l}\right|_{1\to3} \begin{bmatrix} 3/4 & \sqrt{3}/4 & -3/4 & -\sqrt{3}/4 \\ \sqrt{3}/4 & 1/4 & -\sqrt{3}/4 & -1/4 \\ -3/4 & -\sqrt{3}/4 & 3/4 & \sqrt{3}/4 \\ -\sqrt{3}/4 & -1/4 & \sqrt{3}/4 & 1/4 \end{bmatrix} \begin{bmatrix} u_1 \\ v_1 \\ u_3 \\ v_3 \end{bmatrix}
$$

Bar $2 \to 3$ This vertical bar going from node 2 to node 3 makes an angle θ equal to $90°$, so $\cos 90° = 0$ and $\sin 90° = 1$. The bar's system of equations is as follows:

$$
\begin{bmatrix} 0 \\ 0 \\ F_{3x} \\ F_{3y} \end{bmatrix} = \left.\frac{EA}{l}\right|_{2\to3} \begin{bmatrix} 0 & 0 & 0 & 0 \\ 0 & 1 & 0 & -1 \\ 0 & 0 & 0 & 0 \\ 0 & -1 & 0 & 1 \end{bmatrix} \begin{bmatrix} u_2 \\ v_2 \\ u_3 \\ v_3 \end{bmatrix}
$$

Now that we have each bar's system of equations, we need to assemble the structure's global system. The structure has a total of three nodes, and each node has two degrees of freedom, so the size of the system is $3 \times 2 = 6$. In this system, the forces and displacements need to appear in the position given by their DOF number. To make this clear, let's make a table with the DOF numbers and the forces and displacements associated with them (Table 16-2).

Table 16-2: DOF Numbers for Each Force and Displacement

DOF	Associated force	Associated displacement
0	$F_{1x} = 0$	u_1
1	$F_{1y} = 0$	v_1
2	$F_{2x} = 0$	u_2
3	$F_{2y} = 0$	v_2
4	F_{3x}	u_3
5	F_{3y}	v_3

If the DOF numbering gives us the position in the system of equations that each force or displacement term needs to occupy, we can start constructing the system like so:

$$
\begin{bmatrix} 0 \\ 0 \\ 0 \\ 0 \\ F_{3x} \\ F_{3y} \end{bmatrix}
=
\begin{bmatrix}
k_{00} & k_{01} & k_{02} & k_{03} & k_{04} & k_{05} \\
k_{10} & k_{11} & k_{12} & k_{13} & k_{14} & k_{15} \\
k_{20} & k_{21} & k_{22} & k_{23} & k_{24} & k_{25} \\
k_{30} & k_{31} & k_{32} & k_{33} & k_{34} & k_{35} \\
k_{40} & k_{41} & k_{42} & k_{43} & k_{44} & k_{45} \\
k_{50} & k_{51} & k_{52} & k_{53} & k_{54} & k_{55}
\end{bmatrix}
\begin{bmatrix} u_1 \\ v_1 \\ u_2 \\ v_2 \\ u_3 \\ v_3 \end{bmatrix}
$$

Note that if we decided to number the degrees of freedom differently, the order of the force and displacement terms would be different but perfectly valid nevertheless.

In this system of equations, we have yet to compute the stiffness terms. The general stiffness term k_{ij} relates the force applied in the ith degree of freedom with the displacement in the jth degree of freedom (the same as we saw earlier in the "Interpreting the Stiffness Matrix Terms" on page 429).

As you can imagine, if the ith and j^{th} degrees of freedom don't belong to the same node or to nodes not joined by a bar, the k_{ij} stiffness term will be zero: there can't be any relation between a force applied in i with a displacement in j. In our example structure, all the nodes are connected, so there won't be zero values in the global matrix (except for those already in the bar's individual matrices). In big structures where a node is connected with only a few others, the resulting stiffness matrices tend to have many zeros.

To compute each of the k_{ij} terms, we need to add all the stiffness values in the bar's stiffness matrices that relate the ith and j^{th} degrees of freedom. For example, to compute k_{00}, we have to account for the stiffness of bars $1 \to 2$ and $1 \to 3$, because those bars add a stiffness relation between the force applied in the DOF 0 and the displacement in the same DOF. To simplify the notation of the $\frac{EA}{l}$ terms a bit, let's use the following aliases:

$$
S_{12} = \left. \frac{EA}{l} \right|_{1 \to 2} \qquad S_{13} = \left. \frac{EA}{l} \right|_{1 \to 3} \qquad S_{23} = \left. \frac{EA}{l} \right|_{2 \to 3}
$$

With this, let's assemble the system's matrix and vector by adding each of the stiffness terms and loads:

$$
\begin{bmatrix} 0 \\ 0 \\ 0 \\ 0 \\ F_{3x} \\ F_{3y} \end{bmatrix}
=
\begin{bmatrix}
S_{12} + \frac{3}{4}S_{13} & \frac{\sqrt{3}}{4}S_{13} & -S_{12} & 0 & -\frac{3}{4}S_{13} & -\frac{\sqrt{3}}{4}S_{13} \\
\frac{\sqrt{3}}{4}S_{13} & \frac{1}{4}S_{13} & 0 & 0 & -\frac{\sqrt{3}}{4}S_{13} & -\frac{3}{4}S_{13} \\
-S_{12} & 0 & S_{12} & 0 & 0 & 0 \\
0 & 0 & 0 & S_{23} & 0 & -S_{23} \\
-\frac{3}{4}S_{13} & -\frac{\sqrt{3}}{4}S_{13} & 0 & 0 & \frac{3}{4}S_{13} & \frac{\sqrt{3}}{4}S_{13} \\
-\frac{\sqrt{3}}{4}S_{13} & -\frac{3}{4}S_{13} & 0 & -S_{23} & \frac{\sqrt{3}}{4}S_{13} & \frac{3}{4}S_{13} + S_{23}
\end{bmatrix}
\begin{bmatrix} u_1 \\ v_1 \\ u_2 \\ v_2 \\ u_3 \\ v_3 \end{bmatrix}
$$

There's one last step required to make this system of equations solvable: applying the external constraint conditions, that is, setting the constrained displacements as zero. This system of equations so far represents the structure without external constraints, but there are some imposed displacements of zero, and we have to force these conditions into its solution. In this case, node N1 has both its x and y displacements constrained, which can be expressed mathematically as follows:

$$u_1 = 0 \quad \text{and} \quad v_1 = 0$$

The N2 node has its y displacement constrained. Thus,

$$v_2 = 0$$

To introduce these conditions in our system of equations so that they appear in the solution, we have to set both the row and columns of the given DOF number as the identity in the system's matrix and a zero in the system's force vector. In this case, the displacements u_1, v_1, and v_2 have the 0, 1, and 3 DOFs assigned to them; let's make those rows and columns the identity vector:

$$
\begin{bmatrix} 0 \\ 0 \\ 0 \\ 0 \\ F_{3x} \\ F_{3y} \end{bmatrix}
=
\begin{bmatrix}
1 & 0 & 0 & 0 & 0 & 0 \\
0 & 1 & 0 & 0 & 0 & 0 \\
0 & 0 & S_{12} & 0 & 0 & 0 \\
0 & 0 & 0 & 1 & 0 & 0 \\
0 & 0 & 0 & 0 & \frac{3}{4}S_{13} & \frac{\sqrt{3}}{4}S_{13} \\
0 & 0 & 0 & 0 & \frac{\sqrt{3}}{4}S_{13} & \frac{3}{4}S_{13} + S_{23}
\end{bmatrix}
\begin{bmatrix} u_1 \\ v_1 \\ u_2 \\ v_2 \\ u_3 \\ v_3 \end{bmatrix}
$$

The force vector values at the constrained indices were already zero (there's no force applied in those degrees of freedom), but if they weren't, we'd have to zero them out as well. With this little algebraic trick, we force

u_1, v_1, and v_2 to be equal to zero in the system's solution. The resulting system matrix is positive definite; thus, the Cholesky numerical method we implemented in Chapter 14 is a good candidate to solve this system.

The structure's system of equations is now assembled and ready to be solved. If we use a linear system resolution procedure, such as Cholesky's factorization, we'll obtain the values for the displacements.

Now that we understand this procedure, let's put it in code.

The Algorithm

In the Structure class, enter the method in Listing 16-4. This method defines our resolution algorithm step-by-step.

```
from functools import reduce

from eqs import Matrix, Vector as EqVector, cholesky_solve
from .node import StrNode
from .bar import StrBar


class Structure:
    --snip--

    def __solve_system_of_equations(self):
        size = self.nodes_count * self.__DOF_PER_NODE
        self.__assemble_system_matrix(size)
        self.__assemble_system_vector(size)
        self.__apply_external_constraints()
        self.__global_displacements = cholesky_solve(
            self.__system_matrix,
            self.__system_vector
        )
```

Listing 16-4: Solving the system of equations

We called __solve_system_of_equations in Listing 16-2, but we hadn't yet defined it. This now complete method outlines the main steps to assemble and resolve the structure's system of equations. Note that we're using many methods we have yet to define; we'll do so in later sections.

We first compute the size of the system by multiplying the number of nodes in the structure by the degrees of freedom for each node, a value we stored in the constant __DOF_PER_NODE in the class.

Then we assemble both the system's matrix and vector using two private methods we'll write later: __assemble_system_matrix and __assemble_system_vector.

The next method we call, __apply_external_constraints, applies the conditions that force the constrained displacements to be zero, similar to the example we did by hand shown earlier.

The last step uses the recently computed system matrix and force vector to find the solution using our Cholesky's solver function: cholesky_solve.

This function needs to be imported from the eqs package. The result we get is the displacement vector in global coordinates.

Assembling the System's Matrix

Let's write the __assemble_system_matrix method. This is probably the most complex piece of code involved in the structural analysis algorithm, but don't worry, I'll walk you through it. First, enter the code in Listing 16-5.

```
class Structure:
    --snip--

    def __assemble_system_matrix(self, size: int):
        matrix = Matrix(size, size)

        for bar in self.__bars:
          ❶ bar_matrix = bar.global_stiffness_matrix()
          ❷ dofs = self.__bar_dofs(bar)

            for row, row_dof in enumerate(dofs):
                for col, col_dof in enumerate(dofs):
                    matrix.add_to_value(
                      ❸ bar_matrix.value_at(row, col),
                        row_dof,
                        col_dof
                    )

      ❹ self.__system_matrix = matrix

    def __bar_dofs(self, bar: StrBar):
        start_dofs = self.__dofs_dict[bar.start_node.id]
        end_dofs = self.__dofs_dict[bar.end_node.id]
        return start_dofs + end_dofs
```

Listing 16-5: Assembling the system of equations matrix

We start by creating a new Matrix instance with as many rows and columns as the passed-in size parameter. Then, we have a for loop that iterates over the bars in the structure. In the loop, we call the global_stiffness_matrix method on each bar and store the resulting stiffness matrix in the bar_matrix variable ❶.

Next, we create a list of all the degrees of freedom numbers included in the nodes of the bar: dofs ❷. To do this without adding too much noise in the __assemble_system_matrix method, we've implemented another private method: __bar_dofs.

This __bar_dofs method uses the ids of the passed-in bar nodes to extract its DOF numbers from the __dofs_dict. After extracting the start and end nodes' DOF numbers, we create a new tuple by concatenating the two DOF tuples. Note that we can concatenate tuples using the + operator.

Now we have a tuple containing the DOF numbers for a given bar's nodes. Recall that this gives us the bar's stiffness term's position in the structure's system of equations matrix: the DOF number is also the index in the system's matrix. Back in __assemble_system_matrix, we use two for loops to cover all the terms in the bar's stiffness matrix. These loops iterate over the matrix's rows and columns and add every visited stiffness value to the structure's global matrix ❸. We use the indices from the enumerations to access the bar's stiffness matrix and the DOF numbers to know the position in the structure's matrix. To make sure you understand this process, take a look at Figure 16-5.

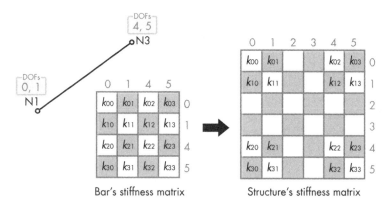

Figure 16-5: Assembling the stiffness matrix

In the figure, we've taken bar $1 \to 3$, whose first node, N1, has the DOFs 0 and 1, and whose second node, N2, has the DOFs 4 and 5. We've annotated the side and top of the bar's stiffness matrix with the degrees of freedom numbers. The stiffness terms in the matrix relate these degrees of freedom. For example, the term k_{21} is in the row that corresponds to DOF 4 and the column that corresponds to DOF 1; this term relates the force applied in DOF 4 with the displacement in DOF 1. These DOF numbers are the indices in the structure's stiffness matrix. The k_{21} term, for instance, is located in the 4th row and 1st column in this matrix.

The last step in Listing 16-5 is to assign the computed matrix to the instance's __system_matrix attribute ❹.

Assembling the System's Vector

We assemble the system's external-force vector using a similar procedure to what we just did with the stiffness matrix. This time, instead of iterating over the bars of the structure, we'll iterate over the nodes: we want to collect the external forces on each of them.

In your file, enter the new private method in Listing 16-6.

```
class Structure:
    --snip--

    def __assemble_system_vector(self, size: int):
```

```
        vector = EqVector(size)

        for node in self.__nodes:
            net_load = node.net_load
            (dof_x, dof_y) = self.__dofs_dict[node.id]

            vector.add_to_value(net_load.u, dof_x)
            vector.add_to_value(net_load.v, dof_y)

        self.__system_vector = vector
```

Listing 16-6: Assembling the system of equations vector

We first create a new Vector sized according to the size parameter (don't
forget we've aliased this class to be named EqVector now).

Next, we have a for loop that iterates over the nodes. For each node we
save its net load in the net_load variable. Then we extract the node's DOF
numbers from __dofs_dict into the dof_x and dof_y variables. Note that we're
destructuring the tuple into these variables; take a look at "Destructuring"
on page 20 if you need a refresher on destructuring.

We then add each of the net load components into the vector variable:
the x component (net_load.u) in the position given by dof_x and the y component (net_load.v) in the position given by dof_y.

Lastly, we assign the vector we've computed to the instance's __system_vector
attribute.

Applying the External Constraints

Lastly, we need to include the external constraints in the structure's stiffness
matrix and force vector. This means that we want those displacements that
are externally constrained to be zero in the final solution vector; if they're
constrained, they can't move. To accomplish this, we can use the algebraic
trick we explored earlier, which consisted of setting the rows and columns
of the associated degrees of freedom as identity rows and columns in the
stiffness matrix and as zero in the force vector.

This is easier done than said, so, without further ado, let's see what the
code looks like. Enter the code in Listing 16-7.

```
class Structure:
    --snip--

    def __apply_external_constraints(self):
        for node in self.__nodes:
    ❶      (dof_x, dof_y) = self.__dofs_dict[node.id]

    ❷      if node.dx_constrained:
                self.__system_matrix.set_identity_row(dof_x)
                self.__system_matrix.set_identity_col(dof_x)
                self.__system_vector.set_value(0, dof_x)
```

```
❸ if node.dy_constrained:
        self.__system_matrix.set_identity_row(dof_y)
        self.__system_matrix.set_identity_col(dof_y)
        self.__system_vector.set_value(0, dof_y)
```

Listing 16-7: Applying the external constraints

To check the existing external constraints, we iterate over the nodes of the structure. For each node, we extract its DOF numbers into the dof_x and dof_y variables ❶. Then we check whether the node has its displacement in the x direction constrained ❷, in which case we do three things:

1. Set the stiffness matrix dof_x row to the identity.

2. Set the stiffness matrix dof_x column to the identity.

3. Set the force vector dof_x value to zero.

We do the same for the displacement in the y direction constraint ❸.

The system is now ready to be solved. Once we have the system's solution in the form of the displacement vector, we can create the structure's solution model.

Creating the Solution

Let's do a quick recap to remind ourselves where we are. We've written a lot of code split among a couple private methods. Figure 16-6 shows a hierarchy of the methods involved in solving the structure.

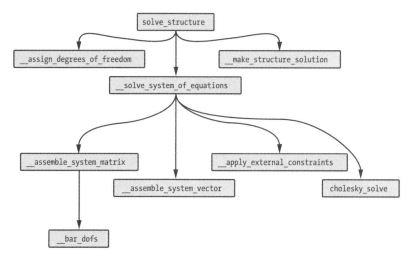

Figure 16-6: Structure resolution code split into a hierarchy

The nodes in this diagram are the methods ordered from left to right according to their execution order. The solve_structure method is the public method defining the main algorithm. If you recall, that method consists of three steps, which are written as private methods:

```
__assign_degrees_of_freedom
```

```
__solve_system_of_equations

__make_structure_solution
```

The second private method, __solve_system_of_equations, is the one with the most submethods, as you can observe in the diagram.

So far we've written all but the __make_structure_solution method, the third and last step in solve_structure. Let's write this method now. It uses the solution to the system of equations (the node's global displacements) to build the structure solution model.

In the *model/structure.py* file, enter the code in Listing 16-8.

```python
from functools import reduce

from eqs import Matrix, Vector as EqVector, cholesky_solve
from geom2d import Vector
from structures.solution.bar import StrBarSolution
from structures.solution.node import StrNodeSolution
from structures.solution.structure import StructureSolution
from .bar import StrBar
from .node import StrNode


class Structure:
    --snip--

    def __make_structure_solution(self) -> StructureSolution:
        nodes = [
          ❶ self.__node_to_solution(node)
                for node in self.__nodes
        ]

      ❷ nodes_dict = {}
        for node in nodes:
            nodes_dict[node.id] = node

        bars = [
          ❸ StrBarSolution(
                bar,
                nodes_dict[bar.start_node.id],
                nodes_dict[bar.end_node.id]
            )
            for bar in self.__bars
        ]

      ❹ return StructureSolution(nodes, bars)

    def __node_to_solution(self, node: StrNode) -> StrNodeSolution:
      ❺ (dof_x, dof_y) = self.__dofs_dict[node.id]
      ❻ disp = Vector(
```

```
        self.__global_displacements.value_at(dof_x),
        self.__global_displacements.value_at(dof_y)
    )
❼ return StrNodeSolution(node, disp)
```

Listing 16-8: Creating the solution model

The first thing we need to do is add a few imports from the `structures` `.solution` package. We also import the `Vector` class from the `geom2d` package.

Note how we add a type hint for the method's returned object. These type hints are preceded by an arrow (`->`) and go between the method or function name and the colon.

Then, using a list comprehension, we map each of the original `__nodes` to the node solution model ❶. We use a private method we have to write: `__node_to_solution`. Given a node, this method looks for its degrees of freedom numbers ❺, creates a vector with the two displacements associated with those DOF numbers ❻, and returns an instance of `StrNodeSolution` using the original node and the vector of global displacements ❼.

Back in `__make_structure_solution`, the next step is an intermediate computation that will simplify the construction of the solution bars. We'll create a dictionary of solution nodes where the key is the `id` of the node and the value is the node itself ❷.

With the help of `nodes_dict`, computing the solution bar model becomes simpler. Using a list comprehension, we map each of the original bars to a `StrBarSolution` instance ❸. To instantiate this class, we need to pass it the original bar and the two solution nodes; thanks to the dictionary we just created, this is a piece of cake. If we hadn't created the dictionary of nodes by ID, we'd need to search the list of solution nodes for a node with a given ID. Performance-wise, this isn't ideal. For each bar, we may need to iterate over the whole list of nodes twice. Creating the dictionary to find nodes by ID is a much wiser option; it allows for a constant-time search of the nodes. This means that, no matter the size of the dictionary, looking up the value associated with a key takes the same amount of time. If the structure has a large number of nodes, this improvement can noticeably decrease the execution time.

Lastly, we instantiate `StructureSolution`, passing it the solution nodes and bars ❹.

The Result

Resolving the structure required quite a lot of code, so we better bring it all together in a single listing for clarity. Listing 16-9 is the complete `Structure` class's code, including the `solve_structure` implementation and every private method we wrote.

```
from functools import reduce

from eqs import Matrix, Vector as EqVector, cholesky_solve
from geom2d import Vector
```

```
from structures.solution.bar import StrBarSolution
from structures.solution.node import StrNodeSolution
from structures.solution.structure import StructureSolution
from .bar import StrBar
from .node import StrNode


class Structure:
    __DOF_PER_NODE = 2

    def __init__(self, nodes: [StrNode], bars: [StrBar]):
        self.__bars = bars
        self.__nodes = nodes

        self.__dofs_dict = None
        self.__system_matrix: Matrix = None
        self.__system_vector: EqVector = None
        self.__global_displacements: EqVector = None

    @property
    def nodes_count(self):
        return len(self.__nodes)

    @property
    def bars_count(self):
        return len(self.__bars)

    @property
    def loads_count(self):
        return reduce(
            lambda count, node: count + node.loads_count,
            self.__nodes,
            0
        )

    def solve_structure(self) -> StructureSolution:
        self.__assign_degrees_of_freedom()
        self.__solve_system_of_equations()
        return self.__make_structure_solution()

    def __assign_degrees_of_freedom(self):
        self.__dofs_dict = {}
        for i, node in enumerate(self.__nodes):
            self.__dofs_dict[node.id] = (2 * i, 2 * i + 1)

    def __solve_system_of_equations(self):
        size = self.nodes_count * self.__DOF_PER_NODE
```

```python
        self.__assemble_system_matrix(size)
        self.__assemble_system_vector(size)
        self.__apply_external_constraints()
        self.__global_displacements = cholesky_solve(
            self.__system_matrix,
            self.__system_vector
        )

    def __assemble_system_matrix(self, size: int):
        matrix = Matrix(size, size)

        for bar in self.__bars:
            bar_matrix = bar.global_stiffness_matrix()
            dofs = self.__bar_dofs(bar)

            for row, row_dof in enumerate(dofs):
                for col, col_dof in enumerate(dofs):
                    matrix.add_to_value(
                        bar_matrix.value_at(row, col),
                        row_dof,
                        col_dof
                    )

        self.__system_matrix = matrix

    def __bar_dofs(self, bar: StrBar):
        start_dofs = self.__dofs_dict[bar.start_node.id]
        end_dofs = self.__dofs_dict[bar.end_node.id]
        return start_dofs + end_dofs

    def __assemble_system_vector(self, size: int):
        vector = EqVector(size)

        for node in self.__nodes:
            net_load = node.net_load
            (dof_x, dof_y) = self.__dofs_dict[node.id]

            vector.add_to_value(net_load.u, dof_x)
            vector.add_to_value(net_load.v, dof_y)

        self.__system_vector = vector

    def __apply_external_constraints(self):
        for node in self.__nodes:
            (dof_x, dof_y) = self.__dofs_dict[node.id]

            if node.dx_constrained:
```

```
            self.__system_matrix.set_identity_row(dof_x)
            self.__system_matrix.set_identity_col(dof_x)
            self.__system_vector.set_value(0, dof_x)

        if node.dy_constrained:
            self.__system_matrix.set_identity_row(dof_y)
            self.__system_matrix.set_identity_col(dof_y)
            self.__system_vector.set_value(0, dof_y)

def __make_structure_solution(self) -> StructureSolution:
    nodes = [
        self.__node_to_solution(node)
        for node in self.__nodes
    ]

    nodes_dict = {}
    for node in nodes:
        nodes_dict[node.id] = node

    bars = [
        StrBarSolution(
            bar,
            nodes_dict[bar.start_node.id],
            nodes_dict[bar.end_node.id]
        )
        for bar in self.__bars
    ]

    return StructureSolution(nodes, bars)

def __node_to_solution(self, node: StrNode) -> StrNodeSolution:
    (dof_x, dof_y) = self.__dofs_dict[node.id]
    disp = Vector(
        self.__global_displacements.value_at(dof_x),
        self.__global_displacements.value_at(dof_y)
    )
    return StrNodeSolution(node, disp)
```

Listing 16-9: The final Structure class

With this code ready, the only missing thing is some unit tests. We need to make sure all the logic we've just written is bug-free. But the code we've written in the previous two chapters has become more complex and requires the interaction of several different classes to work. How do we isolate the parts of the code we want to test?

Advanced Unit Testing: Test Doubles

As our classes get more complex, they'll often rely on other classes and external functions. Here's where unit testing becomes trickier. Unit testing is about isolating a small portion of the logic in the class or function we want to test so that there's one single reason for a test to fail. Testing that things run correctly when they're put to work together is known as *integration testing*. Integration tests are meant to test bigger chunks of the system; with integration tests, we're interested in knowing whether the smaller pieces of a system still work when they interact with each other. We won't be integration testing here, but I encourage you to try it on your own.

Going back to unit tests, let's take our StructureSolution class from the previous chapter. Let's say we want to test its bounds_rect method.

```
def bounds_rect(self, margin, scale=1):
    d_pos = [
        node.displaced_pos_scaled(scale)
        for node in self.nodes
    ]
    return make_rect_containing_with_margin(d_pos, margin)
```

This method delegates most of its logic to make_rect_containing_with_margin and also depends on StrNodeSolution instances to correctly compute their displaced position. If we tested this method as is, we'd be testing make_rect_containing_with_margin and the Node class's displaced_pos_scaled method. Those should both already be unit tested somewhere else. The test could fail for several reasons that are unrelated to the logic in bounds_rect. In this case, we'd be doing an integration test, but we first want to make sure our method works well in isolation using unit tests.

We can test this method without relying on other classes' implementation using test doubles.

Test Doubles

A *test double* replaces a real implementation used in a test. This test double may replace a function, an entire class, or just parts of it. To do the unit test, we replace all the parts of the code that are not being directly tested by the unit test with test doubles. What exactly the test double does depends on what type of test double it is. There are a few flavors.

Dummy   This is the simplest test double. The *dummy* replaces an object whose presence is required but that is never actually used in the test. This could be a parameter to the function, for example.

Fake   A *fake* test double replaces some part of the code; it has a working implementation but takes some shortcuts or is greatly simplified. Say, for example, we have a function that reads a text file and parses a structure model from it. If this function was used in another part of the code we wanted to test, we could create a fake version of it that pretends to read a file, although it really doesn't and creates a structure to return it.

Stub   A *stub* replaces some part of the code and always returns the same value or behaves in a specific way. For example, we could stub our are_close_enough function (that compares floating-point numbers) to always return False in a given test.

Mock   This is a test double that records the way it's being used so that it can be used to make assertions. *Mocks* are probably the most sophisticated and versatile type of test doubles. We can mock entire objects, pass them to our code in place of the real implementation, and then explore how our code interacted with the mock to make sure the right interactions took place. We'll look at a real example of a mock briefly.

Let's now explore how Python allows us to create test doubles. We'll focus on mocking, as mocks are so versatile that we can use them in almost every case where a test double is required.

The unittest.mock Package

The unittest package in the Python standard library includes its own mocking mechanism, found in the unittest.mock package. You can read the package's documentation at *docs.python.org/3/library/unittest.mock.html*, and I recommend you do, as it contains detailed explanations that will help you understand how best to use it. Let's take a quick look at how to use the unittest.mock package's main functionalities.

The Mock Object

Mock is the main class in the unittest.mock package. This class's instances record every interaction they have and provide us with assertions to check those interactions. You can call any method you want in a mock object; if the method doesn't exist, it will be created so we can inspect how many times this method was called or what parameters were passed in. As stated in the documentation,

> Mocks are callable and create attributes as new mocks when you access them. Accessing the same attribute will always return the same mock. Mocks record how you use them, allowing you to make assertions about what your code has done to them.

Let's break that documentation down. An instance of the Mock class being "callable" means that you can "call" it the same way you call a function. Those calls you make on the instance are recorded by the mock. This suggests we can use Mock instances to replace functions.

The documentation also says that mocks "create attributes as new mocks when you access them." This means that when you call a method on a Mock instance, Python will create a new Mock for that method, if it doesn't exist yet, and append it as a new attribute of the instance. Don't forget that mocks are callable: you can call these attributes as if they were methods, and their interactions will be recorded.

Let's take a look at a quick example in Python's shell to start making these concepts a bit more concrete:

```
>>> from unittest.mock import Mock
>>> mock = Mock()
>>> mock()
<Mock name='mock()' id='4548720456'>

>>> mock.some_method('foo', 23)
<Mock name='mock.some_method()' id='4436512848'>
```

In this code we create a new instance of the Mock class and call it like a function. We also call a method named some_method on our mock and pass it two arguments: the string 'foo' and the number 23. Calling some_method has no side effects: it does nothing except for record the call to it; this is because mock methods have no implementation by default. We'll learn later how to make mock methods return something or perform some kind of side effect, but for now just keep in mind that, by default, mocks do nothing but record their usage.

If we call a method from a Mock object that we haven't configured to return anything or perform any kind of side effect, by default it'll return another Mock instance. This is the instance that's stored in the original mock as an attribute.

We can ask this mock whether some_method has been called or not, and with what arguments:

```
>>> mock.some_method.assert_called()
>>> mock.some_method.assert_called_once()
>>> mock.some_method.assert_called_with('foo', 23)
```

All three calls succeed (don't raise an assertion error), but if we asked for arguments that were not passed to some_method,

```
>>> mock.some_method.assert_called_with('bar', 577)
```

we'd get an AssertionError with a helpful message, which would make a test fail and give us the reason why:

```
Traceback (most recent call last):
--snip--
AssertionError: Expected call: some_method('bar', 577)
Actual call: some_method('foo', 123)
```

Likewise, if we asked for the calls of a method that was never called,

```
>>> mock.foo.assert_called()
```

we'd also get an error:

```
Traceback (most recent call last):
--snip--
AssertionError: Expected 'foo' to have been called.
```

Let's not forget that the mock itself is a callable object that records the interactions made with it. Therefore, the following also succeeds:

```
>>> mock.assert_called()
```

Mocking Classes

A common use case for mocks is creating a mock instance of a given class. These mocks let us inspect how the class they're mocking was used and what methods were called on it; we can also use the mock to provide return values for the mocked methods to use in the tests.

To mock a class, we pass it to the spec parameter of the Mock constructor. Let's create a mock for our Vector class:

```
>>> from unittest.mock import Mock
>>> from geom2d import Vector
>>> vector_mock = Mock(spec=Vector)
>>> isinstance(vector_mock, Vector)
True
```

This mock object has its __class__ attribute set to Vector so that it looks like a real Vector instance. It even passes the isinstance test! This mock can be effectively used to replace a real Vector. All of the methods in the Vector class are also defined in this test double. We can call any of them as we normally would:

```
>>> vector_mock.rotated_radians(0.25)
<Mock name='mock.rotated_radians()' id='4498122344'>
```

This time, rotated_radians didn't return a new instance of Vector, as we'd expect. Instead, it returned a Mock instance. Since a mocked class's methods have no implementation, there is no code to perform the rotating operation and return the resulting vector. We can program mock methods to return a predefined value using the mock's side_effect and return_value attributes.

But before we get to that, there's one more thing that's important about class mocks: if we try to call a method that doesn't exist in the class, we'll get an AttributeError. New attributes can be added to a generic mock, but not to a mock of a class. The code

```
>>> vector_mock.defrangulate()
```

yields this:

```
Traceback (most recent call last):
--snip--
AttributeError: Mock object has no attribute 'defrangulate'
```

This is good: we can be sure that if some part of our code tries to call methods that don't exist in the original class, we'll get an error.

Let's now take a look at how we can go about adding a stub implementation or simply a predefined return value for mocks.

Setting Return Values and Side Effects

By setting a mock's return_value, we can make it return something when called:

```
>>> vector_mock.rotated_radians.return_value = Vector(0, 0)
>>> vector_mock.rotated_radians(0.25)
<geom2d.vector.Vector object at 0x10bbaa4a8>
```

Calling rotated_radians now returns an instance of the Vector class: exactly the instance we programmed it to return. From now on, every time this method is called on the mock, it will return the same Vector instance.

Mocks can also execute side effects when called. According to the documentation, a side_effect

> can either be a function to be called when the mock is called, an iterable or an exception (class or instance) to be raised.

Let's first take a look at how a mock can raise an exception. For example, if we needed the cosine method to raise a ValueError, we could do the following:

```
>>> vector_mock.cosine.side_effect = ValueError
>>> vector_mock.cosine()
Traceback (most recent call last):
--snip--
ValueError
```

Note that we're setting the ValueError class itself as the side_effect, but as the documentation states, we can also use a concrete instance, like this:

```
>>> vector_mock.cosine.side_effect = ValueError('Oops')
>>> vector_mock.cosine()
Traceback (most recent call last):
--snip--
ValueError: Oops
```

In this case, every time we call cosine, we get the same ValueError instance. In the previous example, every call produces a new instance of the error.

We can also assign a function to a mock's side_effect attribute. This function receives the parameters passed to the mock function and might return a value. For example, in our `Vector` mock, we could decide to have the `scaled_by` method return the passed-in `factor` parameter:

```
>>> vector_mock.scaled_by.side_effect = lambda factor: factor
>>> vector_mock.scaled_by(45)
45
```

In this case, the `scaled_by` method was passed a `45` as the scaling factor, and this parameter was forwarded to the function defined as the mock's `side_effect` attribute.

This function can perform its own side effect, like saving the parameters it received or printing something to the shell. We can use this function together with `return_value`. If we use the function to perform a side effect but still want to return whatever is set in the `return_value` attribute, the function should return `DEFAULT` (defined in `unittest.mock`):

```
>>> from unittest.mock import DEFAULT
>>> def side_effect(factor):
...     print(f'mock called with factor: {factor}')
...     return DEFAULT

>>> vector_mock.scaled_by.side_effect = side_effect
>>> vector_mock.scaled_by.return_value = Vector(1, 2)

>>> vector_mock.scaled_by(2)
mock called with factor: 2
<geom2d.vector.Vector object at 0x10c4a7f28>
```

As you can see, the `side_effect` function was called, but as it returned the `DEFAULT` value, the call to `scaled_by` returned the vector we set as `return_value`.

The patch Decorator

The *mock* package includes a `unittest.mock.patch` decorator we can use to mock objects in a test function. The `@patch` decorator has the ability to mock objects instantiated in the test function they decorate. The mocks created by the decorator are cleared for us automatically once the function returns, so the mocking is only effective in the context of the function. We have to pass the `@patch` decorator the target we want to mock using the format `'package.module.name'` (this is a string, so don't forget the quotation marks), where `name` can be the name of a class or a function. The decorated function will be passed the mocked target as a new argument:

```
from unittest.mock import patch

@patch('geom2d.circles.make_circle_from_points')
def test_something(make_circle_mock):
    make_circle_mock(1, 2, 3)
    make_circle_mock.assert_called_with(1, 2, 3)
```

In this test we're replacing the `make_circle_from_points` function defined in the *geom2d* package's *circles* module. We have to include the mocked function, `make_circle_mock`, as an argument to the function. Then, in the context of the `test_something` function, we can refer to the mocked function and assert it was called like we do with any other mock.

The `@patch` decorator's main use case is replacing functions or classes that are imported by our test subjects. By using a patch, we force them to import a mock instead of the real dependency.

There is no other easy way of mocking the dependencies of the modules we want to unit test: if the module imports their dependencies, we need a way of replacing that dependency in Python's importing mechanism. The `@patch` decorator does this for us in an elegant manner.

Now let's apply all this knowledge to test our code in isolation: there's no better way of learning how to use test doubles than using them in real use cases. If you're new to using test doubles, you may be a bit confused at this point; that's perfectly normal. As we see mocks in action a couple times, you'll start to grasp the concepts.

Testing the Structure Solution Class

Following the example we introduced earlier of the `bounds_rect` method in the `StructureSolution` class, let's see how we can go about testing it. Remember, the method we want to test is defined as follows:

```
def bounds_rect(self, margin, scale=1):
    d_pos = [
        node.displaced_pos_scaled(scale)
        for node in self.nodes
    ]
    return make_rect_containing_with_margin(d_pos, margin)
```

The method requires that the `StrNodeSolution` class correctly computes its displaced position using a scale and that the `make_rect_containing_with_margin` function returns the correct rectangle using the given margin. We don't need to test those behaviors; that should have been done somewhere else. What we want to do is replace their real implementations with test doubles so that they don't interfere in our tests.

Without further ado, let's create a new file in *structures/tests* named *structure_solution_test.py*. In the file, enter the test setup code, as in Listing 16-10.

```
import unittest
from unittest.mock import patch, Mock

from geom2d import Point
from structures.solution.node import StrNodeSolution
from structures.solution.structure import StructureSolution
```

```
class StructureSolutionTest(unittest.TestCase):

    p_one = Point(2, 3)
    p_two = Point(5, 1)

    def setUp(self):
        self.n_one = Mock(spec=StrNodeSolution)
        self.n_one.displaced_pos_scaled.return_value = self.p_one
        self.n_two = Mock(spec=StrNodeSolution)
        self.n_two.displaced_pos_scaled.return_value = self.p_two
```

Listing 16-10: Structure solution class test: the setup

In this test setup, we're defining two points: p_one and p_two; these are the positions for the mock nodes we create in the setUp method. This setUp method is executed by the unittest framework before each test, which ensures that each test gets fresh mocks; otherwise, mocks would continue to record throughout the tests, breaking the independence between tests.

We define two nodes: n_one and n_two. Then we instantiate node mocks using the StrNodeSolution class as the value for the spec parameter. Each of the node mocks defines one of the defined points as the return value for its displaced_pos_scaled method.

Next, let's write the first test, which will ensure that the two nodes get the displaced_pos_scaled called with the correct value for the scale parameter. After the setUp method, enter the test in Listing 16-11.

```
class StructureSolutionTest(unittest.TestCase):
    --snip--

    def test_node_displaced_scaled_positions_called(self):
        solution = StructureSolution([self.n_one, self.n_two], [])
        solution.bounds_rect(margin=10, scale=4)

        self.n_one.displaced_pos_scaled.assert_called_once_with(4)
        self.n_two.displaced_pos_scaled.assert_called_once_with(4)
```

Listing 16-11: Structure solution class test: first test

We create a StructureSolution instance with a list containing the two nodes defined in the setUp and no bars: we don't need them to test the bounds_rect method, and the StructureSolution doesn't complain if we instantiate it with an empty bars list. If the StructureSolution class initializer complained about getting an empty list of bars, this would have been the perfect case for using the dummy test double: we'd pass the constructor a list of dummy bars. Dummies are used to fill in required parameters, but dummies don't actually do anything or interfere with the test in any way.

Once we've instantiated our StructureSolution, we call the bounds_rect method, our test subject, with values for the margin and scale. Lastly, we assert that `displaced_pos_scaled` was called once with the correct value for the scale in both nodes.

This test ensures that we use the node's displaced positions with the corresponding scale applied to compute the structure solution bounds. Imagine that, by mistake, we confused the `margin` and `scale` parameters when implementing the method:

```
def bounds_rect(self, margin, scale=1):
    d_pos = [
        # wrong! used 'margin' instead of 'scale'
        node.displaced_pos_scaled(margin)
        for node in self.nodes
    ]
    # wrong! used 'scale' instead of 'margin'
    return make_rect_containing_with_margin(d_pos, scale)
```

Our unit test would have warned us:

```
Expected call: make_rect_containing_with_margin([
    <geom2d.point.Point object at 0x10575a630>,
    <geom2d.point.Point object at 0x10575a6a0>], 10)
Actual call: make_rect_containing_with_margin([
    <geom2d.point.Point object at 0x10575a630>,
    <geom2d.point.Point object at 0x10575a6a0>], 4)
```

Congratulations! You've written your first unit test using test doubles. Let's now write a second test that ensures the right usage of the function that computes the rectangle. Enter the code in Listing 16-12.

```
class StructureSolutionTest(unittest.TestCase):
    --snip--

    @patch('structures.solution.structure.make_rect_containing_with_margin')
    def test_make_rect_called(self, make_rect_mock):
        solution = StructureSolution([self.n_one, self.n_two], [])
        solution.bounds_rect(margin=10, scale=4)

        make_rect_mock.assert_called_once_with(
            [self.p_one, self.p_two],
            10
        )
```

Listing 16-12: Structure solution class test: second test

This test is a bit trickier because the `make_rect_containing_with_margin` function is imported by the `StructureSolution` class. To make this class import our mock instead of the real implementation, we have to patch the function's path: `'package.module.name'`, which is, in this case, as follows:

`'structures.solution.structure.make_rect_containing_with_margin'`

But, wait: isn't `make_rect_containing_with_margin` defined in the *geom2d* package? So why are we patching it as if it were in the *structures.solution* package and the *structure* module?

The `@patch` decorator has some rules that define how the path should be given to mock a given object. In the "Where to patch" section, the documentation states

> `patch()` works by (temporarily) changing the object that a *name* points to with another one. There can be many names pointing to any individual object, so for patching to work you must ensure that you patch the name used by the system under test.
>
> The basic principle is that you patch where an object is *looked up*, which is not necessarily the same place as where it is defined.

That second paragraph gives us the key: objects have to be patched where they're looked up. In the case of our test, the function we want to replace is looked up in the `structures.solution` package, in the *structure* module. This may sound a bit complicated in the beginning, but it'll start to make sense after you've done it a few times.

Moving on with our test, the first two lines are identical to the previous one: they create the structure solution and call the function under test. Then comes the assertion, which is done on the parameter passed to the test function: `make_rect_mock`. Remember, the `@patch` decorator passes the patched entity to the decorated function. We assert that the mock was called only once with the list of positions the mocked nodes return and the value for the margin.

You can run these tests using PyCharm, by clicking the green play button to the left of the test class name. Alternatively, you can run them from the shell:

```
$ python3 -m unittest structures/tests/structure_solution_test.py
```

Listing 16-13 shows the resulting code for your reference.

```python
import unittest
from unittest.mock import patch, Mock

from geom2d import Point
from structures.solution.node import StrNodeSolution
from structures.solution.structure import StructureSolution


class StructureSolutionTest(unittest.TestCase):

    p_one = Point(2, 3)
    p_two = Point(5, 1)

    def setUp(self):
        self.n_one = Mock(spec=StrNodeSolution)
        self.n_one.displaced_pos_scaled.return_value = self.p_one
```

```
        self.n_two = Mock(spec=StrNodeSolution)
        self.n_two.displaced_pos_scaled.return_value = self.p_two

    def test_node_displaced_scaled_positions_called(self):
        solution = StructureSolution([self.n_one, self.n_two], [])
        solution.bounds_rect(margin=10, scale=4)

        self.n_one.displaced_pos_scaled.assert_called_once_with(4)
        self.n_two.displaced_pos_scaled.assert_called_once_with(4)

    @patch('structures.solution.structure.make_rect_containing_with_margin')
    def test_make_rect_called(self, make_rect_mock):
        solution = StructureSolution([self.n_one, self.n_two], [])
        solution.bounds_rect(margin=10, scale=4)

        make_rect_mock.assert_called_once_with(
            [self.p_one, self.p_two],
            10
        )
```

Listing 16-13: Structure solution class test: the result

Before we move on, there's one important gotcha we need to take into account. If you take a look at both tests, you may be tempted to remove the duplicated lines,

```
solution = StructureSolution([self.n_one, self.n_two], [])
solution.bounds_rect(margin=10, scale=4)
```

by moving them to the setUp. That seems a reasonable thing to do so that the tests don't need to repeat those lines, but if you want to go ahead and do the refactor, you'll find that the second test now fails. Why?

The answer has to do with how the @patch decorator works. It has to decorate the function where the dependency it's patching gets resolved, and in our case, the make_rect_containing_with_margin function is imported when the StructureSolution class is instantiated. Therefore, at least for the second test, the instantiation of this class needs to happen in the test method, which is annotated with the @patch decorator.

Testing the Structure Resolution Process

Let's now add a few tests to ensure the structure resolution process yields the correct results. For these tests, we'll define the structure in Figure 16-7 in code.

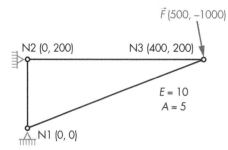

Figure 16-7: Structure for the unit tests

Create a new file in the *structures/tests* directory named *structure_test.py*. In the file, enter the code in Listing 16-14.

```python
import unittest
from unittest.mock import patch

from eqs import Matrix
from geom2d import Point, Vector
from eqs.vector import Vector as EqVector
from structures.model.node import StrNode
from structures.model.bar import StrBar
from structures.model.structure import Structure


class StructureTest(unittest.TestCase):

    def setUp(self):
        section = 5
        young = 10
        load = Vector(500, -1000)

        self.n_1 = StrNode(1, Point(0, 0))
        self.n_2 = StrNode(2, Point(0, 200))
        self.n_3 = StrNode(3, Point(400, 200), [load])
        self.b_12 = StrBar(1, self.n_1, self.n_2, section, young)
        self.b_23 = StrBar(2, self.n_2, self.n_3, section, young)
        self.b_13 = StrBar(3, self.n_1, self.n_3, section, young)

    ❶ self.structure = Structure(
            [self.n_1, self.n_2, self.n_3],
            [self.b_12, self.b_23, self.b_13]
        )

    def test_nodes_count(self):
        ❷ self.assertEqual(3, self.structure.nodes_count)

    def test_bars_count(self):
```

```
    ❸ self.assertEqual(3, self.structure.bars_count)

    def test_loads_count(self):
        ❹ self.assertEqual(1, self.structure.loads_count)
```

Listing 16-14: Structure resolution test

This listing defines the StructureTest test class. In the setUp method, which is called before every test, we define the structure in Figure 16-7. The structure has three nodes: n_1, n_2, and n_3. The last one, n_3, has a load applied to it. We're not adding the external constraints to nodes 1 and 2 yet; we'll see why this is in a minute. Then, we create the bars b_12, b_23, and b_13 between the nodes we just defined; we use the values 5 and 10 for the cross section and Young's modulus. With all these nodes and bars, the structure is finally instantiated ❶.

Next come three simple tests. The first ensures that the structure counts how many nodes it has ❷. The second does the same thing but with bars ❸. The third also does the same, this time with the number of loads applied to the structure ❹.

One of the most complex operations in solving the structure is assembling the stiffness matrix, so let's add a test to check this matrix is properly assembled before we apply the external constraint conditions. Since we haven't yet added external constraints to the structure, the matrix that is passed to the cholesky_solve function is the system's matrix we're looking for. If we mock the cholesky_solve function, the arguments passed to it are the system's stiffness matrix and load vector, which we can capture to make assertions. By mocking this function, our code won't execute the Cholesky's method original code, which is fine because that logic shouldn't interfere with our test. Enter the new test in Listing 16-15.

```
class StructureTest(unittest.TestCase):
    --snip--

❶ @patch('structures.model.structure.cholesky_solve')
    def test_assemble_system_matrix(self, cholesky_mock):
        eal3 = 0.1118033989
        c2_eal3 = .8 * eal3
        s2_eal3 = .2 * eal3
        cs_eal3 = .4 * eal3
    ❷ expected_mat = Matrix(6, 6).set_data([
            c2_eal3, cs_eal3, 0, 0, -c2_eal3, -cs_eal3,
            cs_eal3, .25 + s2_eal3, 0, -.25, -cs_eal3, -s2_eal3,
            0, 0, .125, 0, -.125, 0,
            0, -.25, 0, .25, 0, 0,
            -c2_eal3, -cs_eal3, -.125, 0, .125 + c2_eal3, cs_eal3,
            -cs_eal3, -s2_eal3, 0, 0, cs_eal3, s2_eal3
        ])

        self.structure.solve_structure()
```

❸ `[actual_mat, _] = cholesky_mock.call_args[0]`

❹ `cholesky_mock.assert_called_once()`
❺ `self.assertEqual(expected_mat, actual_mat)`

Listing 16-15: System's stiffness matrix assembly test

We first want the `cholesky_solve` function mocked, so we've added an `@patch` decorator with the path to where this function is looked up: the structures/model/structure package's *cholesky_solve* module ❶. Notice how we pass `cholesky_mock` as an argument to the test method.

Next, we define the expected structure's stiffness matrix: `expected_mat`. This is a 6×6 matrix (three nodes with two degrees of freedom each). I've done the math and assembled the matrix by hand; I suggest you do this as well to make sure you understand the process. There are some auxiliary variables defined for bar $1 \to 3$:

- `eal3` is the $\frac{EA}{l}$ amount
- `c2_eal3` is $\cos^2 \theta \times \frac{EA}{l}$
- `s2_eal3` is $\sin^2 \theta \times \frac{EA}{l}$
- `cs_eal3` is $\cos \theta \times \sin \theta \times \frac{EA}{l}$

The numbers in the stiffness matrices for bars $1 \to 2$ and $2 \to 3$ are straightforward because their angles are $\frac{\pi}{2}$ and 0 radians, respectively. After assembling the global matrix using the three bars' matrices, the result is ❷.

To run the resolution code, we have to call the `solve_structure` method. After executing the solve method, we're interested in knowing which arguments were passed to the `cholesky_mock` function. Mocks have an attribute, `call_args`, a list containing the arguments passed to each of the calls to the mock. Our mock function was called only once, so we want the arguments to this first call.

We destructured `cholesky_mock`'s `call_args` for the first call (`call_args[0]`) and only kept the first one in a variable named `actual_mat` ❸. As you can see, the second element in the left-side list (`[actual_mat, _]`) is an underscore, meaning there is a value for that position in the right-side list (`cholesky_mock` `.call_args[0]`), but we're not interested in saving it.

Then come two assertions. The first one checks that `cholesky_mock` was called only once ❹, and the second compares the expected stiffness matrix with the actual stiffness matrix passed to the `cholesky_mock` resolution function ❺.

In this test, we're ensuring that the Cholesky resolution function gets passed the right structure's stiffness matrix assembled without external constraint conditions applied. Let's now write a new test with these constraints to check that the stiffness matrix is correctly modified to include them. Enter the test in Listing 16-16.

```
class StructureTest(unittest.TestCase):
    --snip--
```

```
❶ @patch('structures.model.structure.cholesky_solve')
   def test_system_matrix_constraints(self, cholesky_mock):
❷     self._set_external_constraints()

       eal3 = 0.1118033989
       c2_eal3 = .8 * eal3
       s2_eal3 = .2 * eal3
       cs_eal3 = .4 * eal3
❸     expected_mat = Matrix(6, 6).set_data([
           1, 0, 0, 0, 0, 0,
           0, 1, 0, 0, 0, 0,
           0, 0, 1, 0, 0, 0,
           0, 0, 0, 1, 0, 0,
           0, 0, 0, 0, .125 + c2_eal3, cs_eal3,
           0, 0, 0, 0, cs_eal3, s2_eal3
       ])

       self.structure.solve_structure()
       [actual_mat, _] = cholesky_mock.call_args[0]

       cholesky_mock.assert_called_once()
❹     self.assertEqual(expected_mat, actual_mat)
```

Listing 16-16: System's stiffness matrix constraints test

This test is similar to the previous one. The cholesky_solve function is patched the same way ❶, and the new mock argument, cholesky_mock, is passed to the test method. Then, we call a private method to add the external constraints to nodes 1 and 2, like they appear in Figure 16-7 ❷. We'll have to write this method after the test.

Then comes the definition of the expected matrix, this time with the external constraints applied ❸. The only terms that are not zero, apart from the ones in the main diagonal, are those that belong to node 3: degrees of freedom 4 and 5. For this reason, only the terms in those row and column indices are nonzero.

The rest of the test is exactly the same as before: we call the solve _structure method on the structure instance. Then we save the matrix argument extracted from the call to cholesky_mock into a variable named actual_mat. Note that we're using a list unpacking for this, where the second item, which is the system's load vector, is ignored by using an underscore. There's the assertion that checks if the Cholesky mock function has been called only once, and the check comparing the actual and expected system matrices ❹.

Lastly, we need to write the _set_external_constraints function that applies the external constraints to nodes 1 and 2. After the method we've just written, enter the code in Listing 16-17.

```
class StructureTest(unittest.TestCase):
   --snip--
```

```
def _set_external_constraints(self):
    self.n_1.dx_constrained = True
    self.n_1.dy_constrained = True
    self.n_2.dx_constrained = True
    self.n_2.dy_constrained = True
```

Listing 16-17: Setting external constraints to nodes

Let's try one last test to check the load vector assembly process. The idea is to follow the structure of the last two tests, but this time checking the load vector. Enter the test in Listing 16-18.

```
class StructureTest(unittest.TestCase):
    --snip--

❶ @patch('structures.model.structure.cholesky_solve')
    def test_assemble_system_vector(self, cholesky_mock):
    ❷ expected_vec = EqVector(6).set_data([
            0, 0, 0, 0, 500, -1000
        ])

        self.structure.solve_structure()
    ❸ [_, actual_vec] = cholesky_mock.call_args[0]

    ❹ self.assertEqual(expected_vec, actual_vec)
```

Listing 16-18: System's load vector assembly test

We patch the cholesky_solve function the same way as before ❶. Then we declare the expected load vector ❷, which this time is easy, as there's only one load applied to node 3.

The rest of the test is similar. The major difference is that this time we're destructuring the second argument of the first call to the cholesky _mock ❸, which is the passed-in vector, the load vector that our code produced. This time we're not asserting that the mock was called once, as we've done in the last two tests; we could, but that condition is already tested. There's no need to repeat the same assertion. What we do want to check is that the actual_vec equals the expected_vec ❹.

We may now run our tests. To do so from the shell, run the following command:

```
$ python3 -m unittest structures/tests/structure_test.py
```

This should produce the following output, if all of your tests passed:

```
Ran 6 tests in 0.004s
```

```
OK
```

We could write a few more unit tests, but we won't be doing so for brevity reasons. Nevertheless, I suggest you come up with more tests and exercise your test doubles skills.

Summary

In this chapter, we developed the structure's resolution algorithm, a complex piece of logic that we split among a few private methods. This resolution process does all the heavy lifting in assembling the structure's global stiffness matrix and vector, applying the external constraints, and solving the resulting system of equations using the Cholesky's procedure we implemented earlier. Once the node global displacements are obtained, they are used to construct the structure solution model. We'll see in Chapter 18 how to produce a graphic result for this solution model.

We also introduced the concept of test doubles, a key technique to write good unit tests by isolating a small part of the code from its collaborators. There are a few different test doubles; Python's *unittest* implementation basically provides us with one: the mock. Nevertheless, this mock implementation is so flexible that it can also be used as a stub or spy. We learned how to use this class and the @patch decorator by using them to test our latest code.

It's now time to focus on reading and parsing structures from text files so we can feed our resolution algorithm with some fine structure definitions. Let's go for it!

17

READING INPUT FROM A FILE

Any engineering application we develop will require some data input. For example, to solve a truss structure using the algorithm we developed in the previous chapter, we first need to construct the structure model. It'd be tedious to manually instantiate the classes to construct the model every time we want to solve a structure; it'd be more convenient to simply pass our app a plaintext file that follows a given and well-defined scheme defining the structure we want to solve. In this chapter, we'll equip our app with a file parser function that reads text files, interprets them, and constructs the model that the app uses internally.

Defining the Input Format

For our application to work, the files we feed it need to have a well-defined structure. The text file has to include the definition of the nodes, the loads applied to them, and the bars of the structure. Let's decide on a format for each of these parts.

The Nodes Format

Each node will be defined in its own line, following this format,

```
<node_id>: (<x_coord>, <y_coord>) (<external_constraints>)
```

where

- *node_id* is the ID given to the node.
- *x_coord* is the x position of the node.
- *y_coord* is the y position of the node.
- *external_constraints* is a set of the constrained movements.

Here's an example:

```
1: (250, 400) (xy)
```

This defines a node with an ID of 1, at position (250, 400), with its x and y displacements externally constrained.

The Loads Format

Loads will be defined separately from the nodes they're applied to, so we'll have to indicate the ID of the node where the load is applied. Having the nodes and loads defined in different lines allows us to simplify the input parsing process by using two simple regular expressions (one for the nodes and another for the loads) instead of one long and complicated regular expression. Each load will be defined on a separate line.

Let's use the following format for loads,

```
<node_id> -> (<Fx>, <Fy>)
```

where

- *node_id* is the node where the load is applied.
- *Fx* is the x component of the load.
- *Fy* is the y component of the load.

Here's an example:

```
3 -> (500, -1000)
```

This defines a load ⟨500, −1000⟩ applied to the node with an ID of 3. We're using the -> character sequence to separate the node ID from the load components instead of a colon so that it's clear we're not assigning an ID to the load itself. Rather, we're applying the load to the node with that ID.

The Bars Format

Bars are defined between two nodes and have a section and Young's modulus. As with nodes and loads, each bar will be defined on its own line. We can give bars the following format,

```
<bar_id>: (<start_node_id> -> <end_node_id>) <A> <E>
```

where

- *bar_id* is the ID given to the bar.
- *start_node_id* is the ID of the start node.
- *end_node_id* is the ID of the end node.
- *A* is the cross-section area.
- *E* is the Young's modulus.

Here's an example:

```
1: (1 -> 2) 30 20000000
```

This defines a bar between nodes 1 and 2, with a cross section of 30 and a Young's modulus of 20000000. This bar is given an ID of 1.

The File Format

Now that we've come up with a format for the nodes, loads, and bars, let's see how we can put them all together in one file. We're looking for a file structure that's simple to write by hand but that's also easy to parse.

One interesting idea is to divide the file into sections, each opened by a header:

```
<section_name>
```

Each section should contain only the lines defining entities of the same type.

Given that our structure definition files will have three different kinds of entities—nodes, loads, and bars—they'll need three different sections. For example, the structure we used for the unit tests in the previous chapter, included here as Figure 17-1, would be defined as follows:

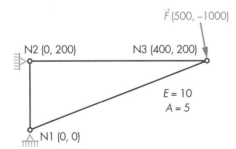

Figure 17-1: Structure from previous chapter's unit tests

```
nodes
1: (0, 0)      (xy)
2: (0, 200)    (xy)
3: (400, 200) ()

loads
3 -> (500, -1000)

bars
1: (1 -> 2) 5 10
2: (2 -> 3) 5 10
3: (1 -> 3) 5 10
```

Now that we've defined a format for our structure definition files, we need to work on a parser. A *parser* is a component (a function or class) that reads text, interprets it, and translates it into a data structure or model. In this case, the model is our truss structure class: Structure. We'll use regular expressions, as we did in Chapter 9.

Finding the Regular Expressions

If we know the structure ahead of time, regular expressions are a reliable way of extracting all the information we need from plaintext. We'll need three different regular expressions: one for the nodes, one for the loads, and one for the bars. If you need a refresher on regular expressions, take a moment to review "Regular Expressions" on page 9. Let's design these regular expressions.

The Nodes Regex

To match nodes defined in our format, we can use the following regular expression:

```
/(?P<id>\d+)\s*:\s*
\((?P<pos>[\d\s\.,\-]+)\)\)\s*
\((?P<ec>[xy]{0,2})\)\)/
```

This is one scary regular expression. It's split between several lines because it was too long to fit in a single line, but you can imagine it as being just one line. Let's break down this regular expression into its parts.

(?P<id>\d+)   This matches the node's ID, a number with one or more digits (\d+), and captures it in a group named id.

\s*:\s*   This matches the colon after the ID with arbitrary and optional spaces around it (\s*).

\((?P<pos>[\d\s\.,\-]+)\)   This matches the node's position coordinates inside the parentheses and captures them in a group named pos. Note that we match the whole expression between the parentheses; that includes the two coordinates and the comma that separates them. We'll split the two numbers in code. We do it this way so that our already monstrous regular expression doesn't become even scarier. Combining regular expressions with Python's string manipulation methods is a powerful technique.

\s* This matches zero or more spaces separating the coordinates group from the external constraints group.

\(((?P<ec>[xy]{0,2})\) This last part matches the external constraints defined between parentheses and captures them in a group named ec. The contents inside the parentheses are limited to the character group [xy], that is, the characters "x" and "y." There's also a constraint in the number of characters allowed, which is any number between 0 and 2 ({0,2}).

We'll see this regular expression in action soon. Figure 17-2 may help you understand each of the subparts in the regular expression.

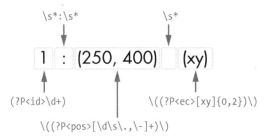

Figure 17-2: Node regular expression visualized

Let's take a look at how to parse the loads.

The Loads Regex

To match loads written with the format we defined, we'll use the following regular expression:

```
/(?P<node_id>\d+)\s*->\s*\(((?P<vec>[\d\s\.,\-]+)\)/
```

This regular expression isn't quite as scary as the previous one; let's break it down into its subparts.

(?P<node_id>\d+) This matches the node ID and captures it in a group named node_id.

\s*->\s* This matches the -> character sequence and the optional blank spaces around it.

\(((?P<vec>[\d\s\.,\-]+)\) This matches the entire expression between the parentheses, where the force vector components are defined. The character set [\d\s\.,\-] inside the parentheses is allowed; this includes digits, spaces, dots, commas, and minus signs. Whatever is captured is stored in a capture group named vec.

Figure 17-3 is a breakdown of the regular expression's different parts. Make sure you understand each of them.

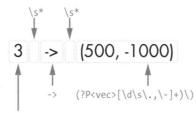

Figure 17-3: Load regular expression visualized

Lastly, let's take a look at the regular expression for the bars.

The Bars Regex

To match bars written using the format we defined earlier, we'll use the following regular expression:

```
/(?P<id>\d+)\s*:\s*
\((?P<start_id>\d+)\s*->\s*(?P<end_id>\d+)\)\)\s*
(?P<sec>[\d\.]+)\s+
(?P<young>[\d\.]+)/
```

This regular expression was also broken down into several lines because of its length, but you can imagine it as being written in one line. Let's break it down piece by piece:

(?P<id>\d+)   This matches the ID assigned to the bar and captures it in the group named id.

\s*:\s*   This matches the colon character and the optional blank space around it.

\((?P<start_id>\d+)\s*->\s*(?P<end_id>\d+)\)   This matches the two node IDs separated by the -> character sequence and the optional space around it. The IDs are captured in the groups named start_id and end_id. This whole expression is required to appear between parentheses.

\s*   This matches the optional blank space between the last parenthesis and the next value, the section.

(?P<sec>[\d\.]+)   This captures a decimal number and assigns it to the group named sec.

\s+   This matches the required blank space between the last parenthesis and the next value, the Young modulus. Recall that, in this case we need at least one space. Otherwise, there would be no way to know where the value for the section ends and the value for the Young modulus begins.

(?P<young>[\d\.]+)   This captures a decimal number and assigns it to the group named young.

This is the largest and most complex regular expression we've seen in the book. Figure 17-4 should help you identify each of its parts.

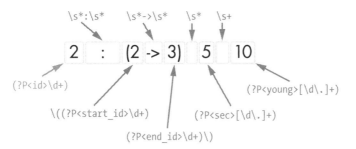

Figure 17-4: Bar regular expression visualized

Now that we have our regular expressions, let's start writing the code to parse our structure files.

Setup

Right now, our *structures* package has the following subdirectories:

```
structures
   |- model
   |- solution
   |- tests
```

Let's create a new package folder named *parse* by right-clicking *structures* and choosing **New ▶ Python Package**. If you're doing this from outside the IDE, don't forget to create an empty *__init__.py* file in the folder. Our *structures* package directory should look like the following:

```
structures
   |- model
   |- parse
   |- solution
   |- tests
```

We're ready to start implementing the code. We'll first implement the logic for parsing nodes, loads, and bars. Each will be defined in its own function along with unit tests. Then, we'll put it all together in a function that reads the entire file's contents, splits it into lines, and parses each line into the right model class.

Parsing Nodes

We'll start with the nodes. In *structures/parse*, create a new file named *node_parse.py*. In this file, enter the code in Listing 17-1.

```
import re

from geom2d import Point
from structures.model.node import StrNode


__NODE_REGEX = r'(?P<id>\d+)\s*:\s*' \
               r'\((?P<pos>[\d\s\.,\-]+)\)\s*' \
               r'\((?P<ec>[xy]{0,2})\)'


def parse_node(node_str: str):
 ❶ match = re.match(__NODE_REGEX, node_str)
    if not match:
        raise ValueError(
            f'Cannot parse node from string: {node_str}'
        )

 ❷ _id = int(match.group('id'))
 ❸ [x, y] = [
        float(num)
        for num in match.group('pos').split(',')
    ]
 ❹ ext_const = match.group('ec')

 ❺ return StrNode(
        _id,
        Point(x, y),
        None,
        'x' in ext_const,
        'y' in ext_const
    )
```

Listing 17-1: Parsing a node from a string

We start by defining the regular expression we saw earlier. It needs to be broken down into multiple lines because it's too long for a single line, but since we're using the continuation backslash character (\), Python will read all the contents into a single line.

Then comes the parse_node function, which accepts a string parameter as input. This string should be formatted following the node's format we defined earlier. We look for a match in the node_str string against the node's regular expression ❶. If there's no match, we raise a ValueError with a message that includes the offending string so that it's easier to debug errors.

Then we extract the ID from the capture group named id and store it in the _id variable ❷.

Next, we parse the x and y position coordinates: we read the contents of the pos capture group and split the string using the comma character.

```
match.group('pos').split(',')
```

This yields the two strings representing the numbers defining the node's position.

Using a list comprehension, we map each of the strings to a float number:

```
[x, y] = [
    float(num)
    for num in match.group('pos').split(',')
]
```

Then we destructure the result into variables x and y ❸.

The last named capture group is ec. It contains the definition of the external constraints. We read its contents and store them in the variable ext_const ❹. Lastly, we create the node instance passing it all the parameters it expects ❺. We pass the ID, the position point, a None for the loads (this will be added later), and the external constraints. The external constraints are added by checking whether the character "x" or "y" is in the constraints string. For this, we use Python's in operator, which checks whether a given value exists in a sequence. Here's an example:

```
>>> 'hardcore' in 'hardcore programming for mechanical engineers'
True

>>> 3 in [1, 2]
False
```

Let's use some unit tests to make sure our code parses nodes correctly.

Testing the Node Parser

Let's create a new test file in the *structures/tests* directory named *node_parse_test.py*. In the file, enter the code in Listing 17-2.

```
import unittest

from geom2d import Point
from structures.parse.node_parse import parse_node


class NodeParseTest(unittest.TestCase):
❶   node_str = '1 : (25.0, 45.0)    (xy)'
❷   node = parse_node(node_str)

    def test_parse_id(self):
        self.assertEqual(1, self.node.id)

    def test_parse_position(self):
```

```
        expected = Point(25.0, 45.0)
        self.assertEqual(expected, self.node.position)

    def test_parse_dx_external_constraint(self):
        self.assertTrue(self.node.dx_constrained)

    def test_parse_dy_external_constraint(self):
        self.assertTrue(self.node.dy_constrained)
```

Listing 17-2: Testing the parsing of a node

This file defines a new test class: NodeParseTest. We've defined a string with the correct format so we can test whether we can parse all of its parts. That string is node_str ❶. We've written all of our tests to work with the node that results when we parse the string ❷; we did this to avoid repeating the same parsing operation in every test.

Then we have a test to ensure the ID is correctly set in the resulting node, another one that checks the node's position, and two more to test whether the external constraints have been added or not.

Let's run our tests to make sure they all pass. You can do so from the IDE or from the shell with the following command:

```
$ python3 -m unittest structures/tests/node_parse_test.py
```

Let's now work on parsing the bars.

Parsing Bars

In *structures/parse*, create a new file named *bar_parse.py*. In this file, enter the code in Listing 17-3.

```
import re
from structures.model.bar import StrBar

__BAR_REGEX = r'(?P<id>\d+)\s*:\s*' \
              r'\((?P<start_id>\d+)\s*->\s*(?P<end_id>\d+)\)\s*' \
              r'(?P<sec>[\d\.]+)\s+' \
              r'(?P<young>[\d\.]+)'


def parse_bar(bar_str: str, nodes_dict):
❶   match = re.match(__BAR_REGEX, bar_str)
    if not match:
        raise ValueError(
            f'Cannot parse bar from string: {bar_str}'
        )

❷   _id = int(match.group('id'))
❸   start_id = int(match.group('start_id'))
```

```
❹ end_id = int(match.group('end_id'))
❺ section = float(match.group('sec'))
❻ young_mod = float(match.group('young'))

❼ start_node = nodes_dict[start_id]
   if start_node is None:
       raise ValueError(f'Node with id: ${start_id} undefined')

   end_node = nodes_dict[end_id]
   if end_node is None:
       raise ValueError(f'Node with id: ${start_id} undefined')

❽ return StrBar(_id, start_node, end_node, section, young_mod)
```

Listing 17-3: Parsing a bar from a string

The regular expression to match the bar definition (__BAR_REGEX) is a bit long and complex. Make sure you enter it carefully. We'll write some unit tests later, so any error here will come to light there.

We've written the parse_bar function, which takes two parameters: the string defining the bar and a dictionary of nodes. In this dictionary, the keys are the IDs of the nodes, and the values are the nodes themselves. The bar needs to have a reference to its end nodes, so these have to be parsed first and then passed to the parse_bar function. This adds a constraint in the way we parse structure files: nodes should appear first.

As with the nodes, we start by matching the passed-in string against our regular expression ❶. If there is no match, we raise a ValueError with a helpful message including the string that couldn't be parsed.

Next, we retrieve and parse the capture groups: id parsed as an integer ❷, start_id ❸ and end_id ❹ parsed as integers, and sec ❺ and young ❻ parsed as floats.

Then we look for the start node in the nodes dictionary ❼ and raise an error if it's not found: we can't build a bar whose nodes don't exist. We do the same thing for the end node, and then we create and return the bar instance in the last line ❽, passing it all the parsed values.

Let's test this code.

Testing the Bar Parser

To test the bar parsing process, create a new file in *structures/tests* named *bar_parse_test.py*. Enter the new tests in Listing 17-4.

```
import unittest

from structures.parse.bar_parse import parse_bar


class BarParseTest(unittest.TestCase):
❶ bar_str = '1: (3 -> 5) 25.0 20000000.0'
```

```
❷ nodes_dict = {
       3: 'Node 3',
       5: 'Node 5'
   }
❸ bar = parse_bar(bar_str, nodes_dict)

   def test_parse_id(self):
       self.assertEqual(1, self.bar.id)

   def test_parse_start_node(self):
       self.assertEqual('Node 3', self.bar.start_node)

   def test_parse_end_node_id(self):
       self.assertEqual('Node 5', self.bar.end_node)

   def test_parse_section(self):
       self.assertEqual(25.0, self.bar.cross_section)

   def test_parse_young_modulus(self):
       self.assertEqual(20000000.0, self.bar.young_mod)
```

Listing 17-4: Testing the parsing of a bar

In this test, we define a bar using its string representation ❶. The parse
_bar function requires a dictionary containing the nodes by ID as its second
argument; we create a dummy (recall the types from the 16 page 447) called
nodes_dict ❷. This dictionary contains the two node IDs mapped to a string.
Our parsing code doesn't really do anything with the nodes or even check
their types; it simply adds them to the bar instance. So for the tests, a string
mocking the node is enough.

Again, we parse ❸ first and store the result in the bar variable. We then
create five tests that check that we've correctly parsed the ID, both start and
end nodes, the cross section, and Young's modulus.

Run the tests to make sure they all pass. You can do so from the shell:

```
$ python3 -m unittest structures/tests/bar_parse_test.py
```

Lastly, we need to parse the loads.

Parsing Loads

We'll now write a function to parse the load strings, but we won't apply the
loads to the nodes here. That'll happen later when we put all the pieces together.

Create a new file in *structures/parse* named *load_parse.py*. Enter the code
in Listing 17-5.

```
import re

from geom2d import Vector

__LOAD_REGEX = r'(?P<node_id>\d+)\s*->\s*' \
              r'\((?P<vec>[\d\s\.,\-]+)\)'


def parse_load(load_str: str):
❶   match = re.match(__LOAD_REGEX, load_str)
    if not match:
        raise ValueError(
            f'Cannot parse load from string: "{load_str}"'
        )

❷   node_id = int(match.group('node_id'))
❸   [fx, fy] = [
        float(num)
        for num in match.group('vec').split(',')
    ]

❹   return node_id, Vector(fx, fy)
```

Listing 17-5: Parsing a load from a string

In this listing we define the regular expression that matches the loads as __LOAD_REGEX. Then comes the parse_load function, which first looks for a match in the passed-in string (load_str) ❶. We raise an error if the string doesn't match __LOAD_REGEX.

The regular expression defines two capturing groups: node_id and vec. The first group is the ID of the node where the load needs to be applied. We convert the value for this first group into an integer and store it in the node_id variable ❷.

To extract the force components, we split the value matched by the vec capture group and then parse each part, convert it to a float value, and use destructuring to extract the components into the fx and fy variables ❸.

Lastly, we return a tuple of the node ID and a vector with the force components ❹.

Let's test this logic to make sure it parses loads correctly.

Testing the Load Parser

In the *structures/tests* folder, create a new file named *load_parse_test.py*. Enter the test code in Listing 17-6.

```
import unittest

from geom2d import Vector
```

```
from structures.parse.load_parse import parse_load


class LoadParseTest(unittest.TestCase):

    load_str = '1 -> (250.0, -3500.0)'
    (node_id, load) = parse_load(load_str)

    def test_parse_node_id(self):
        self.assertEqual(1, self.node_id)

    def test_parse_load_vector(self):
        expected = Vector(250.0, -3500.0)
        self.assertEqual(expected, self.load)
```

Listing 17-6: Testing the parsing of a load

This test defines a string representing a load applied to a node with an ID of 1 and whose components are $\langle 250.0, -3500.0 \rangle$. The string is stored in the load_str variable and passed to the parse_load function.

In the first test, we check that we've correctly parsed the node ID, which is returned by the function as the tuple's first value. Then, we check that we've correctly parsed the tuple's second value, the vector. These two simple tests are enough to make sure our function does its job.

Run the tests from the IDE or from the shell:

```
$ python3 -m unittest structures/tests/load_parse_test.py
```

Now that we have functions that can parse the structure's individual parts from their string representations, it's time to put them together. In the next section, we'll work on a function that reads all the lines of a structure definition file and generates the corresponding model.

Parsing the Structure

Our structure files define each entity on its own line, and entities appear grouped by sections. If you recall, we defined three sections for the three different entities we need to parse: nodes, bars, and loads. Here's the previous example of a structure file:

```
nodes
1: (0, 0)      (xy)
2: (0, 200)    (xy)
3: (400, 200)  ()

loads
3 -> (500, -1000)

bars
```

```
1: (1 -> 2) 5 10
2: (2 -> 3) 5 10
3: (1 -> 3) 5 10
```

Because these files will mostly be written by hand, it would be nice if we allowed the inclusion of comments: lines that are ignored by the parsing mechanism but explain something to someone reading the file, just like comments in code.

Here's an example:

```
# only node with a load applied
3: (400, 200) ()
```

We'll borrow Python's syntax and use the # symbol to mark the start of a comment. Comments will have to appear on their own lines.

Overview

Because we'll need to write a few functions, it may be helpful to have a diagram of the structure parsing process with the function names annotated after the steps. Take a look at Figure 17-5.

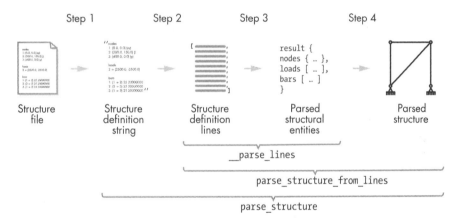

Figure 17-5: Structure parsing process

In this diagram, we show each step of the parsing process. We start with a structure file defining the structure in plaintext following our standard format.

The first step is to read the file contents into a string. We'll implement this part in our application in Chapter 19.

The second step consists of splitting the big string into multiple lines.

The third step is parsing those lines into a dictionary of the structural primitives. This step is handled by the private __parse_lines function.

The fourth and final step is aggregating those parsed structural items into a structure instance.

The parse_structure_from_lines function is a combination of steps 3 and 4: it transforms a list of definition lines into a complete structure. The parse _structure function goes one step further and splits a single string into multiple lines.

Setup

In the *structures/parse* directory, create a new file named *str_parse.py*. The *structures* package should now look like this:

```
structures
  |- model
  |   | ...
  |- parse
  |   |- __init__.py
  |   |- bar_parse.py
  |   |- load_parse.py
  |   |- node_parse.py
  |   |- str_parse.py
  |- solution
  |   | ...
  |- tests
  |   | ...
```

Let's start the implementation with a function that determines whether a line in the file is blank or a comment. This function will let us know whether a given line can be ignored or whether it has to be parsed.

Ignoring Blank Lines and Comments

In *str_parse.py*, enter the code in Listing 17-7.

```python
__COMMENT_INDICATOR = '#'



def __should_ignore_line(line: str):
    stripped = line.strip()
    return len(stripped) == 0 or \
            stripped.startswith(__COMMENT_INDICATOR)
```

Listing 17-7: Function to determine the lines that need to be ignored

We define a constant, __COMMENT_INDICATOR, with the # character for its value. If we ever want to change the way comments are identified, we'll simply need to edit this line.

Next is the __should_ignore_line function. This function receives a string and removes any surrounding blank spaces (in other words, it strips the string). Then, if the line has a length of zero or starts with the comment indicator, the function returns a True value, and a False otherwise.

Parsing the Lines

Now that we have a way to filter out the lines that don't need to be parsed, let's look at the ones that do. We're going to define a function that receives a list of strings representing the lines and identifies whether the line is a section header ("nodes," "bars," or "loads") or an entity. In the case of a section header, the function will set a flag to keep track of the current section being read. The rest of the function will take care of parsing each line using the corresponding parser.

In the file *str_parse.py*, enter the code in Listing 17-8.

```
import re

from .bar_parse import parse_bar
from .load_parse import parse_load
from .node_parse import parse_node

__COMMENT_INDICATOR = '#'
__NODES_HEADER = 'nodes'
__LOADS_HEADER = 'loads'
__BARS_HEADER = 'bars'


def __parse_lines(lines: [str]):
❶ reading = ''
❷ result = {'nodes': {}, 'loads': [], 'bars': []}

    for i, line in enumerate(lines):
      ❸ if __should_ignore_line(line):
            continue

        # <--- header ---> #
      ❹ if re.match(__NODES_HEADER, line):
            reading = 'nodes'
        elif re.match(__BARS_HEADER, line):
            reading = 'bars'
        elif re.match(__LOADS_HEADER, line):
            reading = 'loads'

        # <--- definition ---> #
      ❺ elif reading == 'nodes':
            node = parse_node(line)
            result['nodes'][node.id] = node
        elif reading == 'bars':
            bar = parse_bar(line, result['nodes'])
            result['bars'].append(bar)
        elif reading == 'loads':
            load = parse_load(line)
```

```
            result['loads'].append(load)
        else:
            raise RuntimeError(
                f'Unknown error in line ${i}: ${line}'
            )

    return result


def __should_ignore_line(line: str):
    --snip--
```

Listing 17-8: Parsing the lines

We first add three variables with the names of the file headers: __NODES
_HEADER, __LOADS_HEADER, and __BARS_HEADER. These constants define the names
of the sections.

Then comes the __parse_lines function definition, which takes one parameter: the list of lines in the structure file. The function declares a variable named reading ❶. This variable indicates what structure section the later
loop is currently in. For example, when its value is 'bars', the subsequent
lines should be parsed using the parse_bar function until the end of the file
or a new section is encountered.

Next comes the definition of the result dictionary ❷. It's initialized with
three keys: 'nodes', 'loads', and 'bars'. We'll add the parsed elements to
this dictionary, in their corresponding key's collection. Loads and bars are
stored in a list and nodes in a dictionary, with the keys being their IDs. We
store nodes mapped to their keys in a dictionary because both loads and
bars refer to them by ID in the structure file; thus, when we link them, it'll
be more convenient to look them up by ID.

Next is the loop that iterates over the lines' enumeration. Recall that
Python's enumerate function returns an iterable sequence that includes the
original objects along with their index. We'll use the index only if we encounter an error, using the line number in the error message to make looking for the error in the input file easier. The first thing we do with each line
is check whether it's blank or a comment ❸, in which case we skip it using
the continue statement.

Next, we have a couple of if-else statements. The first block of them is
for matching header lines ❹. When a line is found to match one of the three
possible headers, we set the reading variable to the header's value. The later
if-else statements evaluate reading to determine which structural element
to parse ❺. If reading has the value 'nodes', we use the parse_node function to
parse the line and store the result in the result dictionary, under the 'nodes'
key:

```
result['nodes'][node.id] = node
```

The same goes for bars and loads, but remember that in their case, they're stored in a list:

```
result['bars'].append(bar)
```

The function then returns the result dictionary.

We've implemented a function that reads a sequence of text lines and converts each of them into a structure class instance (what we know as parsing). These instances represent the nodes, bars, and loads of the structure. The function returns a dictionary that bundles these instances by type. The next step is using these parsed objects to construct a Structure instance.

Splitting the Lines and Instantiating the Structure

Given the contents of a structure file as a string, we want to split this string into its lines. We'll pass those lines to the __parse_lines function we wrote earlier, and using the parsed objects we can construct an instance of our Structure class.

In the *str_parse.py* file, before the __parse_lines function, enter the code in Listing 17-9.

```
import re

from structures.model.structure import Structure
from .bar_parse import parse_bar
from .load_parse import parse_load
from .node_parse import parse_node

__COMMENT_INDICATOR = '#'
__NODES_HEADER = 'nodes'
__LOADS_HEADER = 'loads'
__BARS_HEADER = 'bars'


def parse_structure(structure_string: str):
❶   lines = structure_string.split('\n')
    return parse_structure_from_lines(lines)


def parse_structure_from_lines(lines: [str]):
❷   parsed = __parse_lines(lines)
    nodes_dict = parsed['nodes']
    loads = parsed['loads']
    bars = parsed['bars']

❸   __apply_loads_to_nodes(loads, nodes_dict)

    return Structure(
```

```
❹ list(nodes_dict.values()),
    bars
)


def __apply_loads_to_nodes(loads, nodes):
❺ for node_id, load in loads:
        nodes[node_id].add_load(load)

--snip--
```

Listing 17-9: Splitting the lines

We've written three new functions. The first of them, parse_structure, splits the passed-in string into its lines ❶ and forwards those lines to the parse_structure_from_lines function defined afterward.

This second function, parse_structure_from_lines, passes the lines to __parse_lines and saves the result in a variable called parsed ❷. It then extracts the contents of this result dictionary to the variables: nodes_dict, loads, and bars.

The loads are defined separately from the nodes they're applied to; thus, we need to add each load to its respective node ❸. To do this, we've written another small function: __apply_loads_to_nodes. Recall that the loads were defined using the format

```
1 -> (500, -1000)
```

and are parsed by our parse_load function as a tuple consisting of the node ID and the load components as a vector:

```
(1, Vector(500, -1000))
```

It's important to keep this in mind to understand the loop in __apply _loads_to_nodes ❺. The loop iterates over the load tuples, and on each iteration, it stores the node ID and load vector into the node_id and load variables, respectively. Because our nodes are stored in a dictionary whose keys are the node IDs, applying the loads is a piece of cake.

Once the loads have been applied to the nodes (back in parse_structure _from_lines), the last step is to return an instance of the Structure class. The class's constructor expects a list of nodes and a list of bars. The bars are already parsed as a list, but the nodes were in a dictionary. To turn the values of a dictionary into a list, we simply need to use Python's list function on the dictionary values, which we extract using the values() method ❹.

With this, our parsing logic is ready!

The Result

For your reference, Listing 17-10 shows the complete code for *str_parse.py*.

```python
import re

from structures.model.structure import Structure
from .bar_parse import parse_bar
from .load_parse import parse_load
from .node_parse import parse_node

__COMMENT_INDICATOR = '#'
__NODES_HEADER = 'nodes'
__LOADS_HEADER = 'loads'
__BARS_HEADER = 'bars'


def parse_structure(structure_string: str):
    lines = structure_string.split('\n')
    return parse_structure_from_lines(lines)


def parse_structure_from_lines(lines: [str]):
    parsed = __parse_lines(lines)
    nodes_dict = parsed['nodes']
    loads = parsed['loads']
    bars = parsed['bars']

    __apply_loads_to_nodes(loads, nodes_dict)

    return Structure(
        list(nodes_dict.values()),
        bars
    )


def __apply_loads_to_nodes(loads, nodes):
    for node_id, load in loads:
        nodes[node_id].add_load(load)


def __parse_lines(lines: [str]):
    reading = ''
    result = {'nodes': {}, 'loads': [], 'bars': []}

    for i, line in enumerate(lines):
        if __should_ignore_line(line):
            continue

        # <--- header ---> #
        if re.match(__NODES_HEADER, line):
```

```
                reading = 'nodes'
            elif re.match(__BARS_HEADER, line):
                reading = 'bars'
            elif re.match(__LOADS_HEADER, line):
                reading = 'loads'

            # <--- definition ---> #
            elif reading == 'nodes':
                node = parse_node(line)
                result['nodes'][node.id] = node
            elif reading == 'bars':
                bar = parse_bar(line, result['nodes'])
                result['bars'].append(bar)
            elif reading == 'loads':
                load = parse_load(line)
                result['loads'].append(load)
            else:
                raise RuntimeError(
                    f'Unknown error in line ${{i}}: ${{line}}'
                )

    return result


def __should_ignore_line(line: str):
    stripped = line.strip()
    return len(stripped) == 0 or \
           stripped.startswith(__COMMENT_INDICATOR)
```

Listing 17-10: Parsing the structure

Before we move to the next section, open the *__init__.py* file in *parse*, and enter the following import:

```
from .str_parse import parse_structure
```

This allows us to import the parse_structure function like this,

```
from structures.parse import parse_structure
```

instead of this slightly longer version:

```
from structures.parse.str_parse import parse_structure
```

Let's make sure our parsing function is working correctly by implementing some automated tests.

Testing the Structure Parser

To make sure the parse_structure function works as expected, we'll now add a few unit tests. First, we want to create a structure definition file to use in the test. In the *structures/tests* directory, create a new file, *test_str.txt*, with the following contents:

```
# Nodes
nodes
1: (0.0, 0.0)      (xy)
2: (200.0, 150.0)  ()
3: (400.0, 0.0)    (y)



# Loads
loads
2 -> (2500.0, -3500.0)



# Bars
bars
1: (1 -> 2) 25 20000000
2: (2 -> 3) 25 20000000
3: (1 -> 3) 25 20000000
```

We've added comment lines and some extra blank lines; our function should ignore those. Create a new test file: *str_parse_test.py* (Listing 17-11).

```
import unittest

import pkg_resources as res

from structures.parse import parse_structure


class StructureParseTest(unittest.TestCase):

    def setUp(self):
        str_bytes = res.resource_string(__name__, 'test_str.txt')
        str_string = str_bytes.decode("utf-8")
        self.structure = parse_structure(str_string)
```

Listing 17-11: Setting up the structure parsing test

The file defines a new test class: StructureParseTest. In the setUp method, we load the *test_str.txt* file as bytes using the resource_string function. Then, we decode those bytes into a UTF-8 encoded Python string. Lastly, using parse_structure, we parse the structure string and store the result in a class attribute: self.structure.

Testing the Node Parser

Let's add some test cases to ensure the structure that we parsed from the *test_str.txt* file contains the expected nodes. After the setUp method, enter the first tests (Listing 17-12).

```
import unittest

import pkg_resources as res

from geom2d import Point
from structures.parse import parse_structure


class StructureParseTest(unittest.TestCase):
    --snip--

    def test_parse_nodes_count(self):
        self.assertEqual(3, self.structure.nodes_count)

    def test_parse_nodes(self):
      ❶ nodes = self.structure._Structure__nodes
        self.assertEqual(
            Point(0, 0),
            nodes[0].position
        )
        self.assertEqual(
            Point(200, 150),
            nodes[1].position
        )
        self.assertEqual(
            Point(400, 0),
            nodes[2].position
        )

    def test_parse_node_constraints(self):
        nodes = self.structure._Structure__nodes

        self.assertTrue(nodes[0].dx_constrained)
        self.assertTrue(nodes[0].dy_constrained)

        self.assertFalse(nodes[1].dx_constrained)
        self.assertFalse(nodes[1].dy_constrained)

        self.assertFalse(nodes[2].dx_constrained)
        self.assertTrue(nodes[2].dy_constrained)
```

Listing 17-12: Testing the structure parsing: the nodes

We've written three tests. The first one checks that there are three nodes in the structure. The next test ensures that those three nodes have the correct position.

There's one interesting thing to note here. Since the __nodes list is private to the Structure class, Python uses a trick to try to hide it from us. Python prepends an underscore and the name of the class to the name of its private attributes. The __nodes attribute will therefore be called _Structure__nodes, and not __nodes as we'd expect. This is why, to access it from our tests, we use this name ❶.

The third and last test checks if the external constraints in the nodes have the right values as defined in the structure definition file. Let's run the tests. You can click the green play button in the IDE or use the shell:

```
$ python3 -m unittest structures/tests/str_parse_test.py
```

A success message should be displayed in the shell.

Testing the Bar Parser

Let's now test if the bars are also parsed correctly. After the test cases we just wrote, enter the ones in Listing 17-13.

```
class StructureParseTest(unittest.TestCase):
    --snip--

    def test_parse_bars_count(self):
        self.assertEqual(3, self.structure.bars_count)

    def test_parse_bars(self):
        bars = self.structure._Structure__bars

        self.assertEqual(1, bars[0].start_node.id)
        self.assertEqual(2, bars[0].end_node.id)

        self.assertEqual(2, bars[1].start_node.id)
        self.assertEqual(3, bars[1].end_node.id)

        self.assertEqual(1, bars[2].start_node.id)
        self.assertEqual(3, bars[2].end_node.id)
```

Listing 17-13: Testing the structure parsing: the bars

The first test asserts that there are three bars in the structure. The second test checks that every bar in the structure is linked to the correct node IDs. Same as before, to access the private list of bars, we need to prepend _Structure to the attribute name: _Structure__bars.

I invite you to add two more tests that check that the values for the cross section and Young's modulus are correctly parsed into the bars. We won't include them here for brevity reasons.

Run the test class again to make sure our new tests also pass. From the shell, run this:

```
$ python3 -m unittest structures/tests/str_parse_test.py
```

Testing the Load Parser

Let's add the two last tests to ensure the loads are properly parsed. Enter the code in Listing 17-14.

```python
import unittest

import pkg_resources as res

from geom2d import Point, Vector
from structures.parse import parse_structure


class StructureParseTest(unittest.TestCase):
    --snip--

    def test_parse_loads_count(self):
        self.assertEqual(1, self.structure.loads_count)

    def test_apply_load_to_node(self):
        node = self.structure._Structure__nodes[1]
        self.assertEqual(
            Vector(2500, -3500),
            node.net_load
        )
```

Listing 17-14: Testing the structure parsing: the loads

In these two last tests, we check that the number of loads in the structure is 1 and that it's being correctly applied to the second node.

Let's run all the tests to make sure all pass:

```
$ python3 -m unittest structures/tests/str_parse_test.py
```

If your code is well implemented, all the tests should pass, and you should see the following in the shell:

```
Ran 7 tests in 0.033s
```

```
OK
```

Test Class Result

We've done a few tests, so Listing 17-15 shows the resulting test class for your reference.

```python
import unittest

import pkg_resources as res

from geom2d import Point, Vector
from structures.parse import parse_structure


class StructureParseTest(unittest.TestCase):

    def setUp(self):
        str_bytes = res.resource_string(__name__, 'test_str.txt')
        str_string = str_bytes.decode("utf-8")
        self.structure = parse_structure(str_string)

    def test_parse_nodes_count(self):
        self.assertEqual(3, self.structure.nodes_count)

    def test_parse_nodes(self):
        nodes = self.structure._Structure__nodes
        self.assertEqual(
            Point(0, 0),
            nodes[0].position
        )
        self.assertEqual(
            Point(200, 150),
            nodes[1].position
        )
        self.assertEqual(
            Point(400, 0),
            nodes[2].position
        )

    def test_parse_node_constraints(self):
        nodes = self.structure._Structure__nodes

        self.assertTrue(nodes[0].dx_constrained)
        self.assertTrue(nodes[0].dy_constrained)

        self.assertFalse(nodes[1].dx_constrained)
        self.assertFalse(nodes[1].dy_constrained)

        self.assertFalse(nodes[2].dx_constrained)
        self.assertTrue(nodes[2].dy_constrained)

    def test_parse_bars_count(self):
        self.assertEqual(3, self.structure.bars_count)
```

```
def test_parse_bars(self):
    bars = self.structure._Structure__bars

    self.assertEqual(1, bars[0].start_node.id)
    self.assertEqual(2, bars[0].end_node.id)

    self.assertEqual(2, bars[1].start_node.id)
    self.assertEqual(3, bars[1].end_node.id)

    self.assertEqual(1, bars[2].start_node.id)
    self.assertEqual(3, bars[2].end_node.id)

def test_parse_loads_count(self):
    self.assertEqual(1, self.structure.loads_count)

def test_apply_load_to_node(self):
    node = self.structure._Structure__nodes[1]
    self.assertEqual(
        Vector(2500, -3500),
        node.net_load
    )
```

Listing 17-15: Testing the structure parsing

Our structure parsing logic is ready and tested!

Summary

In this chapter, we first defined a format for our structure files. It's a simple plaintext format that can be written by hand.

We then implemented functions to parse each of the lines in our structure files into its appropriate structural element: nodes, loads, and bars. Regular expressions were the stars of the show; with them, parsing well-structured text was a breeze.

Lastly, we put everything together into a function that splits a big string into its lines and decides which parser to use for each line. We'll use this function to read structure files and create the structural model that our truss resolution application will work with.

It's now time to work on producing the output diagrams for the structure solution. That's exactly what we'll do in the next chapter.

18

PRODUCING AN SVG IMAGE AND TEXT FILE

When we solve one of our truss structures, we construct a new model with the solution values. If we want to explore the stress on each bar or the displacement of each node, we need to produce some kind of output with this information. Diagrams are one good way of displaying the information that results from engineering calculations, but we may also want a text file with the detailed values.

In this chapter, we'll write a module for our structural analysis application that produces both a vector image with all the relevant pieces of data in the solution, and a simpler textual representation of the structure solution.

Setup

Let's add a new package in *structures* named *out*; this package will contain all the solution output code. Your *structures* package directory should now look like this:

```
structures
  |- generation
  |- model
  |- out
  |- parse
  |- solution
  |- tests
```

We'll start by implementing the function that produces an SVG image from the structure solution. Let's create a new Python file named *svg.py* and another one named *config.json* that'll contain the configuration for the drawing. Your *out* directory should now contain the following files:

```
structures
  |- out
      |- __init__.py
      |- config.json
      |- svg.py
```

As usual, don't forget to include an *__init__.py* file if you didn't use the IDE.

From Structure Solution to SVG

When our output code is finished, it should produce diagrams like the one in Figure 18-1. Although you can't see it in the print version of the book, the compression bars are red, and the tension bars are green. The external forces are yellow, and we're using purple for the reactions.

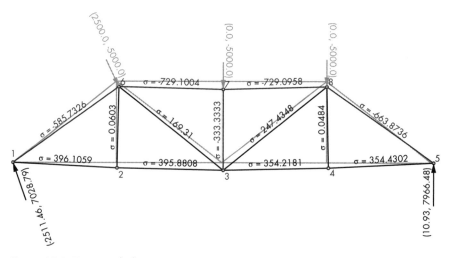

Figure 18-1: Truss result diagram

This image was generated using the code we're going to write together in the rest of this chapter.

The Configuration File

Once your code is ready and working, you may want to play with the diagram's colors and sizes to get a result you find satisfying. We want to have the liberty of changing these colors without needing to read through our code, so we'll move them to a separate configuration file, like we've already done in Chapter 9 and Chapter 12. In fact, any parameter we want to tweak can be placed in the configuration file. We'll include things such as the radius of the nodes, their stroke width, and the margin of the image in the configuration, among others.

Figure 18-2 illustrates some of the properties we want to be configurable and the values we'll assign them. Colors are represented using hexadecimal values prefixed with a #.

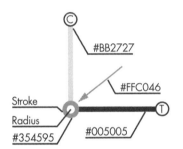

Figure 18-2: Output configuration values

Open the *config.json* file we just created and enter the configuration values in Listing 18-1.

```
{
    "sizes": {
        "margin": 170,
        "node_radius": 5,
        "stroke": 4,
        "arrow": 14
    },
    "colors": {
        "node_stroke": "#354595",
        "back": "#FFFFFF",
        "traction": "#005005",
        "compression": "#BB2727",
        "original": "#D5DBF8",
        "load": "#FFC046",
        "reaction": "#4A0072"
    },
    "font": {
        "family": "sans-serif",
```

```
        "size": 14
    }
}
```

Listing 18-1: The default configuration for our output image

These configuration values are the defaults we'll use when no others are given. Feel free to personalize your app's diagrams using different colors, sizes, or text font.

To do this, we need a way of reading the configuration JSON file into our main *svg.py* script. Let's write a function to do this. In *svg.py*, enter the code in Listing 18-2.

```
import json

import pkg_resources as res


def __read_config():
    config = res.resource_string(__name__, 'config.json')
    return json.loads(config)
```

Listing 18-2: Reading the configuration JSON file

The __read_config function uses resource_string from the pkg_resources package (from Python's standard library) to load our *config.json* file into a string. Then, we use json.loads to parse the string into a dictionary. We'll use this function later.

Let's now see how we can allow the user to pass some parameters to the application; these will modify how the resulting diagram is drawn.

The Settings

We have the configuration, which contains values that determine how the diagram will look. These values are defined by the application, and users don't need to worry about them. We allow users to pass a configuration dictionary to the application with values that override the default configuration.

Apart from the configuration, there are some other values our application needs to draw the solution diagram for a given structure. These values include the scales used to draw the geometry and loads, for example. We can't guess these beforehand, so we need the user to provide them to the application.

Let's call these one-time values *settings*. We'll pass our function a settings dictionary, but these settings won't have default values because there are no sensible defaults we can use here; they completely depend on the structure being computed and what the user wants the result to look like. Does the user want to exaggerate the deformations? Or do they want to see the deformations without a scale to get an idea of what the deformed structure actually looks like? We can't guess this ourselves, and thus, we'll let the user of the app decide on these values.

We've included all the settings we want to make available to the user in Table 18-1.

Table 18-1: Output Settings

Name	Type	Purpose
scale	Number	Changes the scale of the resulting drawing
disp_scale	Number	Changes the scale of the node displacements
load_scale	Number	Changes the scale of load representation
no_draw_original	Boolean	Specifies whether to draw the original geometry

Let's write a function to validate that the dictionary contains values for all these settings. In your *svg.py* file, enter the function in Listing 18-3.

```
--snip--

__expected_settings = (
    # scale applied to the diagram
    'scale',
    # scale applied to the node displacements
    'disp_scale',
    # scale applied to the load vectors
    'load_scale',
    # boolean to decide whether to draw the original geometry
    'no_draw_original'
)


def __validate_settings(settings):
    for setting in __expected_settings:
        if setting not in settings:
            raise ValueError(f'"{setting}" missing in settings')
```

Listing 18-3: Validating the settings dictionary

This __validate_settings function ensures all the expected settings are in the settings dictionary. If any of the functions are not, we raise an error with a message for the user. Let's now write the function to produce the SVG image.

The Solution Drawing Function

In the *svg.py* file, before the __read_config function, enter the code in Listing 18-4.

```
import json

import pkg_resources as res
```

```
from geom2d import AffineTransform
from graphic import svg
from structures.solution.structure import StructureSolution


def structure_solution_to_svg(
        result: StructureSolution,
        settings,
        _config=None,
):
    __validate_settings(settings)
    default_config = __read_config()

❶   config = {**default_config, **(_config or {})}

❷   viewbox = result.bounds_rect(
        config['sizes']['margin'],
        settings.scale
    )
    transform = AffineTransform(sx=1, sy=-1, tx=0, ty=0)

❸   return svg.svg_content(
        size=viewbox.size,
        primitives=[],
        viewbox_rect=viewbox,
        transform=transform
    )


--snip--
```

Listing 18-4: Structure solution to SVG function

We define the structure_solution_to_svg function, but it doesn't draw anything yet; it just produces an empty SVG image. The function receives three parameters: the structure solution (a StructureSolution class instance), the settings dictionary, and the configuration dictionary. The configuration dictionary is optional, so we give it a default value of None.

In the function, we first validate the passed-in settings using the function we wrote in the previous section. If the validation fails, we raise an error and halt execution of the function.

Next, we load the default configuration using the __read_config function.

The next step is merging the passed-in configuration dictionary with the default one ❶. The dictionaries are merged using Python's dictionary unpacking operator: **. If a and b are dictionaries, using {**a, **b} will create a new dictionary containing all the entries from a and b. If there's a key that's in both dictionaries, the version in b, the second dictionary, is kept. Therefore, in our usage, if a configuration value is given by the user, this overrides the default one. We store the merged configuration dictionary in the config variable.

NOTE *The dictionary unpacking operator was added in Python version 3.5. You can read more about it in PEP-448:* https://www.python.org/dev/peps/pep-0448. *PEP stands for "Python Enhancement Proposal." These are the documents the Python community writes to propose new features for the language, among others.*

Next, we compute the viewbox for the SVG image using the structure solution's bounding rectangle ❷. If you recall, the StructureSolution bounds_rect method's first parameter is the margin for the bounds, and the second is the scale. We take the value for the margin from the configuration and the scale from the settings.

We then create an affine transformation that we'll use to flip the image's y-axis so that it points up.

Lastly, we create and return the SVG image using svg_content from our svg package ❸. The size of the image is given by the viewbox size; the list of primitives is empty at the moment. In the next sections, we'll fill this list with the SVG primitives that represent the nodes, bars, and loads. First, though, let's look at captions.

Captions

We're going to use captions in a few places: to note the bars' stresses, to number the nodes, and to give forces coordinates. Positioning these captions is going to be a bit tricky since we'll want to rotate them so they align with the element they caption, as you can see in Figure 18-3.

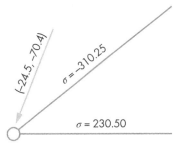

Figure 18-3: Captions in our diagram

Furthermore, since we applied an affine transformation to the SVG image that flips the y-axis, the captions we add will also be flipped, and if we don't undo that flip, they'll be impossible to read. We'll correct this by scaling the caption so that its y-axis is flipped back.

Create a new Python file in *structures/out* named *captions_svg.py*. Your *out* directory should look like the following:

```
out
 |- __init__.py
 |- captions_svg.py
 |- svg.py
```

In this new file, enter the code in Listing 18-5.

```
from geom2d import Point, Vector, make_rotation, make_scale
from graphic import svg
from graphic.svg import attributes


def caption_to_svg(
        caption: str,
        position: Point,
        angle: float,
        color: str,
        config
):
❶ font = config['font']['family']
   size = config['font']['size']

   rotation = make_rotation(angle, position)
   scale = make_scale(1, -1, position)
❷ transform = rotation.then(scale)

❸ return svg.text(
       caption,
       position,
       Vector(0, 0),
       [
           attributes.fill_color(color),
           attributes.affine_transform(transform),
           attributes.font_family(font),
           attributes.font_size(size)
       ]
   )
```

Listing 18-5: From captions to SVG

We implement a function named caption_to_svg. This function has five parameters: the caption's text, a point at which the caption is located, the angle it's rotated, the color, and the configuration dictionary.

We'll extract the font family and size from the configuration dictionary. The first two lines save these values into the font and size variables, respectively ❶.

The next thing we do is compute an affine transformation that scales and rotates the caption. We first generate the rotation with the make_rotation function and then the scaling with the make_scale function; lastly, these are combined into a single transformation ❷. Note how both transformations are done with respect to the caption's position point (see Figure 18-4). This is key. If we scaled and rotated the caption around the global origin (the ⟨0, 0⟩ point), it would appear somewhere unexpected in the drawing.

Position ... $\sigma = -310.25$ ... $\pi/6$

Figure 18-4: Caption rotation

Lastly, we create the SVG text element using the `svg.text` function, passing it the caption, the center point, a zero displacement vector, and a list of attributes ❸. In the attributes we include the fill color, the transformation, the font family, and the font size.

The Bars

Let's now work on producing the SVG code to draw the original and deformed bar geometries. Bars are straight lines, so representing them won't be too complicated. In the *out* directory, create a new file named *bar_svg.py*. Your *out* directory should look like the following:

```
out
|- __init__.py
|- bar_svg.py
|- captions_svg.py
|- svg.py
```

As we know, both the original and deformed bar geometries are straight lines. We'll start by writing a helper function to generate the SVG segments that represent bars, both in their original and deformed states. In the file, enter the code in Listing 18-6.

```
from math import sqrt

from graphic import svg
from graphic.svg import attributes


def __bar_svg(geometry, color, cross_section):
❶ section_height = sqrt(cross_section)
❷ return svg.segment(
       geometry,
       [
           attributes.stroke_color(color),
           attributes.stroke_width(section_height)
       ]
   )
```

Listing 18-6: Single bar to SVG

We've written the `__bar_svg` function to generate an SVG segment using the passed-in geometry, which should be an instance of our `Segment` class; we've also passed in the color to use and the cross section of the bar.

Why do we need the cross-section value? We'll use a line thickness that roughly represents the cross section of the bar so that bars with a larger cross section are drawn with a thicker line. Figure 18-5 shows our approximation: we're computing the line thickness as if it was the side of a square cross section.

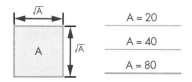

Figure 18-5: Calculating line thickness from the cross section

In the section_height variable, we store the height of the bar as if its section was square ❶. This value is computed from the square root of the bar's cross section.

Lastly, we return an SVG segment using the passed-in geometry and adding two attributes: the stroke color and the line thickness we've computed ❷.

Let's continue and write the first version of the bars_to_svg function. In your file and before the __bar_svg function we just wrote, enter the code in Listing 18-7.

```
from math import sqrt

from graphic import svg
from graphic.svg import attributes
from structures.solution.bar import StrBarSolution


def bars_to_svg(bars: [StrBarSolution], settings, config):
    should_draw_original = not settings.no_draw_original
❶   original, final, stresses = [], [], []

    for bar in bars:
❷       if should_draw_original:
            original.append(original_bar_to_svg(bar))
❸       final.append(bar_to_svg(bar))
❹       stresses.append(bar_stress_to_svg(bar))

    # Ordering is important to preserve z-depth
❺   return original + final + stresses


def __bar_svg(geometry, color, cross_section):
    --snip--
```

Listing 18-7: Bar to SVG

In this listing, we merely outline the main algorithm to generate SVG primitives representing the bars. There are three functions that do most of the work, but we haven't written them yet: `original_bar_to_svg`, `bar_to_svg`, and `bar_stress_to_svg`. We'll write these shortly.

Our `bars_to_svg` function first saves the negated value of the `no_draw _original` setting in the `should_draw_original` variable. If `should_draw_original` is true, our function will also include the segments representing the original bars.

Next, we declare three empty lists: `original`, `final`, and `stresses` ❶. The first one, `original`, stores the segments that represent the original bars; the second one, `final`, contains the final or solution bars; and the last list, `stresses`, stores the stress captions. We'll put all the SVG primitives we generate in these lists.

We then iterate through the bars. For each one, if `should_draw_original` is true, we append the result of `original_bar_to_svg` to the `original` list ❷; `original_bar_to_svg` is a function we haven't written yet that generates the SVG segment for the original bar. We append the SVG representing the solution bar to the `final` list ❸ and the stress caption to `stresses` ❹.

After the loop, the three lists are filled with the SVG primitives that represent the bars of the original and solution structures. We concatenate and return those lists ❺. As noted by the comment in the code, the order here is important: the elements that appear last in the list will be drawn on top of the rest. We want the original bars to be behind the solution bars; thus, they need to appear first in the list. You can imagine these bars as being distributed by layers, as depicted in Figure 18-6.

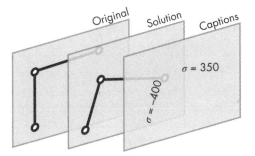

Figure 18-6: Drawing the bar SVGs in layers

Let's write the three functions we used to generate the SVG primitives.

Drawing the Original Bars

For these functions, we're going to use a technique we explored in the "Functions Inside Other Functions" section on page 28. We'll define them as internal functions inside the `bars_to_svg` function so they gain access to the parameters passed to `bars_to_svg`. This spares us from having to pass around the `settings` and `config` dictionaries. The resulting internal functions will have a shorter parameter list, which makes them simpler. As the functions are effectively kept private in bars_to_svg, only the host function has access to them.

Let's write the original_bar_to_svg function first. In your file, enter the missing code in Listing 18-8.

```
from math import sqrt

from graphic import svg
from graphic.svg import attributes
from structures.solution.bar import StrBarSolution


def bars_to_svg(bars: [StrBarSolution], settings, config):
    def original_bar_to_svg(_bar: StrBarSolution):
    ❶ color = config['colors']['original']
    ❷ return __bar_svg(
            _bar.original_geometry,
            color,
            _bar.cross_section
        )

    --snip--

    # Ordering is important to preserve z-depth
    return original + final + stresses


def __bar_svg(geometry, color, cross_section):
    --snip--
```

Listing 18-8: Original (nonsolution) bar to SVG

We've written the original_bar_to_svg function inside the bars_to_svg function, at the beginning of it. This function requires only one argument: a bar from the solution structure (of type StrBarSolution), which contains the original bar inside its original_geometry attribute.

First, we extract the color for the original bar from the configuration dictionary ❶. Then, we return the result of calling the __bar_svg function with the original bar's geometry, the color, and the bar's cross section ❷.

Drawing the Solution Bars

Now let's write the code to draw the solution bars. These will have a different color depending on if their stress is compressive or tensile. In the bars_to_svg function, after the original_bar_to_svg function we just wrote, enter the missing code in Listing 18-9.

```
from math import sqrt

from graphic import svg
```

```
from graphic.svg import attributes
from structures.solution.bar import StrBarSolution


def bars_to_svg(bars: [StrBarSolution], settings, config):
    def original_bar_to_svg(_bar: StrBarSolution):
        --snip--

    def bar_to_svg(_bar: StrBarSolution):
        return __bar_svg(
          ❶ _bar.final_geometry_scaling_displacement(
                settings.disp_scale
            ),
          ❷ bar_color(_bar),
          ❸ _bar.cross_section
        )

    def bar_color(_bar: StrBarSolution):
        if _bar.stress >= 0:
            return config['colors']['traction']
        else:
            return config['colors']['compression']

    --snip--

    # Ordering is important to preserve z-depth
    return original + final + stresses


def __bar_svg(geometry, color, cross_section):
    --snip--
```

Listing 18-9: Solution bar to SVG

The bar_to_svg function returns the result of calling __bar_svg with the
displaced bar as first argument, computed using the final_geometry_scaling
_displacement method we implemented in the StrBarSolution class ❶. The sec-
ond argument is the color, which we compute using another function that
we implemented later in the code: bar_color ❷. The third and last argument
is the bar's cross section ❸.

The bar_color function returns the correct color from the configuration
dictionary depending on the sign of the bar's stress. Note, once again, how
we don't need the config dictionary to be passed to this function. We already
have access to it because we are inside the bars_to_svg function.

Drawing the Stress Captions

Lastly, we need to draw the stress captions. These are a bit tricky to position inside the drawing, but we solved the hardest part earlier in the caption_to_svg function.

Enter the missing code in Listing 18-10.

```
from math import sqrt

from geom2d import Vector
from graphic import svg
from graphic.svg import attributes
from structures.solution.bar import StrBarSolution
from .captions_svg import caption_to_svg

__I_VERSOR = Vector(1, 0)
__STRESS_DISP = 10
__DECIMAL_POS = 4


def bars_to_svg(bars: [StrBarSolution], settings, config):
    def original_bar_to_svg(_bar: StrBarSolution):
        --snip--

    def bar_to_svg(_bar: StrBarSolution):
        --snip--

    def bar_stress_to_svg(_bar: StrBarSolution):
    ❶ geometry = _bar.final_geometry_scaling_displacement(
            settings.disp_scale
        )
        normal = geometry.normal_versor
    ❷ position = geometry.middle.displaced(normal, __STRESS_DISP)
    ❸ angle = geometry.direction_versor.angle_to(__I_VERSOR)

    ❹ return caption_to_svg(
            f'σ = {round(_bar.stress, __DECIMAL_POS)}',
            position,
            angle,
            bar_color(_bar),
            config
        )

    def bar_color(_bar: StrBarSolution):
        --snip--

    --snip--

    # Ordering is important to preserve z-depth
```

```
    return original + final + stresses


def __bar_svg(geometry, color, cross_section):
    --snip--
```

Listing 18-10: Bar stress to SVG

We import Vector from *geom2d* and the caption_to_svg function we implemented earlier in this chapter. Then, we declare three constants:

- __I_VERSOR is the $\hat{i}$ versor to represent the horizontal direction.

- __STRESS_DISP is the distance we use to separate the caption from the bar's geometry.

- __DECIMAL_POS is the number of decimals we use to format the stress values.

Then comes the implementation of the bar_stress_to_svg function. The first thing we want to do in this function is compute the geometry of the bar we're adding a caption to, with exactly the same scale as the drawing itself ❶. We want our caption to be aligned with the drawing of the bar; thus, we need its geometry as a reference.

Next, we compute the bar's geometry normal versor; we need this direction to compute the caption's position. Then, we compute the caption's origin point, called position, by displacing the bar's middle point in the direction of the normal versor an amount equal to __STRESS_DISP ❷. Figure 18-7 illustrates this.

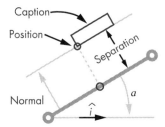

Figure 18-7: Positioning the bar caption

We also need the bar's angle with the $\hat{i}$ versor ❸; this is the angle we'll rotate the caption to align it with the bar.

Now that we have the center point and the rotation angle, we simply need to return the result of calling the caption_to_svg function with these values as arguments ❹. For the caption's text, we use the Greek letter σ (sigma), which is typically used to refer to mechanical stresses, followed by the bar's stress value rounded to four decimals.

Lastly, note that the label color is the same as the bar, and thus we get it from the bar_color function.

The Result

After all the code we've written, your *bar_svg.py* file should look like Listing 18-11.

```python
from math import sqrt

from geom2d import Vector
from graphic import svg
from graphic.svg import attributes
from structures.solution.bar import StrBarSolution
from .captions_svg import caption_to_svg

__I_VERSOR = Vector(1, 0)
__STRESS_DISP = 10
__DECIMAL_POS = 4


def bars_to_svg(bars: [StrBarSolution], settings, config):
    def original_bar_to_svg(_bar: StrBarSolution):
        color = config['colors']['original']
        return __bar_svg(
            _bar.original_geometry,
            color,
            _bar.cross_section
        )

    def bar_to_svg(_bar: StrBarSolution):
        return __bar_svg(
            _bar.final_geometry_scaling_displacement(
                settings.disp_scale
            ),
            bar_color(_bar),
            _bar.cross_section
        )

    def bar_stress_to_svg(_bar: StrBarSolution):
        geometry = _bar.final_geometry_scaling_displacement(
            settings.disp_scale
        )
        normal = geometry.normal_versor
        position = geometry.middle.displaced(normal, __STRESS_DISP)
        angle = geometry.direction_versor.angle_to(__I_VERSOR)

        return caption_to_svg(
            f ' = {round(_bar.stress, __DECIMAL_POS)}',
            position,
            angle,
            bar_color(_bar),
```

```
            config
        )

    def bar_color(_bar: StrBarSolution):
        if _bar.stress >= 0:
            return config['colors']['traction']
        else:
            return config['colors']['compression']

    should_draw_original = not settings.no_draw_original
    original, final, stresses = [], [], []

    for bar in bars:
        if should_draw_original:
            original.append(original_bar_to_svg(bar))
        final.append(bar_to_svg(bar))
        stresses.append(bar_stress_to_svg(bar))

    # Ordering is important to preserve z-depth
    return original + final + stresses


def __bar_svg(geometry, color, cross_section):
    section_height = sqrt(cross_section)
    return svg.segment(
        geometry,
        [
            attributes.stroke_color(color),
            attributes.stroke_width(section_height)
        ]
    )
```

Listing 18-11: Bar to SVG result

Make sure your code looks the same as Listing 18-11, because we won't be writing unit tests in this chapter. Covering our SVG generation functions with tests would be a great idea; there is quite a bit of logic here. But to keep the chapter a reasonable length, we won't be doing it.

Now it's time for the nodes.

The Nodes

In the *out* directory, create a new file named *node_svg.py*:

```
out
  |- __init__.py
  |- bar_svg.py
  |- captions_svg.py
  |- node_svg.py
```

```
|- svg.py
```

In this file, enter the code in Listing 18-12.

```
from geom2d import Circle, Vector
from graphic import svg
from graphic.svg import attributes
from structures.solution.node import StrNodeSolution
from .captions_svg import caption_to_svg


def nodes_to_svg(nodes: [StrNodeSolution], settings, config):
❶ def node_to_svg(node: StrNodeSolution):
        radius = config['sizes']['node_radius']
        stroke_size = config['sizes']['stroke']
        stroke_color = config['colors']['node_stroke']
        fill_color = config['colors']['back']

❷     position = node.displaced_pos_scaled(settings.disp_scale)
❸     caption_pos = position.displaced(Vector(radius, radius))

        return svg.group([
❹         svg.circle(
                Circle(position, radius),
                [
                    attributes.stroke_width(stroke_size),
                    attributes.stroke_color(stroke_color),
                    attributes.fill_color(fill_color)
                ]
            ),
❺         caption_to_svg(
                f'{node.id}', caption_pos, 0, stroke_color, config
            )
        ])

❻ return [
        node_to_svg(node)
        for node in nodes
    ]
```

Listing 18-12: Node to SVG

We first import a few things—make sure you get them all. Then, we define the nodes_to_svg function with the list of StrNodeSolution instances and the settings and config dictionaries as input parameters. This function maps each node in the nodes list to its SVG representation, which is obtained by calling an internal function: node_to_svg ❻. The mapping is done using a list comprehension.

The `node_to_svg` internal function operates on a single node, and it has access to the host function parameters ❶. The first thing it does is save some configuration parameters in variables.

Next, we compute the displaced position of the node ❷ and the position for the caption, which will be the node's ID ❸. The caption's position is obtained by displacing the node's position an amount equal to its radius both horizontally and vertically. Figure 18-8 illustrates this.

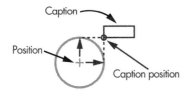
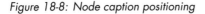

Figure 18-8: Node caption positioning

The `node_to_svg` function returns an SVG group consisting of a circle representing the node itself ❹ and the caption ❺.

Our nodes are ready! Let's add their external reaction forces.

The Node Reactions

We'll also include the reaction forces of the externally constrained nodes in our SVG diagram. We'll represent these as arrows with a caption, similar to Figure 18-9.

Figure 18-9: Node reaction

Since we'll draw external loads and reactions the same way, let's write a function that draws a `Vector` geometric primitive as an arrow with a caption; that way we can use it for both cases.

Drawing Vectors

In the *out* directory, create a new file named *vector_svg.py*. Your *out* directory should look like the following:

```
out
 |- __init__.py
 |- bar_svg.py
 |- captions_svg.py
 |- node_svg.py
 |- svg.py
 |- vector_svg.py
```

In this file, enter the code in Listing 18-13.

```
from geom2d import Point, Vector, Segment
from graphic import svg
from graphic.svg import attributes
from .captions_svg import caption_to_svg


__I_VERSOR = Vector(1, 0)
__CAPTION_DISP = 10
__DECIMAL_POS = 2


def vector_to_svg(
        position: Point,
        vector: Vector,
        scale: float,
        color: str,
        config
):
 ❶ segment = Segment(
        position.displaced(vector, -scale),
        position
    )
 ❷ caption_origin = segment.start.displaced(
        segment.normal_versor,
        __CAPTION_DISP
    )

    def svg_arrow():
        pass

    def svg_caption():
        pass

 ❸ return svg.group([
        svg_arrow(),
        svg_caption()
    ])
```

Listing 18-13: Vector to SVG

We define three constants:

- __I_VERSOR is used to compute an angle with the horizontal direction.
- __CAPTION_DISP is the separation between the vector's baseline and the caption.
- __DECIMAL_POS formats the vector coordinates using a fixed number of decimals.

Then comes the vector_to_svg function, which has the following arguments:

- position is the vector's base point.
- vector is the vector itself.
- scale is applied to the vector to shorten or lengthen it.
- color is the stroke and font colors.
- config is the configuration dictionary.

In the function, we create a segment to represent the vector's baseline ❶. The start point for the segment is the passed-in position displaced by the vector (also passed as an argument to the function) and using a scale of -scale. We want the vector's arrow located at the origin point; thus, the end point for the segment is in the opposite direction of the vector. You can see this configuration of the vector segment points illustrated in Figure 18-10.

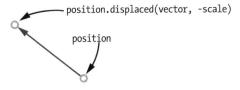

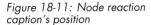

Figure 18-10: Vector segment end points

We also compute the caption's origin point using the segment's start point displaced in the normal direction of the segment's direction ❷ (see Figure 18-11).

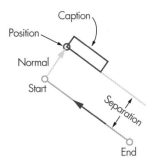

Figure 18-11: Node reaction caption's position

Then there are two functions we haven't implemented yet: svg_arrow and svg_caption. These are the functions that will draw the arrow and the caption. We'll get to them shortly.

Lastly, we return an SVG group consisting of the results of the svg_arrow and svg_caption functions ❸.

Let's implement the two missing functions. Enter the missing code in Listing 18-14.

--snip--

```python
def vector_to_svg(
        position: Point,
        vector: Vector,
        scale: float,
        color: str,
        config
):
    segment = Segment(
        position.displaced(vector, -scale),
        position
    )
    caption_origin = segment.start.displaced(
        segment.normal_versor,
        __CAPTION_DISP
    )

    def svg_arrow():
        width = config['sizes']['stroke']
        arrow_size = config['sizes']['arrow']

    ❶ return svg.arrow(
            segment,
            arrow_size,
            arrow_size,
            [
                attributes.stroke_color(color),
                attributes.stroke_width(width),
                attributes.fill_color('none')
            ]
        )

    def svg_caption():
    ❷ return caption_to_svg(
            vector.to_formatted_str(__DECIMAL_POS),
            caption_origin,
            vector.angle_to(__I_VERSOR),
            color,
            config
        )

    return svg.group([
        svg_arrow(),
```

```
        svg_caption()
    ])
```

Listing 18-14: Vector to SVG

The svg_arrow function first saves the width and arrow_size configuration values inside variables. Then it returns our SVG arrow primitive, passing it the segment, the arrow_size for both the arrow width and length, and the list of attributes including the stroke color and width ❶. Recall that our svg.arrow function draws the arrow located at the segment's end point.

The svg_caption function returns the result of calling the svg_caption function with the caption string, origin point, rotation angle, color, and configuration dictionary ❷. The caption with the right format is computed using our Vector class's to_formatted_str method. This method isn't implemented yet, so let's write it to create a string with the vector components and norm.

Open the *geom2d/vector.py* file and enter the code in Listing 18-15.

```
class Vector:
    --snip--

    def to_formatted_str(self, decimals: int):
        u = round(self.u, decimals)
        v = round(self.v, decimals)
        norm = round(self.norm, decimals)

        return f'({u}, {v}) with norm {norm}'
```

Listing 18-15: Vector to formatted string

We'll also need a similar method in the Point class to format the position of the nodes in the text representation of the solution. Open *geom2d/point.py* and enter the code in Listing 18-16.

```
class Point:
    --snip--

    def to_formatted_str(self, decimals: int):
        x = round(self.x, decimals)
        y = round(self.y, decimals)

        return f'({x}, {y})'
```

Listing 18-16: Point to formatted string

Now that we've implemented a way of drawing vectors with a caption for their coordinates, let's use our implementation to display the node reactions.

Drawing the Reaction Forces

In the *out* directory, create a new file named *reaction_svg.py*. Your *out* directory should look like the following:

```
out
|- __init__.py
|- bar_svg.py
|- captions_svg.py
|- node_svg.py
|- reaction_svg.py
|- svg.py
|- vector_svg.py
```

In this newly created file, enter the code in Listing 18-17.

```
from structures.solution.node import StrNodeSolution
from structures.solution.structure import StructureSolution
from .vector_svg import vector_to_svg


def node_reactions_to_svg(
        solution: StructureSolution,
        settings,
        config
):
    def reaction_svg(node: StrNodeSolution):
    ❶  position = node.displaced_pos_scaled(settings.disp_scale)
    ❷  reaction = solution.reaction_for_node(node)
    ❸  return vector_to_svg(
            position=position,
            vector=reaction,
            scale=settings.load_scale,
            color=config['colors']['reaction'],
            config=config
        )

    ❹  return [
        reaction_svg(node)
        for node in solution.nodes
        if node.is_constrained
    ]
```

Listing 18-17: Node reactions to SVG

In this file, we define `node_reactions_to_svg`. Each externally constrained node in the structure solution is mapped to its SVG reaction using a list comprehension ❹.

We're using an inner function to produce the SVG representation of each solution node: `reaction_svg`. This function first obtains the displaced position of the resulting node (with disp_scale applied) ❶. Then it asks the solution structure for the reaction in the node ❷. With these pieces of information, we can create the SVG representation of the reaction vector using the vector_to_svg function ❸.

The Loads

The last things we want to draw in the result image are the loads applied to the structure.

In the *out* directory, create a new file named *load_svg.py*. Your *out* directory should look like the following:

```
out
  |- __init__.py
  |- bar_svg.py
  |- captions_svg.py
  |- load_svg.py
  |- node_svg.py
  |- reaction_svg.py
  |- svg.py
  |- vector_svg.py
```

In *load_svg.py*, enter the code in Listing 18-18.

```
from geom2d import Vector, Point
from graphic import svg
from structures.solution.node import StrNodeSolution
from .vector_svg import vector_to_svg


def loads_to_svg(nodes: [StrNodeSolution], settings, config):
    def svg_node_loads(node: StrNodeSolution):
      ❶ position = node.displaced_pos_scaled(settings.disp_scale)
      ❷ return svg.group(
            [
                svg_load(position, load)
                for load in node.loads
            ]
        )

    def svg_load(position: Point, load: Vector):
      ❸ return vector_to_svg(
            position=position,
            vector=load,
            scale=settings.load_scale,
            color=config['colors']['load'],
            config=config
        )
```

```
❹ return [
      svg_node_loads(node)
      for node in nodes
      if node.is_loaded
  ]
```

Listing 18-18: Loads to SVG

In this file, we define a function, loads_to_svg, receiving three arguments: the StrNodeSolution list and the settings and config dictionaries. The function relies on two inner functions: svg_node_loads and svg_load. We use a list comprehension to map each node that has external loads in the passed-in nodes list to its SVG representation ❹. We use the is_loaded property of each node to filter the nodes that are externally loaded.

The svg_node_loads internal function first gets the displaced position of the solution node ❶ and then returns an SVG group of all the loads in the node ❷. Each load is mapped to an SVG vector using the second internal function: svg_load.

The svg_load function is straightforward: it simply calls the vector_to_svg function passing the appropriate parameters ❸.

With this, we have all of our SVG generation code ready! We just need to put it all together, and we can finally start drawing structure solutions.

Putting It All Together

Let's now open the *svg.py* file and add the functions we've written into the structure_solution_to_svg function. Enter the missing code, following Listing 18-19.

```
import json

import pkg_resources as res

from geom2d import AffineTransform
from graphic import svg
from structures.solution.structure import StructureSolution
❶ from .bar_svg import bars_to_svg
  from .load_svg import loads_to_svg
  from .node_svg import nodes_to_svg
  from .reaction_svg import node_reactions_to_svg


def structure_solution_to_svg(
        result: StructureSolution,
        settings,
        _config=None,
):
    __validate_settings(settings)
    default_config = __read_config()
```

```
config = {**default_config, **(_config or {})}

viewbox = result.bounds_rect(
    config['sizes']['margin'],
    settings.scale
)
transform = AffineTransform(sx=1, sy=-1, tx=0, ty=0)

❷ svg_bars = bars_to_svg(result.bars, settings, config)
svg_nodes = nodes_to_svg(result.nodes, settings, config)
svg_react = node_reactions_to_svg(result, settings, config)
svg_loads = loads_to_svg(result.nodes, settings, config)

return svg.svg_content(
    size=viewbox.size,
    ❸ primitives=svg_bars + svg_nodes + svg_react + svg_loads,
    viewbox_rect=viewbox,
    transform=transform
)
```

--snip--

Listing 18-19: Structure solution to SVG

First, we import the bars_to_svg, loads_to_svg, nodes_to_svg, and node
_reactions_to_svg functions ❶.

Then, inside structure_solution_to_svg, we call each of the functions to
generate the corresponding SVG code ❷. The results are stored in svg_bars,
svg_nodes, svg_react, and svg_loads. These are concatenated in one list that we
pass to the svg_content function ❸. The order is important: the SVG primitives toward the end of the list will appear in front of those at the beginning
of it.

The Final Result

If you've followed along, your *svg.py* file should be similar to Listing 18-20.

```
import json

import pkg_resources as res

from geom2d import AffineTransform
from graphic import svg
from structures.solution.structure import StructureSolution
from .bar_svg import bars_to_svg
from .load_svg import loads_to_svg
from .node_svg import nodes_to_svg
```

```python
from .reaction_svg import node_reactions_to_svg


def structure_solution_to_svg(
        result: StructureSolution,
        settings,
        _config=None,
):
    __validate_settings(settings)
    default_config = __read_config()

    config = {**default_config, **(_config or {})}

    viewbox = result.bounds_rect(
        config['sizes']['margin'],
        settings.scale
    )
    transform = AffineTransform(sx=1, sy=-1, tx=0, ty=0)

    svg_bars = bars_to_svg(result.bars, settings, config)
    svg_nodes = nodes_to_svg(result.nodes, settings, config)
    svg_react = node_reactions_to_svg(result, settings, config)
    svg_loads = loads_to_svg(result.nodes, settings, config)

    return svg.svg_content(
        size=viewbox.size,
        primitives=svg_bars + svg_nodes + svg_react + svg_loads,
        viewbox_rect=viewbox,
        transform=transform
    )


def __read_config():
    config = res.resource_string(__name__, 'config.json')
    return json.loads(config)


__expected_settings = (
    # scale applied to the diagram
    'scale',
    # scale applied to the node displacements
    'disp_scale',
    # scale applied to the load vectors
    'load_scale',
    # boolean to decide whether to draw the original geometry
    'no_draw_original'
)
```

```
def __validate_settings(settings):
    for setting in __expected_settings:
        if setting not in settings:
            raise ValueError(f'"{setting}" missing in settings')
```

Listing 18-20: Structure solution to SVG

We have everything that we need, but before we put it to work in the next chapter, let's also prepare a textual representation of the solution.

From Structure Solution to Text

A visual diagram helps us understand the structural deformations; because we color the bars depending on the stress they're subject to, it's also a good way to see which bars are compressed and which are stretched. At the same time, it may be simpler to study the numeric results in a text format, and we may want to have them do some other calculations. The formats are complementary, and our structural analysis program will output both.

We will write the displacement of each node in a text file using the following format:

```
NODE 25
    original position: (1400.0, 150.0)
    displacement: (0.1133, -0.933) with norm 0.9398
    displaced position: (1400.1133, 149.067)
```

If the node has external constraints, we want to check its reactions as well. In this case, we can include one last line:

```
NODE 1
    original position: (0.0, 0.0)
    displacement: (0.0, 0.0) with norm 0.0
    displaced position: (0.0, 0.0)
    reaction: (-283.6981, 9906.9764) with norm 9911.0376
```

The bars will follow this format:

```
BAR 8 (25 → 9) : ⊕ TENSION
    Δl (elongation) = 0.0026
    ε  (strain)     = 1.045e-05
    σ  (stress)     = 209.0219
```

Let's write a function that generates this plaintext representation of a structure solution.

Structure Solution's String

Before we write the function that generates the plaintext representation, let's write a useful helper function that takes a list of strings and returns a single string with all those strings concatenated by a "newline" character.

We want to define each of the result values as a string of its own, but the function we'll implement returns one and only one string, which is then written into a file.

Let's create a new file for this helper function. In your *utils* package, create a new Python file named *strings.py*. This package should now have the following contents:

```
utils
|- __init__.py
|- lists.py
|- pairs.py
|- strings.py
```

In this *strings.py* file, enter the function in Listing 18-21.

```
def list_to_string(strings: [str]) -> str:
    return '\n'.join(strings)
```

Listing 18-21: List to string

This list_to_string function maps a list of strings into a single string where each entry is separated from the next using the '\n' (newline) character.

Let's now outline the text output function's logic. First, create a new *text.py* file inside the *structures/out* package, which now should have the following files:

```
out
|- __init__.py
|- bar_svg.py
|- captions_svg.py
|- load_svg.py
|- node_svg.py
|- reaction_svg.py
|- svg.py
|- text.py
|- vector_svg.py
```

In this *text.py* file, enter the code in Listing 18-22.

```
from structures.solution.bar import StrBarSolution
from structures.solution.node import StrNodeSolution
from structures.solution.structure import StructureSolution
from utils.strings import list_to_string

❶ __DECIMAL_POS = 4
```

```
__SEPARATION = ['----------------------------------------', '\n']


def structure_solution_to_string(result: StructureSolution):
❷ nodes_text = __nodes_to_string(result)
❸ bars_text = __bars_to_string(result.bars)
❹ return list_to_string(nodes_text + __SEPARATION + bars_text)


def __nodes_to_string(result: StructureSolution):
    pass


def __node_to_string(
        result: StructureSolution,
        node: StrNodeSolution
):
    pass


def __bars_to_string(bars: [StrBarSolution]):
    pass


def __bar_to_string(bar: StrBarSolution):
    pass
```

Listing 18-22: Structure solution to text

In this listing, we import the StrBarSolution, StrNodeSolution, and Structure Solution classes, as well as the list_to_string function. We define two constants, one to specify the number of decimal positions we want to use to format the resulting values, __DECIMAL_POS ❶, and a separation string list, __SEPARATION, which we use to separate the different sections in the result string.

Then comes the main function, structure_solution_to_string. This function receives only one parameter: the structure solution. It uses two private functions: one to convert the string representation of the nodes ❷ and another to convert the bars ❸. The results are stored as list strings in the nodes_text and bars_text variables. These lists are concatenated with the __SEPARATION strings in the middle and passed to list_to_string ❹.

After this main function, we define the rest of the private functions, but they've yet to be implemented. Let's do that now.

The Nodes

Let's start with the nodes. Fill the __nodes_to_string and __node_to_string functions with the code in Listing 18-23.

--snip--

```
def __nodes_to_string(result: StructureSolution):
    return [
❶     __node_to_string(result, node)
        for node in result.nodes
    ]


def __node_to_string(
        result: StructureSolution,
        node: StrNodeSolution
):
❷   orig_pos = node.original_pos.to_formatted_str(__DECIMAL_POS)
    displacement = node.global_disp.to_formatted_str(__DECIMAL_POS)
    disp_pos = node.displaced_pos.to_formatted_str(__DECIMAL_POS)

❸   strings = [
        f'NODE {node.id}',
        f'\toriginal position: {orig_pos}',
        f'\tdisplacement: {displacement}',
        f'\tdisplaced position: {disp_pos}'
    ]

❹   if node.is_constrained:
        react = result.reaction_for_node(node)
        react_str = react.to_formatted_str(__DECIMAL_POS)
        strings.append(f'\treaction: {react_str}')

❺   return list_to_string(strings) + '\n'
```

--snip--

Listing 18-23: Nodes to text

The first function, __nodes_to_string, uses a list comprehension to map each node in the result to its textual representation, for which it uses the __node_to_string function ❶. This function requires not only the node but also the entire structure object as parameters. Recall that the reaction force of a node is computed by the structure solution instances, not by the nodes themselves.

The __node_to_string function first obtains the formatted strings for the node's original position ❷, the global displacement vector, and the displaced position. We use the to_formatted_str method from the Point and Vector classes to handle the point coordinates formatting.

Next, we declare a list, strings ❸, where we place the strings we just obtained. Note that, except for the first one, which serves as header, the strings all start with the tab (\t) character. With this, we achieve the nice formatting we defined earlier:

```
NODE 2
    original position: (200.0, 0.0)
    displacement: (0.0063, -0.1828) with norm 0.1829
    displaced position: (200.0063, -0.1828)
```

Next, we generate the reaction force string if the node is externally constrained ❹. For this, we first use the structure solution class to compute the reaction for the given node, then format it using the to_formatted_str method, and lastly append it to the strings list.

The last step is to convert the obtained string list into a single string using the helper list_to_string function with a newline character appended to the end ❺.

The Bars

Let's now fill in the functions for the bars. We'll use some UTF-8 characters to make the text a bit more visual. These characters are optional; you can decide not to add them in your code and just go with the labels. If you decide to use them, we'll explain how to do this in the section "The Unicode Characters" on page 18.

Enter the code in Listing 18-24.

```
--snip--


def __bars_to_string(bars: [StrBarSolution]):
❶   return [__bar_to_string(bar) for bar in bars]


def __bar_to_string(bar: StrBarSolution):
❷   nodes_str = f'{bar.start_node.id} → {bar.end_node.id}'
    type_str = '⊕ TENSION' if bar.stress >= 0 else '⊖ COMPRESSION'
    elongation = round(bar.elongation, __DECIMAL_POS)
    strain = '{:.3e}'.format(bar.strain)
    stress = round(bar.stress, __DECIMAL_POS)

❸   return list_to_string([
        f'BAR {bar.id} ({nodes_str}) : {type_str}',
        f'\tΔl (elongation) = {elongation}',
        f'\tε (strain)      = {strain}',
        f'\tσ (stress)      = {stress}\n'
    ])
```

Listing 18-24: Bars to text

The _bars_to_string function uses a list comprehension to map each bar in the list to its textual representation ❶. This text is produced by the second function, _bar_to_string.

In _bar_to_string, we first prepare some strings ❷ that we later return concatenated using the list_to_string function ❸ and nodes_str indicates the bar's node IDs, with a → character separating them.

The type_str indicates whether the bar is in traction or compression, depending on the sign of the bar's stress. We're using the ⊕ symbol to decorate the TENSION text and ⊖ for the COMPRESSION text. This detail makes the result stand out more to the eye.

Then comes the elongation, strain, and stress strings. These are the bar's result values formatted to have _DECIMAL_POS decimal positions. Here strain is the exception; instead of rounding it, we want to use scientific notation with three decimal positions ('{:.3e}'). The strain is usually a small value, orders of magnitude smaller than the stress, so if we try to round it to, say, four decimal positions, the result will still be zero: 0.0000$. Using the '{:.3e}' format, we'll get things like 1.259e-05 instead.

When formatting values in our engineering applications, we have to be aware of the orders of magnitude. A wrongly formatted value, where the precision required is lost, renders the app useless.

The Unicode Characters

The icons we're using in the code, →, Δ, ϵ, ⊕, and ⊖, are all Unicode characters. Every operating system has a way of inserting these characters. If you do a quick Google search, you should be able to find how to access them in your OS. For instance, macOS uses the CMD-CTRL-spacebar key combination to open the symbols dialog, which is how I inserted those in the code.

You may also insert these characters using their code in a Python string like so:

```
>>> '\u2295 is a Unicode symbol'
'⊕ is a Unicode symbol'
```

If you opt for this alternative, you'll need to replace the characters in the listings with their code. Table 18-2 shows the characters we've used and their Unicode code.

Table 18-2: Unicode Characters

Character	Unicode	Usage
⊕	\u2295	Tension stress
⊖	\u2296	Compression stress
→	\u279c	Separates the node IDs of a bar (1 → 2)
Δ	\u0394	Length increment (Δl)
ϵ	\u03f5	Strain
σ	\u03c3	Stress

Putting It All Together

If you've followed along, your result should look like Listing 18-25.

```python
from structures.solution.bar import StrBarSolution
from structures.solution.node import StrNodeSolution
from structures.solution.structure import StructureSolution
from utils.strings import list_to_string


__DECIMAL_POS = 4
__SEPARATION = ['----------------------------------------', '\n']


def structure_solution_to_string(result: StructureSolution):
    nodes_text = __nodes_to_string(result)
    bars_text = __bars_to_string(result.bars)
    return list_to_string(nodes_text + __SEPARATION + bars_text)


def __nodes_to_string(result: StructureSolution):
    return [
        __node_to_string(result, node)
        for node in result.nodes
    ]


def __node_to_string(
        result: StructureSolution,
        node: StrNodeSolution
):
    orig_pos = node.original_pos.to_formatted_str(__DECIMAL_POS)
    displacement = node.global_disp.to_formatted_str(__DECIMAL_POS)
    disp_pos = node.displaced_pos.to_formatted_str(__DECIMAL_POS)

    strings = [
        f'NODE {node.id}',
        f'\toriginal position: {orig_pos}',
        f'\tdisplacement: {displacement}',
        f'\tdisplaced position: {disp_pos}'
    ]

    if node.is_constrained:
        react = result.reaction_for_node(node)
        react_str = react.to_formatted_str(__DECIMAL_POS)
        strings.append(f'\treaction: {react_str}')

    return list_to_string(strings) + '\n'
```

```
def __bars_to_string(bars: [StrBarSolution]):
    return [__bar_to_string(bar) for bar in bars]


def __bar_to_string(bar: StrBarSolution):
    nodes_str = f'{bar.start_node.id} → {bar.end_node.id}'
    type_str = '⊕ TENSION' if bar.stress >= 0 else '⊖ COMPRESSION'
    elongation = round(bar.elongation, __DECIMAL_POS)
    strain = '{:.3e}'.format(bar.strain)
    stress = round(bar.stress, __DECIMAL_POS)

    return list_to_string([
        f'BAR {bar.id} ({nodes_str}) : {type_str}',
        f'\t∆l (elongation) = {elongation}',
        f'\tε  (strain)     = {strain}',
        f'\tσ  (stress)     = {stress}\n'
    ])
```

Listing 18-25: Structure solution to text

In less than 70 lines of code we've written a function capable of generating a text representation of the structure solution model.

Summary

In this chapter, we implemented the code that creates vector diagrams representing the structure solution model. We split the resulting drawing process into chunks to make the code more manageable, and then we put it all together in the *svg.py* file, specifically, in the structure_solution_to_svg function.

We then implemented a function, structure_solution_to_string, that produces a plaintext representation of the structure solution.

Now we have everything we need to put our application together. In the final chapter, we'll do just that.

19

ASSEMBLING OUR APPLICATION

We've implemented all the pieces of our truss structure application, so now it's time to assemble them into something we can run from the command line. The application we'll write this chapter will parse an input file into the structure model, use the solve_structure method from the Structure class to assemble the solved structure, and then use the functions we implemented in the previous chapter to create an SVG diagram and text file describing the solution.

A General Overview

To get an overview of how we'll assemble the different modules into a final application, let's take a look at Figure 19-1. This figure illustrates the stages that take place when our application is executed.

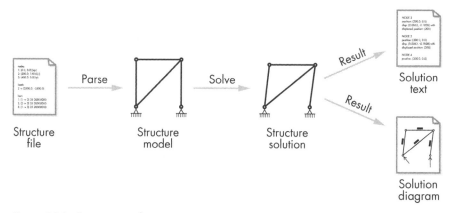

Figure 19-1: Structure resolution steps

First, our application is given a text file defining the structure. This file is formatted according to the rules we defined in Chapter 17. In the first step, we'll read the contents of the file into a string that's then parsed into a model built from our structure classes.

Once the structure model is constructed, the Structure class's solve _structure method does the analysis and creates a structure solution model. If you recall, the StructureSolution class is the top-level entity representing the solution.

The last step is to save the result in the form of a diagram (into an SVG file) and in the form of a text report (into a plaintext file). Thus, our program's output will be two files.

Before we can do anything, though, we first need to set up a new directory for our application.

Setup

First, let's create a new package in the *apps* directory. Name it *truss_structures*. Your directory should look like the following:

```
apps
    |- aff_transf_motion
    |    |- ...
    |- circle_from_points
    |    |- ...
    |- truss_structures
    |    |- __init__.py
```

If you created the package folder as a regular folder, don't forget to include an empty *__init__.py* file to make it a Python package. In the package, let's now add the main file. Create a new Python file named *main.py*, and in it, simply add the following lines:

```
if __name__ == '__main__':
    print('Main')
```

Your *truss_structures* package should now contain two files:

```
truss_structures
  |- __init__.py
  |- main.py
```

In this chapter, we won't be using a run configuration inside our IDE; we'll instead rely on a bash script that wraps the program. Let's prepare the script now so we can use it throughout the chapter. At the top of the project directory, in the *Mechanics* folder, create a new bash file and name it *truss.sh*. Enter the code in Listing 19-1.

```
#!/usr/bin/env bash
PYTHONPATH=$PWD python3 apps/truss_structures/main.py $@
```

Listing 19-1: Bash wrapper script

We have to change the permissions on the file to make it executable. From the shell, run the following:

```
$ chmod +x truss.sh
```

If you run this script from the shell,

```
$ ./truss.sh
```

you should see `'Main'` printed out. We're all set up; let's start coding!

Input Arguments

Our command line application is going to accept a few arguments: the overall scale of the drawing, the scale of the node displacements, the scale of the loads, and whether the original geometry should be drawn (see Table 18-1 on page 497 for a refresher).

We pass these arguments to our program like so:

```
$ ./truss.sh --scale=1.25 --disp-scale=100 --load-scale=0.1 --no-draw-original
```

We want to read these arguments, parse their values, and use a default value if the user doesn't provide a value. We can do this using a handy tool from Python's standard library: *argparse*. Argparse will also generate help messages about the different arguments for the user and validate the passed-in values.

Create a new file in the *apps/truss_structures* package named *arguments.py*. Your *truss_structures* package should now look like this:

```
truss_structures
  |- __init__.py
  |- arguments.py
  |- main.py
```

Enter the code in Listing 19-2.

```
import argparse

def parse_arguments():
❶ parser = argparse.ArgumentParser(
      description='Solves a truss structure'
  )

❷ parser.add_argument(
      '--scale',
      help='scale applied to the geometry (for plotting)',
      default=2,
      type=float
  )

❸ parser.add_argument(
      '--disp-scale',
      help='scale applied to the displacements (for plotting)',
      default=500,
      type=float
  )

❹ parser.add_argument(
      '--load-scale',
      help='scale applied to the loads (for plotting)',
      default=0.02,
      type=float
  )

❺ parser.add_argument(
      '--no-draw-original',
      help='Should draw the original geometry?',
      action='store_true'
  )

❻ return parser.parse_args()
```

Listing 19-2: Parsing the command line arguments

In this file, we define a function named parse_arguments. This function configures an instance of the ArgumentParser ❶ class to identify our arguments and parse them. We pass the constructor a description of what our program does. This will be used as a help message if the user passes in the --help flag, like so:

```
$ ./truss.sh --help
```

This provides the user with the following description:

```
usage: main.py [--help] [--scale SCALE] [--disp-scale DISP_SCALE]
               [--load-scale LOAD_SCALE] [--no-draw-original]

Solves a truss structure

optional arguments:
  -h, --help            show this help message and exit
  --scale SCALE         scale applied to the geometry (for plotting)
  --disp-scale DISP_SCALE
                        scale applied to the displacements (for plotting)
  --load-scale LOAD_SCALE
                        scale applied to the loads (for plotting)
  --no-draw-original    Should draw the original geometry?
```

The first argument we add is --scale ❷; we give it a help message and a default value of 2, and we set its type to be a floating-point number.

Then comes the --disp-scale argument ❸ with a default value of 500. Don't forget that the displacements are usually small compared to the size of the bars, so we'll need a big scale to appreciate them. Each structure solution has a different order of magnitude for the displacements, so this scale is better adjusted by trial and error.

Next comes the --load-scale argument ❹ with a default value of 0.02. This scale will shrink the loads so that they fit inside the drawing.

Last comes the --no-draw-original flag ❺, which controls whether we draw the original structure's geometry. If the flag isn't present in the arguments, we'll draw the original geometry but use a lighter color to keep the focus on the solution drawing. This will look something like Figure 19-2.

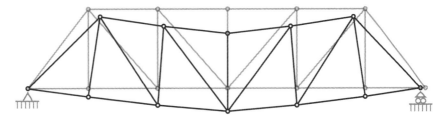

Figure 19-2: Drawing the original geometry (in a lighter color)

The --no-draw-original flag is different than the other parameters: it's not expecting an associated value; we only care whether the flag appears in the parameters list. We add this flag to the parser using the add_argument method with an action parameter. When this argument is found in the arguments list, an action is executed. In this case, we use the 'store_true' action, which simply saves a True value in the argument if the flag is present and a False otherwise. There are a few actions defined in the *argsparse* package, which you can browse in the documentation. We'll need only 'store_true'.

The last line returns the result of calling the `parse_args` method ❻. This method reads the arguments from `sys.argv`, which is where Python stores the arguments passed to a program, and parses the values following the rules we defined earlier.

The result is a dictionary-like structure with the values for the parameters. As we'll see later, the names for the keys of the dictionary are the same as the arguments, but without the initial dashes (`--`) and with underscores instead of the middle dashes. For example, `--load-scale` becomes `load_scale`, a much more Pythonic name for a variable. In addition, the dash isn't allowed for variable names in Python.

Let's now write the code that generates the application's output files.

Generating the Output

We prepared two functions in the previous chapter that generate both the SVG and text solution representations. We'll use these functions in the app and write their results to an external file.

First, create a new file named *output.py*. Your *truss_structures* package should now look like the following:

```
truss_structures
 |- __init__.py
 |- arguments.py
 |- main.py
 |- output.py
```

In *output.py*, enter the code in Listing 19-3.

```
import os

from structures.out.svg import structure_solution_to_svg
from structures.out.text import structure_solution_to_string
from structures.solution.structure import StructureSolution


def save_solution_to_svg(solution: StructureSolution, arguments):
❶  solution_svg = structure_solution_to_svg(solution, arguments)
    __write_to_file('result.svg', solution_svg)


def save_solution_to_text(solution: StructureSolution):
❷  solution_text = structure_solution_to_string(solution)
    __write_to_file('result.txt', solution_text)


def __write_to_file(filename, content):
❸  file_path = os.path.join(os.getcwd(), filename)
❹  with open(file_path, 'w') as file:
```

```
file.write(content)
```

Listing 19-3: Handling the structure output

We define three functions: one for saving the solution into an SVG image file (save_solution_to_svg), another one that saves the solution in a text file (save_solution_to_text), and a third function that creates a new file and saves it in the current working directory (__write_to_file).

The save_solution_to_svg function calls the structure_solution_to_svg function from the previous chapter ❶ and passes the generated SVG string to the __write_to_file function. Note that we pass the command line argument's dictionary to this function; these are the settings we use to generate the SVG vector image. For this to work, we have to make sure the command line arguments are parsed using the same name as the settings expected by structure_solution_to_svg. After the SVG diagram is created, we use __write_to_file to create a file named *result.svg* in the program's working directory.

The save_solution_to_text function is similar to save_solution_to_svg: it produces the text result using the structure_solution_to_string function ❷ and then writes the results to a *result.txt* file.

In __write_to_file, the first thing we do is figure out the file path by joining the current working directory with the filename (which should already include the extension). We then store the file path in the file_path variable ❸. Lastly, we use the with block to open the file in write mode ('w'), which creates the file if it doesn't exist, and then we write the passed-in content string to the file ❹.

We're almost done! We just need to stitch the input, resolution, and output together.

The Main Script

Let's head back to the *main.py* file. Open it and enter the code in Listing 19-4 (you can delete the print('Main') line we wrote earlier).

```
import sys
import time

import apps.truss_structures.output as out
from apps.truss_structures.arguments import parse_arguments
from structures.parse.str_parse import parse_structure_from_lines

if __name__ == '__main__':
❶ arguments = parse_arguments()
❷ lines = sys.stdin.readlines()

    start_time = time.time()

❸ structure = parse_structure_from_lines(lines)
❹ solution = structure.solve_structure()
```

```
out.save_solution_to_svg(solution, arguments)
out.save_solution_to_text(solution)

end_time = time.time()
elapsed_secs = end_time - start_time
❺ print(f'Took {round(elapsed_secs, 3)} seconds to solve')
```

Listing 19-4: Main script

In the "if name is main" block, we parse the arguments passed to the script from the command line. To do this, we use our parse_arguments function ❶, which we import from the *arguments.py* module. If this parsing fails, because a required flag was left out or something similar, the execution halts, and a helpful message is sent to the user.

Once the arguments are parsed, we read all of the lines passed to the program via the standard input and save them in the lines variable ❷.

Next, we parse those passed-in lines to create the structure model using the parse_structure_from_lines function ❸ we developed in Chapter 17. Once we have the structure model, we call its solve_structure method to compute the solution ❹.

Then, we call the two functions we wrote in the previous section to produce the output files: save_solution_to_svg and save_solution_to_text.

Lastly, we calculate the time the program took to run to have it as a reference and compare how long it takes to solve structures of different sizes. We stored the time in the start_time variable before we started to parse and compute the structure. We also stored the time in end_time just after generating the output files. Subtracting start_time from end_time yields the elapsed seconds, the amount of time our app took to produce the results. We print this resulting time in seconds before the application execution finishes ❺.

I'm sure you're as excited as I am to try our new app. Let's write a structure file by hand and solve it.

Trying the App

Let's create a structure file to try the app. Figure 19-3 illustrates four common truss configurations found in bridges. From these standard designs, we'll pick the Warren typology for our first test. We'll write a file by hand defining a structure following this configuration of the bars in the truss.

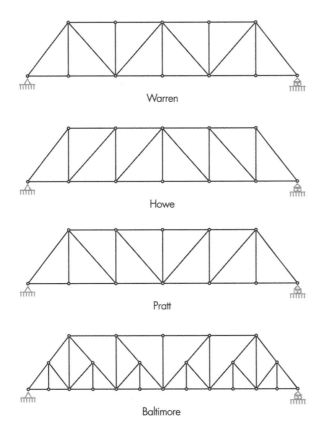

Figure 19-3: Truss typologies

Create a new file named *warren.txt* inside *apps/truss_structures*. Enter the following structure definition:

```
# Warren truss with 4 spans

nodes
# lower nodes
1: (0.0, 0.0) (xy)
2: (400.0, 0.0) ()
3: (800.0, 0.0) ()
4: (1200.0, 0.0) ()
5: (1600.0, 0.0) (y)
# upper nodes
6: (400.0, 300.0) ()
7: (800.0, 300.0) ()
8: (1200.0, 300.0) ()

loads
6 -> (2500.0, -5000.0)
7 -> (2500.0, -5000.0)
8 -> (2500.0, -5000.0)
```

```
bars
# horizontal bars
1: (1 -> 2) 20.0 20000000.0
2: (2 -> 3) 20.0 20000000.0
3: (3 -> 4) 20.0 20000000.0
4: (4 -> 5) 20.0 20000000.0
5: (6 -> 7) 20.0 20000000.0
6: (7 -> 8) 20.0 20000000.0
# vertical bars
7: (2 -> 6) 15.0 20000000.0
8: (3 -> 7) 15.0 20000000.0
9: (4 -> 8) 15.0 20000000.0
# diagonal bars
10: (1 -> 6) 30.0 20000000.0
11: (6 -> 3) 30.0 20000000.0
12: (3 -> 8) 30.0 20000000.0
13: (8 -> 5) 30.0 20000000.0
```

Alternatively, to avoid writing all this yourself, you may copy and paste the contents of the file provided in the code that accompanies the book. Figure 19-4 might help you visually understand how the nodes and bars are arranged in our Warren structure example file.

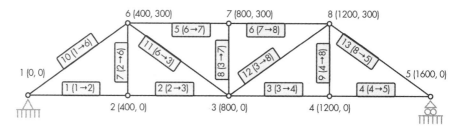

Figure 19-4: Warren truss structure to test our app

Now it's time to solve this structure and see the beautiful results our app produces. From the shell, run the following:

```
$ ./truss.sh --scale=1.25 --disp-scale=250 < apps/truss_structures/warren.txt
```

This should print to the shell:

```
Took 0.058 seconds to solve
```

In the previous command, we execute the bash script that wraps our code and passes it two arguments: a global drawing scale of 1.25 and a displacement scale of 250. The other arguments will use their default values, which if you recall are a load scale of 0.02 and False for the --no-draw-original flag.

Two new files should have appeared in your project, at the same level as the *truss.sh* bash file: *result.svg* and *result.txt*. If you open the second, the textual representation of the solution, you'll see something like Listing 19-5.

```
NODE 1
    original position: (0.0, 0.0)
    displacement: (0.0, 0.0) with norm 0.0
    displaced position: (0.0, 0.0)
    reaction: (-7513.0363, 6089.8571) with norm 9671.1981

--snip--

NODE 8
    original position: (1200.0, 300.0)
    displacement: (0.0185, -0.0693) with norm 0.0717
    displaced position: (1200.0185, 299.9307)


-------------------------------------------
```

```
BAR 1 (1 → 2) : ⊕ TENSION
    Δl (elongation) = 0.0156
    ε  (strain)     = 3.908e-05
    σ  (stress)     = 781.5951

--snip--

BAR 13 (8 → 5) : ⊖ COMPRESSION
    Δl (elongation) = -0.0124
    ε  (strain)     = -2.473e-05
    σ  (stress)     = -494.5523
```

Listing 19-5: Warren truss plaintext solution

The plaintext solution report is useful for checking all the solution values. For instance, you can check the reactions in nodes 1 and 5 (the externally constrained nodes). The node with an ID of 1 (NODE 1), which is externally constrained in both the horizontal and vertical directions, has an approximate reaction force of $\vec{R} = \langle -7513, 6090 \rangle$. The displacement of this node is necessarily zero. The node with an ID of 5 (NODE 5), which is constrained only in the vertical direction, has a displacement vector of $\vec{u} = \langle 0.055, 0.0 \rangle$.

Take a look at the section of each bar section now. You can readily identify the compressed and elongated bars and check their elongation, strain, and stress values. This report gives us all the data we need if we want to analyze the structure under the given loads.

The best part is inside the *result.svg* file. Open the resulting image in your favorite browser. Your result should look like Figure 19-5.

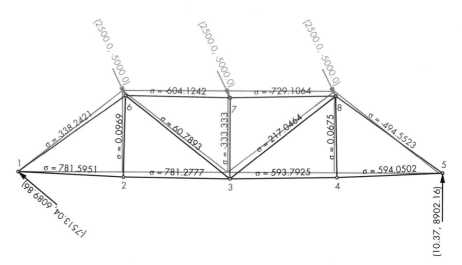

Figure 19-5: Warren solution diagram

As you can see on your screen, the bars are colored in red if subject to compression and green if subject to tension. The captions aligned to the bars indicate their stress. The original geometry is drawn in the background using a light-blue color, which gives us a better visualization of how the loads deform the structure.

NOTE *You can view SVG images in PyCharm, but if we try to open and visualize our diagrams inside the IDE, you'll be surprised to see them upside down. Don't panic: you haven't gotten it wrong. It's just that (as of the 2021.1 version) PyCharm doesn't support the* transform *attribute we added to the SVG, which, if you recall from earlier, we require to flip the y-axis. I recommend using a browser instead.*

Can you see the difference in the bars' line thickness? Using line thickness to represent the cross section of the bars helps us identify the bars of the structure that can withstand a greater load. The stress labels we added to the bars allow us to readily inspect the stress on each bar, giving us one of the most important pieces of information upfront. We can gather quite a bit of information from just a single glance at our diagram; this is precisely the value of these sorts of graphical representations.

To understand what the arguments to our program do, let's play around with them and see what kind of results we can get.

Playing with the Arguments

Let's first check what happens if we pass the `--no-draw-original` flag:

```
$ ./truss.sh --scale=1.25 --disp-scale=250 --no-draw-original
  < apps/truss_structures/warren.txt
```

If you open the *result.svg* image in your favorite browser, you should see the image in Figure 19-6.

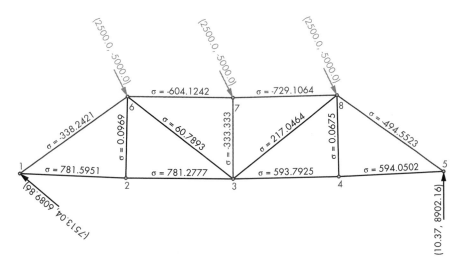

Figure 19-6: Warren solution diagram without original geometry

Without the original geometry we can see the deformed structure with less clutter; at the same time, we cannot see how the nodes and bars are moving relative to their original position.

What about using a larger displacement scale? Let's try the following:

```
$ ./truss.sh --scale=1.25 --disp-scale=500
    < apps/truss_structures/warren.txt
```

Using a displacement scale of 500 exaggerates the deformations so we can see them clearly. The diagram should now look like Figure 19-7.

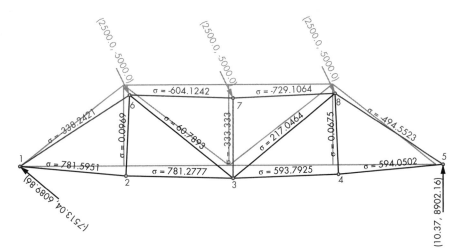

Figure 19-7: Warren solution diagram with a larger displacement scale

We haven't used the loads diagram yet; we've been using the default value of 0.02. Let's try to edit this value to see its effect:

```
$ /truss.sh --scale=1.25 --disp-scale=400 --load-scale=0.01
  < apps/truss_structures/warren.txt
```

If we use a load scale of 0.01, half of what we've used so far, you can see that the load vectors' lengths have shrunk, as in Figure 19-8.

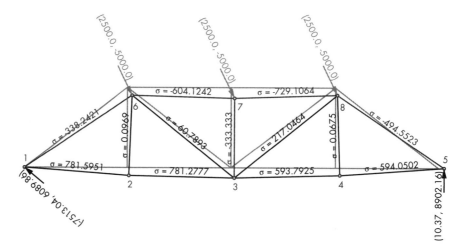

Figure 19-8: Warren solution diagram with a smaller load scale

As you can see, the load scale is important for the correct visualization of the load vectors. A small value shrinks the vectors so much that there's no space for their labels to be nicely placed. You can try a larger load scale, say 0.5. The labels should disappear from the diagram. In this case, the vectors we draw are so long that their centers lie outside the drawing bounds, and therefore, the load caption that we place toward the start point is simply not visible.

Solving a Large Structure

In the *apps/truss_structures* directory of the code distributed with the book is a file, *baltimore.txt*, that defines a Baltimore truss structure with 10 spans. Copy this file into your project, in the same folder. Alternatively, you can create and write the file by hand (Listing 19-6):

```
# Baltimore truss with 10 spans

nodes
# lower nodes
1: (0.0, 0.0) (xy)
2: (200.0, 0.0) ()
3: (400.0, 0.0) ()
4: (600.0, 0.0) ()
```

```
5: (800.0, 0.0) ()
6: (1000.0, 0.0) ()
7: (1200.0, 0.0) ()
8: (1400.0, 0.0) ()
9: (1600.0, 0.0) ()
10: (1800.0, 0.0) ()
11: (2000.0, 0.0) ()
12: (2200.0, 0.0) ()
13: (2400.0, 0.0) ()
14: (2600.0, 0.0) ()
15: (2800.0, 0.0) ()
16: (3000.0, 0.0) ()
17: (3200.0, 0.0) ()
18: (3400.0, 0.0) ()
19: (3600.0, 0.0) ()
20: (3800.0, 0.0) ()
21: (4000.0, 0.0) (y)
# middle nodes
22: (200.0, 150.0) ()
23: (600.0, 150.0) ()
24: (1000.0, 150.0) ()
25: (1400.0, 150.0) ()
26: (1800.0, 150.0) ()
27: (2200.0, 150.0) ()
28: (2600.0, 150.0) ()
29: (3000.0, 150.0) ()
30: (3400.0, 150.0) ()
31: (3800.0, 150.0) ()
# upper nodes
32: (400.0, 300.0) ()
33: (800.0, 300.0) ()
34: (1200.0, 300.0) ()
35: (1600.0, 300.0) ()
36: (2000.0, 300.0) ()
37: (2400.0, 300.0) ()
38: (2800.0, 300.0) ()
39: (3200.0, 300.0) ()
40: (3600.0, 300.0) ()

loads
1 -> (0.0, -500.0)
2 -> (0.0, -500.0)
--snip--
40 -> (0.0, -500.0)

bars
# zig-zag bars
```

```
 1: (1 -> 22) 20.0 20000000.0
 2: (22 -> 3) 20.0 20000000.0
 3: (3 -> 23) 20.0 20000000.0
 4: (23 -> 5) 20.0 20000000.0
 5: (5 -> 24) 20.0 20000000.0
 6: (24 -> 7) 20.0 20000000.0
 7: (7 -> 25) 20.0 20000000.0
 8: (25 -> 9) 20.0 20000000.0
 9: (9 -> 26) 20.0 20000000.0
10: (26 -> 11) 20.0 20000000.0
11: (11 -> 27) 20.0 20000000.0
12: (27 -> 13) 20.0 20000000.0
13: (13 -> 28) 20.0 20000000.0
14: (28 -> 15) 20.0 20000000.0
15: (15 -> 29) 20.0 20000000.0
16: (29 -> 17) 20.0 20000000.0
17: (17 -> 30) 20.0 20000000.0
18: (30 -> 19) 20.0 20000000.0
19: (19 -> 31) 20.0 20000000.0
20: (31 -> 21) 20.0 20000000.0
# left diagonal bars
21: (32 -> 22) 20.0 20000000.0
22: (32 -> 23) 20.0 20000000.0
23: (33 -> 24) 20.0 20000000.0
24: (34 -> 25) 20.0 20000000.0
25: (35 -> 26) 20.0 20000000.0
# right diagonal bars
26: (37 -> 27) 20.0 20000000.0
27: (38 -> 28) 20.0 20000000.0
28: (39 -> 29) 20.0 20000000.0
29: (40 -> 30) 20.0 20000000.0
30: (40 -> 31) 20.0 20000000.0
# vertical bars
31: (2 -> 22) 20.0 20000000.0
32: (3 -> 32) 20.0 20000000.0
33: (4 -> 23) 20.0 20000000.0
34: (5 -> 33) 20.0 20000000.0
35: (6 -> 24) 20.0 20000000.0
36: (7 -> 34) 20.0 20000000.0
37: (8 -> 25) 20.0 20000000.0
38: (9 -> 35) 20.0 20000000.0
39: (10 -> 26) 20.0 20000000.0
40: (11 -> 36) 20.0 20000000.0
41: (12 -> 27) 20.0 20000000.0
42: (13 -> 37) 20.0 20000000.0
43: (14 -> 28) 20.0 20000000.0
44: (15 -> 38) 20.0 20000000.0
```

```
45: (16 -> 29) 20.0 20000000.0
46: (17 -> 39) 20.0 20000000.0
47: (18 -> 30) 20.0 20000000.0
48: (19 -> 40) 20.0 20000000.0
49: (20 -> 31) 20.0 20000000.0
# lower horizontal bars
50: (1 -> 2) 20.0 20000000.0
51: (2 -> 3) 20.0 20000000.0
52: (3 -> 4) 20.0 20000000.0
53: (4 -> 5) 20.0 20000000.0
54: (5 -> 6) 20.0 20000000.0
55: (6 -> 7) 20.0 20000000.0
56: (7 -> 8) 20.0 20000000.0
57: (8 -> 9) 20.0 20000000.0
58: (9 -> 10) 20.0 20000000.0
59: (10 -> 11) 20.0 20000000.0
60: (11 -> 12) 20.0 20000000.0
61: (12 -> 13) 20.0 20000000.0
62: (13 -> 14) 20.0 20000000.0
63: (14 -> 15) 20.0 20000000.0
64: (15 -> 16) 20.0 20000000.0
65: (16 -> 17) 20.0 20000000.0
66: (17 -> 18) 20.0 20000000.0
67: (18 -> 19) 20.0 20000000.0
68: (19 -> 20) 20.0 20000000.0
69: (20 -> 21) 20.0 20000000.0
# upper horizontal bars
70: (32 -> 33) 20.0 20000000.0
71: (33 -> 34) 20.0 20000000.0
72: (34 -> 35) 20.0 20000000.0
73: (35 -> 36) 20.0 20000000.0
74: (36 -> 37) 20.0 20000000.0
75: (37 -> 38) 20.0 20000000.0
76: (38 -> 39) 20.0 20000000.0
77: (39 -> 40) 20.0 20000000.0
```

Listing 19-6: Baltimore truss structure definition

Note that, in this code, we apply the same load to every node, but we've left out some of the load lines. If you write this by hand, you should include those load definition lines.

Let's pass the file defining this large structure to our program:

```
$ ./truss.sh --scale=0.75 --disp-scale=100 --load-scale=0.2
  < apps/truss_structures/baltimore.txt
```

The output produced by the program should look something like the following:

```
Took 0.106 seconds to solve
```

Even for the Baltimore typology with 40 nodes and 77 bars, the computation time is a fraction of a second. If you open the *solution.svg* file, you'll see something like Figure 19-9.

Figure 19-9: Baltimore solution diagram

Now that you've gotten this far, spend some time playing with your application. Try with different structures and parameters to check the results.

Summary

In this chapter, we took all of the structural analysis modules we've been building in the previous chapters and assembled them into a command line application that solves truss structures. Our app reads structure files from the standard input and produces two result files: one is a vector diagram representing the solution, and the other is a plaintext report including all the relevant values.

This is the last chapter in Part V of the book. It's been an intense couple of chapters, but I hope the result has paid off. We've made up a format for files that defines a structure, written a function to parse it into our model, implemented the resolution algorithm that generates the solution model, coded a way to export this solution into a diagram and text report, and, finally, assembled all of it into a final application.

We chose an application that solves truss structures to exemplify the process of writing engineering applications, but we could have chosen any other topic—heat transfer, fluid dynamics, beam analysis, and so on. The process and techniques are the same. The knowledge you've acquired should empower you to write code that works with any engineering domain you might encounter.

This is also the last chapter in the book. I hope you've enjoyed learning about how to build engineering applications, split them into modules, and, of course, test them. All that's left is for you to start creating your own apps. As mentioned in the introduction of the book, the only way to become an expert is by doing: build many apps, learn from your mistakes, and then build some more. Good luck!

BIBLIOGRAPHY

[1] Dustin Boswell and Trevo Foucher. *The Art of Readable Code*. O'Reilly Media, 2011.

[2] Tirupathi R. Chandrupatla and A.D. Belegundu. *Introduction to Finite Elements in Engineering*. Prentice Hall, 1997.

[3] James M. Gere and Stephen P. Timoshenko. *Mechanics of Materials*. Brooks/Cole Engineering Division, 1984.

[4] Erwin Kreyszig. *Advanced Engineering Mathematics*. John Wiley & Sons, 1999.

[5] Eric Lengyel. *Mathematics for 3D Game Programming and Computer Graphics*. Cengage Learning PTR, 2012.

[6] Robert C. Martin. *Clean Code: A Handbook of Agile Software Craftsmanship*. Pearson Education, 2009.

[7] Burkhard A. Meier. *Python GUI Programming Cookbook*. Packt Publishing, 2017.

[8] J. L. Meriam and L. G. Kraige. *Engineering Mechanics: Dynamics*. Wiley, 2006.

[9] J. L. Meriam and L. G. Kraige. *Engineering Mechanics: Statics*. Wiley, 2006.

[10] Singiresu S. Rao. *The Finite Element Method in Engineering*. Elsevier, 2005.

[11] William F. Riley and Leroy D. Sturges. *Engineering Mechanics: Statics*. Wiley, 1995.

[12] Tarek Ziadé and Michał Jaworski. *Expert Python Programming*. Packt Publishing, 2016.

INDEX

resistant element, 388
reusability, 308
rich-text editor, 205, 235
rotation
    pivot, 189
row vector, 340
run configuration, xxxvi, 236

S

Scalable Vector Graphics, *See* SVG
scientific notation, number, 526
screen space, 184
script, 4
segment
    direction, 103
set
    `add`, 12
    `difference`, 12
    `remove`, 12
    `union`, 12
side effect, 24
silent fail, 109
simulation, 289
    ahead of time, 290
    motion, 297
    real time, 290
    system, 288
    time delta, 291
static equilibrium, 389, 417
stiffness, 397
stiffness matrix, 398
strain ϵ, 393
stress σ, 393
stress-strain diagrams, 393
string, 211
    `join`, 214
structure, 388
    external constraint, 395
    external support, *See* external
        constraint
    node, 395
    two-force member, 397
SVG, 204
    attributes, 206, 215
    circle, 221
    group, 225
    line, 217
    polygon, 222
    polyline, 223

rect, 219
text, 224
`transform`, 208
`viewBox`, 207
system of equations
    matrix form, 337, 360

T

TDD, *See* Test-Driven Development
template, 210
    placeholder, 210
test
    assertion, 91
    fixture, 98
    subject, 91, 98
test double, 447
    dummy, 447
    fake, 447
    mock, 448
    stub, 448
test-driven development, 371
time loop, 291
Tkinter
    `Button`, 269
    `Canvas`, 270
    `Entry`, 268
    `Label`, 268
    main loop, 267
    widget, 266
traceback, 94
truss structure, 388
tuple
    `count`, 13
    `index`, 14
type hints, 45–46
    `float`, 46
    `int`, 46
    `str`, 46

U

ultimate strength, *See* ultimate stress
ultimate stress, 394
Unicode characters, 525–526
unit testing, 90–91
    three golden rules, 97–99
        Controlled Environment, 98
        One Reason to Fail, 98
        Test Independence, 99

Unix
    prompt, *See* terminal
    shell, *See* terminal
    terminal, 50
unpacking, *See* destructuring
UTF-8 encoding, 213
utils package, 134

V

vector
    angle, 81
    norm, 74
    normal, 75
    normalize, 75
    parallelism, 81
    perpendicularity, 81
    unit, 75
vector image, 204
version control system, xxix
visibility diagram, 308

W

winding number algorithm, 140
Windows Subsystem for Linux, 50
working directory, 259
World Wide Web Consortium (W3C), 204
wrapper class, 276

X

XML, 205
    namespace, 205

Y

yield strength, *See* yield stress
yield stress, 394
yielding, material, 394
Young's modulus, 392

UPDATES

Visit *http://borisv.lk.net/latex.html* for updates, errata, and other information.

COLOPHON

The fonts used in *Hardcore Programming for Mechanical Engineers* are New Baskerville, Futura, The Sans Mono Condensed and Dogma. The book was typeset with LATEX 2_ε package nostarch by Boris Veytsman *(2008/06/06 v1.3 Typesetting books for No Starch Press)*.

The book was produced as an example of the package nostarch.

RESOURCES

Visit *https://nostarch.com/hardcore-programming-mechanical-engineers/* for errata and more information.

More *no-nonsense books from*  **NO STARCH PRESS**

BEYOND THE BASIC STUFF WITH PYTHON

Best Practices for Writing Clean Code

BY AL SWEIGART
384 PP., $31.95
ISBN 978-1-59327-966-0

EFFECTIVE C

An Introduction to Professional C Programming

BY ROBERT C. SEACORD
272 PP., $49.95
ISBN 978-1-7185-0104-1

HOW COMPUTERS REALLY WORK

A Hands-On Guide to the Inner Workings of the Machine

BY MATTHEW JUSTICE
380 PP., $39.95
ISBN 978-1-7185-0052-5

ALGORITHMIC THINKING

A Problem-Based Introduction

BY DANIEL ZINGARO
408 PP., $49.95
ISBN 978-1-7185-0080-8

COMPUTER GRAPHICS FROM SCRATCH

A Programmer's Introduction to 3D Rendering

BY GABRIEL GAMBETTA
248 PP., $49.99
ISBN 978-1-7185-0076-1

REAL-WORLD PYTHON

A Hacker's Guide to Solving Problems with Code

BY LEE VAUGHAN
306 PP., $34.95
ISBN 978-1-7185-0062-4

PHONE:
800.420.7240 OR
415.863.9900

EMAIL:
SALES@NOSTARCH.COM

WEB:
WWW.NOSTARCH.COM